SON OF THE ALHAMBRA

Portrait of Don Diego Hurtado de Mendoza (1540) by Titian. Pitti Gallery, Florence. (Photograph courtesy of Soprintendenza alle Gallerie, Firenze.)

SON OF THE ALHAMBRA

Don Diego Hurtado de Mendoza,
1504–1575

BY ERIKA SPIVAKOVSKY

University of Texas Press, Austin & London

International Standard Book Number 0-292-70093-8
Library of Congress Catalog Card Number 78-138633
© 1970 by Erika Spivakovsky
All rights reserved
Manufactured in the United States of America
Type set by G&S Typesetters, Austin
Printed by Capital Printing Company, Austin
Bound by Universal Bookbindery, Inc., San Antonio

PREFACE

NEARLY FOUR HUNDRED YEARS AGO Ambrosio de Morales wrote the
first biographical notes about Diego Hurtado de Mendoza; they fill
just a page or two of the dedication of a book to him. Still briefer
notices about Mendoza appeared in 1604, 1607, and 1608, in works
by Sandoval, Taxander, and Bermúdez de Pedraza, respectively.
The first edition of Mendoza's poems came out in Madrid in 1610,
carrying no biographical sketch. The first and second editions of
Mendoza's *Guerra de Granada* (Lisbon. 1627, and Madrid, 1674)
were issued with a story of his life as skimpy as that by Morales.
It was written in 1627 by Baltasar de Çúñiga, and the biographical
sketches from the eighteenth century by Mayans i Siscar and
Sédano, more wordy but hardly more informative, were based on it.

Mendoza's name survived until the middle of the nineteenth
century on the strength of his (assumed) authorship of the *Lazarillo de Tormes*, his poetry, and the *Guerra de Granada*, but his life
story remained practically unknown up to the 1840s, when at last
the Royal Archives of Spain and other countries opened their doors
to researchers. From then on publications of Mendoza's correspondence and studies about him followed each other rapidly.
Adolfo de Castro y Rossi, Cayetano Rosell, Antonio Paz y Melia,
Pascual de Gayangos, E. Señán y Alonso, and Cristóbal Pérez
Pastor in Spain; Karl Lanz, Karl Stahr, Ferdinand Wolf, J. J. I.
von Döllinger, August von Druffel, J. Fesenmair, and Walter
Friedensburg in Germany and Austria; George Ticknor and William Knapp in the United States; Charles Graux and R. Foulché-
Delbosc in France; and others—I do not claim completeness for
this list—contributed to this growing interest in Mendoza. Their
studies usually were biographical introductions to their editions of

Mendoza's writings. Fesenmair and Señan y Alonso published their essay-length studies as booklets.

Simultaneously, Mendoza as a historic personality was met with more frequently in the more thoroughly researched histories of Charles V, Philip II, and the papacy that appeared during the nineteenth and the beginning of the twentieth century. Inevitably, however, every new report of Mendoza was accompanied by inaccurate data, confusion, and misunderstanding. No full-scale biography was written, although Adolfo de Castro, who called Mendoza "the great historical personage of Spain in the century of Charles V," announced in 1854 that he was writing "the Life and Eulogy of this eminent author, which in due time will be published" (ed. *Poetas líricos*, p. xix), a promise left unfulfilled although Castro lived until 1898. Pérez Pastor (1833–1908) had similar plans that he did not carry out.

The momentum of the Mendoza revival continued into the beginning of the twentieth century despite A. Morel-Fatio's shattering—on insufficient grounds—of the traditional attribution of *Lazarillo de Tormes* to Mendoza (1886). But once Mendoza was deprived of his popular appeal as author of the first picaresque novel, while his other works, as well as the increasingly available information on his life, unfortunately were being submerged in esoteric scholarship—available only in widely scattered publications, difficult of access—interest in him slackened for several decades. Then it reawakened during the 1930s.

Roger B. Merriman, professor of history at Harvard University, at work on *The Rise of the Spanish Empire* (vols. 3 and 4, 1925–1934), suggested to his student and assistant at the time, Garrett Mattingly, that he write the Mendoza biography that was so unaccountably lacking. Merriman undertook part of the work himself, still researching and writing up to the time of his death about Don Diego and the *Guerra de Granada*. (The late Professor Mattingly told me this, adding that Merriman's material and notes on Mendoza were accidentally destroyed.)

In 1935 Robert Selden Rose, professor of Romance languages at Yale University, and his doctoral student Alberto Vázquez y Medina published *Algunas Cartas* (a selection of Mendoza's letters from Venice, Siena, and Rome), and in 1941 appeared the first volume of *Vida y Obras de Don Diego Hurtado de Mendoza* (Ma-

drid, 1941–1943), 3 vols., by Angel González Palencia and Eugenio
Mele. Mendoza's irrepressible personality, so urbane, witty, and
modern, first appeared to me in his letters as published in *Algunas
Cartas* and *Vida y Obras*, vol. 3, kindling my wish to share this impression with English readers.

My attempt to write this biography was greatly encouraged by
Professor Selden Rose and Professor Garrett Mattingly, who recommended my project to the Radcliffe Institute for Independent
Study. Radcliffe's two grants, 1962–1964, enabled me to use the
resources of the Harvard College Libraries and to visit archives, as
well as places associated with Mendoza, in Spain and Italy.

The late Professor Selden Rose most generously entrusted me
with all the material on Mendoza that he collected some thirty
years ago when he intended to write a biography of Mendoza together with Dr. Vázquez, a plan they later abandoned. As will be
seen from the source references in the footnotes marked "Rose-
file," in many instances I drew on this unpublished material,
mainly for the letters Mendoza wrote Charles V from Venice and
for the correspondence of Duke Cosimo I de' Medici with Mendoza
and others. In the Archive of Simancas, I read the originals of
many of the letters published by Selden Rose and González Palencia as well as those in the "Rose-file," and I collected additional material there, as well as in Madrid and in Siena.

Professor Mattingly of Columbia University, in the last year of
his life, was an inspiring mentor of my efforts, offering constructive
ideas in the area of Renaissance diplomacy.

The writing of this book, especially in parts of chapters two, six,
and nine, was much furthered also by Professor Paul Oskar Kristeller of Columbia University, to whom I am greatly indebted for
deepening my understanding of Averroism and for many other
helpful suggestions and generously given advice.

Among officials of European archives who spared no effort in
finding letters of Mendoza and other source material for me were,
in Siena, Dr. Sem Falcini, vice-director of the State Archives in the
Palazzo Piccolomini; in Madrid, the Rev. Padre D. Pedro Longás
Bartibás, director of the Instituto de Valencia de Don Juan, and
Sr. D. Ramón Paz, director of the manuscript division of the Biblioteca Nacional; in Simancas, Sr. D. Ricardo Magdaleno Redondo,

director of the Archive, and Señorita Concha Alvarez Terán, Señora Adela González Vega, and Señorita Ascención de la Plaza, unfailingly helpful *archiveras*. Sr. D. Julian Alvárez Zurro, photographer of the Archive of Simancas, excellently photographed and transcribed many documents for me. To all of them I am immensely grateful.

I must give a special expression of thanks to the director of the Museum of the Alhambra in Granada, Sr. D. Jesús Bermúdez Pareja, professor of Arabic at the University of Granada. Professor Bermúdez was able to figure out (from some biographical data I told him) the approximate place of Mendoza's residence during the War of Granada, a fact not known before; he showed me the remains of the palace of the Count of Tendilla where Don Diego was born; and he most helpfully arranged to have Tendilla's portrait and the site of the palace photographed for me. With his unbounded enthusiasm for the Alhambra and for all of the Mendozas linked with its history, Don Jesús gave me much picturesque and useful information about the Mendozas and their circle in Granada.

Any errors in judgment, and in the interpretation and compilation of facts, are of course mine.

I am deeply grateful to Mrs. Mary I. Bunting, president of Radcliffe College, for founding the unique Radcliffe Institute, which gave me the opportunity for completing this book; to Miss Constance E. Smith, dean of the Institute, for her invaluable encouragement and advice; and to Mrs. Rene Bryant, Mrs. Jean Radcliffe, Miss Doris Lorentzen, and other former and present members of the Institute staff for their unvaryingly kind helpfulness.

I could never have undertaken to write this book but for the endless patience of my husband, Tossy Spivakovsky, and of Ruth, our daughter, who grew up with this preoccupation of mine. Both have given me valuable and constructive criticism and constant encouragement to complete my task. Ruth, as well as her husband, Dr. Paul H. Voorhis, deserve the credit for trying to eliminate my foreign-sounding locutions and for devoting great care and interest in trying to make the manuscript generally readable.

E. S.
Westport, Connecticut

A Note on the Text

The names of internationally known figures such as Charles V, Philip II, Paul III, are anglicized; those of lesser-known personages, such as Don Pedro de Pacheco, are left in their Spanish or Italian forms. With the exception of François I, who is called Francis I, other Francises remain "Don Francisco de Mendoza," etc. The Catholic sovereigns and their children I prefer to call by their Spanish names, Fernando, Isabel, Juana.

Many ancient Spanish family names still in use, such as González, Sánchez, and López, were not written with accents in the fifteenth and sixteenth centuries. To be consistent I apply the modern accentuation, except in quotations where such names are given in the spelling copied exactly from original manuscripts.

The spelling in the quotations that appear in the chapter notes might look full of errors to the nonspecialist unfamiliar with Spanish texts of the sixteenth century. Accents were rarely in use at that time (Mendoza never made any); *u, v, b,* are interchanged, apparently at random, often in one and the same document; *h* appears in unexpected places; modern *j* is usually *x*. I transcribed all quotations as exactly as possible from: (1) original manuscripts—the texts furnished me by Simancas have, however, modern punctuation and capitalization; (2) *Algunas Cartas*, edited by Vázquez and Selden Rose, the major source book for this study; and (3) other printed sources that vary in their reproductions of the original orthography. The more recent publications tend to adhere closely to the original spelling in their documentation. Translations of foreign-language sources are my own, unless otherwise noted.

CONTENTS

ILLUSTRATIONS

Portrait of Mendoza by Titian, *frontispiece*

SON OF THE ALHAMBRA

1. BACKGROUND

And this I say as philosopher and as
Moor of Granada, or as a Marrano . . .
Don Diego[1]

Mendozas and Pachecos

Don Diego Hurtado de Mendoza was born in the Alhambra of Granada in 1503 or 1504[2] into a family that a few decades earlier had played a crucial role in launching the Spanish monarchy on the path to world power. He was the last son of aging parents. If his mother, Doña Francisca Pacheco, survived this birth of her eighth living child, it was for a few years only. His father, a man in his sixties, Don Iñigo López de Mendoza, second

[1] "Y esto hablo como philosopho y como moro de Granada, o como marrano." Mendoza to the Bishop of Arras, Rome, September 1, 1548. Alberto Vázquez and R. Selden Rose, ed., *Algunas Cartas de Don Diego Hurtado de Mendoza, 1538-1552*, p. 119. Cited hereafter as *AC*.

[2] The year of Mendoza's birth is not usually given as 1504, but the following remarks by him narrow the date down to this year: Mendoza to Jerónimo Zurita, Granada, December 1, 1573: "he casi setenta años," Diego José Dormer, *Progresos de la historia en el reyno de Aragón*, p. 502. In another letter, dated Sept. 20, 1568, Mendoza says he is sixty-four years old: *Biblioteca de autores españoles (BAE)* XXI, *Historiadores de sucesos particulares*, ed. Cayetano Rosell, I, xxviii. And in his last will, August 6, 1575, he says of himself that he is "71 años o poco mas," *Memorias de la Real Academia Española* (MRAE), ed. C. Pérez Pastor, X, 153–194; also Angel González Palencia and Eugenio Mele, *Vida y obras de Don Diego Hurtado de Mendoza* (GP) II, 385.

Count of Tendilla, was the first Christian governor of the Moorish kingdom. After enduring for 250 years as the only Islamic state in Spain, Granada had been conquered in 1492 to the glory of the Catholic Sovereigns at the Mendozas' instigation and, largely, thanks to their support. This Count of Tendilla and his uncle, the Grand Cardinal Pedro González de Mendoza "whose opinion and prudence governed the Catholic Sovereigns,"[3] joined by other members of their family—a group of about two dozen great lords, each a master of many vassals and able to raise a large private army— had been at the side of the royal couple since Queen Isabel's war of succession (1474–1479). The residence where Don Diego first saw the light of day, a Moorish palace in the sophisticated style of the Royal House, which it adjoined, was given his father by Fernando and Isabel as one of his rewards for his service in the Granadine war.[4]

It had taken the Mendozas almost eight hundred years to fight their way from the narrow confines of their mountain passes in the Pyrenees, over the vast tablelands of Old and New Castile, and finally to the sierras of Granada. The original seat of the family was a small mountain estate in the Basque province Alava. In a cold and humid climate, the ancient estate Divina, later called Mendoça (perhaps from Mendioz, meaning "cold mountain"),[5] lies in the shelter of the Sierra of Badaya, one of the most impenetrable of regions.[6] Rough-hewn are the ruins of the old Mendoza castle, still standing about seven miles west of Vitoria, typical of a rough land inhabited by bands of shepherds, ferocious men unsubdued by any invaders, be they Romans, Goths, or Arabs.[7] Christianity

---

[3] Francisco Henriquez de Jorquera, *Anales de Granada*, ed. Antonio Marín Ocete, I, 279.

[4] In addition to his tenure as *alcaide* and captain-general in Granada, Tendilla received fifty percent of the income the Moorish kings and queens had drawn from the pasture lands in the Sierra Nevada. J. Caro Baroja, *Los Moriscos del Reino de Granada*, p. 98.

[5] Cristina de Arteaga y Falguera, *La Casa del Infantado, Cabeza de los Mendoza*, p. 6.

[6] Gregorio de Balparda y las Herreras, *Historia crítica de Vizcaya y de sus fueros*, II, 203 *et passim*.

[7] According to H. Lautensach, *Maurische Züge im geographischen Bild der Iberischen Halbinsel*, p. 24, Alava is the only Basque region without a trace of Arabic or Germanic topographical names.

entered the region peacefully, brought by monks fleeing the Moors. Through the first three centuries of Arab rule in Spain, this martial people lived in daily expectation of Moorish attacks from the no man's land south of the castellated Alavan-Castilian frontier. The first of the warrior-lords of Alava adding "Mendoza" to his name was Don Lope López de Mendoza, who since 1124 served Castile's Queen Doña Urraca as majordomo. Either this Mendoza or his younger brother was in the direct line of Don Diego's ancestors.[8] Though called *ricos hombres* ("rich men"), the Mendozas were at first comparatively small lords. Over the centuries, they added to their landed estate in almost every generation by marrying heiresses.[9] Not infrequently, this happened two or three times to a single landowner, with the death, usually in childbirth, of his successive wives. Also, the kings of Castile often rewarded their services with territorial grants. Lands became increasingly available as the Christians reconquered them from the gradually retreating Muslims. With the new owners of latifundia came their herds of sheep and cattle, which transformed the empty Castilian tableland into a great wool-producing center, leading to the powerful organization of Spanish transhumance, the base of the growing wealth of the House of Mendoza. By the fourteenth century, these descendants of rugged, single-minded frontier fighters, now a highly educated court aristocracy, formed one of the leading five or six Castilian lineages. They established themselves in Guadalajara, from then on the permanent seat of the family.

The first known poet among them, Don Diego's great-great-grandfather, Don Diego Hurtado de Mendoza (1365–1404), still

[8] Balparda, II, 321–325 *et passim*. Cf. also Diego Gutiérrez Coronel, *Historia genealógica de la casa de Mendoza*, ed. A. González Palencia, vols. I and II; Gerónimo Gudiel, *Compendio de algunas historias de España* (1577); F. Fernández de Bethencourt, *Historia genealógica y heráldica de la Monarquía española, Casa Real, y Grandes de España*; Francisco Layna Serrano, *Historia de Guadalajara y sus Mendozas en los siglos XV y XVI*; F. Rodriguez García, *Crónica del Señorio de Vizcaya*, pp. 45, 46.

[9] The Castilian hereditary laws since Alfonso X granted females succession to the throne as well as to other titles of the nobility, reflecting a tradition going back to the earliest times of the Reconquest that preserved the seignorial houses through the distaff side. If a woman had no brothers, she inherited not only her father's property but also his name and title, which she could bestow on her husband to "raise" him. "Hurtado" and apparently also "Mendoza" continued through the female line.

untitled, owned the estates of Mendoza, Hita, Buitrago, the Hermandades of Alava, and many other localities, and he was Chief Royal Justice, majordomo of the King, *alcaide* (castellan) of many fortresses, and Chief Admiral of Castile.[10] With his son and heir, the famous poet Don Iñigo López de Mendoza (1398–1458), Don Diego's great-grandfather, who attained the Marquisate of Santillana,[11] the Mendozas advanced to the first rank of the entire nobility. Santillana shone also as a patron of writers and scientists, setting an example which, among his fourth-generation descendants, Don Diego alone emulated to a similar degree.

The Marquis inspired the first tentative efforts of the literary movement of humanism in Spain, which Don Diego was not only to continue, but of which this great-grandson became the very embodiment. He commissioned a translation of the *Aeneid;* he introduced the Italian sonnet, and sometimes he used the content matter of the classics as thematic material for his poetry, although, unlike his progeny, the older poet and protohumanist was ignorant of both Latin and Greek.

Santillana's titles and major landholdings went to the first of his seven sons, another Don Diego Hurtado de Mendoza, whom the Catholic Kings created Duke of Infantado in 1475; this ducal house was to remain the titular head of all the subsequent branches of the Mendozas. But the intellectual tradition continued with the second son, Don Diego's grandfather Don Iñigo López de Mendoza, and still more splendidly so with the fifth of Santillana's sons, the above-mentioned Grand Cardinal, Don Pedro González de Mendoza (1428–1495), to whose great position the older brothers deferred.[12]

The Cardinal, Don Diego's outstanding great-uncle, besides laying the foundation for the Spain of Don Diego's time, also largely formed the lives of his grandfather and father (the Cardinal's elder brother and nephew, respectively). With Don Pedro González as

---

[10] A sample of his work in *Critical Anthology of Spanish Verse*, ed. E. Allison Peers, p. 51.

[11] Gutiérrez Coronel, *Historia genealógica*, pp. 172–178; Vicente García de Diego, ed. *Marqués de Santillana, Canciones y Decires.*

[12] Francisco de Medina y de Mendoza, *Vida del Cardenal D. Pedro de Mendoza, Memorial Histórico Español (MHE)*, VI; Abelardo Merino, *El Cardenal Mendoza*; Layna Serrano, *Historia de Guadalajara*, II, 36–74, 301–317.

Chancellor of Castile (he headed the political councils first of Enrique IV, then of the Catholic Kings), the Mendozas reached the highest level of influence that the family was ever to have.[13] Their name gained in renown during the following century when its proud bearers, many of them serving Charles V and Philip II at all times, carried it into the wider world of the Spanish Empire, but these monarchs, increasingly absolutist, drew their political advisers chiefly from the lower classes.

Under Enrique IV, the "Impotent," whose reign (1454–1474) was plagued by civil wars culminating in his deposition (his enemies raising to King his half-brother Alfonso, a boy of eleven), the Mendozas supported the legitimate monarch. Against Enrique's declared heir apparent, his daughter Juana, the opposing faction promoted the succession of Isabel, his half-sister, to the throne of Castile, but the Mendozas stood by Juana; in 1467, they took charge of the Infanta, then five years old, caring for her in Buitrago at the house of Don Diego's grandfather, the Count of Tendilla I. Even when on Alfonso's sudden death Enrique IV was forced to agree to Isabel's succession, Don Diego's grandfather, more consistent than the wretched King in supporting his legal rights, still upheld Juana's side. In Buitrago, where the little girl still lived in his castle, the Count of Tendilla nailed a large poster to the Cathedral proclaiming the rights of the King's legitimate daughter; then he rode defiantly into Ocaña, the temporary abode of Isabel, and stuck the same notice to the very door of her residence.[14]

But near the end of 1469, Isabel married Fernando, the heir presumptive of Aragon. In the face of this *fait accompli*, the Mendozas' interest in the Infanta Juana cooled. Though ostensibly still taking her side, they returned her to her father, starting now to listen to the attempts of rapprochement that the intelligent young princely couple made them. They waited, so it appears, for the highest bid. The only one truly loath to change sides must have been Don Diego's grandfather, a man of high principles, as we will see.

[13] The rise of the Mendozas in the context of the Castilian aristocracy is traced by L. Suárez Fernández, *Nobleza y Monarquía: Puntos de vista sobre la Historia castellana del siglo XV.*

[14] Ibid., p. 163; Layna Serrano, *Historia de Guadalajara*, II, 143.

In the Mendoza empire of territories and titles of duke,[15] marquis, and count, the honor of a Cardinal of the Church was still
lacking. The closest Spanish aspirant to the cardinalate was at the
present time Alfonso de Carrillo, the Archbishop of Toledo, primate
see of all the Spains—the Mendozas' enemy, and the life-long rival
of Don Pedro González. Perhaps it was one of Fernando de Aragon's cleverest moves when, in 1473, he procured Don Pedro's nomination as cardinal. Though the clan still did not desert Enrique IV,
the majority of them were from then on resolved, tacitly as yet, to
help Isabel in the future.[16]

On Enrique's death in December, 1474, many Castilian towns,
Madrid and Burgos among them, rose at once in support of Juana.
The King of Portugal (her mother's brother) swiftly entered the
country with a large army, occupying the towns of Toro and
Zamora, which had invited him in. Now the Mendozas were ready
to swing their faction openly to Isabel's side. While the young
royal couple laid siege to Toro, the second Marquis of Santillana
brought virtually his entire House into their camp, his army increasing the Isabeline to match the Portuguese in numbers. But the
two Iñigos, Don Diego's grandfather and father, were conspicuously absent, a fact revealing the first Count of Tendilla's unusual
intransigence. Apparently, he did not share the clan's consensus to
desert Doña Juana, and he had also prevented his eldest son, who
was his comrade-in-arms, from switching his allegiance.[17] In the
following year, however, the serious danger in which the Isabeline
party found itself may have moved the recalcitrant Count of Ten-

15 The duke among them was Don Beltrán de la Cueva, Duke of Albuquerque
(alleged father of the Infanta Juana, la "Beltraneja"), who was married to a
daughter of the second Marquis of Santillana.

16 Suárez Fernández, Nobleza y Monarquía, pp. 170–172.

17 In the document presenting the title of Duke of Infantado to the second
Marquis of Santillana, drafted in the encampment in front of Toro on July 22,
1475, Fernando and Isabel express their gratitude to seventeen members of the
House of Mendoza, individually naming each one, except the Count of Tendilla
and his older son. In contrast, his younger son (Don Diego's uncle and namesake, then Bishop of Palencia) is punctiliously mentioned there; since the Bishop
never left the side of his Cardinal-uncle, the monarchs thanked him because he
was his (as well as the recently named Duke's) nephew. They do not mention
the Bishop's father even in this connection, although the fathers of all the others
of the Mendoza brothers and cousins are specified in this document. Layna Serrano, Historia de Guadalajara, II, 186–189, 475–477.

dilla to reconsider, for he and his son joined Fernando's forces in the battle near Toro in March 1476, where they defeated the Portuguese and the large faction of the Castilian nobility allied with them.[18]

Yet even with all the Mendozas now behind them, the Sovereigns' war of succession took three years longer. The eventual victory of the future Catholic Kings is unthinkable without their support. So, in the last instance, a cardinal's hat was responsible for the course of Spain's subsequent history, its unification, and its resultant emergence as a world power.

This great-uncle of Don Diego rose from Archdeacon in Guadalajara as a boy of twelve to Bishop of Calahorra (1454), to Bishop of Sigüenza (1467), to Archbishop of Seville (1473), and to Cardinal the same year. After the death of his rival Alfonso Carrillo, he also became Archbishop of Toledo (1482). Parental direction was responsible for his clerical career; it was usual for at least one of the younger sons, with or without a spiritual inclination, to enter the Church. Don Pedro happened to be as secular a man as his brothers; choosing not to restrain his own nature, he was, in addition to being a master in statecraft, a warrior of personal courage, taking to the field in many campaigns. Two of his three illegitimate sons, proudly acknowledged, became heads of powerful titled families,[19] and he lived in princely magnificence.

In 1479, just when Isabel's victory in the war of succession had secured her Castilian throne, Fernando succeeded to the throne of Aragon-Valencia-Catalonia. Except for Granada, still held to be impregnable, all of Spain was unified, at least dynastically. With the Cardinal's encouragement (and most of the Castilian nobility

---

[18] Ibid., pp. 190–193.

[19] The Catholic Kings raised the Cardinal's eldest son, Don Rodrigo de Mendoza, to Marquis of Cenete and Count of the Cid and Jadraque, titles comprising enormous territories in Granada and Valencia. The Marquis' heir was his daughter Doña Mencía de Mendoza, second Marchioness of Cenete, whose first husband was Henry, Duke of Nassau, after whose death she married Don Fernando de Aragón, son of the King of Naples, who was Duke of Calabria and had formerly been married to Queen Germaine de Foix, second wife and widow of Fernando, the Catholic King. The Cardinal's second son, Don Diego de Mendoza, was named Count of Melito; he became a celebrated commander whose most famous descendant was his granddaughter Doña Ana de Mendoza, later the wife of Don Ruy Gómez de Silva, Prince of Eboli.

now behind him), the sovereigns at last attempted the conquest of Granada. Their triumph brought all of Spain under their rule. But there was as yet no central organ of Spanish power to express this union. Although the Queen of Castile and the King of Aragon intervened de facto in governing each other's patrimony, the legal basis for this connubial collaboration remained thinly defined. To reinforce this tenuous unity, Cardinal Mendoza counseled the monarchs to introduce the Inquisition to Castile (it existed, inactively, in Aragon where it was now being revived); and he created the office of Inquisitor-General of Spain, the first federal agency, as it were. He picked Fray Tomás de Torquemada for that function, the sinister personality who has become the symbol for that era of persecution.

Two, three generations later, the Spanish Inquisition would appear an eternal institution to Don Diego, as static as the principle of monarchy and just as normal, natural, and necessary, although he was prudent enough to protect himself from its terror. Yet the "Holy Office" was an almost casual creation of his great-uncle, a man who had no paltriness in his spirit, always advocating prudence, conciliation, and tolerance, and who could not have foreseen that he was letting loose a legacy of persecution that would last for almost 350 years. His motives in establishing the Inquisition were those of a statesman. The occasion for creating this new instrument of unification, analogous to the political, had arisen through the infiltration of the Spanish Church by converted Jews. In the fifteenth century, after a series of pogroms, with resulting waves of baptism in 1391, many *conversos*, some of them *marranos* (secretly, still Jewish believers), had taken clerical positions, high and low. In a bizarre development, former rabbis (and their descendants) had become Catholic priests, bishops, and confessors of kings. The enemies of the newly converted (including some of these converted themselves, denouncing their own brethren) were gripped by a persecuting fervor unmatched until then, calling for the extirpation of the "heresy" of those who were no longer Jews.

This is not the place to go deeper into the history of that odious organization. It is touched on here only to illuminate the climate in which Cardinal Mendoza, a notably humane man, set the scene and chose the directors for the ensuing bloody drama of the Inquisition, a tragedy he had not intended to write. On the contrary, in 1478, when he could no longer avoid listening to complaints about the anarchy prevailing in the Church on account of the "Judaizers," he advocated peaceful measures for improving the situation. He published a catechism spelling out the belief and duties of the Christian, stressing education as the most desirable means for consolidating the faith.[20]

All this notwithstanding, the first fires of the Inquisition were lit in 1482 in Cardinal Mendoza's own diocese, Seville, site of the first *auto de fé*. The Cardinal, occupied in marshalling the forces for the Granadine war, was not present at those spectacles. Besides, once the Holy Office was established, he had no hand in its jurisdiction. Yet those events occurred under his aegis, as did ten years later the expulsion of the Jews, while at the same time he, his family, and virtually his entire class of aristocrats were protecting many actual and former Jews who managed the grandees' estates and served them in countless positions of trust. Could he not have prevented the horror, now incipient, soon to pervade the Spain he had united? Perhaps so, if the professed aim of the persecutors had not been the purification of the Church—and if his own life had been more saintly. He must have felt unable to speak up against the violent forces he had inadvertently set in motion in the name of administrative reform, because he himself, unscrupulous beneficiary of multiple bishoprics and sinner against the vow of continence, was an obvious symbol of the Church's corruption.

Don Diego's grandfather Don Iñigo López de Mendoza[21] (born in Guadalajara 1419 or 1420, died 1479), second son of the first Marquis of Santillana, was made Count of Tendilla by Enrique IV in 1465. As a boy of eighteen, he joined his father in one of the occasional frontier skirmishes against the Moors; during the fighting he saved Santillana's life and felled the Moorish commander at the same time. This established Don Iñigo's fame of greatest military prowess among the seven brothers. Married young (at nineteen or twenty), spending his life in political and military service to the crown, he is described as devoted to letters no less

[20] Henry Charles Lea, *A History of the Inquisition in Spain*, I, 155, 156. Merino, *El Cardenal Mendoza*, pp. 150, 151, 155. On the Inquisition in general, see Henry Kamen, *The Spanish Inquisition*.
[21] Layna Serrano, *Historia de Guadalajara*, II, 22–30.

than to the sword, although he left no writings. Spain's link with
the Renaissance continued through him: as one of the few Castilian warriors knowing Latin, he was sent to Rome in 1455 as
Enrique IV's ambassador to Pope Nicholas V and his successor,
Calixtus III. In 1459/60, the King once more sent him as his envoy
to the new Pope Pius II, who had convened a Congress in Mantua
for all Christian monarchs to join him in planning a Crusade.

On that occasion, Don Iñigo, annoyed that the French ambassador had taken precedence over him, insisted on a more honorable
seat for himself as the Castilian King's representative. Entering
the clerical assembly with an escort of armed vassals, he took it
upon himself to remove the French ambassador bodily from the
seat he had not been willing to yield—another incident showing
the haughtiness and intransigence of Don Diego's grandfather.
Some of his grandson's actions at the papal court about ninety
years later will seem to be astonishingly similar.

The long and fortunate life of Don Diego's father, also a Don
Iñigo López de Mendoza (1442?–1515), the second Count of Tendilla (and from 1512, Marquis of Mondéjar), so overshadowed that
of his father that during the sixteenth century historians believed
both Iñigos to be one person.[22] (Pope Paul III, the former Alexander Farnese, distinguished them both, however. When he was
in a good mood, he would never fail to remind Don Diego—who
like his father and grandfather was ambassador to popes—that he
definitely remembered his father and almost remembered his
grandfather. To be exact, Farnese was not born until six or seven
years after the time of the first Tendilla's second and last embassy.)[23]

The second Tendilla, sometimes called "the great Tendilla,"[24] re-

---

[22] Ambrosio de Morales, *Las antigüedades de las ciudades de España*. In his
dedication to Don Diego (GP III, 470–474), Morales says that Santillana was
Don Diego's grandfather, p. 471. Gutiérrez Coronel, *Historia genealógica*, II,
332, attributes several events from the second Tendilla's life to the first Tendilla.
For more details on the confusion of father and son, see Layna Serrano, *Historia
de Guadalajara*, II, 22, 23, 226.

[23] Mendoza to Charles V, from Rome, May 3, 1547, in J. J. I. v. Döllinger,
Beiträge zur politischen, kirchlichen und Kulturgeschichte, I, 53; *Nuntiaturberichte aus Deutschland (NB)*, XI, 771.

[24] Layna Serrano, *Historia de Guadalajara*, II, 227. On Tendilla II, see ibid.,

sembled his grandfather, the first Marquis of Santillana, in his intellectual interests, display of magnificence and patronage, and perhaps also in temperament. He seems to have been more conciliatory and prudent than his impetuous father, who was his senior by scarcely more than nineteen years. Until his father's death in 1479, he accompanied him to all his battles and ambassadorial missions. His first wife, who was his first cousin, Doña Marina Lasso de Mendoza, died childless in 1477 (but, in accord with the centuries-old Mendoza procedure, she left him estates). Soon after his marriage to his second wife, Doña Francisca Pacheco, in 1480, the Count took part in the Granadine war, interrupting this service from the end of 1485 until 1487, when he went as ambassador of the Catholic Sovereigns to Italy. Pope Innocent VIII hailed him as "peacemaker in Italy"—perhaps the finest honor any Mendoza ever earned. On his return, he brought with him Italian-trained architects to finish *a la antigua* ("in antique style") the College of Santa Cruz, founded by his Cardinal-uncle in Valladolid. Originally designed as a Gothic structure, the college was the first building in Spain to show neoclassic lines.[25] In his entourage also came the Italian humanist and Latin teacher Pietro Martire d'Anghiera (known to English readers as Peter Martyr), the first of Italian intellectuals seeking greener pastures in Spain. So, Count Iñigo, contributing to the introduction in Spain of the Renaissance in architecture and letters, laid the basis for a thorough Latinist education for his sons and daughters and their entire generation. Occasionally the Count composed Latin verse, but he is best known for his rôle in the war of Granada.

In 1483 Tendilla saved Alhama, a town in the mountains southwest of Granada, and then an isolated Christian stronghold over thirty miles inside Moorish territory.[26] In 1489 he conquered Baza, defeating the Moorish Princes Cidi Yahia and Ben Omar, father and son, heroic defenders whom, after his victory, he persuaded to accept conversion. These Arabic chieftains (later known as Don

pp. 292–299, 301; José Cepeda Adán, "Andalucía en 1508: Un aspecto de la correspondencia del Virrey Tendilla," *Hispania* 22 (Madrid, 1962); Antonio Marín Ocete, *El Conde de Tendilla, primer Capitán general de Granada*, soon to be published by the Patronato de la Alhambra y Generalife.

25 Pedro Aguado Bleye, *Manual de Historia de España*, II, 246, 247.
26 Layna Serrano, *Historia de Guadalajara*, II, 264.

Pedro de Granada and Don Alonso de Granada y Venegas) kept their desertion into the Christian camp secret so as to lure many of their trusting followers into military traps. This *coup de grâce* to the Moorish side eventually led to the bloodless surrender of Granada, which also was negotiated by the Count of Tendilla. On the second day of January, 1492, he, with a few other notables, planted on the Torre de Vela, highest tower of the Alhambra, his Cardinal-uncle's silver cross, the royal Castilian banner with its lions and castles, and the standard of Santiago.[27] For the rest of his life— another twenty-three years—he was to command this kingdom.

Don Diego's future mother, Doña Francisca Pacheco, whom the Count brought into his new hereditary estate on the Alhambra in 1492, was no blood relation of the Mendozas, but almost four hundred years before Don Diego's birth, one of her paternal ancestors, the Jewish doctor Ruy Capón, was physician and treasurer of Queen Doña Urraca when his paternal forebears also attended that Queen's court. There seems to have been no poetic or other literary heritage on her side—only traditions of political expertise and boundless ambition. Her father, Don Juan Pacheco, Marquis of Villena and Maestre of Santiago (1419–1474), was for many years a favorite of Enrique IV.[28] He was reared from boyhood as Enrique's page and close friend, but his lineage was not then equal in rank to that of the ancient Castilian families. About 1443, however, in the year after his marriage to Doña María Portocarrero, one of the richest heiresses, he emerged as a great power next to the throne. In 1445, by obtaining the Marquisate of Villena, former crown land of King Juan of Aragon, he had lifted himself to the front rank of all the grandees.

His wife, Don Diego's maternal grandmother, was of Moorish-

27 María del Carmen Pescador del Hoyo, "Cómo fué de verdad la toma de Granada," *Al-Andalus* (*A-A*) 20, fasc. 2 (1955): 283–344.

28 Contemporary chroniclers were either violently biased against Juan Pacheco or presumably in his pay. See the bibliography on him in Aguado Bleye, *Manual*, II, 5–28; see also J. F. O'Callaghan, "Don Pedro Girón, Master of the Order of Calatrava," *Hispania* 21 (Madrid, 1961): 345, n. 8. Alonso de Palencia, *Crónica de Enrique IV*, ed. A. Paz y Melia, is hostile toward Pacheco; Hernando del Pulgar, *Crónica de los Señores Reyes Católicos Don Fernando y Doña Isabel*, is friendly.

Jewish descent. Among her ancestors was Doña María Ruiz, a Jewess of beauty and wealth, and a Cordobese noble, Don Hernando, forebears she shared with the future Catholic King Fernando, who was her cousin. (King Fernando's mother, the Queen of Navarre, Aragon, and Sicily, was Doña Juana Enriquez, aunt of Doña Francisca Pacheco.) Doña María Portocarrero is described as a woman of great qualities and authority. She is said to have been so devoted to her husband that she adopted his tremulous way of speech. Their thirteen or fourteen children married into the families of the Mendoza, Ponce de León, Aguilar, Dukes of Alba and many others; so practically the entire higher nobility of Spain owed their "taint" of "impure" blood mostly to this couple.[29]

During the lifetime of Juan Pacheco, the Mendoza family bitterly opposed him. At one time Pacheco had conquered their town of Guadalajara and made the King sequester all the Mendoza properties that he could reach. This storm lasted more than a year, and the brothers Mendoza withstood it, holding out in their castle of Hita, which was besieged by Pacheco's troops. Near the end of his life Pacheco regretted the continuous feud, and tried to win the Mendozas by ties of marriage. In 1471 he affianced his young daughter Francisca to the ten-year-old grandson of the second Marquis of Santillana (the boy was Don Diego Hurtado de Mendoza [1461–1531] "el Grande," later the third Duke of Infantado), but this agreement must have been broken through new hostilities. In 1472 Pacheco himself, after a year or two as widower, married a young girl from their clan, the daughter of Pedro Velasco, Count of Haro.

Yet the Mendozas continued on the opposite faction even after Don Juan Pacheco's death in 1474. Pacheco's son, the second Marquis of Villena (later, first Duke of Escalona), fought against them on the side of Juana. But in 1480, after the Isabeline victory, the Marquis of Villena gave the second Count of Tendilla his still unmarried sister Francisca with a dowry of three and a half million maravedis and the fortress and town of Jumilla.[30] The two stirpes had at last concluded peace.

---

[29] On the descent of Pacheco's wife, see Julio Caro Baroja, Los Judíos en la España moderna y contemporánea, III, 288.

[30] For data on Doña Francisca Pacheco, see GP I, 4; Gudiel, Compendio, p. 90; Fernández de Bethencourt, Historia genealógica, II, 186, 187.

Childhood in Granada

Count Iñigo and his wife, as far as we know, had three children before moving to Granada: Doña María, born in the 1480s (who in 1503 married her cousin Don Antonio Hurtado de Mendoza, Count of Monteagudo); Don Luis Hurtado, heir to the marquisate (1489–1566); and Don Antonio (1491?–1552), the later Viceroy of Mexico and Peru. The remaining five children of this couple, born within the Alhambra compound, were Doña María Pacheco (?–1531); Don Bernardino (?–1557); Don Francisco (?–1544); Doña Isabel (?–?); and lastly, Don Diego.[31]

Of the "Palace of Tendilla," only the foundations remain.[32] Rows of reddish brick, less than two feet high, remnants of ancient walls, trace the original design of the vanished house. Their long, low lines serve as dividers for flower beds. The oblong pool that once formed the heart of the palace, resembles the slightly larger pool in the "Court of Myrtles" nearby. It is set in gardens of a beauty defying description. Once, arcaded passages and graceful colonnades, similar to those preserved in the royal house, also enclosed this gleaming pool. Now, the alcoves, vaulted ceilings, stucco walls, are gone; the view from the site, once framed within the arches of double and triple partitioned windows, ranges without limit from the towers of the Alhambra in the foreground to the Cerro del Sol with its hillside, the Generalife; it embraces the hills of the Albaicin and Sacromonte and loses itself in the distant sierras. Flowering shrubs and trees fill the spaces that once housed

---

[31] Tendilla II also had at least three illegitimate children, the first of them, Rodrigo, apparently from the time between his two marriages. In 1489, the ninth year of his marriage to Doña Francisca, the Count made a testament asking his wife for mercy to take care of "don rrodrigo mi fijo" in the event of his death. In his final testament in 1515, only a "natural" son, Pedro, appears; possibly he was born after the Countess had died. From that late time seems to hail also a daughter, María de Mendoza, whom her half brother Don Antonio, then Viceroy of New Spain, took with him to Mexico.

[32] Antonio Gallego y Burín, *La Alhambra*, p. 198. During the time of Philip V, the owner of the house, a latter-day Count of Tendilla, who had taken the Austrian side in the War of the Spanish Succession, destroyed his palace rather than allow the Bourbon King or his entourage to lodge there. I am indebted for this information to Don Jesús Bermúdez Pareja, director of the Museum of the Alhambra.

princely retainers and menials, women's quarters, baths, stables, and patios. The Count of Tendilla, first Christian host of this mansion of Arabic princes, used to entertain his guests in Moorish fashion, bidding them squat on silken rugs laid on floors of polychrome tiles.[33] He and his family adapted themselves to Arab customs without delay, and he was content to remain in this newly won territory. Sixteen years after the conquest, in 1508, he disclosed that he had not crossed the Sierra Morena for many years, having all but become a native of this region.[34]

Tendilla's conciliatory manner had endeared him to the proud people of Granada who were, in fact, unbeaten. Their rulers had sold them out to the Christians without allowing them to fight for their city; the conquerors (led by Tendilla) stole through the back door of the Alhambra to take possession from Boabdil, the last King of the Nasirid dynasty. Stealthily, through the night, the troops had filed in, one by one, to occupy the towers and bastions of the Red Fortress. But when the Granadines awoke to the sight of the silver cross planted on the tower of the Alcazaba, and the presence of Christian occupation troops on and around the Alhambra, Count Iñigo's soft-spoken words and promises calmed their anger and fear. He left them undisturbed in their customs and daily pursuits; his civilian co-administrator Don Hernando de Zafra was equally tolerant, and his ecclesiastical collaborator, the first Archbishop of Granada, Fray Hernando de Talavera, was, by all accounts, a saintly man. On the advice of the Mendozas, the Catholic Sovereigns had granted the Moors complete freedom of religion and customs. They promised not to establish the Inquisition in Granada, and they even left the people in possession of their small arms (lances, daggers, bows and arrows, slingshots), sequestering only all cannon.[35]

Granada, whose environment was an important factor in making

---

[33] During, for example, the visit of Dr. Hieronymus Münzer. See *Boletín de la Real Academia de la Historia (BRAH)* 80 (1924), "Viaje por España y Portugal en los años 1494 y 1495," translated from the Latin by Julio Puyol, p. 32.

[34] Letter dated June 18, 1508, in Cepeda Adán, "Andalucía en 1508," p. 32.

[35] *Colección de documentos inéditos para la Historia de España (DIE)* VIII, "Capitulación de la toma é entrega de Granada (1491)," pp. 421–436, especially items 12, 14, 17, 30, and 32, for the Muslim question.

Don Diego the philosopher who understood the mentality of Moor and Marrano, was then a mercantile center with a polyglot population. Until the invading armies ravaged the flourishing countryside, it had been thriving in sericulture and horticulture. The working people and the small traders, mostly Arabs but also Jews, inhabited the Albaicin; on this hill's summit, level with the Alhambra fortress across the deep gorge of the Darro River, stood the largest mosque and another palace of the Arabic kings. The peace treaty with Boabdil had left also the numerous Jews of "Granada, the Albaicin, and its suburbs" undisturbed, but this situation was the first to be reversed. A scant three months after the conquest, the Jews were given notice to submit to baptism or, under penalty of death, leave within another four months not only Granada but also all of newly united Christian Spain. Many Moors considered this a warning to them as well, for a great number of them left by their own choice at the same time (ten years before the edict for their own expulsion was issued). Even so, the basic composition of the population did not change much. After the Jews' expulsion, the vacant houses of the exiles stood ready to receive incoming Christian settlers, and lately it has been noted that many of these new settlers were, in fact, Marranos. Escaping from the Inquisition now established in all other parts of Spain, these baptized Jews soon filled many places left behind by the Jews who chose emigration. Similarly, many Moors electing to remain bought houses and estates at enforced bargain prices from emigrating Moors.[36]

At the start of its new life, Granada and its hinterland had to adjust to a shift chiefly among the middle classes. The Moorish kings and aristocrats were simply replaced *in toto* by the conquerors who seized all large estates as their spoils.[37] The bulk of the Muslim population remained: workers, artisans, peasants, and small shopkeepers—those elements of the populace who have no-

[36] On Jews in peace treaty, see *DIE* 8, item 38, p. 433; and Miguel Angel Ladero Quesada, "Dos Temas de la Granada Nazari," *Cuadernos de Historia* 3 (1969): 321–345. On Moorish emigration, see Alfredo Bustani, ed. *Fragmento de la época sobre noticias de los Reyes Nazeritas o Capitulación de Granada y emigración de los andaluces a Marruecos,* p. 50. On vacant houses ready for settlers, see M. Gaspar Remiro, "Granada en poder de los Reyes Católicos; primeros años de su dominación," *Estudios Históricos de Granada,* pp. 214–215. On Marrano immigration, see J. Caro Baroja, *Razas, Pueblos y Linajes,* p. 110.

[37] Caro Baroja, *Moriscos,* p. 98.

where else to go. Soon the Moorish kingdom settled down to its usual ways, the majority of the people now "vassals" of new Christian landowners. Always poor, producing the same wealth for their new lords that formerly had flowed into the pockets of the Muslim King and his satellites, the workers and serfs in the mountain villages and on their Albaicin, with its honeycomb of tiny houses, did not find their life changed too much—at least not during the first seven years—under the moderate regime of Tendilla, assisted by Zafra and Talavera. But when Cardinal Mendoza, whose conciliatory counsel had guided the peace treaty, died in 1495, his successor as supreme adviser to the Kings, Fray Francisco Ximénez de Cisneros (who owed his appointment to Mendoza's recommendation), prevailed upon Fernando and Isabel to rescind their solemn guarantee of letting the Muslims exercise their religion and preserve their customs "forevermore" (*para siempre jamás.*)

In 1499 Cisneros himself came to Granada to enforce baptism on the entire population. He hurled thousands of Arabic books into bonfires, irreplaceable manuscripts on religion, politics, and law.[38] By some twist of legality, he succeeded in consecrating the Great Mosque on the Albaicin, symbol of the identity of Granada's Moors, as the Church of San Salvador. Cajoling and bribing many people, he stunned them into conversions en masse. Soon it was apparent that the conversions were no more than skin-deep, and Cisneros turned from persuasion to persecution. He sent many principal citizens to prison, others he drove to flight; finally he touched off armed resistance in the more valiant. Late one night they left their silk-weaving looms, dyeing vats, tanneries, and cobbler, bake and butcher shops and assailed Cardinal Cisneros' residence (a stronghold in downtown Granada). At daybreak they were on the verge of storming it when Count Iñigo arrived with a superior force and dispersed them. Offended at seeing their trusted governor rescue their enemy, the Moors withdrew behind the walls of the Albaicin

[38] Miguel Lafuente de Alcántara, *Historia de Granada*, IV, 162, says that Cisneros burned 1,025,000 priceless Arabic manuscripts. On actions of Cisneros, see Henry Charles Lea, *The Moriscos of Spain*, pp. 29–36, and Lea's bibliography on Cisneros, ibid., pp. 36, 37, n. 1. Further: Esprit Fléchier, *Histoire du Cardinal Ximènez*; Karl Joseph von Hefele, *The Life of Cardinal Ximénez*; Comte de Cedillo, *El Cardenal Cisneros*; L. Fernández de Retana, *Cisneros y su siglo.*

(which, by the peace treaty, Christians were forbidden to climb to prevent them from peering into Moorish homes). They chose forty men among themselves and established their own government. Entrenching themselves on top of their hill, they faced the Alhambra fortress defiantly from there. The revolt lasted ten days. To regain the people's confidence, Count Iñigo sent them his esquire with his own shield as a customary token of peace, but the shield was returned to him, stoned to pieces. Only Fray Hernando de Talavera succeeded in appealing to the rebels. In all of the seven years, he had patiently worked to convert the Muslims by kindness and good example, never by coercion. Now he walked humbly among them, unprotected by an escort, and having calmed the Moors, he opened a new avenue for the Count.

Tendilla's dramatic gestures toward reestablishing his good relations with his people have become legendary. When he rode onto the major square on the Albaicin among the seething throngs, he tore his red bonnet from his head and threw it into their midst as his ultimate sign of peaceful intentions. It is said that the Moors, seeing the shining bald pate of their Viceroy for the first time, were so stupefied that many did not recognize him. (In later years the Count was to wear a white wig.)[39] They picked up the bonnet, kissed it reverently, and handed it back to him. But when the Count requested them to surrender their arms so that he could leave Granada for the court to prevail upon the King and Queen to pardon them, the Moors refused. The monarchs, they declared, could not be trusted since they had broken the peace agreement. In order to gain their confidence, the Count now offered to leave his wife and children as hostages with them for his word. While the Moors demurred, Count Iñigo, who did not wish to let them out of his sight as long as they held on to their weapons, sent for the Countess.

Doña Francisca would have been waiting for her husband in the safety of her mansion behind the strong walls of the Alhambra fortress. When the Count's lieutenants appeared before her with the strange request to join him in the Moorish quarter, she went back with them to the Albaicin at once, taking two of her small children with her. Despite the Moorish mob that had recently been

[39] I am grateful to Sr. Don Jesús Bermúdez for showing me Count Iñigo's portrait. It is presently in the Washington Irving Room of the Arabic Royal Palace and is reproduced here by his kind permission.

so angry, Countess Francisca moved into a house next to the Great Mosque, staying there as long as her husband was absent from Granada. Overwhelmed by the Tendilla couple's trust and chivalry, the Moors surrendered their arms; then Count Iñigo traveled to Seville to plead with the Catholic Kings for better treatment of the Moors. Probably he also effected at the same time the removal of Cisneros from Granada.[40]

It is the only time Don Diego's (future) mother is mentioned individually. This manifestation of courage, this obedience to a husband's wishes, is impressive. She must have freely shared her husband's tolerance of the Moors and his humane convictions.

Though the town reverted to its former calm, the example of the revolt on the Albaicin sparked similar revolts in the surrounding mountains. The Alpujarras southeast of Granada were thickly sprinkled with Moorish villages whose inhabitants (frugal mountaineers who grew mulberry trees and cultivated silkworms), like the town's people, had never been fought or subdued. Soon, a mountain war was ablaze. It fell to the Count of Tendilla, assisted by Gonzalo Fernández de Córdoba (the later "Great Captain" who had learned warfare under Tendilla) and to King Fernando in person to fight this rekindled war in the new theater with superior force. By 1501 Christian victory was total. Now the Catholic Kings dropped all pretense of tolerance. Availing themselves anew of Cisneros' counsel, in 1502 they decreed that every Moor in the kingdom of Granada had to undergo baptism, or, under penalty of death, leave Castile—a law little different from that applying to the Jews ten years earlier (except that it did not touch the Moors of Valencia, Aragon, and Catalonia). The cross was now erected in every mosque, and the Moors who remained and became converted—the majority—were called "Moriscos" from then on. But under the tolerant administration of Tendilla and his successors, the law on the books remained one thing and its execution quite

---

[40] See the sources in note 38, above. For more on Count Iñigo's actions, see Cepeda Adán, "Andalucía en 1508," pp. 3–28; GP I, 3–26; Luis del Mármol Carvajal, *Historia del rebelión y castigo de los moriscos del reyno de Granada,* in *BAE* XXI, *Historiadores* I, 155; Layna Serrano, *Historia de Guadalajara,* II, 291. Don Diego himself, in *Guerra de Granada,* also in *BAE* XXI, *Historiadores* I, 70, does not mention the Countess in describing this episode, saying only that the Count gave his sons as *rehenes* ("hostages").

another. For almost seventy years, the Moriscos succeeded in circumventing this law. When Don Diego returned to Granada in 1569, the same mountain war was being fought all over again by the grandsons and great-grandsons of the parties involved in 1500, under the same basic conditions that had prevailed a year or two before his birth.

By the time Don Diego was only about four years old, his mother apparently was not living. In 1508 the Count's eldest son Don Luis, then nineteen, was spending the summer with his household—he probably was already married—in Alhama, and his father sent Don Luis' little brothers, the *hermanillos*, along with him to escape the summer heat in Granada. A friend of the Count, who lived not far from Alhama, wrote Count Iñigo, inviting the children to his house, and the father, replying that they had already gone with Don Luis, seemed to regret that Don Yñigo Manrique's invitation had come too late. "For all my sins," he wrote, "they need someone who is kind to them. I know well that they would have fared better in the house of Señora doña Ysabel whose hands I kiss [the wife of the addressed, presumably], than in a place where [the grown-ups] do not yet know what children are."[41]

The Count does not mention his wife in this correspondence, nor in other letters of that year. But the *hermanillos*—too young to be in college or doing page-service at the royal court—were still in their father's house and in need of kindness. They would be Don Diego, about four years old, and the older Don Francisco and Doña Isabel, children still. Apparently the atmosphere around Don Luis was not a kind one to children; the young man was not yet a father.[42] In later years, Don Luis and Don Diego were never close. The elder brother brought law suits against the younger for the regulation of their properties; and we are told, also, that Don Luis resented being a head shorter than Don Antonio, the second of the brothers.[43] The impression is that Don Luis, as the future head of

[41] Cepeda Adán, "Andalucia en 1508," p. 36.

[42] His first son, who did not survive, was born perhaps a year or two later; the second son, his heir Don Iñigo, was born in 1511; Caro Baroja, *Moriscos*, p. 142.

[43] G. Avalos Guzmán, *Don Antonio de Mendoza*, p. 24. See also "Crónica de Don Francesillo de Zúñiga," *BAE* XXXVI, "Curiosidades bibliográficas," ed. Adolfo de Castro, p. 16: ". . . Fué este marqués [Mondéjar II] devoto y liberal;

the Mondéjar-Tendilla branch of the Mendoza clan, carried himself pompously, lacking humor—the kind of person who would regard children as pests.

Having lost his mother so early, Don Diego must have been thrown chiefly upon the affection of his aging father, who was spending the rest of his energies mostly in intellectual pursuits, surrounded by humanists, many of them learned Moriscos and Marranos.[44] But the Count often went on inspection tours of the coastal fortifications, and he also undertook several military campaigns. In his old age, he sold some of his property to raise a private army and valiantly marched his famous banner against unruly Andalusian grandees at Gibraltar who had broken away from King Fernando.[45] (For this contribution, the Catholic King raised the Count to Marquis of Mondéjar.)[46]

Perhaps his father's frequent absences were the reason that Diego regarded the estate of sympathetic neighbors as his second home early in life. On the Generalife lived the former Moorish prince, Ben Omar (Don Alonso de Granada y Venegas), *alcaide* of this summer palace of the Nasirid kings. He had married Count Iñigo's cousin Doña María (or Juana) de Mendoza and raised a family— at least a son, Don Pedro de Granada Venegas y Mendoza—of the approximate age of Don Diego.

The buildings and gardens of the Generalife cover a hillside on the neighboring mountain, separated from the Alhambra hill by a deep ravine. A secret door on the north side of the Alhambra fortress led (and leads) to the well-camouflaged former royal path connecting both places that Don Diego must have crossed many

---

parescía caña fístola siempre; riyó pocas veces, regañó infinitas; tuvo cuatro hermanos, los dos siete palmos mas altos que él. . . ."

[44] Previous to 1492, Count Iñigo had a Jewish majordomo and a Jewish physician; afterwards they and others may have continued to stay with him as *conversos*. See Fritz Baer, *Die Juden im christlichen Spanien*, I, part 2, 348, 426.

[45] In the Mendozas' quartered emblem, a red diagonal stripe, edged in gold on a field of green, appears on the top and bottom fields; the two lateral golden fields have in azure letters the legend *Ave Maria Gratia Plena*, which was earned by their ancestor Garcilaso de la Vega in the battle of Salado against the Moors. Tendilla II surrounded this traditional coat of arms with eight points, representing the star of Bethlehem, and the lettering *Buena Guía* ("Good Guide").

[46] GP I, 14, 20.

times.[47] In his years of absence, much later, Don Diego was to consider the Generalife—decidedly not the Alhambra—his home.[48] "Home" (*mi casa*) was not just a nostalgic figure of speech: this is disclosed by the fact that he lived there when he returned to Granada as an old man. In his correspondence from Granada during 1569–1572, as well as in the *Guerra de Granada*, the only local person he mentions with any sympathy is the then-living owner and heir of the same house, Don Alonso de Granada Venegas y Rengifo, whom Don Diego calls his *compañero*.[49] Whether Mendoza had a certain right to a lease on one of the estates on the Generalife (none is mentioned in his father's testament nor in his own), or whether he later rented a house on those grounds, or had an invitation for life to retire there—whatever the legal arrangements, it was his home, a sign that this half-Moorish family had close ties with him.

Catholic orthodoxies did not hold Don Diego in thrall; he showed little need for religion—an atypical trait in a Spaniard. Neither the Virgin Mary nor the Saints appeared in his vocabulary. Would his exceptional childhood environment have influenced him into developing such an unusual attitude? Perhaps this happened in part because Doña Francisca had not been there to instill in her youngest son a worship of Mary. Despite her remote non-Christian descent, the Countess, like all Castilian noblewomen of her generation, must have been a devout Catholic, and a mother is possibly the most important influence in raising her child in religious devotion and belief. Instead, the elders who guided the young Diego,

---

[47] On title to Generalife, see Antonio Gallego Morell, ed. *Casa de los Tiros: Guías de los Museos de España*, XI, 13; Luis Seco de Lucena, *La Alhambra como fué y como es*. Don Alonso's wife was a daughter of Francisco Hurtado de Mendoza; on her parentage, see "Romancero sobre don Alonso Granada y Venegas," in "Romancero General," II, ed. A. Durán, *BAE* XVI, 130. On the connecting path between the Alhambra and the Generalife, see Jesús Bermúdez Pareja, "El Generalife después del incendio de 1958," in *Cuadernos de la Alhambra* 1 (1965): 9–39, esp. p. 14.

[48] Mendoza to Arras, Siena, March 14, 1551: ". . . mostrarle hecho el servicio y tenerme con esto por pagado, y quando otra cosa no pueda contentarme, con salir en juego, y que mis emulos a lo menos no me ayan estoruado; esto e yrme con Dios a Genalarife." *AC*, p. 215.

[49] Mendoza to Cardinal Espinosa, Granada, June 29, 1570, GP III, p. 458.

or whose behavior served him as an early example, were his father, an intellectual man, and his friends of similar stamp. This peculiar circumstance of Mendoza's childhood may be a reason for his later individuality and originality. He could become the future irreverent writer so easily because he was allowed to grow up uncowed by religious mysteries, frankly enlightened in the house of his exceptionally tolerant and imaginative father. Also, one of his two eldest sisters, both women of outstanding intelligence who had received a humanist education, was still at home (María Pacheco, who did not marry before 1510); and his nurse, the "Señora Montalto," was presumably a Morisca. (Seventy years later, Don Diego's favorite servants in Granada still were "New Christians.")[50] But since the New Christians of his environment literally had been touched by few, if any, drops of holy water at their recent mass baptism, Don Diego grew up among a probably somewhat cynical company.

By coincidence, he was born just when Spain's greatest champion of Catholicism, the Queen of Castile, was silenced. No appeal to religion was to be heard again with similar emphasis and power until Philip II reached the maturity and influence of middle age. Queen Isabel was dead. The body of the venerated monarch rested only a few steps away from Diego's house, in the Franciscan convent that the Count of Tendilla had installed in the Arabic palace adjoining his own. (It is now the Parador of San Francisco.) Her tombstone stood in the same small chapel that contained Doña Francisca's sepulcher. The conqueror of Granada and the wife of her Viceroy in that kingdom lay under a graceful *ajimez*—a window similar to one above the Lion's Court, divided by two slender columns into three round-arched partitions. The wall of the chapel still showed (and show today) Hispano-Mauresque traceries. There, as in the Alcázar, decorative inscriptions, elegantly interlaced with foliage patterns, spell in Arabic letters "God, the only victor"; others praise a Granadine king.[51]

[50] On the nurse, see GP III, 265, 266. In Mendoza's testament, among servants remembered for back pay and legacies, were "New Christians"; see C. Pérez Pastor, *Memorias*, pp. 153–194, fol. 814.

[51] The bodies of Queen Isabel and King Fernando were transferred under Don Luis' direction in 1521 to the royal chapel of the new Cathedral of Granada. There is no trace of the tombs of Mendoza's parents in the old chapel on the Alhambra.

Whenever the boy visited the graves, perhaps from filial piety or ceremonial duty, would the religious atmosphere have attracted or cowed him? Or would he rather have checked his progress in Arabic—the language now officially despised, but not yet forbidden —by trying to decipher the script on the wall? Presumably a precocious and observant child, tended at every step by nurses, grooms, and retainers, all drawn from the recently "converted" people, he must have been aware that the Queen's edict against the Moors had remained a dead letter. Neither did the late Queen, who could not conquer the hearts of the Moriscos, have the power to direct the path of his own personal religiosity. He had absorbed his spirit of doubt and criticism early—if not with the milk of his (possibly) Morisca nurse, then perhaps as an attentive listener to his father's conversations.

The shrine was to the right of Tendilla's house; to the left, further down, stood (and stands) the old Alcazaba fortress, where a garrison of hundreds of soldiers was stationed under the Count's command. Between the chanting of the monks on the one side, and martial music, drums, trumpets, on the other, Diego was exposed to the two contending forces that sought to determine his life. But it is possible that even then neither the cloister nor the military attracted him—at least far less than the books, manuscripts, and mathematical instruments he would have found in his father's Arabic house. As a philosopher, he would often quote Aristotle: "From an upward movement and another, going downward, results the diagonal; for this we must look."[52] Perhaps his early location between two extremes predisposed him toward his ideal of the middle way.

As the youngest child, Don Diego was forced to compete at great odds with the achievements of his elders. He may have tried, consciously or unconsciously, to overcompensate for the head start the others had, not only in time and opportunity but even, unfairly as it seems, in money. This does not refer to the universal heir, Don Luis, who, under the law of primogeniture, received literally everything. (Either the Count was not wealthy enough or the time had passed to establish more than one *mayorazgo*, or entailed estate, per family. His grandfather, the Marquis of San-

[52] Mendoza to Arras, Rome, February 11, 1550. *AC*, p. 198.

tillana, had been able to found seven *mayorazgos*, even though the six of the *segundones* were of relatively modest size.) Oddly, Don Antonio, an adult at the time of his father's death, received twice as much income-producing property as his young brothers Francisco and Diego; also Bernardino received a legacy that, although not specified in his father's testament, seems to have been larger than that of those least favored. An *hijo bastardo*, Don Pedro, in his turn, was dismissed with a lump sum of 100,000 maravedis— no more than the annual amount conceded to Francisco and Diego each.[53] Yet this was not simply a parental caprice. The younger sons were destined for the Church. If any of them took after their great-uncle, theirs could be the most lucrative of all businesses. The second and third sons, selected for political careers as courtiers, perhaps already engaged to be married by parental contract, required a higher guaranteed income than the future clerics, who would be gaining benefices in the course of their careers.

It has been variously asserted and denied that Don Diego was ever destined for a career in the Church,[54] but it is unlikely that Count Iñigo had intended another future for him. Both his financial provision for Diego—similar to that of the older ecclesiastic-to-be, Francisco—and his Cardinal-brother's name, with which he had honored his youngest son, point in the clerical direction.[55]

[53] GP I, 43; III, 265, 266.

[54] Cf. GP I, 69–71.

[55] Don Diego's uncle, Diego Hurtado, at first Bishop of Palencia, then Archbishop of Seville and Cardinal, who had grown up under the protection of the Grand Cardinal without ever acquiring a similar political or even personal eminence, died on September 13, 1502, leaving two sons. He had been very close to his brother, Tendilla II. In his testament, the Count ordered ten thousand masses said for the soul of his brother Diego, the same commemoration accorded the souls of his first and second wives. GP I, 22; III, 256.

2. FORMATIVE YEARS, TO 1529

Oh that we were still so young as in Toledo!
Don Diego in 1549[1]

Educational Climate

AMONG ALL OF HIS MANY BROTHERS, half brothers, and first cousins, Don Diego is the only one who left evidence of intellectual activity. We have little information of the kind of education predisposing him for that. His only autobiographical remarks known to us are those he made later in life to Ambrosio de Morales, one of Philip II's official chroniclers, who dedicated a book to him. (Morales, an archeologist, numismatist, and a generally erudite person, was interested in studying Mendoza's famous collection of ancient coins. Don Diego taught him all he knew about it; some of his treasures he gave him, others he let him borrow, just as he generously lent out his books and manuscripts to other scientists and men of letters who enjoyed his patronage. Probably he gave him money, because this is, after all, the duty of maecenases.) In order to document the testimonial preface of his book, Morales asked Don Diego some questions about his studies. Mendoza told the author that he had studied Latin, Greek, and Arabic in Granada and Salamanca, and later there the civil and canonical law; he had followed this by traversing a good part of

[1] ". . . vieramonos en Toledo tan jovenes . . . ," R. Foulché-Delbosc, ed., *Archivo de Investigaciones Históricas (AIH)* II, 193.

Spain in search of ancient sculpture, much of which he dug up; and then he had gone to Italy.[2]

Don Diego gives no dates for his studies in Granada and Salamanca, but possibly he remained in Granada during the life of his father. Count Iñigo (then the Marquis of Mondéjar) died in July, 1515. When he was laid to rest next to the sepulcher of his wife in the Franciscan convent on the Alhambra, all his sons accompanied the funeral procession. Since Don Diego was around twelve, the usual age for commencing college studies, it seems likely that he departed for Salamanca shortly afterward.

Determining Mendoza's exact movements as a boy and young man may be guesswork, but this much is clear: he lived his formative years during an unusual, open period in Spain, the splendor of which has been overshadowed by the later Spain of the Counter Reformation and by the next century's "Golden Age" of great literature. It is now recognized more generally that, for Spain, the first half of the sixteenth century was a unique time, a sort of reprieve. By the beginning of the era, the Inquisition, under the reign of Queen Isabel, was on its way toward establishing a tyranny over the minds of the people. About sixty years later, Philip II ended the era by taking up the process which the Queen's death had interrupted.

Don Diego was a product of the interregnum, when conditions in Spain were often chaotic. At first, the nominally united country almost fell apart because Fernando of Aragon's influence on the Catholic Queen's kingdom ended with the accession to the Castilian throne of Queen Juana and her husband, Philip the Fair of Habsburg, Duke of Burgundy, Archduke of Austria. With Philip's sudden death (1506), Fernando took over the regency of Castile in the name of his widowed and incompetent daughter. But the King was much more interested in territorial expansion than in suppressing the thoughts of Castilians and Aragonese. After his death in 1516, a series of regents alternated in Spain with infrequent, short appearances of the new King, Charles I (who was the Emperor Charles V). During many years when Charles was absent, Francisco de los Cobos, the easy-going minister of finance, was the

2 GP III, p. 472.

de facto ruler. Until Philip II's return in 1559 as King, Spain had no consistent, single, strong authority.

During the early part of that time, foreign influences—that of Erasmus and the Italian Renaissance—could enter Spain relatively unchecked. That intellectually splendid period of the Spanish Renaissance for the first time enabled a Castilian feudal noble to become a full-fledged secular intellectual. To be sure, this continued to be unusual. Mendoza practically stepped out of his class when he followed his real interests. Aside from the poet Garcilaso de la Vega (also one of Mendoza's—more distant—relatives), or Luis de Avila y Zúñiga (his friend and colleague in the Emperor's service, who was a fluent though not profound writer), few nobles wrote outstanding works. By and large, this abortive enlightenment was carried along by the relatively small middle class that furnished the professional educators and writers, many of them "Erasmians," people of sometimes humble or uncertain, often *converso*, origin. Among the lights of a slightly older generation are Juan Luis Vives, Juan de Sepúlveda, Antonio Agustín; among the younger, Jerónimo Zurita and Juan Páez de Castro. But in this "open" period, irrational, mystic movements, like illuminism, were also able to spread. And stiff-necked scholasticism could find new voices to champion tradition—it was the era as well of Domingo de Soto and Melchor Cano.

Since Don Diego had already learned Latin, Greek, and Arabic in Granada, he could hardly have studied with Peter Martyr, Count Iñigo's most famous protégé, Latin teacher of Don Luis and perhaps of his other brothers. Martyr, who conducted a Latin school for the young nobles at court, was to be found wherever the itinerant royal court stopped for a while—Valladolid, Burgos, Seville, Madrid, and even in Tordesillas, residence of the mad Queen. In 1511, when the court spent more than six months in Seville, Count Iñigo joined King Fernando for the duration of his residence in Andalusia.[3] He may have brought Diego, then six or seven, along with him for some elementary grounding in Latin. Martyr finally settled in Granada not long before he died there in 1526, but by then Don Diego had long left his native town.

---

[3] Peter Martyr to Pedro Fajardo, March 15, 1511: ". . . mi Conde de Tendilla en estos momentos lo tenemos a él presente en la corte . . . ," in "Epistolario de Pedro Martir de Angleria," *DIE* 10 (1953), 348.

Another, more versatile, noted educator formed part of Count Iñigo's household during Don Diego's childhood—Hernan Núñez, the so-called Greek Commander, who taught Greek and Arabic, as well as Latin, and who stayed there at least until 1509 and possibly longer.[4] He might have been the one to give the very young Diego a rudimentary knowledge of Greek. Simultaneously, or later, the boy continued his study with an unknown teacher in downtown Granada.

In those years, we are told, the *hijos* of the Count of Tendilla "every day walked down the hill from the Alhambra into town to be taught by a teacher of grammar." (*Hijos* might refer to Don Diego and Don Francisco, but possibly also to Don Pedro, the illegitimate son, and perhaps Doña Isabel.) The *hijos* were accompanied by the future religious poet Fray Luis de Granada, who was of the same age as Don Diego and who served as page in the Count's household. One of his duties was to carry the books of the young lords as he trudged behind them on their way to and from school, but he studied together with them.[5]

Intermittent Appearances in Spain and Italy

Don Diego's adolescence fell into the early years of the reign of Charles I, the young Habsburg of Flemish birth, who was still in Flanders in 1516 when he took up his heritage on the death of his grandfather, King Fernando. The Mendozas were alert to the new era: Don Antonio formed part of a group of Spanish officials hastening at once to Flanders to attach themselves to the boy-king. This group included Francisco de los Cobos, old Count Iñigo's former protégé, who had succeeded Hernando de Zafra as secretary for civilian affairs in Granada. His trip with Don Antonio signifies the start of their close association in the coming administration; Cobos and the Mendozas were to help each other to the lion's share of Royal-Imperial power. Since the young monarch's

---

[4] Aguado Bleye, *Manual*, II, 223.

[5] This story has been doubted, possibly because it seems incongruous to think of Mendoza and Fray Luis de Granada as having shared juvenile impressions and education in such a close contact. But Don Pedro de Granada, first Marquis of "Campo-Rey" or Campotéjar, son of Don Alonso de Granada Venegas, stated that he learned this from Fray Luis personally. Luis Muñoz, *Vida y virtudes del venerable . . . Fray Luis de Granada*, pp. 15, 16.

suite was preponderantly Flemish, this nucleus of wide-awake Andalusians started serving from the bottom. In ten to fifteen years the Spaniards were all to come out on top.

In 1517, when Charles, seventeen, visited Spain for the first time, Don Diego was in all likelihood still in Salamanca. The young foreign-born monarch's first contact with his mother's country was not successful. The Spaniards disliked his looks, his slowness of speech, his ignorance of the "Romance" language; and one and all disapproved of the Flemings in his entourage who conducted themselves indiscreetly, grabbing powerful positions in Spain, extorting financial contributions. When Charles left the country in May 1520 in order to accept his new dignity of German Emperor-elect, Spain's resentment exploded in revolt: the civil war of the Comunidades (communities) spread from Toledo over most of Castile, that of the Hermandades (brotherhoods) over Valencia.[6]

Of Don Diego we know nothing during the two years the war raged throughout the country. If he was not any more at school, he might have been with one or another of his brothers. Don Antonio did not accompany the King this time; he stayed behind to marry and settle down on his estate.[7] Both he and Don Bernardino were soon to appear as military assistants to the Marquis Don Luis in Granada; in the King's name they put down the Comunero revolt in the few places it had caught on in the Morisco kingdom. Don Diego might have done military service at their side. Or possibly he might have gone to Rome with Don Francisco who served Pope Leo X as chamberlain.[8] He was not, we may be sure, with his sister Doña María Pacheco, wife of the first leader of the

---

[6] For new studies of the Comunero movement, see José A. Maravall, *Las Comunidades de Castilla: Una primera revolución moderna*; Juan Ignacio Gutiérrez Nieto, "Los Conversos y el movimiento comunero," *Hispania*, no. 94 (Madrid, 1964); Joseph Pérez, "Pour une nouvelle interprétation des 'Comunidades' de Castille," *Bulletin Hispanique* 65, nos. 3–4 (1963): 238–283; J. H. Elliott, *Imperial Spain*, pp. 135–153; John Lynch, *Spain under the Habsburgs*, I, 36–45; Aguado Bleye, *Manual*, II, 412–430; Gregorio Marañón, *Antonio Pérez*, I, 126, 127. Still good is H. L. Seaver, *The Great Revolt of Castile: A Study of the Comunero Movement of 1520–1521*, especially the bibliography given in the introduction.

[7] Avalos Guzmán, *Don Antonio*, p. 25; also A. Scott Aiton, *Antonio de Mendoza: First Viceroy of New Spain*.

[8] Seaver, *The Great Revolt*, p. 331.

Comuneros, Don Juan Padilla. The heroine of the movement, she kept up the rebellion in Toledo even after the defeat of the Comunidades by the Royalists and the execution of Padilla. In the end, her own townspeople surrendered and she had to flee for her life to Portugal.[9] Doña María's amazing individuality and talent (no less than her youngest brother, she knew Latin, Greek, mathematics, history, and poetry), indirectly throws light on the personality of Don Diego. Like his sister, he was apt to do something shockingly unexpected.

Although her brothers petitioned Charles V for clemency in Doña María's behalf, he never forgave this turbulent woman.[10] From this we might guess that Don Diego, whatever side he may have felt sympathy for during the conflict, did not fight for the Comuneros at any time. Had he done so, the Emperor would not later have given him his complete trust for twenty-two years.

In Italy, says Morales, "you took part in the war, in the rank suitable to your person. You divided your year this way: In summer you assisted in the War. In winter you went to Rome and to Padua and to other universities."[11] But when did Mendoza first go to Italy? Twice, he says in his old age, he had seen Rome in times of *sede vacante*.[12] One of these occasions was the conclave after the death of Paul III (1549–1550); the other, doubtful, occasion might refer to one of the conclaves following the deaths, respectively, of Leo X in December 1521, of Adrian VI on September 13, 1523, or of Clement VII on September 25, 1534. During 1534, though, Don Diego was in Charles V's personal service, and the Emperor happened to be in Spain. It is more plausible that he chanced to be in Rome at the preceding *sede vacante*, 1523, when Clement VII was elected. He recalls later that the father of Cardinal Salviati had introduced both him and the young Cardinal into the service of Clement VII. He does not mention in which capacity he served

---

[9] GP I, 42. See also Antonio Martín Gamero, *Historia de la Ciudad de Toledo*; Prudencio de Sandoval, *Historia de la vida y hechos del emperador Carlos V*, vol. I, book 9, chap. 27.

[10] All the followers of Doña María, even her servants who had accompanied her to Portugal, were able to purchase their pardons from the Emperor. Fidel Fita, "Los judaizantes españoles," *BRAH* 33 (1898): 326.

[11] GP III, 471.

[12] Mendoza to Cardinal Espinosa, Granada, September 19, 1569; GP III, 451.

the Pope, or precisely when.[13] If at the beginning of Clement's reign, Don Diego could have combined his attendance at the papal court with his studies at the Sapienza, the university of Rome. But he may just as well have been in Rome at the death of Leo X in 1521.

The evidence is uncertain, too, about the dates and places of his participation in "the War," that is, the endless contest between France and Spain for the possession of Italy. The Spaniards, aptly, felt "the War" to be a permanent institution. In the early twenties, the balance of the seesawing struggle seemed to favor the King of France, Francis I; in 1524, the Most Christian King's troops had dispelled the Imperial army, which was laying siege to Marseilles, and in October of that year Francis I was seizing Milan.

In the *Guerra de Granada* (written 1571 or 1572), Don Diego compares the later Christian armies under Philip II's lieutenants unfavorably with "the many disciplined and reputable armies in which I found myself, led by the Emperor Don Carlos, the others by King Francis of France."[14] He refers to the campaigns of Charles V in which he had taken part—the conquest of Tunis in 1535, and the invasion of Provence in 1536, where the French armies did not come out to meet the Imperials in battle. But unless he had confronted the king of France in an earlier campaign (that of Spain's recapture of Navarre in 1521, perhaps), he could not have seen Francis I at war except at the battle of Pavia of 1525. There, the Spanish commander Antonio de Leiva provoked the French King to an encounter between French and Imperial troops on the outskirts of Pavia. According to Sandoval, Francis I had his horse killed under him and fell to the ground. The first to seize the King was Juanes de Urbieta, a Basque soldier "from the troop of Don Diego de Mendoza." Later on, the chronicler refers to "another" man-of-arms from *Granada*, Diego de Avila,[15] which implies that the regiment of Juanes de Urbieta—the one commanded by Don Diego de Mendoza—was precisely the one from Granada. Even though there is nothing else to support this identification, Sandoval's reference cannot possibly apply to anyone

[13] Mendoza to Arras, Rome, December 1, 1549; *AC*, p. 137.

[14] Quoted from edition by Manuel Gómez Moreno in *MHE*, XLIX, 147. (*G. de Gr.*)

[15] Sandoval, *Historia*, II, 87.

else. True, the name "Don Diego de Mendoza" seems ubiquitous in Spanish history, but at Pavia in 1525, none of Don Diego's homonyms could have taken the place of "Don Diego de Mendoza from Granada."[16] It is therefore quite safe to assume that he was at Pavia, leading his own detachment "suitable to his rank," as Morales had indicated. But he did not do anything of particular distinction, because Sandoval does not mention him again.

Later that year, we find Mendoza in Toledo. The young emperor had summoned the Cortes there, just when the bulk of his victorious army was returning from Italy with the royal prisoner. The unexpected extent of the victory made these Cortes a triumphant occasion. Ambassadors from France, England, Portugal, Venice, Africa, and even Persia were present; so were the Papal legate Salviati, almost all the Castilian grandees, and lastly, Charles Lannoy, the Imperial Viceroy of Naples, who had conveyed the captive king to Spain and left him confined in Madrid. The whole world gathered in small Toledo, the town still largely battered from María Pacheco's fatal reign of only three years before. Among this beehive of people appeared two young men, Don Diego and Don Fernando Alvarez de Toledo, later the third Duke of Alba.

In September 1549, when the then Duke of Alba was at the Emperor's court in Brussels, Don Diego wrote to him from Rome: "Regarding [a frivolous allusion] we are still so green as we were in Toledo."[17] And in the same letter: "Oh that we were still so young as in Toledo!" Also, in April 1551, to the same, from Siena: "You must see to it that your history be corrected by this wicked secretary [Don Diego himself], unless you want him to publish how badly you behaved in the alley of Toledo, where I gave an example of my manliness, which now shines splendidly in these republics."[18] These references point to the Cortes of 1525.

16 For example, the Duke of Infantado, over seventy and ailing with gout, was in Guadalajara at the time; another namesake, also an old man, the Conde de Mélito, Viceroy of Valencia, was not at Pavia, either; and the Duke of Infantado's grandson and namesake was five years old in 1525; besides, at that time no other Diego de Mendoza came from Granada.

17 ". . . tan verdes nos estamos como in Toledo . . . ," *AIH* 2: 193.

18 ". . . quan mal se huvo con la callejuela de Toledo, donde yo di el exemplo de mi virtud . . . ," *AIH* 2: 537.

At no other period of their lives would Don Diego, then about twenty-one, and the future Alba, about eighteen, have been "so green" together—certainly not when Medoza met Don Fernando (who was Duke of Alba then, and married) again in Toledo, in the not so joyful winter of 1538/39. The events in the "alley of Toledo" that Mendoza alludes to were doubtless amorous adventures, a result of which, presumably, was the future Duke of Alba's illegitimate son.[19]

The time of these Cortes was for many Spaniards the best time of the entire century.[20] They had reason to rejoice in the presence of their young King, a favor so seldom granted them. Much as they formerly disliked him, now they appreciated him. He had shown clemency to so many participants in the Comunidades that the grievances of the few whom he never pardoned did not count. The people were grateful, also, that he had worked hard to become a Spaniard. Now he spoke to them in "Romance," and he bowed to the wish of the Cortes—it happened to coincide with his own— when he decided to marry his beautiful cousin Isabel, the wealthy princess of Portugal. The Cortes also demanded that all government officials in the Empire be replaced by Spaniards. Charles V, in order to obtain the Imperial dignity, had given the Germans his oath to put and keep Germans in all leading positions; he did not commit himself on this point to the Castilian Cortes. But a look at his domains not too many years later shows Spaniards in all important positions of the World Imperium (except for the Granvelles, father and son, from Burgundy, but they were glad to identify with the Spanish ruling caste). Not the least of these positions would be held by two presently carefree "green" fellows

[19] See the notices about "El prior Don Hernando de Toledo, hijo bastardo del Duque de Alba," in Mariano D. Berrueta, *El gran Duque de Alba*, pp. 59–73. On p. 64, the approximate date of the illegitimate son's birth is speculated to be 1527 or 1528; it might as well have been 1526.

[20] The "anonymous" author of *Lazarillo de Tormes* gave this mood expression almost thirty years later when he let Lázaro conclude with these nostalgic words: "This was the same year when our victorious Emperor entered the famous town of Toledo and had the Cortes there, with great rejoicing and feasts as you may have heard. For at that time I was prosperous and at the summit of all good fortune." Diego Hurtado de Mendoza, *La Vida de Lazarillo de Tormes*, *Biblioteca Universal*, LXXIX, 78.

who in 1525 expressed their exuberance chasing the young wenches of Toledo.

The Emperor set King Francis free under humiliating peace conditions. Then, in the exalted mood of a great victor (as far as his cautious nature would lend itself to such a mood), he went off to marry his princess in Seville and take her on their honeymoon to Granada.

Spain was still jubilant, but Italy and much of Europe were in a different mood. In their eyes, the unfortunate royal prisoner was at least the moral victor. Almost the entire non-Imperial world joined Francis I in the "League of Cognac," signed in 1526 between France, Pope Clement VII, Milan, Genoa, Florence, and Venice, while England and the Turks looked on with sympathy. The world was anxious to dispatch the Emperor's power from Italy. They saw the current situation correctly as the last opportunity to prevent Charles V from growing into the "universal" monarch.

Against that coalition, Charles de Lannoy's armies, in thirty ships with eight thousand men, returned to Italy, and so, probably as one of the captains, did Don Diego. Forty-five years later, he praises the prowess of these armies. In the *Guerra de Granada* he shakes his head at the poor showing the Christian Spaniards were making in the face of a much smaller number of Moriscos, and recalls: "What a sight this is for those in the know who have seen Don Antonio de Leiva challenging the entire League [of Cognac] of forty thousand infantry, nine thousand cavalry—and the city [Milan] hostile besides. He encircled it with only seven thousand infantry, resisted the enemies, laid siege to the citadel, and in the end he took it, throwing out the enemies, and pursuing those who were strong and united, the flower of Italy, soldiers and captains![21]

The outstanding Spanish general to whom Don Diego fondly tenders posthumous laurels is Don Antonio de Leiva; greater admiration he showed none of the many other generals he had known. (Leiva had learned warfare as a boy in the Moorish War of 1500–1501 under Count Iñigo and the Great Captain.) But Don Diego makes no mention of any distinguished military action of

[21] *G. de Gr.*, p. 166.

his own. He declares only that he had "seen" Leiva in action. Perhaps he was already training himself to be the exemplary historian of war, the "Spanish Sallust," he was later to become.

Student in Italy

Again it is Morales who gives us the only information about Mendoza's studies in Italy: "You had eminent teachers, such as Agustin Nypho, Montesdoca, and others. You listened to their lectures on logic, philosophy, and mathematics.[22]

Agostino Nifo (1473–1546) taught at the Roman Sapienza until the great upset by the sack of Rome (1527), so Don Diego, whose presence in Rome by October 1526 is noted by the Imperial ambassador,[23] would have attended Nifo's courses in the fall and winter of 1526/27. It was Don Diego's last chance to sit at Nifo's feet, for in May 1527 Charles V's Spanish and German armies descended on Rome and destroyed the university as well. Professors and students fled for their lives, as did half the population, including writers, artists, cardinals, ambassadors, princesses, Jews (some of them refugees in the great Spanish exodus of 1492), and even resident Spaniards (like Sepúlveda who escaped to Naples) and Germans. Many refugees rushed down the Tiber to Civitavecchia where they embarked for Pisa—among them Machiavelli, who died six weeks later.

The winter in Rome before the sack was not the most tranquil time for studies, either. On September 20, 1526, the Colonna family, traditional partisans of the Emperor, attacked the quarter of the Vatican with four thousand Italian soldiers; they gave Pope

[22] GP III, 471.

[23] The Imperial ambassador, Don Ramiro Núñez de Aguilera, to Charles V, letter no. 576 in Calendar of State Papers (Cal. St. P.), Spanish, ed. Gayangos, III (1525–1526): 953: ". . . don Francisco de Mendoça, brother of Diego Hurtado, took the other day to Spain the detailed account of the occurrences here . . ." From the same time might be an undated remark from Sepúlveda, Spanish humanist (1490–1573), that he had known the brothers Francisco and Diego in Rome; cf. L. de Torre y Franco Romero, "Don Diego Hurtado de Mendoza no fué el autor de la 'Guerra de Granada,'" BRAH 64 (1914): 478. Sepúlveda, who served the Pope as official translator of Aristotle, also experienced the "sack"; he had the misfortune of being put out of the Castle Sant'Angelo (where he had taken shelter with the papal household) because he was Spanish. Angel Losada, Juan Ginés de Sepúlveda, pp. 60, 61.

Clement (still allied with the French), who locked himself for safety in the Castle of Sant'Angelo, a foretaste of the impending greater disaster. In the changed political climate it seems unlikely that Don Diego was still "serving" Clement VII as he had done before the League of Cognac. Probably he avoided the papal court, and, as long as the halls of learning were still standing through the winter of 1526, he let nothing interfere with his attendance at Nifo's lectures on Averroës.[24] "I always upheld the part of Averroës against Domingo de Soto and against Saint Thomas," he later told of his learned discussions at the Council of Trent.[25]

Professor Nifo, who taught a particular kind of rationalism somewhat equivocally known as Averroism, was after the recent death of Pomponazzi (1525) the leading authority on Aristotle. Don Diego must have been aware of the great controversy between Nifo and Pomponazzi about the meaning of Averroës' commentaries on Aristotle,[26] but he did not name Pomponazzi among his teachers. His library included several of Pomponazzi's works, however, copies of which had been burned by the Inquisition. He owned the 1525 edition of Pomponazzi's collected writings, including *De immortalitate animae*, as well as a manuscript copy of *De incantationibus* (1520), and the printed edition of 1567, containing the same work and *De fato*. This shows that his interest in Pomponazzi accompanied him through his life.[27]

It is idle to speculate whether Mendoza may have listened to Pomponazzi, who taught at Bologna in his later years, or where he studied with Montes de Oca (Padua or Rome), and when.[28] What counts is the result of his education at various Italian schools: he had learned a great deal, whether inside lecture halls, or without.

---

[24] On Nifo as Mendoza's teacher, see GP I, 59–61.

[25] ". . . en las disputas tenía siempre contra y contra Santo Tomas la parte de Averroe . . .," Mendoza to a relative at court, from Rome, May 6, 1549, *AC*, p. 124.

[26] On the dispute between Nifo and Pomponazzi, see Karl Werner, *Der Averroismus in der christlich-peripatetischen Psychologie des späteren Mittelalters*, pp. 130-148; see also Etienne Gilson, "Autour de Pomponazzi," *Archives d'Histoire doctrinale et littéraire du Moyen-Age* 28 (1961): 163–279, especially pp. 236–253.

[27] GP I, 299–301; III, 485, 528, 558.

[28] On Montes de Oca, see Marcial Solana, *Historia de la filosofía española*, II, 288.

He called himself a philosopher. His later works show that he was an Aristotelian. And he himself says that he mastered the theories of Averroës.

In Italian schools between 1520 and 1530, the leading philosophy was a secular Aristotelianism. It had been studied there since the early fourteenth century under the guidelines of the commentaries of Averroës (1126–1198), the Arabic-Andalusian sage from Córdoba. The basic positions of this so-called Averroism are usually understood as:

1. The unity of the intellect. Averroës considers the "passive intellect" as being one for all men, a single immortal substance separate from the body. The implication is that the individual soul (a *vis cogitativa*) as differentiated from the "passive intellect" and inseparable from the body, is mortal.

2. Averroës interprets Aristotle's statement in the *Physics*—that motion is in existence from eternity—as meaning that the world is eternal, thus opposing the religious concept of God's creation, His beginning the world.

3. Averroës was thought to have presented his statements—which are equally heretical to Muslim, Jewish, and Christian orthodoxy—under the concept of a "double truth"; that is, even though theological and philosophical statements are diametrically opposed, both may be true. This "double truth," in itself a denial of the absolute authority of Revelation, again offends all three religions.

It is now known that the theory of the "double truth" is not found in Averroës, and that not all schools or all teachers interpreted the "Averroist" doctrines in the same way.[29] But this is beside the point when we consider the time of Don Diego and his exposure to these various teachings. His professor Agostino Nifo in his own youth openly argued for the concept of the unity of the intellect in all mankind, showing little regard for the contrary Christian-Aristotelian doctrine of Saint Thomas Aquinas. In the fifth Lateran Council of 1513, however, all philosophical schools were forbidden

---

[29] For a definition of "Averroism" in the sixteenth century, see Paul Oskar Kristeller, "Paduan Averroism and Alexandrism in the Light of Recent Studies," *Renaissance Thought II: Papers on Humanism and the Arts*, pp. 111–118. Also William F. Edwards, "The Averroism of Iacopo Zabarella," *Atti del XII Congresso Internazionale di Filosofia*, IX, 91–107.

to teach that the human soul is mortal, that the intellect of all men is only one, and that there can be a distinction between theological and philosophical truth. Thereafter, Nifo became more moderate in tone, but he never dropped his Averroist studies. He edited Averroës' works and engaged in his great debate with Pomponazzi.[30]

Don Diego had grown up among people who concealed their true religion while paying lip service to another. Now he listened to Italian teachers who professed themselves pious Catholics but with every subtlety led him to follow the commands of reason to the very limits. For instance, the Sevillan Montes de Oca (alias Juan Hispano, the other teacher remembered by Mendoza) is called "the most genuine representative of Averroist peripatetism in Spain in the sixteenth century." Montes de Oca claimed that "there is no natural or philosophical reason to consider the soul immortal."[31] With teachers like "Montesdoca" and Nifo, under the pretext of criticizing unchristian doctrines, Don Diego was now studying and assimilating these very doctrines. In speculative thinking he had found his true element. Schooling himself to cover up his intellectual tracks, he cherished his freedom of inquiry—and he would do so all his life. He might have become an Averroist, or even an agnostic, but this is unlikely. We will see later that he was basically religious—at least we can believe this if we take his words to the Bishop of Arras, concerning the "salvation of his soul," at face value. Yet a certain influence from his studies of Averroës, however elusive, can be traced in the manifestations of his thought. His later literary distinction owes much to the undefinable dissentient element in his writings, which in turn is a result of his thorough acquaintance with several "unchristian" doctrines.

Though he did not mention it to Morales, Mendoza also studied in Siena. Our information, inadequate and contradictory, comes from Sienese historians, Sozzini, Bardi, and Pecci, who wrote after Mendoza had finished his rule as Governor of Siena. For reasons to be discussed later, their histories are biased. Sozzini, without any foundation, calls him "bastard-born." His contemporary Bardi does not make such a statement, but Pecci, a later

[30] See Werner, *Der Averroismus*, pp. 117, 130–148.
[31] Solana, *Historia de la filosofía española*, p. 288.

writer, follows suit with the same slander. Sozzini also calls Mendoza a friar who left the cloister. This is taken up by the two others—and, knowing nothing about this, we are unable either to deny or accept this statement. Further, Sozzini says Mendoza came to study in Siena for two years, graduating as a doctor. Bardi, though agreeing that Don Diego stayed in Siena for two years, does not mention his studying. According to Bardi, Don Diego achieved nothing there but led a life as a playboy, maintaining himself in style at the court of his friend, the Duke of Amalfi, Alfonso Piccolomini d'Aragona, then the captain-general of Imperial forces in Siena. Pecci, again copying Sozzini, agrees that Mendoza was studying but says nothing about a doctorate.[32]

The chroniclers, speaking of "two" years, do not spell out the dates. From the Duke of Amalfi's appointment as captain-general in 1527, we may infer that Mendoza stayed in Siena from 1527 to 1529. Perhaps the Sienese historians would have revealed more had they not been hampered by the fact that Don Diego, as a student in Siena, apparently used the name "Andrea."[33] For unknown reasons, he wished to be incognito. Even as a student, it seems, he started to conceal manifestations of his intellectual activities—a process that continued through his entire life. He wrote, but did not publish; he published, but left pamphlets and books anonymous; he spread gossip in letters to friends, with the warning not to quote him as source—he would deny his statements; he even sent anonymous letters of bold advice and criticism to Charles V.[34]

Bardi tells an anecdote that is probably true, since Sienese oral tradition has a way of staying alive. When Don Diego was in Siena as a young man, says Bardi, he made friends with gentlemen of his ilk, liberal spenders and playboys. "It happened once," he continues, "that in Postierla square he entered a grocery shop with many of his young friends to buy three marzipans. Mounting

---

[32] Alessandro Sozzini, "Diario delle cose avvenute in Siena dai 20 luglio 1550 ai 23 giugno 1555," *Archivio Storico Italiano (Arch. Stor. Ital.)* 2: 456. Angelo Bardi, "Istorie senesi del 1512 al 1556," MS in the Biblioteca Comunale of Siena, quoted in GP I, 66, 67. Gio. Antonio Pecci, *Continuazione delle memorie storiche critiche della città di Siena fino agli anni MDLII raccolte . . .* , III, 177, quoted in GP I, 68.

[33] A. Liberati, "Onoranze rese a Don Diego di Mendoza nella sua venuta a Siena," *Bullettino Senese di Storia Patria (Bull. Sen.)* 18: 364–368.

[34] See Appendix.

some steps he held out these marzipans, and said: 'Whoever wants some must pay reverence to me,' and to each who bowed and knelt before him, he gave a piece of marzipan." Writing after 1552, Bardi comments, "This was a forecast as to how the thing he did in jest turned out later to be a reality."[35]

[35] For the marzipan story, see GP I, 66, 67. Another example of oral tradition is the story told me by the vice-director of the archives that the reading room of the Sienese State Archives in the Palazzo Piccolomini is said to have been Don Diego's bedchamber.

3. IN THE EMPEROR'S SERVICE, 1532–1538

The Emperor, whom I took as my master
Don Diego[1]

The New Vassal of His King

Don Diego's departure from Siena in 1529 coincided with, or was the result of, the Peace of Cambrai, concluded on August 5, 1529. The Marquis of Vasto (who had won the Republic of Genoa, with its mighty fleet under Prince Andrea Doria, over to the Imperial side), and Antonio de Leiva's victories over the French in Northern Italy had ended the current "second" war between Habsburg and Valois in a triumph for the Imperials. The war had left Lombardy devastated, its agriculture ruined, Milan and other towns ransacked, and the citizens dying of famine and plague; but this interruption in the "War of Italy" found Charles V nearly the universal lord of Christendom. He summoned the Pope to Bologna to crown him "Holy Roman Emperor." With a glittering entourage (now preponderantly Spanish), Charles V sailed from Barcelona on the galleys of Andrea Doria and arrived August 12, 1529, in Genoa, his new vassal city, where Don Diego met the Imperial party.

Again, as at the Cortes of Toledo in 1525, Imperial fortunes had

[1] ". . . el Emperador, a quien he tomado por señor . . .," Mendoza to Arras, July 16, 1551. *AC*, p. 255.

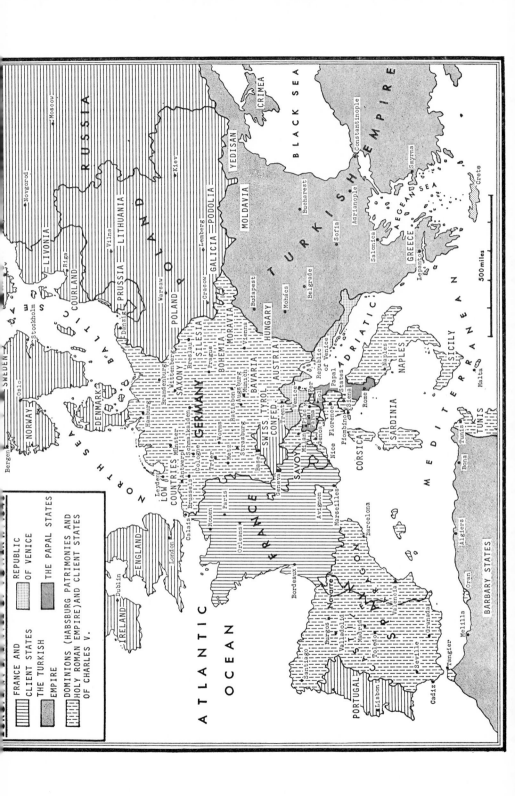

reached a crest. Again, the Spaniards had cause to exult, and those
so inclined celebrated in debauchery. This time, Don Diego's companion in frivolity was not the young Alba, but his older friend
from Granada, Francisco de los Cobos, the Emperor's secretary.
Then fifty-two, Cobos had just been given the Encomienda Mayor
de León by Charles V.[2] A brilliant administrator, the new Comendador was equivalent to both Prime Minister and Finance Minister.
Born in Ubeda, near Granada, of minor gentry, he had been raised
(criado)[3] in the house of Hernando de Zafra, the Secretary of the
Alhambra Precinct for Civilian Affairs and a neighbor of the Mendozas. In 1508 Cobos himself stepped into Zafra's position at the
latter's death, and presumably he had Count Iñigo to thank for the
start of his career. Working in close collaboration with the Captain-
general of Granada, he remained loyal to the five brothers Mendoza; in 1522 he married their cousin Doña María de Mendoza
(then fourteen years of age to his forty-five), a sharp-witted person
in her own right, the "patrona" of Don Diego's letters from Venice.
Affable and always helpful, Cobos constantly used his great influence with the Emperor in favor of the Marquis of Mondéjar's
brothers. Don Diego often declared later that he and his brothers
were all Cobos' "creatures."[4]

The elderly *bon vivant* (who had left his wife in Spain) and the
young Aristotelian roamed Genoa, where fairs and festivities
greeted the Imperial visit, in search of adventures. In several letters from Venice in 1540, Mendoza reminds Cobos of their adventures at the fair of Genoa—reminiscences similar to the earlier ones
with the Duke of Alba but phrased somewhat more respectfully.[5]
Mendoza's name occurs also in a few chronicles of the Emperor's
visit, showing that he stayed with the party until the end of the
ceremonies in Bologna.[6] Among other high Imperial officials pres-

---

[2] On Cobos' encomienda, see Pedro Girón, *Crónica del Emperador Carlos V*,
ed. Juan Sánchez Montes, p. 8. For a detailed study of Cobos, see Hayward
Keniston, *Francisco de los Cobos: Secretary of the Emperor Charles V.*

[3] It was the custom to *criar* in the royal house and the houses of the grandees
the sons of other families, so creating strong bonds of dependence and vassalage.
Also the prelates used to *criar* the future churchmen.

[4] *AC*, pp. 33, 62, 83, *et passim*.

[5] Cf. *AC*, p. 56 (footnote 4), p. 66. These mentions of Genoa can refer to no
other period before 1540.

[6] For example, Gaetano Giordani, *Cronaca della venuta e dimora in Bologna*

ent there, whose friendship he might have cultivated at that time, was Nicolas de Perrenot, Sieur de Granvelle, who, like Cobos, was to become a tireless advocate on Mendoza's behalf at the ear of the Emperor.

Don Diego did not follow Charles V into Germany and Flanders. Instead, he went to Portugal to see his sister Doña María Pacheco, who was ailing and died in 1531. That year, back in Granada, he attended the final lawsuit about his inheritance. He sold Don Antonio his property, the township of Alhendín, whose pasture lands would have paid him 100,000 maravedis annually according to his father's instructions, which Don Luis, executor of the will, apparently did not carry out. Don Antonio paid Don Diego 2,200,000 maravedis for the estate—the total of his share.[7]

For a man who had seen the great world and wished to play a part in its control, this was a small sum. His entire capital came to less than three thousand ducats (as ambassador his annual salary would range from two thousand to five thousand ducats, and even that, for his style of living, was too little). Thus, he was poor—one good reason for him to enter the Emperor's service. By this time, among those who had known him in Rome, he had the reputation of being miserably poor and of having "no talent except to talk and say funny things."[8] An adherent of the Toledos directed these deprecating words to Cobos, but this staunch friend of Mendoza no doubt had a higher opinion of him, and so had Granvelle. The Burgundian, a legally trained mind, and the Andalusian, a financial wizard, both recognized in others what they themselves lacked—intellectual genius. If Don Diego's family ties were not enough to

del Sommo Pontefice Clemente VII per la coronazione di Carlo V Imperatore, tells how on Dec. 5, 1529, twenty-two caballeros took part in a joust before the Pope and Emperor, naming Don Diego de Mendoza among them. P. Giovio, *La vita di Gonsalvo Fernando di Cordova: Il gran Capitano,* p. 157, recalls an evening in Bologna when he had dinner with the two "very famous captains, Don Diego di Mendoza and Signor Anton de Leva"; also Nicolas Hogenberg, *The Procession of Pope Clement VII and the Emperor Charles V* (a contemporary engraving reproduced in facsimile by Sir William Stirling Maxwell) mentions Mendoza's presence in Bologna.

[7] GP I, 58.

[8] Cardinal García de Loaísa to Cobos, Rome, November 14, 1531, *DIE* 14 (1849): 256.

place him at the court, these two powerful men must have helped him enter the Emperor's inner circle some time in 1532.

As it happened, many Spanish nobles left Spain that year to join the Emperor's armies in Austria. Charles V and his brother Ferdinand (the "King of Rome," ruler of the Austrian possessions of the Habsburgs), accompanied by many Lutheran soldiers, were marching against Soliman on a "Crusade." Ever since the Peace of Cambrai and the coronation, Imperial policy had been firmly set to deal with the danger of Ottoman Imperialism. (To win the German princes' support in this cause, Charles V, at the recent German Diet, had been quite conciliatory with the Protestants, concluding the "Peace of Nuremberg" with them.) For a decade he had watched the Turks gain military victories on land and at sea. They continued to advance steadily in Hungary and on all the shores of the Mediterranean, as long as the Christians persisted in fighting each other. In 1529 the Sultan had stood outside the walls of Vienna with a huge army, but unexpectedly he raised the siege, retreating voluntarily from Vienna without seeking battle. Apparently the great Pasha had overestimated the odds against him. But in the summer of 1532 he was again expected to advance near Vienna.

That was the time when the flower of Spain—nobles and caballeros—went over to join Charles V. A great wave of enthusiasm swept them along. So many cavalry left the country, carrying so much wealth with them, that the Empress (who acted as Regent of Spain in her husband's absence) became alarmed at losing them, but Charles V said he would be glad to receive them all.[9] The young Duke of Alba, recent successor to the title, was among them, as well as members of all the great Houses. The bulk was made up of "those who have little."[10] This appears to be the time Don Diego went over too—from then on to continue at the Emperor's side.

For Don Diego, now about twenty-eight, it was time to start his political career. All his brothers held high positions—they had started much earlier in life than he. Don Luis, second Marquis of Mondéjar, though he never quite filled the boots of old Count Iñigo, ruled the Alhambra and Granada adequately and was raising a large family. Don Antonio, the Empress' chamberlain, future Vice-

9 José María Jover, *Carlos V y los Españoles*, pp. 122, 123.
10 Girón, *Crónica*, p. 175.

roy of Mexico and Peru, would soon embark on his way to the New World. He was also a family man, and so was Don Bernardino, best known for his long tenure as Commander of all the Spanish galleys. And Don Francisco, though not much older than Don Diego, was advancing fast in the Church. Charles V favored him greatly; he appointed him Vicar of his armies, and gave him several Spanish abbeys and eventually the bishopric of Jaén, one of the richest benefices in Spain. Around the age of forty, in 1542, Don Francisco was named a Cardinal, but shortly thereafter he died.

Seeing his brothers climbing to their respective high offices almost effortlessly, Don Diego must have found it difficult, if not impossible, to follow in their footsteps. They filled all the seemingly available positions. Their marriages to heiresses had probably been arranged by their father. And the Church? Could a second Mendoza chase after abbeys, bishoprics, and cardinalates? Unless they were grandsons of the reigning Pope, two brothers were unlikely to reach the cardinalate simultaneously. (Such an unusual situation arose later in Mendoza's life, when he had to deal with the three Cardinal grandsons of Paul III.) For these reasons Don Diego, although he had at one time been in Clement VII's service, had little impetus to steer his ambition in the direction of the Church.

The uncertainty of his goal in early life had left him free, however, to develop in any direction, together with the growth of Spain as the new center of a world empire. From his humanist point of view, there had never been a more auspicious time to rebuild the world after the Roman model. His deep knowledge of antiquity would help him to understand the concept of empire; the special glory to his mind was that Spain now was called on to direct, and attempt to enlarge, this new-old Imperium. Those who stood near the throne could have a hand in shaping this changing world, and Mendoza's lengthy education had equipped him for such a task— in addition to the baggage he already carried, namely, his family's tradition of living and dying for their kings, of not only advising and directing them but also of defending their honor at all costs.

When Don Diego swore his oath of fealty to Charles V, he did so in the tradition of his ancestors, vassals to their lieges, the kings of León, later those of Castile: he considered the Emperor his liege in his quality of Charles I, King of Spain, in the medieval concept of a servant who had chosen his master.

From then on, until the summer of 1535, we have no record of Mendoza's whereabouts except for his own words stating that he was serving the Emperor.[11] Though this gives us no individual details, at least he is not lost from view. In the absence of diplomatic assignments—which would have been documented—"serving" the Emperor meant just that, to be the master's servant in the palace, as a valet, as a waiter. Wherever Charles V went, there was Don Diego. Soon after he had joined him on his intended drive against Soliman, the Emperor arrived in Vienna on September 23, 1532, but the Turks, who dreaded a winter campaign, were complaining that Charles V had not come earlier when they expected to fight him and had just turned around to start their march home.

Thus the armies of East and West did not meet this time. To the disappointment of the Imperial cohorts, their energies unused, their appetites for booty unappeased, their wages unpaid, the armies of Charles V had to march back peacefully with their King and his court. Homeward bound, but in the slowest possible stages, they traveled over the Brenner pass on a peaceful tour of northern Italy, where the Emperor alternated political conferences with sightseeing. In April, 1533, almost four years to the day after he had taken leave of his young wife to attend the coronation, Charles V returned to Barcelona, followed by an armada of thirty-four ships bringing the Duke of Alba, Cobos, Granvelle, the rest of the court (Don Diego, though unnamed, among them), and fifteen hundred Spanish soldiers. After some initial unrest caused by these troops who refused to disband without pay and by the riotous reaction of the Barcelonian populace, harassed by the burdens of the presence of the court and disorderly armies, Charles V spent most of the two years he was to remain in Spain in raising funds for his postponed crusade. To this effect, a few months after his arrival he held Cortes at Monzón for the representatives from Aragon, Catalonia, Biscay, Roussillon, and Cerdaña[12] (all of them reluctant to vote him increased subsidies for his war machine), and he summoned the Castilian Cortes to Madrid for October, 1534.

---

11 "haviendo servido XX años," Mendoza to Arras, April 9, 1552. *AC*, p. 307. On April 14, 1552, Mendoza says in his *Instrucción* to Pedro Ximénez that he has served His Majesty "XX años." *AC*, p. 351.

12 A valley in the Spanish Pyrenees, not to be confused with the island of Sardinia (Cerdaña or Cerdeña in Spanish), also a Spanish possession at that time.

Since there is no reason to assume that Don Diego might at any time have escaped the service he had sworn to render, he must have been with the Emperor through 1533 in Barcelona and Monzón. Early in 1534 he would have been moving with his master and the court on their leisurely tour through Old Castile. He had made no "name" for himself as yet, so the Emperor's chroniclers, their fists weary of scratching interminable lists of notables' names down on paper, rarely singled him out from "the group of young caballeros around the King's person," or "a number of gentlemen from the Emperor's household." This was his time of apprenticeship; specifically he learned to know the Emperor's mind; his long schooling was now being completed by a training in "business" (negocio), that is, politics. When he suddenly emerged from obscurity a few years later, he was ready to deal with foreign kings and governments, and he was equal to foreign, often hostile, diplomats. He knew how to defend his Emperor's interests and how to improvise his policy, if necessary, on the spur of the moment. In these unsung years he also formed his circle of devoted friends, the nucleus of which would carry him through later years of royal disgrace. He was in daily contact with such men as Cobos, Granvelle, Alba, Gonzalo Pérez, Gutierre López de Padilla, Luis de Avila y Zúñiga, and with all the consejos (councils), ambassadors, and the higher clergy, who also traveled with the Emperor.

Throughout his preoccupations with the internal administration of Spain, world events held the Emperor's primary interest. In the summer 1534, the Turks were spreading out in the Mediterranean: Their Admiral Kheireddin-Barbarossa conquered Tunis, driving out the Moorish king, Muley Hacen, who was Charles V's tribute-paying vassal. In September of that year, Pope Clement died, to be succeeded by Paul III, the illustrious old Alexander Farnese, Dean of the College of Cardinals.

By October 21, when the Emperor confronted the Castilian Cortes in Madrid, his new objectives were clear in his mind: Barbarossa was to be driven from Tunis, and the new Pope to be gained as an ally in this crusade. Although Cardinal Tavera, the new Archbishop of Toledo, argued against a far-flung and costly expedition against Tunis, the Emperor found less resistance to war subsidies in Madrid than at the earlier Cortes of Monzón. Despite the fact that Castilian finances were sliding and the boom through the new commerce with the overseas empire slackening, Castile provided Charles V with the means to raise new armies and build a new fleet, a task concerning Don Diego directly.[13]

Tunis

The moment of confrontation of the two greatest powers in the world, East and West, arrived at last in 1535. Charles V was thirty-five when he marshaled the Christian world on his crusade against the crescent. Never again would he come so close to seeing his aspirations to universal monarchy fulfilled. From Portugal to Germany, from papal Rome to Savoy, Europe was with him. True, France, England, and even Venice were absent—but at least they did not stir. The medieval device of "crusade" still served to ensure the new Pope's assistance and blessing; it swayed Castile, unwilling at first to continue paying the bills, to make common cause with Lutherans.

The "crusade" propaganda blinded men to the fact that the cross did not go against the crescent as such: the crusade was only a power clash between two imperialisms. In 1535 the Turkish empire comprised the territories of Greece, the Balkans, Hungary, Egypt, Rhodes, Algiers, and, since 1534, Tunis. Parts of the Spanish empire—Sicily and Naples—and the southern and eastern coasts of Spain had never been as vulnerable to Muslim piracy as now. Charles V's limited though realistic aim, therefore, was to do away with "Barbarossa," Admiral Kheireddin, who, as Soliman's vassal, dominated the Mediterranean. To that effect, his Sacred Catholic Majesty made secret efforts before the campaign to win the "infidel pirate" over to his side; but should Barbarossa not agree to an understanding, Charles V arranged to have him murdered. He entrusted one of his officers with the orders of bribery or murder—grim alternatives to be used at the discretion of one man. Charles V's wretched servant did not get far under such a burden. In Barbarossa's lair he was soon unmasked as a spy and put to death.[14] When the Emperor then decided to carry out his plan of conquering Tunis, his motive was political rather than religious:

[13] The aforegoing information about the Emperor's movements between January 1533 to May 1535 is contained in Girón, *Crónica*, pp. 27–56.

[14] Arthur I. Andrews, "The Campaign of the Emperor Charles V against Tunis" (Doctoral dissertation, Harvard University, 1905), pp. 70–73.

he was content merely to reinstall his vassal, the former Moorish King of Tunis.

Charles V's timing was unusually fortunate. In the five years since the Peace of Cambrai, the thin fabric of European peace had almost worn through, but it still held, though the Emperor knew that Francis I's patience was near breaking. The Emperor had not ceded Milan to him, and Pope Clement, after his niece married the French King's second son, had once more encouraged French aspirations. At the same time, King Henry VIII of England was upsetting the equilibrium in Christendom still further; he had voided his marriage to Charles V's aunt, Catherine of Aragon, taken another wife, and subsequently broken with Rome as an heretic. Yet, ominous as the situation had been, Clement's death suddenly improved it. Paul III started his reign by proclaiming a strict neutrality. The new Pope persuaded France to respect the crusade by at least abstaining from any contemplated offensive in Europe for the time being. He sent galleys to join the campaign against Barbarossa.

The Emperor had been raising armies from the beginning of winter 1534, and a vast ship-building program was under way. The outfitting and equipment of this Spanish fleet were to serve as a model for all Spanish armadas to follow in the sixteenth century. That Don Diego had a hand in this, remained unnoticed. Don Luis, the Marquis of Mondéjar, was in charge of gathering Spanish troops, ships, and provisions; it is rarely mentioned that his entire House helped him, but never, that his youngest brother probably did the heavy work. It was perhaps the first time for Don Diego to be called on to do administrative rather than personal service for his master. To anyone unaware of this early part of Mendoza's career, it is astonishing to find him later, in his postambassadorial years, outfitting several armadas for Philip II. But he was very much at home in assembling ships and shipwrights from Guipúzcoa, flour for hardtack from Malaga, bacon from Andalusia, wine from many regions, saltpeter from Murcia and Almería, iron arms from Bilbao, and even, as a last item, fresh and salted fish from the port of embarcation. As late as 1567, when he pored over the financial accounts of an armada he was then managing, Don Diego recalls his experiences of the preparatory stage of the Tunis campaign.[15]

---

[15] ". . . dende el armada de Tunez aca que yo maquerdo . . .," Mendoza to

June 10, 1535, was the great day when all the Christian forces of the Empire assembled in the port of Cagliari of Sardinia. The Emperor had sailed from Barcelona with the Spanish, Portuguese, and Genoese fleets; the Marquis of Vasto had brought the Spaniards from the kingdoms of Naples and Sicily, the papal galleys, and the Germans. More than thirty thousand troops in all, about half of them Spanish, crossed over to North Africa in about twenty-four hours in brilliant summer weather. They landed not far from the ruins of old Carthage, from where they prepared to assault the strong fortress of La Goleta ("Little Neck"). Tunis stands at the inland end of a round bay which is cut off from the sea except for a narrow strait, and La Goleta protected this strait and the approach to Tunis beyond the lakelike bay.

After a siege of three and one-half weeks, the Christians took the fortress in an amazing bombardment that brought down one of the mighty square towers of the Moorish fortifications. This opened the approach to Tunis, and the bulk of Barbarossa's fleet, eighty-two sail that stood in the inland bay, also fell into their hands. After that, the actual conquest of Tunis was relatively easy, the more so because Barbarossa's many thousands of Christian captives freed themselves and communicated with their approaching rescuers.

The crusade has countless chroniclers who cite scores of names of practically all the notable participants. Why was Don Diego not especially noticed? As before, he was "lost" among the other young gentlemen around the Emperor's person, and, in addition, his older brothers overshadowed him now. Except for Don Antonio, who had already gone to America, all of them were present. Don Francisco, like Don Diego, also is mentioned no more than incidentally,[16] but Don Luis, supreme commander of the Spanish cavalry, drew special attention because he was the first serious casualty, having been wounded (though not fatally) in battle before the capture of La Goleta. Also Don Bernardino is noted in all the histories: after victory, Charles V installed him as governor of La Goleta.

Philip II, Laredo, October 25, 1567, Archivo General de Simancas (Arch. Sim.), Estado, legajo 149, folio 298.

16 Alonso de Santa Cruz, *Crónica del Emperador Carlos V*, III, mentions as going along on the crusade "el Marqués de Mondéjar y tres hermanos, D. Francisco, D. Bernardino y D. Diego . . .," p. 259.

Insignificant beside such great captains, Don Diego was also lost in the crowd of all the other prominent men of the Empire, such as his protectors Cobos and the elder Granvelle; and the spotlight shone on the martial heroes of his own generation, the Marquis of Vasto, the Duke of Alba, and Don Ferrante Gonzaga, all of whom earned laurels in this campaign. They were great commanders in important Imperial positions, while Don Diego, despite his assistance in so many wars, had not distinguished himself as they had. But unlike the others he maintained that he was not by profession a military man.[17]

Yet though he drew no attention to himself, Don Diego exercised all his faculties there. He served not only in the preparation and administration of the campaign, but he also fought in the group of young Castilian nobles surrounding the person of the Emperor, especially in a famous battle when only twelve of them charged on horseback into a squadron of "eighty proud Moorish cavalry" (on this occasion the famed poet Garcilaso de la Vega was wounded).[18] Doubtless he belonged to the few Spanish "philosophers" who discussed Averroës with the dethroned King Muley Hacen (who had joined the besiegers), and he received Arabic books from that Moor.[19] Best of all, he wrote a Latin narrative of the Tunisian campaign—his first reported literary work.[20] Though this paper has never been found, an anonymous "Relación" exists that is written in a style like his; it is the only document, written by an an eyewitness, that points out the great flaw of the campaign—the

[17] ". . . esto es lo que pido, y no exercito ni mano en las armas, no siendo mi profesion . . .," Mendoza to Arras, April, 1549 (the dating is erroneous; the content of this letter places it among those of September, 1547). *AIH* 2 (1911).

[18] *Vida de Garcilaso de la Vega, DIE* 16 (1850): 65, 66.

[19] On conversations of Muley Hacen with the Spanish philosophers, see Paolo Giovio (Iovii), *Historiarum sui temporis,* II, book xxxiv, p. 238.

[20] Unless his Spanish translation of *Sirus* is an earlier work; see Foulché-Delbosc, "Les oeuvres attribuées a Mendoza," *RH* 32 (1914); 21. This is a Latin comedy by Dominicus Crispus Ramnusius of Pistoia, a manuscript of which (the Latin text, not Don Diego's translation) is now in Salamanca, Biblioteca Universitaria, MS 2648 (formerly it was in Madrid, Biblioteca de Palacio, MS 465). At the end is a note by a later hand that the Count of Tendilla's son, "Didacus Mendozius Hurtado," translated this comedy into "lingua vulgari." I am grateful to Professor Paul Oskar Kristeller for sending me this information.

reason for the escape of Barbarossa. A writer of such an objectivity in reporting, and readiness to offer criticism, resembles Mendoza.[21] This frankness may well be the cause of the writer's anonymity— at once, the parallel with the "Letter of Busseto" (1543), and the *Guerra de Granada* suggests itself. Though the letter of Busseto (highly critical of the Emperor), and the *Guerra* (indirectly critical of Philip II's personnel, though not of the King himself), are also anonymous, it is known that Mendoza wrote them. In his later years, Don Diego had the deserved reputation of being one of the most serious critics of the Spanish monarchs. Such an attitude does not appear suddenly; an apprenticeship leads up to it. The document in question looks like an example of an early exercise in historical criticism; it appears to be motivated by the anonymous author's reasonings about "the flaw." Only one with an inner compulsion to isolate the truth in complex circumstances would resort to such work.

Even if Don Diego did not write that report, it is likely that he shared the view it expresses. Since "Barbarossa, rather than Tunis, was the Emperor's real objective,"[22] the "pirate's" escape was much more than an embarrassment: the immediate consequence was that the danger to the Spanish coasts suddenly increased. While the city of Tunis itself was simply falling into the Emperor's lap, Barbarossa managed to get away in time and reach a reserve fleet of fourteen galleys and two foists he had waiting at Bona. (It must be understood that the mighty Christian fleet stood between Tunis and Bona!) This way, Soliman's great admiral not only survived and recuperated his forces, but later in the summer he even emerged undiminished from Algiers, making his presence more heavily felt on the coasts of Spain than before, "so that," as Empress Isabel wrote to her husband, "nothing else is spoken of here."[23]

Was this what the flower of Christian Europe had come to

21 "Lo de la Goleta y Túnez, año de 1535," Anonymous, in *DIE* 1; 159–206. See E. Spivakovsky, "Lo de la Goleta," *Hispania* 23 (1963): 366–379.

22 Roger B. Merriman, *The Rise of the Spanish Empire*, vol. 3, *The Emperor*, p. 315.

23 ". . . el daño que se hace en éstos por este enemigo se sienta más agora que en otro tiempo; y de manera que no se habla en otra cosa . . ." Empress Isabel to Charles V, September 24, 1535, in J. M. Jover, *Carlos V*, p. 136.

achieve on its so widely heralded crusade? True, they had liberated a great number of Christian captives, many of them smarting in *mazmorras* (underground silos), according to a horrible Muslim custom. But another Moor, even though a friendly one, now sat on the throne of Tunis (and not even for long, as it would turn out), and Barbarossa was still at large with an undamaged fleet of his own.

The campaign ended with a significant meeting of Christian and Moorish civilizations. The Moorish king, whose throne Charles V was glad to restore, was "legal" inheritor of this privilege only because he had helped kill his father and several brothers, blinding his other brothers. His own son was to drive him from the throne of Tunis later, burning out his father's eyes,[24] but not destroying his ambition. In 1548 Muley Hacen traveled through Italy in quest of renewed help from Charles V to regain his throne once more, and Don Diego had occasion to meet the mutilated former King in Rome.

But when Muley Hacen entered his castle of Tunis in 1535 at the side of his Christian friends, he would have found all his priceless possessions intact if Charles V's soldiery had not preceded him. Barbarossa and all his Turks and Moors had not destroyed his pharmacy full of fragrant ointments and spices "so rare [according to Giovio] that the very names of these things were still unknown to the Christians.[25] They had preserved his precious collection of colors: lazulite, purple, and Indian gum, essentials for the dyeing of exquisite cloth and silk; and they had carefully guarded an invaluable collection of Arabic manuscripts. But the invading conquerors destroyed everything, trampling underfoot what they did not tear, loot, spill, or burn.

Some books were rescued, nevertheless—at least Don Diego obtained some from the King. In his *Guerra de Granada* he refers to what he had read in Arabic books from the land of Granada "and those from Muley Hacen, King of Tunis."[26]

[24] Christian Spanish kings do not seem to have used this particular method of gaining a throne since A.D. 931, when Ramiro II of Leon blinded his brother.
[25] Iovii, *Historiarum*, book xxxiv, p. 245.
[26] ". . . lo que hallé en los libros arábigos de la tierra y los de Muley Hacén, rey de Túnez . . .," *G. de Gr.*, p. 3.

First Official Appointment

Part of the Christian world now expected Charles V to move
against Constantinople as a step toward conquering Jerusalem. But
the Emperor's more realistic goal was the conquest of Algiers, a
military necessity in Spain's interest, planned for the following
year. The Empress, in the name of his Spanish subjects, had urged
Charles V in this direction for years, and thanks to Barbarossa's
escape from under his hands, the problem had now become acute.
Chiefly to raise funds for the new project, the Emperor went from
Tunis on a triumphant tour through Italy, where he traveled with
his court in slow stages from toe to top. All his domains paid him
substantial tributes. The Imperials danced, masqueraded, jousted,
and hunted. They made their way under triumphal arches, amid
rejoicing throngs of people who liked to crane their necks at a rare
gala event. Don Diego, still inconspicuous to posterity, went along.
Had the new African campaign taken place when intended, he
would doubtless have taken part in it—and he would still have
been relatively unnoticed. But the deaths of the Duke of Milan and
of Queen Catherine of England changed the political and military
situation and with it the Emperor's plans.

The death of Francesco Sforza was bad news. The last Duke of
Milan by grace of Charles V, he had married the Emperor's young
niece Christina of Denmark, but left no heir, and so Milan again
became a bone of contention. The news reached the Imperials at
the end of the year on their way from Sicily to Naples. It meant
that for the Emperor, "the War," soon to kindle into the so-called
third war between himself and France, was a foregone conclusion.
At this juncture, he might have ceded Milan to one of the French
princes, and peace would have been preserved. But neither the
Empress nor Cobos and Granvelle, who tried to dissuade him, nor
Pope Paul III in his earnest desire for neutrality and peace could
move Charles away from his decision to fight Francis I again. His
old war lords, Andrea Doria at sea and Antonio de Leiva on land,
understood their master best at this time; they advocated the invasion of Provence—the next (disastrous) enterprise on which Imperial substance and men were wasted.

Before it came to that, when the Imperials had just set out from
Naples for Rome, they learned that the Emperor's aunt had died in

England. This, ironically, was good news for him though it ended the tragic life of Queen Catherine, the wife repudiated by Henry VIII. As long as this unjustly treated lady, humbly but heroically, continued to exist, her nephew was greatly embarrassed in his relations with Henry VIII. He did not acknowledge the validity of Henry's second marriage, continuing to refer to Queen Anne Boleyn as "concubine." But Catherine's death cleared the situation. While the entire Imperial party donned heavy mourning for Charles V's aunt the rest of their way to Rome, the Emperor started to ponder new ways of winning Henry's alliance in the coming war with France. Soon it was learned—after the momentous encounter of Pope and Emperor in Rome at Easter—that the "concubine" had followed the first wife in death; she had been beheaded on orders of the King who was already legally married to an English woman, Jane Seymour. Charles V could acknowledge the "second" Queen of England without scruples, and now a new marriage tie with the Tudor family was feasible for him. Henry VIII's daughter, the Princess Mary, had as a child been engaged to Charles V. Now the Emperor decided to claim Mary for a close relative, his brother-in-law Dom Luis (brother of Empress Isabel), the Infante of Portugal. The plans for this match and for the newly projected alliance with England matured between Rome, Siena, and Florence, where celebrations and festivities repeated themselves without end. At Asti, on June 21, 1536, amid the drums and preparations for the impending war, Charles V instructed Don Diego Hurtado de Mendoza to join Eustace Chapuys, his regular ambassador in England, and to propose the match between Princess Mary and the Infante of Portugal.[27] But before the new ambassador could start on his journey, he took part in the Provençal campaign.

The Imperials invaded the south of France, trying to pursue the French who retreated, scorching their own earth. It was a war of attrition that bogged the invaders down. When they finally decided to turn back, exhausted, starving, and ailing, Antonio de Leiva himself, and thirty thousand Imperial troops perished. One of the few tragic casualties in a minor skirmish (there were no major

[27] *Cal. St. P.*, Spanish, Henry VIII, 1536–1538, vol. 5, part 2, nos. 64, 65, June 21, 1536.

battles) was the poet Garcilaso de la Vega, the most intrepid of the young warriors, who had been wounded in former campaigns. Don Diego, who commanded a Spanish *bandera* of 215 men,[28] there found himself for the last time at the side of Don Antonio de Leiva, the greatest soldier he had known.

The end of the inglorious withdrawal saw the Emperor with his court in Genoa, among the remnants of the Imperial armies—a catastrophic contrast to the jubilant days seven years back, when Charles V had stopped in the same city on the way to his coronation. The Spaniards embarked there for the journey home, bypassing, not without difficulty, the Turkish and French fleets in Marseilles. They arrived in Barcelona early in December.

Possibly to avoid a repetition of the mutiny and unrest provoked by his last homecoming to Barcelona, Charles V had ordered the Empress and her court to await him at Tordesillas, the residence of his mother (who was by no means so neglected as it is usually assumed). Hence, Don Diego was among the hundreds of caballeros now crowding into the somewhat narrow confines of mad Juana's palace where the royal party stayed until the end of the year.[29] He then went with the court to Valladolid, waiting through January and February until weather would permit sailing the Gulf of Biscay. On March 2, 1537, he left the Emperor's court at Valladolid on his way to England.

Mission to England

Ready to go to England ever since the middle of 1536, Don Diego set foot there almost a year later, after an uncomfortable crossing. In London, fifty "great gentlemen" rode out in a solemn procession to greet him—perhaps the first time he was honored individually in this manner. Henry VIII lodged the new ambassador with his entourage in his palace, assigning him the room directly above the King's own.[30]

Now thirty-three, Mendoza was at last making a step toward his political career, but his first mission left hardly any impression in

[28] *DIE* 16: 252.

[29] Girón, *Crónica*, pp. 80–86.

[30] On Mendoza's crossing, see R. Villa, "El Emperador Carlos Quinto y su corte," *BRAH* 45: 467. For his reception in London, see *Lettere inédite di Monsignor Giovanni Guidiccioni da Lucca*, June, 1537, pp. 137–138.

politics, in history, nor even, apparently, on himself. By the time Charles V's ambassador arrived with the marriage proposal for Henry VIII's daughter, the Emperor's plan had become obsolete. Men's minds had moved faster than post horses and galleys. In the past summer, at the moment the Emperor was galloping into a renewed war with France, it had seemed strategically important to him to woo the King of England, but the urgency had passed. After his Provençal campaign had ended in failure, Charles V was predisposed toward greater caution, opening his mind gradually toward a possible agreement with Francis I. Never given to radical changes, he did not quite withdraw his English proposal, but neither did he implement it. He let the affair drift, always withholding some enigmatic "powers" from Mendoza and his colleague Chapuys, preventing them from concluding any negotiations. Even when he furnished them with these powers, he ordered the envoys to conceal the fact that they had the documents and to do nothing without first referring everything to him.[31] Caught in the sluggish waters of that make-believe business, Don Diego was to trifle away two years of his life—important years to a maturing man—in useless service. He languished in a climate he found miserable, in surroundings that depressed him.

"I am well," he wrote Cobos on February 20, 1538, after three-quarters of a year had passed, "and although it is not really cold here, I am as dead from the cold as if I were in Russia—and the health of this place is no better. The bell scares me every time it tolls [probably, the bell announcing the passing-by of a plague victim on the way to burial], and then I follow your advice and flee for fifteen miles . . ."[32]

Many reports of Don Diego's infrequent interviews with Henry VIII and the Princess are published in English in the Calendar of State Papers, as is the official correspondence connected with this

[31] A "power" was a document written on parchment, folded, and tied with a cord of red silk, with the monarch's leaden seal clearly legible, covering the knot of the tassel. Charles V to Mendoza and Chapuys, Barcelona, February 2, 1538: "As to your excuses for not mentioning the powers in your possession, we entirely approve of them and find them good and plausible . . ." Cal. St. P., Henry VIII, vol. 13, part 1, no. 212, p. 498. This excerpt, and all subsequent quotations from the Spanish, French, or Italian correspondence in this Calendar are in the English translation provided by the C. St. P. editors.

[32] AC, p. 1.

mission. Chapuys and Mendoza apparently worked together in perfect harmony. The two envoys' joint letters to Charles V are usually drafted by Don Diego, the more frequent letters to Queen-Regent Marie in Brussels by Chapuys. But Don Diego signed only the missives to which he contributed.[33] Eustace Chapuys (1499–1556), a lawyer and orator of middle-class background from Savoy, had been at his post in London since 1529. He was the only sympathizer with the Spanish side to witness the downfall of Queen Catherine, Anne Boleyn's ascendancy and, following the annulment of her mother's marriage, the downgrading of Princess Mary's status to that of "illegitimate" daughter of the King, along with various other forms of diminished respect. As Don Diego was wont to do with the Granvelles, he played down his own preeminence of family rank, warmly recommending Chapuys to his own patron, Cobos.[34]

After the first half-year Don Diego's mission grew somewhat more complicated, though no more auspicious. On October 12, 1537, a son was born to King Henry, and Mendoza was the first person to kiss the hands of the future King of England.[35] Now, Princess Mary was only second in line to the throne, a fact surely to lessen still further the Emperor's dwindling interest in her marriage to his House. But only twelve days after the birth of the future Edward VI, the King lost his third wife. Mendoza, the ambassador "last come,"[36] assisted at Jane Seymour's funeral, and immediately became instrumental in new matrimonial offers from the Habsburgs, now aimed at the King's own person. The Emperor had Don Diego offer Henry VIII his niece Christina of Denmark, the young dowager duchess of Francesco Sforza, who presently lived at the court of her aunt, the Queen-Regent Marie, in Brussels. This does

[33] For example, the letter to Queen-Regent Marie, May 27, 1537, *Cal. St. P.*, Spanish, supplement to vols. 1 & 2, p. 452: "This was written in the name of Diego de Mendoza and myself, but it seemed to him better that I should sign it alone. (signed) Eustace Chapuys."

[34] Chapuys comes to life in Garrett Mattingly's *Catherine of Aragon*, pp. 280–414.

[35] Morysine from Brussels to London, March 16, 1553: "Don Diego told him he had a great desire to go there to kiss the King's [Edward VI's] hand, which he said he did the first of all others, the late King's Majesty having done him that favor . . .," *Cal. St. P.*, Henry VIII, pp. 256–257.

[36] *Cal. St. P.*, Henry VIII, vol. 12, no. 1060, p. 2.

not mean that Charles V really wanted Christina to marry the English King; the plan only helped his politics of the moment. In an aftermath of fatigue following the "third war," Charles V and Francis I began working toward an understanding, and as long as the Emperor was seeking peaceful relations with France, it suited him to hold Milan in apparent readiness either for the Princess Mary, should she marry Dom Luis of Portugal, or for the King of England himself, in case he wed the dowager of Milan.

Don Diego, who knew by now, if he had not known it from the outset, how futile his mission was, implored the Emperor to let him return to Spain, but his master did not permit this. "Although you, Don Diego, desire to return," Charles V wrote him, "you must remain there now that this negotiation with France is on foot, so that the English will not be offended and lose hope. We shall permit you to return as soon as feasible."[37]

The new policy of pacification was working out; in November, 1537, the French and the Imperials entered a temporary truce. At the same time, the Emperor had diplomatic successes elsewhere: favorably for him, the Turks were at last coming to blows with the Venetians, and Venice, still neutral during the Tunis campaign, was driven directly into the Imperial camp. Charles V now formed the "Holy League" against the Turks that he had long desired, concluding an alliance with Paul III and Venice in February, 1538. Temporarily, a new European equilibrium was established. This gave the Emperor cause to agree with the efforts of the Pope in entering the great "truce with France of ten years," to be contracted in Nice in the presence of Paul III, on June 15, 1538. Still, while Charles V was solidifying his power on the Continent, it was in his interest to keep by means of the marriage offers some hold over England.

Henry VIII displayed no more eagerness than Charles V to agree to any of the forwarded plans for matrimony. He delayed the discussions about Princess Mary on the pretext of some unsettled decisions concerning the dowry. And his own person he was unwilling to commit unless he first saw the dowager duchess of Milan.

[37] Charles V to the ambassadors in England, Nov. 9, 1537, from Monzón, *Cal. St. P.*, Spanish, supplement to vols. 1 & 2, p. 454.

Perhaps Henry playacted, but after Holbein brought him Christina's portrait from the court in Brussels, he seemed genuinely interested in the match. Christina's likeness pleased him so much that he summoned Don Diego and Chapuys to Hampton Court in February, 1538. On that visit, Don Diego also met, as he was to live and see, the next three reigning monarchs of England: Edward, the baby prince, four months old; Mary, a young lady who performed for the ambassadors with great skill on the lute and the spinet; and Elizabeth, at five years a very pretty girl.[38]

For a short while in March, the warmth of the Imperial ambassadors' reception in the King's residence contrasted favorably with the cool treatment shown the French ambassadors. But by mid-April the improved mood revealed itself as illusory. Henry VIII was becoming annoyed by the truce of Charles V and Francis I that was foreshadowed in the news, and his ministers at once transmitted his defiance to Charles V's men. "You two imagine perhaps," Cromwell addressed the Imperial ambassadors, "that we ought to do anything the Emperor asks of us, out of fear of the meeting which is to take place at Nice; but you are very much mistaken if you think so, for even if a league were formed against us between Pope, Emperor, and King of France, we should not care a fig for it." While Don Diego and Chapuys were spoken to so rudely by Cromwell and his colleagues, the King had the French ambassador with him, regaling him and offering him the choice of four of his royal country seats for the summer.[39]

Possibly Henry VIII resented especially the alliance with the Pope. The old wounds of his break with the Church had not healed. Continuing to give the Imperial ambassadors the cold shoulder, he directed his marriage-feelers toward the religiously divided principalities of Germany; this turn of politics led some time later to his marrying the Princess Anne of Cleves. Don Diego's mission was definitely finished. But just as it had taken him so long to go to England, so would his leave-taking extend endlessly. He sought every occasion, participating in every ceremony, so as to keep up

[38] Chapuys to Queen Marie, February 23, 1538, *Cal. St. P.*, Spanish, vol. 5, part 2, no. 213, pp. 506, 507; no. 214, pp. 508, 509.

[39] Ibid., no. 223, pp. 522, 523; for treatment of French ambassador, see Chapuys and Mendoza to Charles V, ibid., no. 225, pp. 528, 529.

the nonexistent political importance of his visit: there was a round of conferences with the ministers, farewell interviews with King and Princess, and a frustratingly long wait for his passports.

By this time the truce of Nice was concluded and trumpeted throughout the world, with the Emperor's intention to scare the Turk as well as the remaining independent states of Europe. All of them, however, regarded the improbable alliance between these two arch-rivals with utmost suspicion. It would not take the world too long to see their disbelief well justified. The English professed their doubts from the outset. Cromwell and other ministers, in a conference with Don Diego and Chapuys, declared themselves shocked to hear that Charles V contemplated a peaceful journey through France. "They lowered their heads, and remained, as it were, stupefied and astonished, without uttering one single word more about that or any other affair."[40]

Then Mendoza paid his farewell to Henry VIII. "The King asked me how I intended to return to Spain, by land or sea. I answered resolutely and at once that my intention was to make a land journey, passing through France. This the King was astonished to hear." (The trip of his Emperor through France was in fact decided on only more than half a year later, and completed more than a year afterwards; and even then it took the world by surprise.) As was the custom in international diplomacy, the King gave Don Diego a parting gift, four-hundred pounds sterling.[41] At this end of his mission, he found Henry VIII in a bewildered mood, filled with uncertainty about the new European situation since Charles V and Francis I had met privately in Aigues Mortes.

Before he left England on the first day of September, Mendoza had occasion to further the already established friendly relations with the French ambassador. And at last, while waiting for good weather in order to set sail from Dover, he requested another audience with the King, who happened to be in the same place, but Henry VIII curtly denied an interview.

So his visit came to an end with a snub from the English King.

[40] Chapuys and Mendoza to Charles V, *Cal. St. P.*, vol. 6, part 1, no. 7, pp. 15, 16.
[41] Ibid.

Don Diego had nothing to show for the time spent in England. "And never do they give you a charge of importance." Yet he was rewarded by earning the Emperor's complete approval for his conduct. He had proved that he could carry out orders as an accomplished master of dissimulation and diplomacy, adapting himself flexibly to every change in official politics. But on himself his stay in that country left no imprint. No memory of London is reflected in any of his later works. The rhymed "Epistle to Don Gonzalo" shows why. He was simply disgusted. "What good is it to be born in Spain . . . if we have to die in a foreign land? I do not like this country any better than you would like anything that's sour! All we get here is grey hair, and colic, and kidney stones, headaches, catarrhs, and hemorrhoids . . . Here, where we see nothing but fog and rain or perpetual thunder—how far is Spain from such darkness!"

> Serving kings—smoke and vain hopes!
> They never give you anything important to do![42]

In 1545, in Trent, when he spoke to Massarelli about his interesting life, he told the amiable secretary of the Legates about his service to the Emperor in Spain, Tunis, Italy, and Germany, saying not a word about England.[43]

Since it had been the Dowager Queen-Regent Marie's idea to marry young Christina to Henry VIII, she was perhaps the only person who still believed that both the English King and her brother had been serious about the proposal. She pressed her new visitor for detailed information, but Don Diego, who had arrived at the court of Brussels on his way to Spain, was fed up with the

---

[42] "Epístola á Don Gonzalo," *Obras poéticas*, ed. W. Knapp, p. 467.
> Ni es más á mi gusto aquesta tierra,
> que el vuestro suele ser lo que es acedo . . .
> Adonde nunca vemos sino niebla,
> ó llover, ó tronar perpetuamente . . .
> servir á reyes, residir en corte,
> es todo humo de esperanzas vanas,
> y no os darán jamás cosa que importe . . .

[43] *Concilium Tridentinum (Conc. Trid.)*, ed. S. Merklé (1901); A. Massarelli, *Diaria*, I, 181.

whole affair. "The Queen never stops asking me for information," he wrote to Cobos. Don Diego was unable to escape the Emperor's younger sister, a most energetic woman. His orders were to stay at her court and accompany her on a trip to meet Francis I and his Queen, Eleanor, the older, gentler, sister of Charles V and Marie. The prospect dismayed him. "I begged her to send me on. She replied that I am to go on the same trip she wants to make, that is, the trip to France. Although this is not far, it is costly, and I am broke! I beg you," he implored Cobos, who was in Spain, "get me out of here before that. Tell them I am needed over there!"[44]

Was it the personality of Queen Marie, or the situation in Flanders that was so disagreeable to Don Diego? Perhaps both. When he came to the court in Brussels, the province of Flanders was near open revolt against Imperial oppression. Two years before, at the height of the Provençal campaign, Queen Marie had imposed a contribution of 2,000,000 gold florins on the Low Countries, of which Flanders was to pay its share of 400,000. The other provinces paid up, but the city of Ghent refused, and the Queen put the leaders of Ghent in jail, intending to keep them there until they produced the money. The Ghenters petitioned, repeatedly, for the freedom of their citizens, referring to their ancient civic privileges, according to which they could not be forced to pay any tributes. In the end they made Charles V so angry that he decided to go straight to Flanders (instead of Italy, for the new "Holy League" crusade) "in order to put his hand on the Ghenters so heavily as to flatten them."[45]

The despairing citizens of Ghent then decided to offer themselves to Francis I. But their timing was poor, for the French king, having only recently concluded the truce with Charles V, did not wish to break the friendship. For one thing, Francis I still hoped for Milan. For another, as a king he did not want to let mere citizens decide to whom they should belong. If he allowed the throne of his colleague to be shaken, he might feel his own position less secure. Therefore, Francis informed the Emperor of his Ghenters' intended treason; he even showed him their letter. His rebuttal increased the

44 Mendoza to Cobos, Breda, September 4, 1538, *AC*, pp. 6–8. Also translated into English in *Cal. St. P.*, vol. 6, part 1, pp. 43–44.

45 Sandoval, *Historia* (edition of 1604), book 23, xiv, p. 81.

Ghenters' despair; complaining that the Emperor and his sister were destroying their liberties, they now resolved to die.[46]

This was the mood in the Netherlands when Don Diego arrived there. After his ennui in England, he now found himself in an even less desirable situation at the somber court of the "Christian widow," as the Dowager Queen of Hungary wished to be called. The Queen-Regent, an efficient, even virile governor on the Emperor's behalf, in her younger years had Erasmian, even nearly Protestant sympathies; yet, as regent in behalf of her brother, she relentlessly adopted severe measures, persecuting without mercy any dissenters in the name of the old religion.[47]

It is small wonder, then, that Don Diego prayed for any pretext to leave that bigoted court. "Get me out of here—say I am needed over there . . ." But he did not ask for the impossible. If he had to stay on and travel part of the way in the Queen's entourage, philosophically he said: "If I have to go along on the same trip, everything will be all right for me."[48] As it happened, his resignation was appropriate. He made the first stage of his homeward journey as far as Compiègne together with the Queen and her court; with the party traveled her niece Christina, whose plans for remarriage still kept him busy during the six weeks of the journey at new meetings—without any new ideas—with the English ambassadors to Francis I, Wriothesley and Vaughan, who accompanied the French royal couple to their meeting with Queen Marie. As a memento of his excursion into France, Don Diego received a gold chain from the French King; on the same day, Francis I gave Cornelius Scepperus, another Imperial ambassador, a chain of twice the value, a fact revealing Mendoza's inferior status at that time as a simple "gentilhomme de la maison de l'Empéreur."[49]

Don Diego arrived in Toledo by November 26, while the Cortes were in progress. The French ambassador at the court of Charles V wrote Francis I that Don Diego had come, "who did well in describing the great cheer Your Majesty gave the Queen of Hun-

---

[46] Ibid.

[47] See Jane de Iongh, *Mary of Hungary*.

[48] *AC*, p. 8, ". . . todo sera uno . . ."

[49] *Catalogue des Actes de François I* (Paris, 1889), III, 633, Rose-file.

gary."[50] The English ambassador, who had left Toledo at the same time, remarked to Henry VIII "I suspect that Don Diego's coming hath done no good, because we find more coldness [from Charles V] than afore his coming."[51]

The Emperor, then, was making fast retribution for the snub Henry VIII had given Don Diego. He was obviously satisfied with his ambassador's conduct. From the Imperial point of view, Mendoza's mission was a success. His stay in England had accomplished exactly what the Emperor intended: it had lent a semblance of sincerity and respect to the proposals; at the same time, Mendoza had shown himself a master of courteous temporizing. Tiresome as his service had been, he would now reap his reward. Charles V appointed him his sole permanent ambassador in Venice —one of the highest diplomatic positions in the Empire, currently held by an eminent veteran minister, Don Lope de Soria.

[50] Castelnau, Bishop of Tarbes, to Francis I, November 26, 1538, *Cal. St. P.*, XIII, part 2, no. 914.
[51] Thomas Wyatt to Henry VIII, ibid., no. 974.

4. VENICE, 1539–1540

I curse myself day and night for
having left Venice.
Don Diego in 1552[1]

Arrival in Venice

MENDOZA'S INSTRUCTIONS as Imperial Ambassador to the
Doge of Venice, 1539, included keeping Venice within the
Holy League (concluded by Emperor, Pope, and Doge), preventing
any private peace settlement between Venice and the Turks, and
watching the activities of French agents in Venice.[2] Francis I sent
a new ambassador to Venice at the same time; despite his current
friendship with Charles V, his instructions to Monseigneur Pellicier
were precisely the reverse. The Frenchman, Don Diego's opposite
number, arrived early in August—commissioned to win Venice
away from the League with Emperor and Pope, to effect a reconciliation between Venice and Turkey, to ally the Republic to
France, and to keep a good watch on the activities of the Imperials
in Venice and Italy.[3]

Venice, where Mendoza was to stay for a longer continuous
period than anywhere else during his adult life, was one of the few
places in Italy he had not seen before, and the Venetian Republic,
in turn, had hardly heard of him. But Mocenigo, the Venetian

---

[1] Mendoza to Arras, April 9, 1552, *AC*, pp. 308, 309.
[2] GP I, 89–100.
[3] J. Zeller, *La diplomatie française vers le milieu du XVIème siècle*, p. 43.

ambassador at Charles V's court, looked the Emperor's new envoy over carefully: "He is a noble from a principal Castilian family, highly esteemed and favored by Charles V. Notably, he is related by marriage to the Comendador Mayor." (The Venetian hit the mark there: doubtless, Cobos had been instrumental in Don Diego's new appointment.) "He is," concludes Mocenigo, "a man of letters and learning and very pleasant conversation. Also, he is most favorably disposed toward Venice."[4]

Whatever his disposition may have been, Mendoza's first impression of Venice was one of disappointment. Western Christendom's earliest model of applied imperialism since the Romans, the Venetian empire, consisting of parts of Dalmatia and Greece, enjoyed the highest standard of living on the backs of those foreign peoples it exploited. Its wealth was proverbial. In the last decades, however, Venice had seen bad days. In 1509 the entire Christian world had made war on it, from which the Republic had only partially recovered with the help of its Turkish commerce. (The Ottoman Empire was the best market for the rich Venetian cloths of scarlet and carmoisin, gold and silver brocades, elaborate jewelry. It provided the raw materials Venice needed, raw silk and grain.) Meanwhile, the new Atlantic trade routes were gradually transforming the Adriatic, formerly one of the most important centers of navigation, into a backwater. Venetian decline was impending, though the world did not know it—an old reputation is hard to kill. Now it was war time again, and Venice, cut off from the grain supply of its colonies, as well as from the export of Turkey, was plunged into poverty and unprecedented famine. Also, a dry summer had caused an unusually bad harvest in the nearby Venetian terra firma and islands, Burano, Torcello. Reduced to beggary, starving peasants fell back on the city people. Loading their barges with their families, the aged, the sick, the babies, they rowed down to the Rialto, the route they customarily took to deliver their produce to market. It is said that for many days and nights the destitute country folk provided a scene of utmost misery; at last the harassed Senate gave them emergency shelter and temporary relief in an abandoned monastery.[5]

4 *Venetianische Depeschen vom Kaiserhofe* (*Ven. Dep.*), I, 311.
5 P. Marcello, *Vite de' Prencipi di Vinegia*, pp. 182, 183.

Under such conditions, the reception parade escorting Mendoza along the Grand Canal on the day of his arrival, July 25, 1539, could not have been as pleasurable as former visitors used to describe their first glimpse of the world-renowned waterway. Possibly, the canal was still thronged with floats full of beggars. "My arrival here coincided with the worst possible situation," he wrote the Emperor, "and it came at a time when things could not be worse."[6] This was, of course, a temporary situation, just as the summer weather, hot and sultry, contributed to make the city, deserted by the gentry, look dismal. Besides, many of the older palaces were in disrepair, their outer walls crumbling, paint and plaster peeling, while a number of such old houses were being torn down to make room for buildings in the new classicist style. Slow decay, unfinished new construction—a passing moment, yet it sufficed to give Don Diego a negative opinion lasting as long as he was to remain there.

The Palazzo near San Barnaba

By contrast, Mendoza's establishment on the Grand Canal was, in keeping with his new rank, the most sumptuous he had as yet presided over. Having departed from Spain practically alone, he hired his *famiglia* ("household staff") from among Spaniards and other Imperials living in the State of Milan through which he passed on his way to Venice. (Among dozens of servants, his chief cook was "half a German." In Rome, in a similar position, he would be housing and feeding more than 120 people.)[7]

His palazzo stood in the parish of San Barnaba, with "a window" looking out on the Grand Canal.[8] Very few old palaces of this district face the water, but one of them is still called "Dell' Ambasciatoro." Perhaps that fifteenth-century palazzo is the former Imperial embassy where Mendoza made his home for seven years: the Palazzo Loredan, at the corner of the Grand Canal and Calle Cer-

---

[6] Arch. Sim., Estado, leg. 1315, Rose-file.

[7] For the assembling of the *famiglia*, see Mocenigo to Signoria of Venice, April 21, 1539, *Ven. Dep.* I, 311. The Marquis of Vasto, who was now the governor of Milan, had a German cook, and Mendoza's cook in Rome, where he was to take his Venetian *famiglia*, was so described by Paolo Giovio, *Lettere*, II, 82; Giovio to Cardinal Alessandro Farnese, May 3, 1547, Rome: "Mensa fuit lucullana militaris e il coquo fu mezzo tudesco . . ."

[8] GP I, 103.

chieri. The graceful front of three lofty stories, unchanged for five hundred years, noble backdrop to the traffic of the main water street, still shows its Gothic face—pointed windows, a loggia ornamented by delicate tracery in stone, and a water gate designed in the same Venetian-Gothic style. It differs from similar fronts of many other almost identical buildings by a pair of statues of young knights in separate niches at the height of the second floor.

The pattern of Mendoza's lordly interiors did not much vary from place to place, except that he accumulated more things with the years. The walls of one of his reception rooms were covered with splendid gold and crimson hangings, presumably Granadine craftsmanship in stamped leather. Another hall was decorated with French tapestries, embroidered with historical scenes; perhaps from the famous craftsmen of Arras, they might have been a gift from his close friends, the Granvelle family. Not yet had he assembled his large collection of paintings and sculpture, which was to include works by Titian and Veronese and many antique Greek and Roman statues, but he had a portrait of his father with him. Of his brothers, Mendoza treasured portraits of Don Francisco, Don Antonio and Don Bernardino, but, significantly, he had apparently none of his eldest brother, Don Luis.[9] Likenesses of Erasmus had probably come his way during his short stay in Flanders. Of his coins, medals, and other *objets d'art*, the nucleus was there, but his collections would be built up substantially from then on. Among curiosities that impressed his visitors were gifts sent by Don Antonio from the New World: Mexican idols of green malachite and of gold; and unusual stones from the Americas.[10] Other things perhaps not too familiar to Venetians were Arabic—astrolabes and planispheres. And he brought a large library with him, but he was to acquire most of the Greek and Latin manuscripts of his famous collection, as well as the first books printed, in Venice. Greek scholars whom he employed in Venice also made for him purchases of Greek and Latin manuscripts in eastern countries.[11]

[9] On Mendoza's paintings and *objets d'art*, see GP III, 244–250.

[10] Amatus Lusitanus, *In Dioscoridis*; in enarratio 119, p. 432, the doctor tells how he was assisting Don Diego's analysis of some stones unknown to the ambassador, gifts from his brother; in enarratio 113, Amatus speaks of idols made from a green stone from the same source (p. 530).

[11] Cf. the catalogue of Mendoza's library in GP III, 481–564.

He made full use of his opportunity to be near the Aldine press. Venice—with Aretino its leading writer—had no censorship. Possibly, Mendoza still took such liberty for granted. This was only the beginning of the century's fifth decade, a time when men's thoughts in many parts of Europe were still free. As the seat of the freest press in the world, the Venetian environment gave Don Diego encouragement for the life-long freedom of his own pen, but whether he ever realized this he did not reveal.

The Holy League

Mendoza's foremost task was to keep Venice in the Holy League. Because of its dependence on the Turkish market, the Republic was a most unwilling partner, but so far it had not been able to withdraw from the alliance. To this crusade, Charles V contributed a hundred galleys, the Venetians the same number, the Pope thirty-six. Together they had a total of 100,000 infantry and 4,500 cavalry. Also, interestingly, the statutes of the League solved the division of Soliman's Empire after anticipated victory: Constantinople would be given to Charles V.[12]

But that crusade is seldom mentioned. Its inglorious end was usually treated with silence. Sixteenth-century historians contradicted each other in trying to explain away the flight of the combined Imperial, Venetian, and Papal fleets from Barbarossa's galleys on the Adriatic. The Allies lost a sea battle at La Prévesa in September, 1538[13]—the same spot, the Gulf of Arta in the Ionian Sea, where Antony and Cleopatra were vanquished by Augustus.

One of the reasons why the combined efforts of Doge, Pope, and Emperor received such a hush must be that each of the three parties to the treaty was in fact double-crossing the others. Behind the scenes, only a year or so before, His Holiness had secretly consented to Turkish support of the French against Charles V. Venice, just as secretly, was already sending out peace-feelers. And late research has brought evidence against the pious Emperor to light—even

<hr />

[12] Santa Cruz, *Crónica*, III, 498.
[13] R. B. Merriman, *The Rise of the Spanish Empire*, III, 321–334, gives a detailed account of this war and a complete bibliography. A recent Spanish account by the Marqués de Mullhacén is in *Carlos V y su política mediterránea*, pp. 135–147.

Charles V had secret dealings with the "Infidel."[14] From 1538 to 1540, Charles V tried to buy Barbarossa over to his side. Neither the miscarried mission to win or to kill Barbarossa before Tunis, nor his conquest of the city, nor the flight of Barbarossa, and the latter's harassment of the Spanish coasts, stopped the Emperor's clandestine attempts at soliciting this corsair's friendship. Now he offered to reinstate Barbarossa in Tunis—although he professed it would pain him to break his faith with Muley Hacen.[15] Among other conditions, such as asking Barbarossa to bring a large quantity of the Sultan's galleys with him and to burn those he could not safely remove, the Muslim admiral was to send his son to Charles V's court as a measure of his good faith, and he was to promise, if necessary, to help Charles V in conquering Venice or Marseilles, or all of France, if the Emperor so desired. Barbarossa declared his readiness to comply with everything except burning the Sultan's galleys.[16] Possibly, he only pretended agreement while keeping the Sultan informed at the same time.

Inviting the Muslim "pirate" to be an ally against France, and even to conquer Venice, Charles V used similar tactics that had proved successful in causing Prince Andrea Doria to desert King Francis I.[17] But in the case of Barbarossa, the secret came out, and the deal fell through. Antonio Rincon, a former leading Comunero who served Francis I as go-between to Sultan Soliman, found out about it and notified the Turkish government.[18] In due course, the news reached the perturbed Republic of Venice. Don Diego had been there only a few months when he heard "a strange tale of a contact between Barbarossa's fleet and a Spanish soldier. A certain Alonso de Alarcón is under suspicion."[19]

With such separate machinations going on, there had to be disunity in the allied camp. No one knew this better than Barbarossa.

---

[14] *DIE* 1: 207–227; Modesto Lafuente, *Historia general de España*, VI, 386–399; Merriman, *Rise of the Spanish Empire*, III, 321, 322, 333.

[15] Lafuente, *Historia general*, p. 390.

[16] Ibid., p. 389.

[17] See "Cómo se adquirió una escuadra en 1528," in F. de Laiglesia, *Estudios históricos*, I, 121–156. Then, the agent was Vasto; in 1537–1540, it was Gonzaga.

[18] Lafuente, *Historia general*, VI, 392 (especially note 2). See also Merriman, *Rise of the Spanish Empire*, III, 333–334.

[19] Mendoza to Charles V, October 19, 1539, Arch. Sim., Est., leg. 1315, Rose-file.

He beat the "crusaders" into flight, Andrea Doria in the lead. The allied fleet, finding refuge in Corfu, blamed each other violently, while Barbarossa and his men, sitting within earshot on a nearby island, openly derided the Holy Leaguers. Yet, despite their mutual recriminations, the Venetians, Genoese, and Spaniards combined their forces once more and conquered a Turkish fortification, Castelnuovo, which seemed to be a convenient base for operations planned for the following year. The Spanish veterans, still numbering four thousand (excluding a motley crowd of women and boys, camp followers who always went along on Spanish crusades), were left as garrison on that place, holding the fort of Castelnuovo over the winter of 1538/39.[20]

When Don Diego left Toledo for Venice in May 1539, the Emperor was worrying about the fact that he had heard no news of the naval situation. He charged Mendoza to find out what was going on as soon as he arrived in Venice, and Don Diego had been in his new post only a few weeks, when he learned and reported the worst.[21] The Turks had retaken Castelnuovo; they had captured or killed all the Spaniards. This boded ill for the continuance of the Holy League. Barbarossa would not have risked coming back up the Adriatic for the reconquest of Castelnuovo, had he not known, by Venice's secret agreement, that the Venetian fleet would stay idle and let him pass.

As the smiling ambassador, ordered to keep Venetian friendship at all costs, Don Diego was obliged to overlook such a flaw in the behavior of his Emperor's unreliable ally. He advised his superiors to overlook it, too. He wrote Cobos:

You over there must always take care to show great confidence in these people here. This will free them of fears they now have; they think His Majesty despises them ever since the fall of Castelnuovo because they made a truce with the Turk, letting him come up the gulf, with-

[20] From documents in Mendoza's accounts it seems that a company of infantry consisted of three hundred men, twenty-five horses, fifty boys, and ten women. Francisco (or Lucas) de Ibarra, Arch. Sim., Contraduría Mayor, first period, 1420, Rose-file. For the conquest of Castelnuovo, see Sandoval, *Historia* (edition of 1604), book 24, pp. 56ff.

[21] Mendoza to Charles V, August 19, 1539, Arch. Sim., Est. Venecia, book 66, Rose-file. Also, GP I, 105.

out sending their fleet against him. They [the Venetians] should be told, if you think it right, that His Majesty thinks their truce was made only as a step toward the general truce, and that he has learned that Barbarossa, coming up the gulf, deceived them step by step. Barbarossa had first promised he would not go past Gallipoli, and they did not know of his coming until it was too late to stop him. If this is not done, I am afraid their fear of the Emperor—always stirred up by those who do not like us here, and by the French, who are never asleep —together with the bad shape they are in, regarding grain, and their hope to get it from the lands of the Turk, all these things together will fill them with despair and really make them join the Turk.[22]

This was applied psychology. If left to Don Diego's influence alone, the Venetians might have stayed loyal to an Emperor who forgave them as magnanimously as his new ambassador tried to do. But words, even the best ones, were not all that was needed. If the Imperials did not quickly come to their aid with grain, Venice would still be lost to the Holy League. Here, then, was Mendoza's dilemma: to exhort the Venetians—who needed peace in order to stay alive—to continue fighting; to explain this paradox to his Emperor, who needed Venice as a buffer state, who had not seen with his own eyes the standstill of commerce, the real famine, and who, on account of the great old reputation of the Republic, would not believe the reports to the contrary; and to make his master understand that his orders could not be executed—but at the same time to persuade him to send help!

He tried to do all this and sincerely implored the Emperor to come to Venice's help. Although he mistakenly believed that Charles V would send the desired assistance, he was realistic enough to calculate that it would take, at best, very long to arrive. This impelled him, seeing how keen Venice was to end the war, to work at delaying its peace as long as possible. "It seems to me," he wrote Cobos, "that I always end up with the most troublesome commission, that is, to temporize, and so I shall strive to do here, if I get support from there [the Imperial court]."

I should be happy [he continues] to see a truce of five to six years, so that we could pull ourselves together and relax, even if it should then start all over again. I fear the lack of money which gets worse every day, and the lack of brave spirits in our people after losing the good

[22] Mendoza to Cobos, September 3, 1539, AC, pp. 9, 10.

ones who were in Castelnuovo. So, my opinion is that, it being so difficult to assemble a new large force strong enough to force the enemy to
join the truce, making us spend every day more and more of the money
we do not have, it would not be a bad idea to join this truce ourselves,
at the least damage and shame possible.

I know well enough that some great spirit might say that, after this
loss [of Castelnuovo] it would be shameful for a Majesty like the Emperor to come to such an agreement, that this would give wings to the
enemy. But those who would risk the most without money and equipment to support them, and who will have to pay dearly for it, are more
often than not just those [who think themselves] "great" minds. I do
think that nothing can strengthen the enemy's wings more than what
this success of Castelnuovo has already done.[23]

The Venetian Government

To Mendoza, the constitution of this Republic vividly illustrated
his concept of the Greek and Roman republics. In his modern
world, he thought it a curious fossil. The ideal ruler for him was an
absolute monarch, guiding his people, according to justice and law,
benevolently, paternally. He deplored the irresolution resulting
from a multiheaded government, and, projecting his own experience of one-man rule, he professed to see individual leadership also
in the real Venetian government, though appearances hid this fact,
and this leader was not the Doge. This elected figurehead drew
Mendoza's mockery:

It is something to see how humble and how
Alone in all greatness on the street
Walks the highest citizen they have.
If you come to his house to speak to him,
You find no one there but him [i.e., the Doge opens the door],
And though he appears before you, you still want to look for him.
    [i.e., the visitor takes him for the servant.]
His belt caught up in a disorderly way,
His dress trailing as long as you please,
His sleeves filled with papers. [The Doge, dispensing with
    secretaries, carries state documents in the sleeves of his toga.]
His stole hangs every which way,
A bonnet flat as a frying pan,
Half slippers on his feet.

[23] AC, pp. 10, 11.

This dress they never change, come what may,
Young, old, rich, or have-nots,
All come and go in one fashion![24]

That Doge, Pietro Lando, had inherited the Holy League from his predecessor and wanted nothing better than to dissolve it. He had been elected the seventy-eighth Doge (since the year 697) a few months before Don Diego's arrival, and he happened to be seventy-eight years old at that time. Doge Lando did not belong to the famous and great, although he had to play on the chessboard of the world against the most brilliant group of masters to be found at one time: Soliman, Francis I, Charles V, and Paul III. Yet in 1539 the Senate of Venice was still of utmost importance in the politics of these monarchs.

The Council of Ten (which with Doge, councillors, and secretaries, numbered in reality almost sixty heads) was composed of very old men, wearing floor-length, loose, full garments, the toga of ancient Rome; as they were sitting or standing side by side, their flowing lines seemed to melt together, expressing their indissoluble community in government, where no individual was allowed to become greater than the others. Yet as uniform as it would look to an outsider, Mendoza noticed that the Senators' unity was not as impenetrable as it was meant to appear. They were split in two factions, and the actual power, he asserted, was concentrated in the hands of one man who apparently did not have more dignity than any other: the same Senator Marco Foscari who once had come as a special ambassador to pay homage to Charles V at Naples. He wrote Cobos on September 3:

Here are two heads working together, and these are the persons whose hands presently govern the affairs of this Republic. One is Marco Foscari, and the other is Juan Dolfin. This Marco Foscari, whose hanger-on is the above Juan Dolfin, is most most French and most most Turk. But though he has a good knowledge of everything, he seems easygoing. He has a son, a Bishop, whom he tries to make Cardinal, wishing to enrich him. It would not be difficult, treating him skillfully, promising him His Majesty's favor, to make him change sides, especially if

[24] From "Epístola á Peña, criada de doña Marina de Aragón, sobre la fundación de Venecia," in *Obras poéticas*, ed. William Knapp, pp. 139–148. ". . . Es de ver cuán humilde . . .," p. 146. Also in C. Malcolm Batchelor, ed., *A tí, Doña Marina*, p. 189.

he obtained some profit or benefice from the Church. Together with him, his large following would also come over to our side. I know somebody who is a great friend of mine and of his who can prove this, and who knows to what length one can go to tempt him.[25]

Senator Foscari (a grandnephew of the famous and unfortunate Doge Foscari of a hundred years back) had warned the Republic when there was still time, not to enter the Holy League. When Venice joined, despite Foscari's advice, he had also prophesied that it would earn nothing but ruin and losses in a war against the Turk.[26] Now, justified by the turn of events, Foscari had become the leader in the peace drive, supported by the majority of public opinion. He distinguished himself from average Venetians by being cultivated and learned, and was no less an Aristotelian than the new young Spanish-Imperial ambassador. No one else could have seen what he so easily recognized: the Republic could preserve the status quo only through peace. The Venetian Empire was at its pinnacle; any military step Venice now took would pull it down. Don Diego, skeptical about Foscari's patriotism, asserted that the Senator took bribes from the French, and that he espoused the Turkish side because he held property in Turkey.[27]

The leader of the pro-Imperial faction seemed also to have been aware that Venice's star was setting, but he drew other conclusions from his insight. Senator Marcantonio Cornaro was firmly attached to the Spanish side, and he appears as a character of much less responsibility than Foscari. First he prodded his country into the war, and at present he desired to keep it in the war. At the same time that Foscari had warned the Republic against the foolhardiness of joining the Holy League, Cornaro called on the Republic to fight for its liberty. His patriotic sentiments, beautifully presented, had then carried the day,[28] while Foscari's prudent and realistic counsel was voted down. But now public feeling was swinging behind the wiser statesman.

It is astonishing to see the illustrious Venetian Cornaro willing to

---

[25] AC, pp. 11, 12.

[26] Giuseppe Cappelletti, *Storia di Venezia*, VIII, book 29, chap. 47, pp. 145–146.

[27] Mendoza to Charles V, April 8, 1541, Arch. Sim., Est. Ven., book 66, Rosefile.

[28] Cappelletti, *Storia di Venezia*, pp. 133–138.

risk a continuation of the war when even Don Diego, the stranger, privately admitted its folly—not only for Venice, but for the Emperor as well. Cornaro apparently was taken in by too great an admiration for the Spaniards. He overestimated their future power because their present far-reaching greatness dazzled him. Probably, also, his self-interest blinded his perception of the whole picture; in his private business he must have been involved with the Spanish wool trade. (Cornaro had formerly served as Venetian ambassador to Spain, a wool-producing country; Venetians often sent as resident envoys to a particular state those patricians who had a commercial interest in the state to which they were accredited.) Only someone whose wealth was based on Spanish wool would have had no personal objection toward remaining in the Turkish war. Another personal tie with Spain was the fact that Cornaro had a Cardinal-uncle of the same name in Rome, and Cornaro's nephew also became a cardinal shortly afterward, both of them partisans of the Emperor who must have recommended the Cornaros to the Pope. (Paul III, striving to preserve neutrality, elevated during his reign an almost equal number of French and Spanish partisans to the cardinalate.)

Foscari's son never received the red hat with which Don Diego had proposed to bait him. Father Foscari was not, apparently, a man to be bought. As soon as Mendoza realized this, he advised the Emperor to withdraw his support from Foscari's son. Although Foscari, according to Don Diego's information, was also to some degree moved by self-interest in advocating peace, his discourses, simple, energetic, and logically convincing, show him as a man of moral principles. Cornaro, who was said to have been a fascinating orator of great eloquence, whose speeches bloom with beautiful phrases in which the words *dignity* and *liberty* abound, appears chauvinistic and emotional by contrast.

Only six weeks after his letter to Cobos, Mendoza observed a complete change in the political orientation of the Venetians.[29] Perhaps his first impression had been misleading, since he revised his opinion drastically. "Four persons who are particularly opposed to the Emperor in the government of Venice have lost their influ-

---

[29] Mendoza to Charles V, October 19, 1539, Arch. Sim., Est., leg. 1315, Rosefile.

ence," he wrote. He found that both Marco Foscari and Juan Dolfin "had fallen very low." A third had been banished for receiving bribes. The fourth, Juan Antonio Venier, who was formerly ambassador to Charles V, was going away on official business. Foscari was said to have refused an appointment as ambassador to the Emperor. "This Signory," he remarked to Cobos, "is like the people. Today they resolve to do one thing, and tomorrow, before one can sit down to write about it, we find they completely reverse their positions, and that's how it is!"[30]

Another change that he reported a few days later sounded more ominous still for one who, like Mendoza, depended on a steady supply of "inside" news. "The Signoria has established an office of Inquisition. Three inspectors are now proceeding against anyone who is giving out information."[31]

The Visit of the Marquis of Vasto

Single-handedly, Mendoza continued his effort to keep the Republic in the war, but at the same time he added another interest to the many he already had. He turned businessman. While the famine lasted, he expected to do a good deed to the city by importing grain, and to himself as well by profiting from the current high prices. For months at a time, he worried about his grain business. And, anticipating the peace between Venice and Turkey—although he did his best to prevent it—he invested in rugs, carpets, and other "divine" things to be ordered from the Orient. The Venetian facilities were too inviting for anyone, even a Spanish nobleman unused to this kind of business, to abstain from commerce. The water-level floor of his house, a lofty apartment, marble-pillared, was a warehouse, a storeroom, the most important room in a Venetian household. Business and private life were merged in this city. The splendor and luxury of a patrician's upper stories rested in more than one sense on the water-level floor foundation of his palazzo. There, the "Merchant of Venice" stored his goods, imported from the East, carried from overseas in Venetian freighters (the largest in the world, of up to four hundred tons) from their ports of origin up the Grand Canal directly to the steps of his own water gate. Soon,

[30] Mendoza to Cobos, October 18, 1539, *AC*, p. 16.
[31] Mendoza to Charles V, October 22, 1539, Arch. Sim., Est., leg. 1315, Rosefile.

Mendoza's own empty ground floor would be filled with sacks of wheat, bales of cloth, and many other commodities.

"I shall die of hunger in this famine," he wrote to Cobos, "if I do not get a cargo of five hundred to six hundred wagonloads of grain from Apulia, because all of my salary goes for bread." He implored Cobos to exert pressure on the Viceroy of Naples (Don Pedro de Toledo, uncle of the Duke of Alba), to send him the grain without fail. At the same time he prodded the Emperor and Cobos to help the Republic. "I am still convinced," he wrote Cobos on October 18, "that they will make their separate peace as long as the enemy will agree to it, even if they go broke in doing so. I am turning preacher, telling them in general and in particular what I know and can do. I am afraid that hunger will move them toward some unwise step, even though it should go against us. At the moment our enemies have no other weapon to harm us with but precisely the lack of wheat. If we could only give them some hope for the future, even with ever so small a quantity of grain, our partisans would take heart and persuade others to our side."[32]

But before he could dispatch this letter, on the next day, the Signoria decided by only one majority vote to offer a separate peace to the Turks. This happened despite his greatest exertions. Almost every other day he had shown himself in the Doge's palace; he exhorted the Venetians, admonishing them to take a leaf from the Spartans, who did not surrender to Xerxes.[33] He made exorbitant promises of wheat. And he still remained hopeful; it was one thing for Venice to propose peace, but the Sultan, he thought, might reject this proposition.

As long as the outcome of these negotiations was not known, he continued to play for time with the Senate. The task was thankless and nearly futile. What good was it to continue telling "these gentlemen" of the great unity of Charles V and Francis I, when they did not believe him and said so, and he had nothing to prove it? He kept promising them that Imperial troops and shipfuls of grain were on their way to Venice, but the Senate, while wisely not commenting on the nonappearance of the troops, asked him ever more pointedly about the promised grain. Trying to keep up these pre-

[32] Mendoza to Cobos, September 3, 1539, *AC*, p. 14; October 18, *AC*, p. 15.
[33] Mendoza to Charles V, October 19, 1539, Arch. Sim., Est. Ven., book 66, Rose-file.

tenses, he had nothing and no one to reassure him throughout the first three months in his new office, until, near the end of November, 1539, relief arrived in the form of heartening news. The Emperor was in France.

Six months earlier, when Ghent had broken out in armed revolt, the city had even asked Francis I for help. But having timed their overtures badly, the Ghenters were now being used by the French King, who tried to overwhelm his life-long antagonist with a display of unusual magnanimity. Divulging to Charles V the treasonable offer of the latter's own native city, he invited the Emperor to travel through France on his way to punish the rebels and to consider France his own country. He did so in the expectation that Charles V would reciprocate with equal generosity and let him have Milan.

By the snail's pace at which events were creeping, the Emperor was ready to start his "hurried" trip in mid-November; withal it took him nine months from the outbreak of the revolt to get to Ghent. By the end of November, Venice heard for the first time of Charles V's actual, peaceful presence in France. The highlight of that unusual trip was the day both monarchs, like brothers, went to worship in the Cathedral of Notre Dame.

For the Emperor, and for his Spaniards all over the world, it was important to make the most of the all-Christian friendship while it lasted. They expected to intimidate the Turks with it and to impress Venice. Perhaps, despite its recent offer of a separate peace, Venice would now be content to remain in the Turkish war. But if many would be impressed by this propaganda journey, not so the Venetians. Steadily they continued to build their separate peace. "These gentlemen," whose principle of state was distrust, were not so easily convinced that Charles V had suddenly become a true friend of his life-long foe and rival.

Don Diego made this so clear to his master that the Emperor at last understood. Venice was still doubting him! Charles V would exploit the situation to the full. He persuaded Francis I to send messengers into the world as tangible proof of their unity. The highest officials were chosen to visit Venice: the French sent Marshal d'Annébaut, governor of Piedmont, and the Emperor sent the

Marquis of Vasto, who was then his greatest general and, since the year before, governor of Milan.

"A great reception is being prepared here for the señor Marquis," wrote Don Diego to Cobos on November 28. "He is arriving on Sunday. He will come just in time to launch our negotiations, and will gain much reputation because these gentlemen will have to throw their lot in with us anyway—the Turks do not want them."[34]

Two days later, Mendoza and his colleague, the French ambassador, in their ceremonial dress of crimson damask and fur-lined velvets, sat as guests of honor among "these gentlemen" next to the Doge on the Bucintoro, as the gala ship was rowed out to Chioggia to receive the Marquis and the Marshal. It was a splendid mark of respect toward the Emperor and King that the Doge and the great "Ten" went such a long way to welcome their deputies; the traditional reception place for royal guests was at the nearby precinct of Sanct Biagio, on the Canal of the Giudecca.

Under the red banner with the winged golden lion that fluttered in the sharp November breeze from the top of the red-lacquered flagpole, Mendoza, on what must have been a chilly and rough ride on the wintry Adriatic, could find comfort, perhaps, in reflecting how favorably many things had recently changed for him. He was now relieved of some of the terrible responsibility. If the Venetians still went ahead with their peace, he would not be the only one to be blamed. Another welcome change appeared in the aspect of Venice, suddenly so different, that even he felt compelled to admire. "The most sumptuous reception was given [the señor Marquis]," he wrote a few days later, "that has ever been made for a prince."[35]

For the first time since the war years, there were parades of decorated gondolas; multicolored carpeting hung from every balcony and window ledge; flowers, garlands, triumphal arches, embellished the city, while masses of people spread a festive air as they watched from roofs, loggias, windows, bridges, and quays. Bells pealed, cannons were fired, music sounded, and the Doge, to be

[34] *AC*, p. 181.
[35] Ibid., p. 21.

sure, had replaced his "shabby bathrobe-type" ordinary garment
with gowns and mantles of goldcloth and ermine, and the "frying-
pan bonnet" with the ducal hat, all gold and jewels—a splendid
doorman of a splendid house.[36]

Don Alfonso d'Avalos, Marquis of Vasto, a handsome personage
with large and somewhat melancholy eyes (as Titian twice por-
trayed him), of a commanding stature, in shining gilded armor
and wearing a golden, red-plumed helmet, on leaving the Imperial
galley and joining the small group on the Bucintoro, made a good
show himself, and the French Marshal was hardly less impressive.
With the visitors aboard, the gala ship headed back toward Venice,
followed by a procession of countless boats; after the guests were
shown the unique view around the Piazzetta, the French party
stepped off close to the French embassy near San Moisé; then the
Bucintoro turned in to go all the way up the Grand Canal, passing
through the old drawbridge of the Rialto, toward the city's own
prepared guesthouse, reserved for kings.[37] Among those who described this procession in glowing terms was Pietro Aretino, then
in the Imperials' pay as publicity writer, who saw Vasto's entry
first-hand from the balcony of his comfortable house on the Grand
Canal.[38]

There is not much literature on the doings of Marshal d'Annébaut on this occasion. One of the reasons for this neglect is the fact
—discovered later—that d'Annébaut used his stay in Venice to
hatch a plot of treason together with the residing French ambassador, undermining future Venetian relations with the Turks. Besides, Aretino, having quit the service of Francis I, ignored the
French envoy, omitting any reference to his former employer.
With the French therefore out of the limelight, the Marquis of

[36] In "Epístola a Peña" (see note 24, above), Mendoza reports that, a thousand years earlier, when the first elected Doge of these islands had nothing to
cover his head with, one of the rough fishermen of that first senate—

    The senate that was covered with rushes,
    Of hard shells the seat was made,
    and fishers' nets were stretched across . . .

—tore off his sleeve and offered it to the Doge; hence the horned, or sleeved,
shape of the Doge's precious hat (worth 198,000 ducats).

[37] Then, the Palazzo d'Este; later, that building became the "Fondaco de'
Turchi"; now it is the Museum of Natural History.

[38] GP I, p. 186.

Vasto, who basked in it (for good measure, he had brought Paolo Giovio along as his guest), had it almost to himself. When he gave his introductory oration in the Hall of the Great Council, so many noblemen crowded in to hear him that halberdiers had to defend the door. Many patricians, though listed in the Golden Book of the Republic and therefore privileged to enter, could not be admitted.[39]

Vasto, with convincing demagoguery and with all the craft of a great commander accustomed to sending his men, with well-chosen words, to their death (Titian immortalized him this way in *Allocution to his Soldiers*), called on the Venetians for a new crusade. Promising not only troop reinforcements, ships, sailors, and grain from the Emperor—sustaining Mendoza's previous promises—he generously threw in, besides, the armies of Bohemia and Hungary, and at the end even those of France, although his colleague in the double embassy, Marshal d'Annébaut, thereafter praised peace among Christendom in very vague terms, without mentioning the crusade.[40] But the glowing words of Vasto caused even the Doge to utter something about the "Holy War" in his response. However, the special wisdom of Venetians consisted in the fact that political decisions could never be made instantly; the real reply to the Emperor's embassy would be given only after several days of deliberation.

During the waiting period, Don Diego entertained the Marquis and his followers in his house. "I remember those seven poets," wrote Aretino to Giovio later, "who, in the house of the Signor Don Diego de Mendoza, the admirable personage, circled around you both [Giovio and the Marquis]: they seemed like little beggar barks surrounding the proper boats."[41] At a gala to which Aretino was invited, Titian, Sansovino, and other leading artists and scholars of Venice would also have been present. And Mendoza took Vasto sightseeing. They visited the Arsenal, the first and traditional thing to do for every new guest. There, a brand-new galley could be launched every morning, although in the current period of stagna-

---

[39] Paolo Giovio, *Historiarum sui temporis*, book 39, pp. 426–428 (German edition).

[40] Ibid., p. 425.

[41] P. Aretino, *Corrispondenza*, II, 206. In *Scrittori d'Italia*, edited by Fausto Nicolini.

tion and recession, ship production had shrunk or even halted. In the evening, they donned masks and went in search of adventure, the Marquis now leading Don Diego, showing him what he so far seemed to have missed in Venice.

"His Excellency," Mendoza reports to Cobos, "saw on the third [day of December] two ballerinas, and inflamed himself so much that on the very same evening he became a bridegroom. We missed you greatly at that wedding, as we do everywhere. But now we see that it does no harm to official business to enjoy the good life at the same time! That's what this devil of a Marquis does, whom the little Venetian wenches visit, in masks, three at a time. But he rules the Venetians [the Senators], over whom he has great authority for his skill and personality." He tells Cobos later, "I am unable to describe the good time the Marquis had and the pranks he played with mask and without, for they are countless and have no equal. I can only say that during most of them he wished for the company of Your Excellency."[42]

Venice was famous for its corruption. A special sort of rhymed Baedeker then available for tourists, *The Directory of Love*, listed names, addresses, and fees (from one or two scudi up to thirty scudi per night) of 215 Venetian ladies. Since, reportedly, there were eleven thousand prostitutes in the city (in a population of about 100,000—roughly, every second female of marriageable age), the guidebook referred only to the most select of the profession. The quarters of San Foscha and San Canciano, officially reserved for the brothels, did not suffice at all. The "triste" women, whose elegance sometimes equaled or even outshone that of the Dogaressa, lived all over town.

It goes without saying that this "devil" of a Marquis was not in the least restrained by having a beautiful and noble wife, the Princess Marina of Aragon. A woman of the same name was the object of an ideal love whom Don Diego had chosen to serve platonically in the way then fashionable, addressing poetry to her. In his bedchamber, concealed under a silken curtain, hung a portrait of her he had commissioned Titian to paint. Usually, such mock devotion was directed to a married woman, and Mendoza's admired lady possibly was the Marquesa del Vasto. But according to some opin-

[42] December 4, *AC*, p. 21; December 16, *AC*, p. 23. Also, GP III, p. 294.

ions he loved a young, unmarried Spanish woman of the same name.[43] Ideal or real love, however, his chivalrous relation with his adored Marina of Aragon did not prevent him from sharing Don Alfonso's escapades.

While the Imperial ambassadors carelessly amused themselves and the French spread their net of treason, the senators lived through a period of stress. Finding themselves so seriously admonished by Charles V to continue on the warpath, they had to come to terms with their own intentions. The Foscari and Cornaro factions engaged in endless night-long debates. Compromise was impossible, the question being either peace or war. In the end, Foscari overstepped his powers, causing an unexpected crisis that Don Diego, prematurely, took to be a victory for the Imperial side.

It had happened this way: The Senate faction favoring the Emperor seemed to have won a lot of ground on account of the double embassy. Since this rather loud-mouthed faction comprised many of the younger members of the general Council, Foscari, afraid that the peace party would lose in the impending vote, proposed to reduce the right of referendum from the three hundred or four hundred who held it now, to about fifty or sixty of the wisest ones. Formerly so prudent, he had not foreseen the uproar that would follow his unprecedented idea. As a result, suddenly, a vote deprived him of all his senatorial honors and privileges. It was as simple as that. In Venice, no one could become too great. The news came out, and Don Diego rejoiced, writing that Marco Antonio Cornaro really carried the day for the party of the Empire.[44]

A day later came an even greater surprise. The 350 voters who so dramatically had protected their traditional right to vote and who counted among their number many of the younger gentlemen who liked to wear the Spanish fashion of short coats and long hose —these apparently unwise dandies, Foscari's disgrace notwithstanding, voted for peace in accordance with Foscari's advice. Even the youngest Venetians were already a thousand years of age!

The official reply given the double embassy was couched in care-

---

[43] See C. Malcolm Batchelor, "Doña Marina de Aragón," in *A tí, Doña Marina*, pp. 55–78.

[44] Mendoza to Charles V, December 12, 1539, Arch. Sim., Est. Ven., book 65, Rose-file.

ful words: the government of Venice professed itself ready to proceed with the war, provided that both their Majesties wanted them to do so. Otherwise they felt unable to join.[45] Evidently, the Venetians had seen through the pretense of Imperial-French friendship. The embassy in their midst may have afforded them the best insight into what they had suspected all along.

As soon as they had pocketed this message, very suddenly, without the Doge and Bucintoro, in a neglect contrasting sharply with the sumptuousness of their arrival, both the French Marshal, and a few days later the Imperial Marquis, hurriedly departed.

The señor Marquis is leaving so suddenly, [Don Diego told Cobos on December 16] and I have such a cold, that I cannot write much. But I want to let you know that this Signoria has given him all proofs of good friendship and goodwill possible. These gentlemen have decided, each time they see the two Majesties united, to join them with all their forces. Meanwhile they will hold the power of the enemy at bay with words. They are not powerful enough to resist him alone, but the condition is that they must get victuals. It is in any case necessary to provide these, and quickly, because they have nothing to eat and do not know where they can get something. It is not right, according to human law, to see one's friends go to ruin. It is even worse to see this in those who are in such need that they might become desperate. I do not say this because I happen to be here and wish to give them pleasure, but because it seems to me that this has to be done, simply to sustain them.[46]

And—despite the professed friendship—taunting the French, he continues, reporting on the retinue of Marshal d'Annébaut: "The French have left the house where they lodged stripped of all rugs and sheets, and they also left behind a very wretched name in their manner of negotiating."[47]

Venice seemed to have depleted itself in its costly entertainment of the guests. A week later, Don Diego reports to the Emperor that the famine was worsening. "Laborers in the arsenal, two days ago, armed themselves and robbed the stores of flour. It is certainly a great pity to see them die of hunger." He found out, also, that Venice still (or again) showed its skepticism about the professed friend-

[45] AC, pp. 22, 23.
[46] Ibid., pp. 22, 23.
[47] Ibid., p. 23.

ship between Charles V and the French King. In his last audience, when he read His Majesty's recent letter aloud to the Senators, stressing this harmony, Don Diego was told that he seemed to have written the letter himself on a blank, signed beforehand by the Emperor.[48]

If the Marquis of Vasto's visit did not particularly help the Emperor's cause, better news for Don Diego's purposes arrived in mid-December. As he had hoped, the Venetian bid for a separate peace had collapsed. The Sultan, whose aim was the destruction of the Republic's colonial empire, found the Venetian ambassador lacking in authority to agree to this. The Venetian envoy returned from Constantinople with none of his objectives attained. Mendoza now employed his wits to prevent the Signoria from appointing a new peace negotiator. Speculating at length about what the Venetians would or would not do, he wrote Cobos on December 19: "Do not leave off writing me often, even if there should be nothing to say, because it gladdens me and gives me confidence to speak with them more freely."[49]

Meanwhile, his grain business looked much less lucrative than anticipated. The Viceroy of Naples let him have only half the amount he had ordered; besides, he sent it from Apulia where the price was highest. "He makes me lose more than six thousand ducats where I thought to gain them thrice doubled."[50]

Cobos promised Don Diego he would prod the Viceroy in behalf of his grain, admonishing him, however, not to expect too much and to beware of extravagance. The report of Mendoza's "magnificence" in Venice had begun to spread. "I take your letters to heart," wrote the magnificent ambassador, "trying to keep my expenses within my salary. I am profiting so much from your admonishings that, if I should turn from prodigal to miser, I can say you ordered me to do so."[51]

Cobos' wife had also written. She was scandalized about Don Diego's reports of extracurricular activities in Venice. "Half of the

[48] Mendoza to Charles V, December 25, 1539, Arch. Sim., Est. Ven., book 65, Rose-file.
[49] AC, p. 61.
[50] Ibid., p. 23.
[51] Ibid., p. 61.

letter of my patroness is full of reprehensions, but I repent nothing. In my life I have not seen a place like this where a man can give a good time to someone he likes. Everything is so well provided here for that."[52]

By December 31, the Signoria, overriding Don Diego's objections, once more supported a new trial for peace. The new envoy, Contarini, received secret instructions by the Council of Ten to sign away, if worst came to worst, the Venetian overseas empire, Nauplia and Malvasia. No one else knew the extent of the sacrifice that Venice was prepared to make. All that leaked out was the amount of reparations they were willing to pay, 300,000 ducats. And no one in Venice knew at the time that one of the scribes serving in the Council of Ten was in French pay: through this channel the Turk was informed as to how far he could go. Don Diego knew no more than anyone else, but he speculated that "Venice is making use of the visit of the Marquis and d'Annébaut for a better deal with the enemy."[53] He did not suspect that Venice would get only the worst deal possible. Meanwhile, rumors that the terms of the agreement would be disastrous circulated freely.

It took six months before there would be any answer. The length of the period of waiting made the city weary. From the end of 1538, when Venice had started to open negotiations, the peace had seemed accompanied by misfortune. The first Venetian envoy died on the way to Turkey. The second was rejected by Soliman because he had not been able to make the exorbitant concessions the victorious Turk had requested. Now, the third ambassador was on the way with his undisclosed instructions, and everyone felt some impending doom in the air. Sansovino, the great builder and sculptor in the employ of the Republic, gave permanent expression to the atmosphere; he was building the Loggetta at the foot of the Campanile of San Marco, and one of the four bronze statuettes in the Loggetta, *La Pace*, bows her head in mourning, as if a symbol from the time of a painful peace. (Aretino invited Don Diego on February 10, 1540, to attend the inauguration of the Loggetta—bidding him to come either in mask or as he usually went.)[54]

[52] Ibid., p. 62.
[53] Mendoza to Charles V, December 31, 1539, Arch. Sim., Est. Ven., book 66, Rose-file.
[54] Aretino, *Corrispondenza*, II, 210–211.

Shady Dealings

Already less than half a year after his arrival, it was obvious that Mendoza had failed in the first two points of his instructions: keeping Venice within the Holy League, and preventing a private peace settlement between the Republic and the Turks. The third point, watching the activities of the French, was a task more lasting, more complex, and, in the end, more rewarding. At the moment, his colleague, the French ambassador Monseigneur Pellicier, who worked at opposing three points, seemed to be successful in his mission just where Don Diego failed: Venice had dropped out of the League; the reconciliation of Venice with the Turks was under way, thanks to secret French efforts, and the French were successful even in spying upon the Imperials. Mendoza was still unaware of the fact that a minor official in his embassy was a spy in the pay of Pellicier. Possibly he did not, at first, distrust the French quite as much as was necessary. He had established at once after the French envoy's arrival a good fellowship with him. Preceding the visit of their superiors, for instance, the two ambassadors had made an excursion to Chioggia, amiably working out the details of the official welcome for Vasto and d'Annébaut. Pellicier was a scholar, a collector of manuscripts and books, and Don Diego was easily prepared to esteem a potential adversary who turned out to be an intellectual.[55] Hence he started somewhat late to become suspicious, but gradually he uncovered a vast French spy net. All the time, however, he watched the openly declared French agents who did business with Constantinople and who passed through Venice on their way to and from Paris several times a year. Among them were Antonio Rincon, the French ambassador to the Sultan; his collaborator Cesare Fragoso; and a certain Cantelmo, special envoy of the King of France to the Turk.

Closely connected with French agents were the Florentine exiles resident in Venice, especially the Strozzi. The house of these enemies of the Medici, wealthy bankers completely at the service of France, was a focus of anti-Imperial intrigue; and secretly coming and going was Lorenzino de' Medici, the murderer of Duke Alessandro de' Medici, first husband of Charles V's daughter, Margaret of Austria. Lorenzino was a fugitive from Imperial justice.

[55] Zeller, *La diplomatie*, p. 43, *et passim*.

It was never spelled out that Don Diego's special task consisted
in doing away with this Medici. Many times throughout the seven
years he stayed in Venice, he gives news about his whereabouts,
promising "to do my best" according to "what Your Majesty
wishes." In September, 1539, Don Diego was already on his trail,
reporting that Lorenzino "changed his lodgings from hour to hour"
and was hard to come by. He did not know the fugitive personally,
and had to arrange a special maneuver by which a go-between
would secretly point the wretched Medici out to him.[56] Despite his
professions of wishing to fulfill the Emperor's order, this task was
not to his taste—as little, probably, as were all his underhand dealings with his secret service. When Lorenzino reappeared in Venice,
making less of an effort to hide himself, Mendoza, averse to cut
down a hunted man, sent him an indirect warning to protect himself better.[57]

It was much more essential to him, and also more difficult, to discover which of the rank-and-file Venetians were in French pay. At
first he had suspected even such high government officials as Senator Foscari of being open to direct bribery. After some time, however, he concluded that he had been wrong.[58] Now he believed it
difficult even to try to tempt them with presents—perhaps he had
tried it and was rebuffed. Instead, he recommended buying one of
the secretaries, who would keep him up to date about the inner
workings of the Council of Ten. But here the French were already
far ahead of him; they had hired a secretary from the Council while
he and Vasto amused themselves. The consequences appeared later
in the disastrous Turkish peace—the discovery of French treason
came only two years afterward.

Difficult as this beginning was, Mendoza made several friends
who knew many important people and enjoyed the full confidence
of Venetians, yet did not disdain being kept on a secret payroll in
return for their usefulness: the ambassador of the Duke of Urbino
and a certain Venetian, Galceran Cepello. Don Diego paid each of

---

56 Mendoza to Charles V, November 28, 1539, Arch. Sim., Est. Ven., book 66,
Rose-file.
57 L. Campana, "Monsignor Giovanni della Casa," *Studii Storici* (*Stud. Stor.*)
17: 426.
58 Mendoza to Charles V, February 9, 1540, Arch. Sim., Est., leg. 1316, Rose-
file.

them six hundred escudos annually for their Imperial friendship, suggesting that the Emperor let him spend altogether four thousand escudos per year (twice the amount of his current starting salary as ambassador) for this kind of news service.[59]

While he went about weaving his own spy network, the French go-between, Cantelmo, stopped in Venice in March, 1540, on his way from Constantinople. All at once, ominous predictions about impending peace flew wildly about, some rumors even hinting at an understanding between Charles V, Soliman, and Francis I. The Senate summoned Don Diego, reproaching him with the report about secret negotiations that the Emperor was supposed to be carrying on with the Turk. Charles V and Francis I, they told him, were allying themselves with the Turk against Venice.

Mendoza went to great effort to convince the Signoria that all such talk was a fabrication. He could do this persuasively, because, at worst, it was only half true. He knew only too well that there was no actual agreement with France—but this angle, wisely, he did not stress. His reaction shows that he was perhaps totally unaware of the Emperor's secret machinations. His reply to the Signoria, in which he tried to "tear their suspicions out by the root," reveals not only his clear conscience, but also his feeling of superiority and moral pride on behalf of his Emperor. To vindicate the honor of his master, he even permitted himself to teach the thousand-year-old Republic a lesson in government (a closely reasoned political view that has escaped attention until now).[60] There, he analyzes the three forms of government in existence: republics (Venice), tyrannies (the Turk), and states ruled by reason and justice (Charles V's Empire and the France of Francis I). A republic, that is, a multiheaded government like Venice, he predicts, "will amble along until it comes to grief . . . all republics suffer from irresolution, and in the end they die of it." Tyranny, keeping

[59] Ibid.

[60] *AIH* II (1911), 162–172. This interesting document has never been commented on. Besides, it is dated erroneously 1546. One of the proofs that the letter is from March 1540 instead of 1546 appears on page 170 with the reference to the Emperor's recent journey through France to pacify his province of Flanders: ". . . como se ve claro por esta passada de su Magd. por Francia a pacificar sus tierras en Flandes . . ."

neither justice nor truth, "will devour you in peace and war, little by little." By contrast, in the Christian monarchies "friend and foe meet truth. The Emperor rules over free peoples, Germans, Italians, Spaniards . . . they cannot be ruled by tyranny but only by reason and religion."

After describing in interesting detail the way Charles V conducts his political business, Mendoza advises the Doge not to rely on what, for example, the Venetian ambassador at the Emperor's court tells him. Unless directly from the lips of His Majesty, or from those who on his orders deal with the business, nothing can be understood correctly. The Serenissimus, therefore, should not rule himself by unfounded reports, for "sometimes you will provide for things which are not necessary, or you will fail to provide what is necessary."

5. GROWING SPANISH-FRENCH HOSTILITY, 1540–1544

Oh ambassadors, you sharp simpletons,
When the Kings intend some deception
They use it first on you!

Don Diego[1]

Conquistador or Pope?

AT THE END OF MAY, 1540, Venice was ready to sign its peace with the Turk. The details of the treaty were not made known for four or five months; their release awaited the new round trip of a Venetian envoy to the Ottoman Porte for ratification by the Sultan. "You will see by the letter to His Majesty," Mendoza wrote Cobos on May 28, "how these gentlemen have agreed so shamefully to their peace. I believe they will ratify it, and I intend to talk to them tomorrow. I shall send you my speech together with the decision. I could do no more, but shall always do what I can and am told to do."

Two days later he told Cobos: "My oratory did little good to make these gentlemen change their minds, although I have written my speech, copy enclosed, and sent it into their Council, as is the custom of doing business hereabouts. I have done what I could, and

---

[1] C. Malcolm Batchelor, ed., *A tí, Doña Marina*, p. 71:
    ¡O embaxadores, finos majaderos,
    que si los reyes quieren engañar,
    comiençan por vosotros los primeros!

I could do no more. Little rugs and pretty things from the Levant will be coming with this peace," he continues, "and I will start life anew, although it is a wretched one without you, and seeing that what I was ordered to do, and have so much desired, has turned out otherwise. Please console me! Since I have nobody else who could do so, if you are satisfied with me I will not care for all the rest."[2]

In Madrid, Cobos, invariably considerate of the welfare of the brothers Mendoza, had anticipated the problem of a "new life" for Don Diego. Don Antonio, now five years in the New World, wished Don Diego would join him, and Cobos, apparently, was not averse to the idea. Having set up a workable government in Mexico City, the Viceroy was at that time undertaking expeditions into unexplored territories. He wanted to head the campaigns personally, but needed a dependable deputy in the Viceroy's palace. His youngest brother, who still had to make his fortune, seemed the right choice.

Don Antonio lived like a king, waited on by sixty Indian servants, escorted by a bodyguard of thirty to forty gentlemen.[3] At the same time he helped Cobos "fill his house with gold."[4] Trade with the new Spanish colonial empire was a monopoly of Spain, to be sure, but for only a very few people in Spain, and Cobos was one of them. Don Antonio had steered the pastel (flax) monopoly Cobos' way; then there was the Mexican trade in wine and black slaves; the monopoly of a pearl fishery in Panama; an annual business in Church bulls for the christianized Indians, worth 300,000 ducats—and Cobos, through Don Antonio, had a large share in most of these and other privileges.[5] The Viceroy's men had just discovered Colombia (named "New Granada" in honor of his city). To proceed with such expeditions, Don Antonio needed government permission and funds, but apparently a hitch had developed—the Council of the Indies started to make difficulties, possibly because there was no one to replace Don Antonio when he absented himself from the government house. Don Diego learned about this directly from his brother, who always worked hand-in-hand with him.

---

[2] May 28, 1540, GP III, 282; May 30, AC, p. 38.

[3] A. Scott Aiton, *Antonio de Mendoza*, pp. 48, 49.

[4] Mendoza to Cobos, London, February 20, 1538, quotes Don Antonio: "a el le hinchiré la casa de oro . . .," AC, p. 4.

[5] Ibid., pp. 4, 5.

Don Diego wrote Cobos on May 12:

The copy of this letter from Don Antonio will show you how important that discovery and conquest is for his advantage and his honor.
Now that you started him off, you must order him to continue. This is
all he wants, and this is what we expect of you, our boss. . . . I beg you
to realize that, having this [opportunity for] conquest is Don Antonio's
whole life; this is what he writes. If I should have to stay in the government [meaning that he should represent the Viceroy in Mexico City
while Don Antonio goes on campaigns], it's all the same to me. You
must decide. It will be a favor for me, and I intend to serve God and
the Emperor and you. I love Don Antonio so much that I will undergo
any kind of job, all the more if it will be to my advantage as well.
This [the peace of Venice] will in any case be resolved one way or the
other before new mail from New Spain can reach us.[6]

This looks as though Don Diego might have been interested in
becoming a conquistador, but nothing was less likely. He simply
felt unable to speak openly of his intention. Vassal of his master,
he had to do what he was asked to do. Also, he would not have
wished to say a direct "no" to one of his brothers, although by now
he was independent of them. No one would be harmed if he used a
little subterfuge to further his own purposes. Practically the same
day Don Diego gave Cobos his half-hearted consent to being used in
the New World, Galceran Cepello, the agreeable Venetian gentleman who was in his secret pay, wrote Cobos a letter that sounds as
though Mendoza had been looking over the writer's shoulder:

The señor Don Diego [writes Galceran Cepello] is not only diligent
regarding his service to the Emperor, but also much more diligent than
any one else who has been here during our time. He is so skillful that
he understands fully as much as can be understood. In his spare time
he has made such progress in his study of Greek that now he can understand, unassisted, Aristotle and other Greek authors [in the origi-
nal]; soon he will be the greatest expert, in these parts, in Greek as
well as in Latin.

All these gentlemen here not only love but also admire him for his
adroitness in negotiating, and for his complete truthfulness. He never
troubles them for favors on behalf of private people, as some of the previous ambassadors have done; he carries out the service of the Emperor
with great gentleness and modesty.

[6] Ibid., pp. 34–36.

Besides this, he studies mathematics; and many times he carries out demonstrations for his teacher. In short, he does all that a perfect and virtuous man can do. And although these things are not news for Your Excellency, I have wanted to write them, because *it would be better to give him the bishopric of Cartagena and keep him in these parts than to send him into the New World* [italics added]. I do not doubt that, if he becomes Cardinal, he will one day be Pope, making the House of Mendoza even more illustrious, although it is already so illustrious that it seems to me nothing can make it more so.[7]

This was indirect strategy; it was clever—and it worked. No more was said of Don Diego's going to America. All the same, as long as he lived in Venice, he did not like it, or at least he so pretended. He had, in truth, to do many disagreeable things there: looking for the corruptible side of every new friend he made, exploiting his venality in the Emperor's service, or enmeshing himself in a spy network that was increasingly complex and full of danger for him. But apart from his shady dealings and official business, he had plenty of time and opportunity to read and study, the life he preferred. He made full use, for example, of his permission to visit the library of Saint Mark's at any hour, even unattended.[8] Posthumously, he would be accused of stealing some precious volumes from Cardinal Bessarion's collection, together with the chains that tied them to the reading stands. The slanderous story had its origin in the fact that he had a secretary borrow one codex from the Marciana for use at the Council of Trent: Massarelli saw it with its telltale chains.[9] But all the books Mendoza had taken out were returned to the library "in a saintly manner."[10]

He found and used in Venice the best-qualified teachers of Greek (presumably, Bernardo Regazzola, known as "Feliciano," who

[7] GP I, 283, 284.

[8] Domenico Molino to Giov. Meursio, Venice, November 3, 1622, in Marquardi Gudii et Claudii Sarracini Senatoris Parisiensis, *Epistolas Ultrajecti*, Lugduni Batavorum, 1711, p. 131, Rose-file.

[9] *Conc. Trid.* Massarelli, *Diaria* I, entry of July 26, 1545, mentions a book from the Venetian collection of Bessarion; according to Charles Graux, *Essai sur les origines du fond grec de l'Escurial*, p. 408, this was a book taken from the Marciana on March 29, 1545, and returned September 26, 1545. Cf. J. Páez to Zurita, ". . . Lo de Dionysio Halicarnassaeo . . . hallé en una librería de Venecia, y lo truximos acá con su cadena . . .," Diego J. Dormer, *Progresos*, p. 405. See also GP I, 261–263.

[10] "Sancte restituit." GP I, 262.

dedicated a commentary on Alexander of Aphrodisias to him)[11]; and of mathematics (presumably, Professor Tartaglia). Scholars and poets sought the honor of dedicating the labor of many years to him. He enjoyed being a Maecenas; his own creativity was stimulated by this environment. He started to translate works of Aristotle directly from Greek into Spanish (this had not been done before), and he encouraged others to use the vernacular; he wrote poetry full of amusing observations; he inspired Titian to make a new departure in his art of portraiture by painting him full-length. Sansovino fashioned a sculpture of him, intended by Mendoza as a gift to Cobos, whom he warned not to display it in his foyer, "otherwise the pages will throw shoe polish in my eyes. . . ."[12] Aretino, besides celebrating him in poems and letters, was cheerful company. Intellectual and artistic riches, not to mention his affluence in his first Venetian year, could well match any wealth he might be able to amass in the New Spain. With peace—much as he had to deplore this peace of Venice officially—the city's trade suddenly revived on a scale he had never seen, and it submerged him. "I am standing here in a labyrinth of crates and bales," he wrote Cobos on June 21, 1540, after the arrival of a Turkish merchantman, "that seems a far bigger labyrinth to me than the peace treaty that these gentlemen have just concluded."[13]

And although he was in no position to increase Cobos' transatlantic businesses still further, he supplied him with—in addition to costly oriental rugs—Venetian specialties, such as eyeglasses (a great many of them: one found the correct ones, it seems, by taking a chance at different types of lenses); for Cobos' wife he ordered Venetian jewelry made with shells (*venericas*).[14]

He therefore had not the slightest intention of exchanging his honored place in the midst of a sophisticated civilization for the raw society of the New Spain. It was interesting enough to read Don

[11] Alexandri Aphrodiciensis, in *Priora Resolutoria Aristotelis Stageritae Explanatio*.

[12] "No quiero perder el derecho de un lugar en la casa de V.S. en que ponga uno de bronze que me hare hazer aqui; mas no sera en el escalera como dezia, porque los pajes no me tiren cerotes en los ojos . . .," *AC*, p. 29. Given his friendship with Sansovino (GP I, 236–239), no one else could have been commissioned by Mendoza for such a bust; nothing is known of that sculpture.

[13] *AC*, p. 41.

[14] Ibid., pp. 41–44.

Antonio's reports of the conquest of strange new territories, but it gave Don Diego more satisfaction to embellish his brother's somewhat primitive prose before he forwarded it to the Emperor, "fixing it up as a royal chronicler should,"[15] than to share such adventures.

Besides, his hopes for a great career in the Old World had never been as high as now. In the midst of so much well-articulated adulation from his circle of sycophants, his dream of the papal tiara in the far future—he was only thirty-six—may not have appeared too utopian to himself. Was it only Galceran Cepello's idea that Mendoza might one day be Pope? There was Don Francisco, ahead of him in the Church. His brother might have been less ambitious than he—this is impossible to ascertain since Don Francisco died in mid-career. Perhaps Don Diego did not see in his brother the qualities of leadership he felt in himself. An active priest, Don Francisco was not, apparently, given to scholarship to the extent Don Diego was. Since the days of Pius II (the great Sienese humanist and poet laureate Enea Silvio Piccolomini), no such highly educated person sat on Peter's throne. Perhaps the young student "Andrea" in Siena, who made his companions kneel for a piece of marzipan, played with the "pope" idea for a long time. Pius II, the same Pope who had tried to slight Don Diego's intrepid grandfather, might have been the hero upon whom he secretly modeled himself. He had enough insight as to how the highest religious office should be used for the benefit of Christendom: from his point of view, entirely in accord with the policies of the Emperor. He knew he was at least as qualified by family, education, and personality for such an office as that (in his eyes) least worthy of Popes, Clement VII, whom he had served as a youth. (We can infer from his remarks about Clement and Cosimo I, the current Duke of Florence, that Mendoza looked with disdain upon the House of Medici. The only Italian aristocracy he seemed to appreciate were the Colonnas and the Gonzagas.) Everything seemed to indicate that perhaps the papacy would be within his reach—at least if he remained unmarried.

Yet he had not given up his wish to marry. When the Viceroy

[15] Mendoza to Cobos, May 1, 1540: ". . . Yo la e afeitado de real coronista . . .," *AC*, p. 33.

of Naples, under renewed pressure from Cobos, let Don Diego have the full amount of grain he had bargained for, Mendoza, delighted with his profits, said he could now look for a wife. "I would marry a little chick if there were a magnificent one," he wrote Cobos on April 7, 1540.[16] Although this sounds facetious, he meant it. Even fourteen years later, at the age of fifty, when he had long buried all hopes for a career in the Church, he still considered marriage.[17]

A Jewess in Venice

At about the same time Galceran Cepello (and Mendoza himself) saw in him a future Pope, a Jewess in the Venetian Ghetto asked His Magnificence, the Imperial ambassador, to become a Jew for her sake. For some reason he had let three months pass before revealing that relationship to Cobos. But since May, 1540, he had called on the Jewess every evening, continuing to do so for months to come.[18] It seems odd that he frequented the Jewish quarter and even formed a strong and long lasting attachment to one of its inhabitants. But a typically Venetian circumstance was the reason.

In Venice, for the first time in his life, Mendoza found himself outside the ranks of high society. After a year or two of his stay there, the law of the newly introduced Inquisition went so far as to forbid any social contact between foreigners—especially the diplomatic corps—and Venetian nobles.[19] But long before this was made official, the suspicious government frowned upon such contact. An ambassador met patrician gentlemen only at state functions, al-though even there personal contact was kept to a minimum, as when Mendoza sent his speeches to the Council in writing. He never met the ladies. He lived in close vicinity to the Grimani, Cornaro, Donato, and Foscari—families of ancient nobility who entertained lavishly at banquets, balls, house concerts, and falcon hunts—but he was not invited. If he had hopes of finding a wife in that society, he soon saw that he was unable to get close enough to

---

16 *Pollina*, literally "any little animal." Mendoza uses the same word of affection for Cobos' son and daughter, *los pollinos. AC*, p. 28.

17 *AC*, pp. 277, 293.

18 Mendoza to Cobos, August 5, 1540, Arch. Sim., Est., leg. 1316.

19 Mendoza to Charles V, July 30, 1541, Arch. Sim., Est. Ven., book 66, Rosefile.

any Venetian family to learn whether there were any daughters, let alone to propose marriage.

Not that he was lonely—he had more people than his "cook Juan" to talk to.[20] With his poets, artists, and scientists, he always had the intelligentsia, equivalent to the city's demimonde, at his beck and call. There was no dearth, either, of the company of the better class of kept women, such as the famous "Aretine," or the well-educated prostitutes of whom Montaigne tells us: for a price —the same price as the "ultimate" favor—such *hetairai* lent themselves to night-long philosophical discussions. But socially, Mendoza was in a desert. He had no occasion to converse with women of the type of his own sisters and cousins, Spanish gentlewomen, whom he used to delight with his wit and his poems at the Emperor's court.

Once, he described a great wedding. There he could at least look at the hidden beauties of the Venetian aristocracy. It must have been an official function to which all ambassadors were invited. Even then, a stranger could not really get acquainted with the ladies. No woman whom he addressed or who joined him in a dance would open her mouth. Instead of saying yes or no, the married women only nodded or shook their heads. Unmarried girls were not present; Venetian custom kept them in haremlike seclusion, in boarding schools or nunneries, until the very day of their weddings.

In the usual absence of the civilizing female element at state functions, Venetians were doltish in their manners. The Senators were not above filling their ample sleeves with tidbits and delicacies from the buffet to take home.[21] And according to Mendoza's testimony, all a gentleman could do at this wedding was to protect the women from being knocked over and shoved aside by the greed of men pushing their way to the table.[22] He was an outsider to that

[20] C. Malcolm Batchelor, ed., *A tí, Doña Marina*, p. 174:
  Ni tengo, ni sé qu'es otro exercicio
  Sino con mastre Juan, mi cozinero,
  Jugar y conuersar como por vicio.
  Con el sólo platico y a él quiero
[21] Thomas Okey, *The Story of Venice*, p. 222.
[22] "Epístola a Peña," in William Knapp, ed., *Obras Poéticas*, p. 148; Batchelor, ed., *A tí, Doña Marina*, p. 191.

type of society, and so it happened that the only woman to attract him was, in her way, an outsider, too.

Conceivably, the mysterious people that his country expelled a dozen years before his birth excited his curiosity. Until his first departure from Spain, he had not seen professing Jews, although *conversos* of both Jewish and Moorish extraction—major components of what there was in Spain of a middle class—surrounded him from infancy.[23] He was able to identify, for the purposes of explaining his concept of liberty of conscience, with the insincerely converted, the Marranos and Moriscos. Whether or not he was aware of his own mixed descent, the embarrassing secret of his family, in Italy he associated matter-of-factly with a number of Jews. The doctor Jacob Mantino, then practicing in Venice, was his regular physician as long as Mantino remained there. After the doctor's departure from Venice, Mendoza called the Marrano physician Amatus Lusitanus to his bedside from Ferrara.[24]

The Ghetto of Venice, where Mendoza sought out the woman, still exists. Its old entrance, on the quay of the rio Cannaregio, is opposite San Geremia. He may have strayed into the place accidentally at first, perhaps on his way to a meeting where someone had promised to point Lorenzino de' Medici out to him; the fugitive lived at one time in Cannaregio quarter, near the Ghetto.[25] The Ghetto was composed of two parts, the Ghetto Vecchio, not closed off from Christian Venice, where among a mixed population, free to move at all hours, some Spanish Jews had found new homes after their expulsion from Spain; and the Ghetto Nuovo, the small round island adjoining the Vecchio beyond a narrow rio, where indigenous Italian Jews and those of earlier immigration from Germany had settled in 1516. The inhabitants of the "new" Ghetto, which in fact was the older Jewish quarter,[26] were locked in from sundown to sunrise.

23 See Antonio Dominguez Ortiz, "Historical Research on Spanish Conversos in the Last Fifteen Years," p. 68; and Francisco Márquez Villanueva, "The Converso Problem: An Assessment," p. 330; in *Collected Studies in Honour of Américo Castro's 80th Year*, ed. M. P. Hornik.

24 Amatus Lusitanus, *Centuriae*, I, curatio 31, p. 100.

25 *Stud. Stor.* 7 (1907): 418.

26 See Cecil Roth, "The Origin of *Ghetto*," *Romania* 60 (1931).

In the spring of 1540, when Mendoza came to know the neighborhood of the "old" Ghetto, only three or four years had passed since the Spanish and the Levantine houses of worship were founded (where they still confront each other, rebuilt in baroque style). The dwellings were low enough to let in sun and air; the little main square, Campiello delle Scuole, had an uncrowded aspect.

The only clue to the Jewess' identity is found in Mendoza's revelation that she inhabited this very locality. On November 24, 1540, he wrote Cobos: "My portrait [by Titian] is ready, and I saw myself. I thought I looked so much worse than when I left [Spain] that, at vesper time, I did not yet dare to go to the Jewish quarter. Now you can understand how I shall feel among Christians."[27] At vesper time, he could not have gone to visit someone in the Ghetto Nuovo, where the gates closed at sunset. Since only those of Spanish descent still lived outside such restriction, it follows that his Jewess, still visible and visitable at dusk, was most likely one of them. His special interest in a woman of Spanish tongue is understandable. From the moment he knew the girl—before he had told Cobos about her—he requested Cobos' wife to send him samplers (lace patterns of intricate Moorish design, presumably) and bags (for the needlework) to be had only in Spain; this suggests that she supported herself by lace making.[28]

On August 5, 1540, in his usual official letter to Cobos, which he expected the "patroness" to read, he said: "Send me the pattern and two bags so that I will not be the unhappiest man in the world." On the same day he added a postscript on an extra sheet of paper that Cobos was not to show his wife:

And if my Señora wishes to snatch this piece of paper as she did the last one, so that she should not find it blank, I must tell you that I made love here three months ago to one of the beautiful women of Italy; she stopped me halfway [saying] that she is a Jewess and could not do anything for me unless I became a Jew. I, who was not far from the one or the other, told her to go ahead, as little was amiss for that. Tell me, please, whether I should circumcise myself. If you think I should, and if you should be coming here, do the same, because since the Jewess is beautiful, it seems a very good bargain to me.[29]

[27] AC, p. 58.   [28] Mendoza to Cobos, June 27, 1540, GP III, 284.
[29] Arch. Sim., Est., leg. 1316; also in GP III, 284, 285; and AC, p. 46.

"I have a garden and a house outside of Venice," he writes from Murano a short time afterwards, "where, if I were an evildoer, one could make assaults; but if the Jewess had her wish, I would quickly move to live in the Sinoga. My dear Sir, in my life I have not seen a more beautiful Jewess, nor a smarter one! She is a woman who has a head." Two weeks later, returning to Venice, he writes: "For the bags which were very pretty, I kiss your hands. The Jewess wore the blue one, and that was no bad use for it." (She must have gone to Murano, evidently, where Don Diego entertained sumptuously in a rented summer house. Aretino visited him there, presenting him with a pair of Majolica vases.) By September 1, Don Diego felt himself close to triumph: "My relations with the Jewess are coming to the boiling point, and I believe we shall make peace without abandoning my religion." (By then, she must have started to resign herself to the fact that he would never become a Jew.) For a while, we hear nothing more about her. But Cobos continued to refer to the gifts Don Diego had requested, and on November 24, Mendoza acknowledged them: "The bags are in the Sinoga. If I thought you would be coming here, I should postpone the day of my circumcision to celebrate a feast for you. Send me some unbleached linen, as this Jewess, before we have yet come to the wedding, gives me a pain in the stomach."[30]

"I shall send you the unbleached linen with this," replied the kindly Cobos from Madrid, "and I believe that the señora Jewess must be the reason you want it. If that is the case, all must be very well employed. God knows that I should like to be present at your circumcision. For the señora Jewess I am sending you another bag, you will give it to her."[31]

She is not mentioned for another two months. They may have quarreled. Although in September he had confidently seen her submission near, he had been mistaken. Even late in November it had not yet come to what he called the wedding. She does not reappear before January 29, 1541: "I kiss my gentle patroness' hands, and may she send me the patterns. Yesterday I went to see the Jew quarter and saw my Jewess. Her house stinks like a galley, and therefore I don't know what to do."[32]

[30] GP III, 288, 289; GP I, 173, 174.
[31] Cobos to Mendoza, February 1, 1541, GP III, 298.
[32] January 29, 1541, GP III, 297.

The Ghetto Vecchio must, in fact, have deteriorated rapidly within only a few months. This was the negative consequence of the recent prosperity coming to Venice through the final peace with the Turk. In October, 1540, when the Venetian trading fleet returned from the Levant, the exact peace conditions were at last revealed, and the terms surpassed all apprehensions. Mendoza had not known that the Republic was forced to cede its Greek possessions Nauplia and Malvasia to Soliman; even the "Ten" had not yet found out why the Turk had insisted on the ultimate terms from the very beginning. The hand of France was not discovered until two years later. Yet, however bad the peace looked, and though the Venetian Empire, so suddenly diminished, was now openly on the decline, it was peace after all. Merchants began to arrive from the Levant, swarming over the reopened sea lanes, lifting the depression, restoring the normality of Venetian trade and industry.

Most of the traders with the East were Jews, descendants of the refugees from Spain who, almost fifty years before, had been allowed to settle in Turkey under the tolerant administration of Sultan Bayazid. The businessmen went to live in the vicinity of their two Sephardic synagogues in the Ghetto Vecchio. This tiny island consisted, literally, of nothing more than the Campiello and a few alleys behind the houses—then no higher than two flights—lining that miniature square. Daily, the place filled with more humanity. Landlords (Christians who lived elsewhere, for Jews were forbidden to own real estate), in great hurry, built additional stories on all houses. A sudden influx like this, hasty and inartistic construction, can create slum conditions almost overnight. Since Don Diego had not gone there for some time, the contrast, the decay, when he saw the place again, suddenly became noticeable to his eyes—and to his nose.

He was undecided, as he says—probably, whether he should drop the girl or take her away from there. He had already been courting her for eight months, an unusually long period of resistance in a time when morals were easy, fast surrender being the rule. But now, at last, she appeared ready to give in; after his last visit on the twenty-ninth of January, she must have moved away from the Ghetto to become his mistress.

Soon he uses a different tone: "I received the unbleached linen," he writes Cobos on March 12, "and if I had to replace what Doña So-and-So can use up—I should call her 'la Signora Ambaxatora,' not the Jewish quarter full of the stuff would suffice; but as God lives, I will keep her until you come this way so that you can get a taste of Jewish virginity."[33] On April 8, he writes: "From the letter to His Majesty you will see the shape of business. I am fine, and I have two Easter celebrations, one after the other, since my Jewess does it on Good Friday, and I, on Sunday."

But although the reference to "my Jewess" with her Easter (presumably a Passover-Seder) celebration sounds idyllic, the affair was, in fact, already starting to break up. His lack of vigor must have had something to do with that. "It is true, my dear Sir," he tells Cobos on May 19, 1541, "that I lost a testicle from a bump I gave myself on a chair, and no help for it. You may sympathize with the Jewess, as I already had her so well trained that not much was lacking for the resurrection of the bones of my grandparents."[34] "My life is as usual," he says on May 29, "although my testicle tires me. Thank God it is a member that is not very necessary." "My pain continues," says the letter of June 30, "so that I can truly be called 'magnificent testicle.'" He notices another time: "What do you want me to write about my happiness? The Jewess is in a heat that is sufficient to burn up herself and my entire clan."[35]

An International Incident

By early summer of 1541 it seemed as if the Emperor were deliberately provoking his old rival, Francis I. Instead of ceding Milan to the Dauphin, as the French King had trusted he would do, it was becoming apparent to all (and the Spaniards had known this all the time), that Charles V wished to invest his own heir, Prince Philip, with the dukedom. Francis I, in turn, had also failed to live up to his vague promises: he never withdrew from his alliance with

[33] March 12, 1541, *AC*, p. 66. See also GP III, 299–300.

[34] Américo Castro interprets this passage as an allusion by Mendoza to the Jewishness of his ancestors. *The Structure of Spanish History*, p. 251.

[35] April 8, 1541, *AC*, p. 67; May 19, *AC*, p. 72; May 29, *AC*, p. 74; June 30, GP III, 306.

Soliman. Imperial officials in Italy expected an increase in French-Turkish friendship. Don Diego hoped to avert the desertion of Venice into that camp by doing what he could do to prevent it.

This was the political atmosphere when the French ambassador to Turkey, Antonio Rincon, traveled once more to the Sultan's Porte. To communicate with Constantinople, the French had to travel over Venice. The direct way, over the Po Valley, between the Venetian terra firma and French-ruled Piedmont, led through the dominion of Milan, still ruled for the Emperor by the Marquis of Vasto. The only alternate route, over the Swiss Alps, was longer and cumbersome. In February, 1541, when Rincon touched Venice on his return from the East, the town was buzzing with rumors that the Emperor would try to have him murdered in the Po Valley. Not taking any chances, the Venetians lent the diplomat an escort of fifty cavalry to see him safely to French territory over the longer route.

Mendoza ridiculed the Signoria for their gullibility. The French were spreading these rumors, he told the Senators, to discredit the Emperor and his ministers in Italy. Charles V ignored the existence of Rincon; there was no need to worry about his security. "I told them they were losing prestige by furnishing this escort," he wrote the Emperor, "and if they were giving this escort to Rincon to help him pass the time on his journey, I suggested that they provide him with a few Senators and men of good conversation."[36]

Don Diego's pleasantry notwithstanding, the following July, Rincon, once more on his way to Turkey, and Cesare Fragoso (an exiled Genoese and his associate in the French service) never reached their earthly destination. Fragoso would have preferred the safer land route, but the "renegade Spaniard," as historians call Rincon, who lately had made that trip over the Alps with some hardship, and for whom "the great weight of his flesh was tiresome," prevailed with his wish to travel more comfortably on the waters of the Po.[37] A fatal decision, for two boatloads of hired, masked bravi had been lying in ambush for him under cover of foliage (such ambushes were standing in preparation all along the

---

[36] Mendoza to Charles V, February 8, 1541, Arch. Sim., Est. Ven., book 66, Rose-file.

[37] Prudencio de Sandoval, *Historia*, book 25, p. 98 (edition of 1604).

course of the Po).[38] The two envoys of the French King were being rowed with two companions in a barge at some distance from their suite when the bandits overpowered them, killing them both. The bodies disappeared in the river, where they were found only two months later.

Charles V, who is said to have spent 150,000 ducats to bring Rincon to justice after twenty years,[39] had secretly ordered the murder of this former Comunero; the Marquis of Vasto had proceeded with his detailed plans only after double-checking his order with the Emperor.[40] But as soon as the murders became known, the Imperials displayed a most innocent attitude. Vasto put on a show of mildly punishing three poor devils of Spanish soldiers who had to assume the guilt.

"When I heard from Vasto about the loss of Rincon and Fragoso," Don Diego wrote to Charles V on July 12, 1541, "I showed this Signoria the letter Your Majesty had written me, in which you ordered me not to interfere with any doings of this Rincon, who was not to be hurt or offended during the duration of the truce." Evidently, Mendoza was completely informed by his secret intelligence of the premeditated attack. "The news of Rincon's and Fragoso's misfortune reached the French ambassador here," Don Diego continues, "touching him so overwhelmingly that he fell down in a swoon behind a chest in his room and came to again with great difficulty, weeping."[41]

Shortly afterward, Charles V passed with his court and a great army through Venetian territory on his way to his long-postponed expedition against Algiers. Mendoza met the Emperor near Trent. He stayed with the court, entering Milan and Genoa in dazzling processions. When the Imperial party embarked, he took leave from his master, and Charles V praised his services, promising to

[38] J. Zeller, *Diplomatie*, p. 249.

[39] *Memorial Histórico Español*, Colección de documentos, opúsculos y antiguedades, vol. 48 (Madrid: Real Academia de la Historia, 1948).

[40] On the Emperor's approval of order to kill, see Gonzalo Jiménez de Quesada, *Anti-Jovio*, introduction by Manuel Ballesteros Gaibros, p. xcvi.

[41] Mendoza to Charles V, July 12, 1541, Arch. Sim., Est., leg. 1317; also Est. Ven., book 66, Rose-file.

bestow on him benefices and honors like those his brothers had already received.[42]

Probably Don Diego did not reveal at court his real feelings about the sinister deeds. Had he reckoned, when he swore fealty to his chosen master, to what iniquities he would have to stoop? Although these murders were not of his doing—his guilt consisted in sharing the secret—the French made him one of the targets of their revenge. He found himself constantly harassed from that time on, his life in danger. The cloak-and-dagger picture usually associated with the dark alleys of Venice became very real in his case. Gone were the carefree days of unlimited movement and adventure. Not for nothing had the French ambassador suffered the shame of swooning behind the furniture. After this, he never let up in his plans for retaliation.

The Emperor, meanwhile, had had his satisfaction. To all appearances he had accomplished his purpose without participating in it. According to his lights, justice had caught up with a traitor, yet, by denying his hand in it, he was still able to postpone the outbreak of the renewal of war with Francis I. He looked forward to dealing with the French later, after his anticipated triumph in Algiers. The French King, deeply offended, could not strike back openly at once where, apparently, no provocation existed. But prepared for any possible French advance, Charles V left the Marquis of Vasto at his post in Milan, while Gonzaga and Alba sailed with him and his armada of three hundred ships under Andrea Doria.

At last, six years after his victory over Tunis, he saw himself ready to break the backbone of Turkish sea power. But the campaign started too late in the season; Algiers turned into a catastrophe. The Emperor and the generals survived, but half the fleet, men and equipment, did not. Yet even so, Imperial propaganda tried to stress the positive aspect of this debacle. Don Diego wrote the Emperor a congratulatory message, rejoicing over His Majesty's safe arrival in Spain. The Venetian ambassador at Charles V's court, Marino Giustiniani, was writing good news about His Majesty to the Signoria; Giustiniani minimized the loss of the Imperial fleet, emphasizing the enormous strength of the Emperor; in fact, he did

---

[42] Mendoza to Charles V, October 4, 1542 (he reminds the Emperor of his promises one year later!), Arch. Sim., Est. Ven., book 65, Rose-file.

everything to reassure Venice about the protective power of Charles V.[43]

But Venetian diplomacy—just like Imperial diplomacy—had a double set of correspondence. In a secret letter, Giustiniani wrote the truth to the Signoria. He told Venice that, because of Mendoza, he had not been quite frank about the real reasons for the failures of Charles V's attack on Algiers. Since Don Diego always learned the contents of Venetian Senate proceedings and then informed the Emperor about them, said the Venetian, he had been careful not to tell them before that Charles V must take all the blame himself for bad timing, bad planning, and bad leadership, strategy, and tactics. (This ambassador had suffered such hardship in the Algerian campaign that he died a few months later, at fifty-three, from its aftereffects.)[44]

The Jewess is not mentioned in the numerous letters to Cobos after May 19, 1541, when Mendoza had told his friend of her fiery unsatisfied temperament. That was the time he started receiving secret news about the forthcoming attack on Rincon. He had become preoccupied, busier than usual and then anxious, as anyone in constant mortal danger might be. If he sought for solace, he found it in Aristotle. At that time he requested Duke Cosimo of Florence, with whom he also was in continuous correspondence, for some commentaries on the works of Aristotle.[45] Cobos, in turn, wondered why Don Diego had stopped asking for bags or patterns or writing gay little reports of his love life. Tactfully, he refrained from questioning, until, about six months later, he could not suppress his curiosity any further. Politely he inquired after the Señora Judía. But Don Diego was in no communicative mood. Querulously, he replied on January 29, 1542: "It is a very miser-

[43] Mendoza to Charles V, Dec. 31, 1541, Arch. Sim., Est., leg. 1317, Rose-file.

[44] "tutto se scia da Don Diego et è poi scripto a sua Cesarea M.tà . . .," Giustiniani to the Dieci, from Bugia, November 10, 1541. Ven. Dep. I, 434–435. On his death, see ibid., p. xiii.

[45] Mendoza asks Cosimo to order one of his secretaries to send him the index of the libraries of San Marco and San Lorenzo, and he wants a commentary of Theodoro Metochite on the works of Aristotle, as well as a book on astrology by Hipparcho. Archivio di Stato di Firenze (Arch. Flor.) Mediceo 2964, Rose-file.

able life. Kidney pains, and fear, and suspicion, and giving audiences to secret agents before dawn: with all that, one forgets about Jewesses and everything else."[46]

That he should have forgotten her was possible, but it was not the whole story. On June 2, 1541, shortly after the Jewess was already finding her relationship with Don Diego somewhat strained, the Signory of Venice issued a law that all Jews still living in Christian territory be moved to the Jewish quarter. The quarter was to be shut in the same way that the Ghetto Nuovo of the German-Italian Jews had been these twenty-four years.[47] The new order caused the old gate between both Ghettos to be torn down, combining both places into one miserable thoroughfare; a new gate was built in the *sottoportico* on the Fondamenta del Cannaregio, where the aperture still is. The old stone framework shows the large round holes where rested the hinges of the heavy wings of the portal. No longer could a Spanish Jewess take an evening walk on the field in front of San Geremia, nor again would a Spanish Jewess be visitable and accessible at dusk or seducible by a pursuer from outside.

On the fate of this Jewess, one can only speculate. About to be left by her seducer, was she now, in addition, harassed by the police, perhaps forced to return to the Ghetto? Would she have been willing to go back—and the community willing to readmit her? The fact is that Don Diego never again mentioned her after the new law went into effect.

Revelation of French Treason

In the wake of Charles V's setback in the Mediterranean, the Imperials marshaled their land forces, preparing for imminent warfare with the French. One of his spies told Mendoza that the King of France intended to attack the Emperor in five places: Navarre, Naples, Milan, Genoa, and Flanders, assisted by the Turks at sea in Naples and Genoa, and on land in Hungary.[48] The war started, in

---

[46] *AC*, p. 85.

[47] Cecil Roth, *History of the Jews of Venice*, p. 61. For a detailed study on Mendoza's affair, see E. Spivakovsky, "A Jewess of Venice," *Chicago Jewish Forum* 19, no. 2 (1960/61): 129–137.

[48] Mendoza to Charles V, March 4, 1542, Arch. Sim., Est. Ven., book 66, Rosefile.

fact, near Venice. French partisans had "subverted" Marano, a place on the Adriatic near Trieste (in Habsburg territory, under King Ferdinand), from within. Near the end of 1541, Marano—indirectly assisted by the French ambassador Pellicier in Venice—proclaimed itself French, raising fleur-de-lis banners. Don Diego suspected Venice of having been an accomplice in the conspiracy. He went before the Senate, urging them to prevent Marano, now that it had defaulted to the French, from coming into the possession of the Turk. He assured the Venetians that he had originally proposed handing over Marano to Venice. For such a service, he told the Signoria, "Venice ought to put up a statue of himself in the Rialto." At the same time he warned them of conspirators who assembled in the neighborhood of Saint Mark, and he asked them to stop selling artillery to Marano.[49]

The Senate denied having a part in this conspiracy, but the truth was that, with the utmost secrecy, Venice was sponsoring the revolt. They had promised a thousand ducats a year to their secret agent for keeping his hands in this conspiracy; to assure themselves of that agent, the Senate threatened both his life and that of his wife, who presumably lived in Venice. Through his own spies, Mendoza found out the whole affair.[50] He lost no time to inform the Emperor secretly that Venice was a partner to the conspiracy of Marano, but the secret leaked out and drifted back into Venice through the Imperial ambassador in France, who had spoken about it to the Venetian ambassador in France. This let Mendoza worry about his reputation with the Signoria. He rushed letters back and forth, requesting the Emperor to deny, officially, that Mendoza ever had entertained such a suspicion.[51]

In his endeavor to keep abreast of all underground activities and to protect his personal safety, Mendoza's health began to suffer. At times his kidney trouble paralyzed him—a condition he kept secret, as he did not wish to lose his chances to marry. He complained to Cobos about "such pain, that sometimes I have no brains left," and

---

[49] January 5, 1542: Arch. Ven., minutes of the Colleggio; January 12, 1542: Arch. Ven. To the Locum Tenenti Patrii Fole Julii, fol. 123; January 3, 1542, Arch. Sim., Est., leg. 1189; all in Rose-file.
[50] Arch. Ven., Senate, fol. 123, Rose-file.
[51] AC, p. 95.

about his "scant safety. I shall try to protect myself as well as I can, but in such a way that I shall not be accused of timidity. It should not be said that I have done something for which I have to be on guard, because this is not the case."[52]

In addition, he was increasingly troubled by financial difficulties. Regularly he alerted Cobos to every ecclesiastical benefice in Spain that fell vacant, hoping to obtain such rewards. (All bishoprics were saddled with mortgage-type rents that Charles V used to add to the income of his ministers without burdening his own purse.) Often he also suggested that Cobos promote him elsewhere.

He was never out of personal danger. Knowing that hired murderers were following him, he engaged a bodyguard of several armed men whom he kept standing by, day and night, in a boat opposite his house on the Grand Canal, in front of San Samuele. But one night as he stepped out of his gondola on to his own water-stairs, an assassin closed in on him. Don Diego escaped with his life only because his guards rushed over in time to overpower the fellow. The man's confession disclosed that ambassador Pellicier had instigated the assault. Pellicier, in turn, had acted on direct orders of Francis I, and Don Diego asked the Emperor to provide a permanent escort of twenty-five or thirty paid men for the security of his house and the dispatches. At his small salary, he wrote Cobos, he could not pay for even four men. "This place is full of French and of bandits, our enemies. Here they are recruiting all the soldiery for ever so many felonies that they are carrying out in Italy and abroad."[53]

While Mendoza was moving uneasily in the shadows of a lurking stiletto, worrying about having damaged his faultless reputation with the Signoria, Imperial prestige in Venice sank low. The aftermath of the Rincon-Fragoso murders, increased anti-Imperial exertions of the Strozzi, the bad impression of the Algerian campaign, still lingering, all served to undo years of his efforts to build up his Emperor's image. Even Aretino, for whose flatteries he duly paid out a yearly pension of two hundred ducats from the Imperial treasury, lately used his pen to extol the French ambassador and his King.

[52] Ibid., pp. 105, 102.
[53] Ibid., p. 104.

But the tide rolls back, and things improve sometimes for the most unexpected reasons. First, Don Diego's colleague in France apologized. This buoyed his mood: "Regarding the ambassador in France," he wrote Cobos on July 1, 1542, "there is no reason to make a fuss if you don't want to, either. To you I trust my life and honor because you are the person who understands all this better than I or any other. The ambassador has written me and I am very well satisfied."[54]

Then came the great exposure of French perfidy. The sensational news, which turned the political wheel, was the discovery of a French-instigated espionage network reaching into the secret councils of the Signoria. The spy web had been the direct cause of the severe peace terms of two years before. By it, the Turks had learned about the Council of Ten's secret orders to Contarini, the Venetian peace ambassador. Contarini was expected to bargain long and hard with the Turks for favorable peace terms, but should this be ineffectual, he was empowered to cede the possessions Nauplia and Malvasia to them—yet only as an improbable very last resort. But thanks to the French, the Turks had known from the outset how far the Venetian could go. This scandal, now, suddenly drove the French underground, into exile, or to the gallows, from high officials down to the lowest hired bandit. Although Don Diego had not yet run out of danger as long as the Strozzi remained in Venice, there was more safety in the future; his personal prestige, and that of Charles V, was bolstered up, soon to become higher than at any time before. The last three years' Imperial policies in Venice were completely vindicated.

Since Don Diego—apparently—had nothing to do with the discoveries, the rehabilitation of his standing was all the greater. French treason, seemingly, had been exposed by accident, through the workings of a love triangle. Agustin Abbondio, a Venetian of good family, had been serving the French as contact. He had collected secret documents from a secretary of the Council of Ten by the name of Cavazza (who drew a secret French pension), selling them to the French ambassador. But Abbondio had an unfaithful wife. One day her lover, a sturdy, upright citizen from Verona,

54 Ibid., p. 99.

Geronimo Martolosso, happened to glance at some papers lying around in the Signora Abbondio's bedroom—letters from that secretary, Nicholas Cavazza, of the Council of Ten. Martolosso understood at once what was going on. Whether his soul was torn by the dilemma of what to sacrifice—the reputation of his beloved or the fatherland—we are not told, but the result was clear: the histories of Venice speak of the "shameless wife" of Abbondio, but of her lover as a "patriot."[55]

Martolosso brought the incriminating documents to the three awesome heads of the Council of Ten. The Inquisition instituted a trial and prosecuted the traitors. Secretary Cavazza, the principal culprit, was soon caught; his brother, who was his accomplice, got away, Agustin Abbondio, the most unfortunate cuckold, escaped to the French embassy, but not for long. Such a crime against the state apparently went beyond any consideration of extraterritoriality. While Venice was in an uproar of fury, suspicion, and fear, the Chief Justice, severely dressed like the heads of the Ten in his black summer-weight toga with a red stole and accompanied by the captains of police, penetrated into Pellicier's palace in the street of San Moisé, not far from the Piazza San Marco. But the French ambassador's retainers drove the unwelcome guests out of the house before they even climbed the main staircase. Consequently, Venetians (so say the stories) made better preparations for a second attempt to get the traitor. They surrounded the French embassy with armed barges (according to the usual account), and so, Pellicier was forced to break his word to the fugitive and hand him over.

So much for the traditional account of Abbondio's capture. But from a report that Mendoza sent to the Emperor—so secret that he did not trust it to the usual couriers but waited six months to send it with his brother, the Admiral Don Bernardino—we learn the truth about his part in arranging the affair.[56]

Don Diego had dealt for some time with both Martolosso and Abbondio as his paid agents. Martolosso, the "lover" of Abbondio's wife, brought Mendoza all the documents he stole from her (as well as from the wife of the murdered Cesare Fragoso). Abbondio, in turn, doubled-crossed Don Diego. On the occasion of the Marano

55 Zeller, *Diplomatie*, pp. 354–375. Also: *Cal. St. P.*, Henry VIII, IX, 135–136.
56 "Instruction for Don Bernardino," Mendoza to Charles V, March 2, 1543, Arch. Sim., Est. Ven., book 65, Rose-file.

conspiracy, when Mendoza thought Abbondio was working for him, he had, in fact, deceived Don Diego, but did not realize that Don Diego found it out. So, with Abbondio still trusting him, Don Diego was able to plan his destruction coolly. He alone (secretly) succeeded in getting Abbondio out of his asylum at the French embassy into the hands of the Venetian police:

I paid certain friends of Abbondio to advise him not to leave [the French embassy]. Abbondio sent to ask me if he should stay in the embassy, and if I thought he was safe. I sent him word that he was safe there, and that all the streets were being watched for him, and all main roads. That night I had two empty boats put in front of the ambassador's house and had them shown to his man, telling him that they belonged to the Signoria and were on the watch for him, and a great many other boats were doing the same thing. When the Chief Justice went to ask for him, two of my men, paid by me, mingled with the Justice's escort. I had ordered my men to start some rudeness, if they could, in the house of the ambassador. And so, with the noisy behavior of these men, a great commotion broke out. I hoped that the Signoria, learning of this, would become hostile to the French.[57]

Mendoza achieved his purpose. The wretched Abbondio, put to torture by the Inquisition, divulged the names of all his accomplices. He was then hanged on the traditional spot between the two columns on the Piazzetta, on September 21, 1542. By the time Abbondio was brought to justice, his protector Pellicier was bereft of all his accomplices. "The only one of them to remain here is the King's ambassador, whom I am unable to chase from Venice," said Don Diego on October 25. "It is better to let him remain; he is a man to do more harm than good to his master." (Five days later, however, Jean du Monluc arrived in Venice to replace Pellicier.) "The French are now incredibly loathed here," wrote the English ambassador in Venice to Henry VIII. "They are called dogs and proditors of the universal Christian State, and monsters."[58]

Mendoza was as gratified about these happenings as he was about the fact that not the slightest trace of his manipulations became known. After a difficult and perplexing beginning in this Ve-

netian pool of espionage, he had achieved mastery, beating
Venetians and French at their own game. He made sure that his
Emperor would learn to what depths he had to stoop for his sake,
but all the same he was glad that the world remained ignorant of
such disreputable deeds.

Now he did not mind remaining in Venice. Having done his part
to discredit the French, he wished to supervise the consequences, to
solidify the Imperial position. In the course of time he uncovered
many other French conspiracies connected with the spy center in
Venice; the net extended to other cities—Padua, Florence, and
Rome. He nipped in the bud, for instance, a plot against the life of
the Marquis of Vasto, and another—in his words—against the Republic of Venice itself. He succeeded also, again by Mephistophe-
lian artfulness, in discrediting the Strozzi to such an extent that
these Florentine exiles were all expelled from Venice.[59]

Yet for a foreigner even in the best, most righteous standing, this
was an unpleasant time in Venice to live through. On September
9, 1542, the cautious attitude of Venetian society against "frater-
nizing" was made official law: "No one of our nobles, of whichever
rank and condition, can under any pretext go to the house of a
stranger or ambassador residing in our city unless it be with the
express permission of all three heads of the Council of Ten. If anyone offends against this law, he will be fined five hundred ducats
and will be excluded from all offices, councils, and governments of
our state for five years." And lest the law should be forgotten, the
Inquisition added: "The present decree will be read and published
in the Grand Council, where it shall be read twice a year, in March
and in September.[60]

In the midst of an increasing xenophobia, Mendoza became dis-
couraged again. The new law closed up all the contacts that had
served him for his private information. "I received your letter," he
wrote Cobos on September 16, "and have nothing to reply except
that, now that these unrests of the French are over, seeing they can
do me little harm, but I them not a little, I should be glad if His
Majesty would give me permission to leave, even if he were to do
me no other favor. I expect neither money nor satisfaction nor es-

[59] Mendoza to Charles V, August 26, 1542, Arch. Sim., Est. Ven., book 65,
Rose-file.

[60] Zeller, *Diplomatie*, pp. 373–374.

tate; and I have had many colds and two slight attacks of paralysis, which I have kept secret in order not to lose all hope of marriage, and enough tough luck." A few weeks later he repeated the story of his paralysis, adding: "and I fear the coming winter."[61]

His political difficulties were a thing of the past. The Republic, deadly scared and wounded, pursued from then on a policy of strict neutrality that it held to for thirty years. Imperial intervention in Venetian affairs was no longer necessary, nor—under the new security system—possible. But although Mendoza felt that anyone else could now safely replace him, the Emperor did not wish to remove him from Venice at that time.

From now on, having less to do, secretly or overtly, Mendoza could devote himself more intensively to his studies. In about 1543, he started building up his collection of books and manuscripts. At various times within those seven Venetian years, he sent his scouts to Mount Athos and Asia to search monasteries for manuscripts. Probably his acquisitions were completed by the time he went to the Council of Trent in 1545. It is unknown when, exactly, Sultan Soliman sent him the precious six boxes with Greek manuscripts (grown, in chroniclers' reports, to a shipload). Mendoza had paid ransom for a Turkish prisoner said to be Soliman's favorite (some say he was Soliman's son), returning him to the Sultan with his compliments. The Greek manuscripts were the Sultan's reward for such a magnanimous gesture of a Christian noble. Mendoza also asked Soliman for some grain supplies for the starving Venetians, a gift that the Sultan added to the manuscripts—this lets us assume the exchange to have taken place during the first or second year of Mendoza's residence in Venice, following the conclusion of peace.[62]

New French-Spanish War

In regard to practical politics, Mendoza, while ever watchful for any reappearance of the French threat to Venice, was now able to reduce his dealing with spies to a secret news service about the

---

61 September 16, 1542, *AC*, p. 105; October 4, Arch. Sim., Est. Ven., book 65, Rose-file.

62 On Mendoza's scouting for MSS, see GP I, 254–257. For the gift from the Sultan, the most reliable source is Ambrosio de Morales, Dedication to *Las antigüedades*, in GP III, 470–472.

Turks. Venice, remaining strictly neutral, was the center for the spy network in the East. Mendoza had many clandestine meetings with oriental go-betweens, who usually came in the garb of friars, and through whom he hoped at this time (the beginning of 1543) to arrange a separate Imperial agreement with Soliman. In the current "fourth," if not perpetual, French-Spanish war, Charles V very much desired to come to private terms with the Sultan, whose army and navy again had gone to assist Francis I. In Mendoza's opinion this was possible through lavish bribery at the Pasha's Porte. He suggested that a sum of forty thousand to fifty thousand ducats be spent on Turkish officials.[63] But just as the Emperor had not succeeded previously, during the "crusade" with Venice, in luring Barbarossa away from his Turkish master, he now failed also in swaying the other Turks to his side. One of the reasons probably was Charles V's lack of funds. He was simply unable, especially during the course of the war, to offer bribes large enough to conform to Don Diego's generous estimate. So, the Turks proceeded with their operations in Hungary and the Mediterranean, while Francis I, as Mendoza had predicted, sent his armies to Italy, up to the frontier of the Milanese and southward toward Spain.

At first the Imperials held their own. They repulsed the French at the approaches to Italy. The Marquis of Vasto, lunging out of his State of Milan, penetrated into Piedmont, occupying Carignano near Turin. Simultaneously, a Spanish army defeated the French at Perpignan. After this promising start, Charles V intended to beat his old enemy all-out and to capture Paris. He left Spain in the spring of 1543, planning to raise money first in Italy and then in Germany.

Don Diego, as he had done on former visits of his master, joined the court in Italy. He remained from May to July at the Emperor's side. During this period, Charles V met again with Paul III, and Don Diego felt qualified to speak his opinion about this Pope's influence in politics. In Venice he had a vantage point for observing him. The Pope, afraid of an increase in Imperial power, had been trying to divert Venice from its neutrality in favor of the French. When Mendoza learned of the relations between Rome and Venice, he used his information to warn the Signoria not to heed the Pope's

---

[63] Mendoza to Charles V, Arch. Sim., Est., leg. 1317, Rose-file.

advice. Apparently the Venetians sympathized with his view. "This Signoria regards the Pope as deceitful," Mendoza had written on February 3, 1543, "and, wherever it would be to his advantage, of little religion and little honesty."[64] So it fell to Mendoza to alert the Emperor to this apparent change in the old Pope's disposition. After the benign support he had given Charles V for his crusade against Tunis, after his effort to establish the Truce at Nice, his joining in the "Holy League," and his consent to the marriage of his grandson Ottavio Farnese with the Emperor's widowed daughter, in Mendoza's opinion Paul III had now gone over to the side of France.

Between June 21 and 26, 1543, each monarch fearful and unwilling to step into the other's territory, Emperor and Pope convened at Busseto, a sort of no man's land, a small sovereign locality about ten miles from Cremona. Each of the parties brought an army of five hundred infantry and additional cavalry beyond the usual number of their respective households. Both lodged in the same castle, the Imperials guarding one of its gates, the papal forces the other.[65] And there, Don Diego witnessed what he felt was another attempt of Paul III to take advantage of Charles V.

The Pope brought the Emperor a portentous proposal: in order to do away for all time with the disturbing problem of Milan, starting point of the ever-recurring war, he asked Charles V to give the duchy of Milan to their common descendants, the young couple Ottavio Farnese and Margaret of Austria. The duchy would remain Italian, but would also belong to Charles V's progeny through his daughter's line. Moreover, the Pope offered a million ducats for Milan. The plan did not seem unreasonable to the Emperor. Many things spoke in its favor, especially the money—only it was not enough. Charles V set the price at two million ducats, a sum to which the Pope was not at once agreeable.

Mendoza and several of the advisers in the Emperor's suite considered him imprudent and self-defeating even to listen to the Pope's offer. Don Diego was all the more alarmed because the Em-

---

64 Ibid.

65 F. López de Gómara, *Annals of the Emperor Charles V*, ed. R. B. Merriman, pp. 114–118. On this meeting, see Walter Friedensburg, "Kaiser Karl V und Papst Paul III," in *Schriften des Vereins für Reformationsgeschichte*, Jahrgang 50, Heft 1, no. 153, p. 59.

peror had just sold Cosimo de' Medici the fortresses of Florence,
Pisa, and Livorno—another unwise deal. Charles V himself had
promoted young Cosimo's elevation as Duke in 1537; Imperial
armies had protected Cosimo's uncertain access to power in Florence; Imperial garrisons had held the fortresses for his own and for
the Emperor's benefit. Now, Charles V, in his insatiable need for
money, had deprived himself voluntarily of his foothold in Tuscany, and in Don Diego's opinion he was at the point of doing even
worse with Milan and possibly Siena, for which the Pope also put
in a bid.

Seeing the impossibility of giving his master unasked advice,
Don Diego wrote him a long letter, unsigned, and had it smuggled
into his bedroom.[66] In it, he harshly reprimanded the Emperor for
not going all out in his war against the French, and for his intention to sell Milan and perhaps also Siena to the Pope. He advised
him to march not only against France, but also to attack Rome at
the same time, adducing historical proofs for the Emperor's right
to divest the Popes of their temporal possessions. The bishops of
Rome, now territorial princes disturbing the Empire, ought, he
said, to be reduced to their ancient state of poverty and spirituality.
Principally, he upbraided the Emperor for doubting his own right
to the possession of Milan:

Your Majesty has reason and right to this kingdom by virtue of its being an Imperial feudatory . . . You have the same right to Italy as to
Flanders and Spain, and consequently to the whole world . . . What
right had the Romans to be lords over almost all the world? What
right had the Goths to Spain, the Franks to France, the Vandals to
Africa, the Huns to Hungary, and the Angles to England? Ambition
sent these peoples out, pure valor made them lords over the properties
of others, and by virtue and good government many of them kept it
until now. Usurpation was violent, retention was violent . . . holding
on to the Empire is violent! . . . As the world was then, it is now. Force
was the only right and reason of the kingdoms; hence the proverb *Jus*

[66] Document B: "Papel de don Diego Hurtado de Mendoza, que se halló en la
cámara del Emperador," in *BAE* XXI, *Historiadores de Sucesos Particulares*, I,
Introduction by Cayetano Rosell, pp. xxii–xxvi. Juan Sánchez Montes, "Franceses, Protestantes, Turcos," *Monografías de Ciencia Moderna* 29 (1951): 78,
disputes the attribution of this paper to Mendoza, but this is the only dissenting
opinion known to me. Sandoval, usually well-informed, published it as Mendoza's in 1604, and internal evidence leaves no doubt that he wrote it.

est in armis . . . One state is as legitimate as the next, only the usurpation of one is older than the other."

Scolding the Emperor for having increased the power and independence of the Duke of Florence, subject to him until now, he warns him strongly not to sell Milan, "the keystone of Italy," to Paul III, and he advises him not to worry about the Turk but let the Germans take care of him.

The Emperor, probably moved by these arguments, did not sell Milan or Siena. But he did not proceed militarily against the Pope. Even if he wished it, he was in no position to do so. The defense against the Turks could not safely be left to the Germans alone. Turkish and French vessels together, as early as the next month, besieged Nice, capturing the city and drawing the Marquis of Vasto's army over there to defend the citadel. Far from being able to attempt a conquest of the Papal States, the Imperials were unable even to dislodge the Turks. Barbarossa spent the winter of 1543/44 with his fleet in Toulon as guests of Francis I on French soil. Proclaiming this concert of Soliman and the Most Christian King as treason to the cause of Christendom, Charles V called on all other Christians for help, even those he feared and despised as heretics. At the Diet of Speier of 1544, he pacified the German Protestants with temporary concessions; he also renewed his alliance with his part-time friend and antagonist, Henry VIII of England. It was expected that the Spanish and German armies under Vasto would conquer Paris soon, where the English would meet them, but no such pincer movement on Paris came to pass. The French defeated the Marquis of Vasto at Cérésole in April, 1544, in a disastrous battle; a German army of six thousand men under Vasto's command perished there.[67] Simultaneously, the English King did not really intend to help Charles V. Henry VIII always feared the Emperor's ambition to become the universal monarch of Christendom.[68] Therefore, the remaining bulk of the Imperial army, having penetrated as far as twenty-four leagues from Paris into French territory, saw itself stranded and isolated, without funds and provisions. But by that time the French were equally exhausted. Chastened

[67] Karl Stallwitz, *Die Schlacht bei Cérésole*, inaugural dissertation, 1911.

[68] Marillac to Francis I, March 13, 1541, reports Henry VIII telling him that "were he [Charles V] the sole monarch in Christendom he would not be satisfied. . . ." *Cal. St. P.*, Spanish, V, 1, xix.

and softened, the rival brothers-in-law were ready for their last mutual peace (Francis I died less than three years later), concluded in Crépy in September, 1544.

The peace treaty preserved the *status quo ante*, but with the promise that Milan should go within a year to the French King's second son, the Duke of Orléans, by his marriage with a niece of the Emperor. As an alternative, the Duke would accept Charles V's daughter Maria with Flanders as her dowry.[69] (The death of the Duke of Orléans one week before the year was up released Charles V from his pledge.)

That way, Charles V enticed his old rival once more with the perpetual bait of Milan, achieving a temporary settlement of great importance for his stature, and for his future plans in Germany. For this solution he could thank Don Diego. The latter's advice not to sell the duchy had put him in a favorable bargaining position.

---

[69] About the Emperor's dilemma whether he would lose less by giving up the Netherlands or Milan, see Federico Chabod, "¿Milan o los Países Bajos? Las discusiones en España sobre la 'alternativa' de 1544." *Miscelánea de Estudios sobre Carlos V y su Época en el V Centenario de su muerte*, Homenaje de la Universidad de Granada, pp. 331–372.

6. TRENT, 1545–1546

Everything here looks like sophistry to me . . .
Don Diego[1]

The Ecumenical Council Convenes

FOR THE DURATION OF THE WAR with France, Mendoza remained at his Venetian post; he continued his watch over the neutrality of the Republic, the machinations of the exiled Strozzi, and also the movements of Lorenzo de' Medici, still at large. The fugitive, who had been in and out of France, fomenting trouble in concert with the Strozzi, was reported to be at the head of a wide French conspiracy whose principal target in the beginning of 1543 was Mendoza himself.[2] Had his men been able to catch him then, Don Diego would apparently have had fewer scruples than before or later about doing away with Lorenzino. "This business," he said on March 2, 1543, "would not be a burden on one's conscience any more because it must now be regarded as punishment and execution of justice rather than vengeance."[3]

But with the end of the war, Lorenzo's supposed influence van-

NOTE: A portion of this chapter originally appeared in *Journal of the History of Ideas* 36 (1965).

[1] "Todo lo de aqui me parece sophisteria . . . ," Mendoza to Charles V, April 14, 1545, Arch. Sim., Est. Ven., book 65, Rose-file.

[2] "Por mar y por tierra . . . ," Rose-file, A-4 (27–30), no identification number.

[3] Ibid., Mendoza to Charles V, March 2, 1543, in Rose-file.

ished, and Mendoza slackened his pursuit again. "It is not my custom to persecute any kind of person," he said in 1544. "I praise the good, and leave the bad alone with their own conscience and remorse."[4] So the tyrannicide continued his hunted life, and Cosimo de' Medici, who had set a large prize on his head, was getting impatient about the fact that his criminal cousin was still not caught. It is entirely possible that Mendoza's lack of zeal in apprehending Lorenzo stemmed as much from antipathy to Cosimo as from compassion for the fugitive. Perhaps he found it repugnant to soil his hands in this matter, doing dirty work for the Duke of Florence whose increased power he resented. (Cosimo's bravi murdered Lorenzino in Venice on February 26, 1548, more than a year after Don Diego's departure.)

After Charles V had concluded peace with France, he entered into truce negotiations with Sultan Soliman, a move Don Diego had advised for years; the result was a truce between East and West of five years' duration. But with this general pacification, to Mendoza's annoyance, the Strozzi, whom he helped expel by the end of 1542, reestablished themselves in Venice in 1544. That June, Don Diego wrote a long letter to the Doge, attempting to persuade him to throw the Strozzi out of Venetian territory.[5] When his official representations had little effect, he resorted once more to underhand dealings. He hired *agents provocateurs* who mingled among the men the Strozzi were recruiting for their armies, causing mutinies.

Privately, during this time, Mendoza was still complaining about his finances. In the spring of 1544, his brother Don Francisco, Bishop of Jaén, died in Speier, Germany, while the Reichstag was being held there. The Bishop had been nominated Cardinal but had not lived to receive the hat. Cobos at once asked the Emperor to give the vacated bishopric to Don Diego "who deserves such a favor from Your Majesty for many reasons,"[6] but Charles V honored instead Don Pedro Pacheco, a first cousin of the Mendozas, with this benefice. Don Diego was deeply disappointed and hurt. He wrote to his master:

[4] Mendoza to the Signoria of Venice, June, 1544, *AIH* (1911), p. 155.
[5] Ibid.
[6] Cobos to Charles V, Valladolid, May 14, 1544, GP I, 158.

Regarding myself, I do not need wordy compliments, because I do what is my duty, and I shall do it. I serve principally for the love of it, with all the diligence and fidelity I have. But since the aim of those who serve is to be honored and prospering, it seems I have much reason to complain of Your Majesty, because in this combination of circumstances you have given me to understand expressly what little merit there is in me. It is your custom to give large benefices to brothers and relatives of the dead, even if they have not served Your Majesty and are not your servants, as I am. I take the liberty of speaking so explicitly, with due humility, because I think that my life will end in the service of Your Majesty as my brother's did.[7]

Whatever his reason, the Emperor preferred to continue Don Diego at his present post, particularly in view of the Council that was now being convoked by Paul III to open in Trent by March 1545.

During the hundred years following the Council of Basel, every succeeding pope had prevented the convocation of another Ecumenical Council, despite (or because of) the fact that the abuses in Rome cried out for reform. This century had seen the establishment of the Atlantic trade routes, the consequent emergence of the world market and the accompanying rise of a rudimentary industrialization, the concurrent development of humanism with its spirit of free inquiry, the consequent lessening of reverence for tradition and authority, and finally the emergence of Protestantism and the attempted revolts of plain people, peasants, and soldiers. All these innovations had contributed to an atmosphere propitious to free thinking in religious matters, but free thought, when leading to doubts that were expressed, was called heresy.

In the time of Paul III, heresy had assumed such proportions with the propagation of Lutheranism, that this Pope could no longer avert a Council. He became the first Pope to favor such a Council in principle: a reaffirmation of the faith, a definition of its unchangeable dogma, seemed to him to be the only means of defeating Protestantism. But he feared the question of abuses. Paul III stood at the end of a long line of secularly ambitious, self-indulgent predecessors, whose domain was territorial rather than celestial.

---

[7] Mendoza to Charles V, September, 1544, Arch. Sim., Est., book 65; also *AC*, p. xx.

The last great Pope of the Renaissance (so called because he combined a brilliant mind with a love of splendor, grandeur, and art)
used his position, with a shameless nepotism extraordinary even
for that age, as a means to found, extend, and preserve, the dynasty
Farnese. He was not the man to reform the excesses of privilege in
his own princely court. Barring any discussion of abuses, however,
not to mention their examination and correction, Paul III willingly
called for the Council. To all appearances, he was as eager for it as
the Emperor.

Charles V wished to sustain his authority over the Lutheran
German princes; to him, the state rather than the faith seemed to
be in danger from Lutheranism; obedience to the established religion was closely interwoven with obedience to the secular monarchy. The beginning of his Imperial reign had coincided with the
start of Luther's attack on the Church, and Charles V had wanted
a Council ever since. In his opinion, the deterioration of the body
ecclesiastic had caused Lutheranism to emerge. Therefore he
wished for such an assembly principally on account of the abuses.

With both Emperor and Pope agreeable to a Council, although
for different reasons, they still could not come to terms regarding
the most convenient location for it. Charles V wished to give the
Lutherans—who would never go to Italy—the possibility to attend
the assembly; he insisted the Council be held on German territory.
Paul III, mindful of the past Councils in Basel and Constance (they
had established the Council's superiority over his predecessors), at
first demanded an Italian town near his observation and potential
control. They compromised on Trent, the small Tyrolean town on
the old Roman road in the valley of the Adige. Nominally of the
German Empire, under the jurisdiction of King Ferdinand, this
southernmost outpost of the Germans was inhabited largely by
Italians.

The Council had already been prematurely called together in
1543. Don Diego had gone to Trent for the first time that January,
in the company of his brother Don Bernardino; they had braved
deep snows over bad mountain roads, but it was a vain effort. The
meeting had to be postponed indefinitely because of the French-
Spanish war. All present left Trent after only a few days, and the
brothers Mendoza returned to Venice.

Early in 1545 the dropped thread was picked up again, although Emperor and Pope found the timing even less convenient. They considered it unwise, however, to admit of their objections. Charles V, his hands now freed from involvements with France and the Turks, was calling a Reichstag in Worms, hoping to win the Protestant princes, ostensibly by persuasion, but in reality by threatening them with his increased power. He was, in fact, preparing war against them. If a Council were to investigate the substance of Christian dogma at this juncture, defining its immutability, the Lutherans would be irreconcilable from the outset. The Pope, in turn, dreading as much as ever an investigation against abuses that was to begin at "the head," was just then contemplating to commit his own greatest abuse, that of investing his son Pier Luigi with two states belonging to the Church, Parma and Piacenza. But despite their reservations, each monarch was victim of his own propaganda; none could now withdraw, and the Council was launched. Each party was fully prepared, though, to obstruct the actual opening. It was a new comedy in the make-believe game of politics in which Mendoza was by then superbly trained. He was once more appointed as Charles V's representative.

Possibly he greeted the change of scene from Venice to Trent with pleasure. In Venice he was still living socially isolated, and somewhat tensely, under the ever-present eyes of a foreign power. But Trent was Imperial territory, almost home to him. The Council's host, the young Cardinal of Trent, Christoforo Madruzzo (1512–1578), a wealthy ecclesiastic prince, was the Emperor's partisan. "Trento" (as Mendoza usually referred to Madruzzo in his correspondence) rode three miles out of Trent with a large escort to welcome the Imperial ambassador when he arrived there on the evening of March 23, accompanying him to his lodging in the Convent of San Lorenzo outside the city walls. Privately, Don Diego judged Madruzzo rather sharply: "Trento is a fool and cannot keep a secret,"[8] but he kept up pleasant social relations with him. He frequented his palace, was his summer guest at Bressanone, and when he fell ill there, he was laid up in the Cardinal's castle in Trent.

---

[8] "Trento es loco . . . ," *AC*, p. 134.

Mendoza's presence contributed much to turn the sleepy provincial Alpine town temporarily into an intellectual world center. He furnished a strictly scholarly background for the theological discussions by putting his collection of printed books and priceless manuscripts at the disposal of all factions, cardinals, scholars, private experts. He established an "Aristotelian" academy as a means to use worthily the waiting period that the Emperor's policies imposed on the assembled churchmen before the Council was allowed to open that December. He used much of the time to write a Latin paraphrase of Aristotle's *Physics*; or perhaps he only finished the lengthy work there, having started it in Venice.[9]

Among young foreign scholars flocking to Trent in search of patrons was Juan Páez de Castro, a doctor of philosophy from Spain, whose few letters to Jerónimo Zurita are the nearest thing we have of a Mendoza "Boswell."

I have the house full of ever so many printed books of Don Diego that I want, and manuscripts too, and his sketchbooks. All here believe that Don Diego will climb very high in position after this Council is over, and that His Majesty will make him bishop, and His Holiness, cardinal. Now we understand the *Mechanica* of Aristotle, making great demonstrations. He has it translated into Romance and has written a glossary; I believe I can help him somewhat. Always he says: "Let us study, Señor Joan Páez." He is so good and humane that you can say "Nihil oriturum" [nobody will be born like this] "alias nihil ortum tale" [also nobody has been born such]; his learning is very varied and unusual; he is a great Aristotelian and mathematician; Latin and Greek [scholar] . . Nobody is his equal. In short, he is in a class by himself.[10]

Another scholar whom Mendoza favored was Conrad Gesner, and still another, Angelo Massarelli, the pleasant gentleman, then thirty-five, whose hobby was preparing essence of roses, and whose famous diary, mainly in Latin, affords us a sense of participation in that world forum. Massarelli was the secretary of Cardinal Santa Croce (Marcello Cervini), one of the three papal legates to the Council. Assuming the functions of a liaison man between his mas-

[9] Mendoza's autograph Latin MS in El Escorial, MS F-II-6, folios 63–242. Cf. GP I, 286, 287.

[10] Páez de Castro to Zurita, July 6, 1545, in Diego J. Dormer, *Progresos*, p. 461. On Páez, see M. Solana, *Historia de la filosofía española*, II, 203–210.

ter and the Imperials, he visited constantly with the Cardinal of Trent and Don Diego on behalf of Santa Croce and the other Legate, Cardinal del Monte. And irrespective of their severe differences in power politics, Don Diego extended his social and scholarly amenities just as courteously to the opposite camp. He invited Massarelli to borrow all the books he wanted for Cardinal Santa Croce and himself; he also lent him part of his collection of ancient coins.[11]

The first dissension between Mendoza and the legates sprang up at once. Paying them his respect after his arrival, he told Del Monte and Santa Croce that he wished to present his commission from the Emperor publicly in an open place, such as the cathedral. The legates declared this to be impossible. The Council was not yet opened, therefore nothing that referred to it should be treated publicly. When Don Diego insisted that, having come in the name and place of Charles V, he had now restored the Council Act, the legates disagreed, but seeing that Mendoza was quick to take offense in the Emperor's name and in his own, they proposed a compromise—the first of many. If Mendoza wished to recite publicly his commission to the head of the Council, he could do so in the morning by addressing Cardinal del Monte—the designated presiding Bishop—in the latter's house with the doors thrown open.[12]

As long as appearances were upheld, Don Diego agreed to this substitute performance. Del Monte, a pleasure-loving, nonintellectual cleric, entertained Mendoza and Cardinals Santa Croce and Trent splendidly at dinner the next day, and afterward they went into the large hall of the Palazzo del Prato, Del Monte's residence, where the doors were left ajar. To all who wished to hear, Don Diego read his document in a loud voice. He explained his presence in Trent, telling them how eagerly the Emperor wanted the examination of the Council to begin. The legates postponed their formal answer for a day, because on the next morning Don Diego decided to go fishing. The following day, with courteous praise for Charles V and Mendoza, the legates emphasized their confidence that the

---

[11] Gesner on Mendoza, in *Bibliotheca Universalis*, I, folio 205. On Massarelli, see *Concilium Tridentinum (Conc. Trid.)*, ed. S. Merklé, Massarelli, *Diaria* I–IV, entry of April 1, 1545.

[12] Massarelli, *Diaria* I, March 26, 1545.

Emperor would not allow any private explanation of religion outside Trent.[13] (This referred to the impending Reichstag at Worms;
the Pope wanted to preclude any repetition of "Religious Colloquia" in Germany, where Lutheran criticism had been granted a
hearing. The colloquia proceeded nonetheless; for example, those
of Ratisbon, January 27–March 20, 1546.)

In the subtlety of Imperial diplomacy, the substance of which
usually consisted in artful delay, Don Diego had official instructions to act on the spot as though he assumed the Council to be in
session. But at the same time the Emperor was in fact withholding
his official consent to the opening because he did not wish to offend
the Lutherans unnecessarily. Don Diego's pose was thus assumed.
He could accuse the legates of stalling, while actually the one who
stalled the procedure was Charles V, whose formal approval for
the opening of the Council was not given before October, when the
Reichstag was over.

The next stumbling block was the question of precedence. Since
Paul III was head and host of the Council (the sessions cost him
about 50,000 ducats annually), Mendoza conceded the Pope's representatives, the two legates present, the first place. (They were to
be joined by the third legate, Cardinal Reginald Pole.) But Don
Diego wished to sit beside the legates, preceding in his turn the
Cardinal of Trent and all other dignitaries of the Church. If the
Emperor were present, he argued, His Majesty would sit next to
the Pope. No one, therefore, must sit between the legates and himself. The legates did not accept this reasoning. A cardinal's dignity,
in their opinion, was equal to a king's—a point that Don Diego,
representing an Emperor-King, did not concede. State and Church
kept on bickering about this, although it was not an actual word
battle. It was carried out by the indefatigable footwork of Massarelli, who hurried to and fro all day between the house of Cardinal
del Monte (where he was four times), and the house of the Cardinal of Trent, with whom Mendoza stayed (where he went five
times).[14]

[13] Ibid.
[14] On the fifty thousand ducats, see Mendoza to Charles V, November 18,
1546, Arch. Sim., Est., leg. 1192, folio 3. On Massarelli's visits, *Diaria* I, April
1, 1545.

Don Diego wrote the Bishop of Arras of his annoyance. (A son of Nicolas Perrenot de Granvelle, Antoine de Perrenot served the Emperor at the side of his mighty father, rising to the same position as the elder Granvelle. He was gradually supplanting the aging and ailing Cobos as advocate of Don Diego at the court, and as recipient of the latter's bulk of informal letters.) It was the legates' intention, said Mendoza, to whittle his resistance down with minor irritations until he would be in no position to represent the Emperor properly. Then they would be able to do with the Council what they wished. Should he show himself difficult or raise trouble, they could say he disturbed the proceedings—exactly what they wanted him to do, so that they might call off the Council altogether. He would not give them such a pretext, however. He would exert great care with them because "giving them occasion for annoyance would damage the service to God and benefit to Christendom, if the Council were not to go ahead. They are men who seize any opportunity, even the smallest, to prevent [a Council]."[15]

With this in mind, he consented to let all cardinals precede him, but he still insisted that he had to precede all the bishops. By Easter Sunday no one was as yet certain as to what Don Diego intended to do during the most sacred service. The legates feared he would create a disturbance; they even considered staying at home rather than provoking a demonstration from his side. But Mendoza settled the question privately with the Cardinal of Trent. "The Cardinal of Trent celebrated the Easter Mass in the Cathedral," tells Massarelli. "He left the castle on horseback with all his familiars, the legates, and the nobles of the city. When he entered the church, all followed him. Cardinal Santa Croce and Cardinal del Monte were wearing roseate capes, the cardinals' insignia and the cross of the Church. Meanwhile the Cardinal of Trent put on his pastoral habit, emerging from the sacristy in a golden pluviale, the bishop's mitre, carrying in his hand the Arm of Saint Vigilio, protector of the town of Trent. All the clerics followed him, then the legates, then the Imperial ambassador, who walked at the right with the Bishop of Cava . . . When they reached the altar, Mass was begun. The legates sat down at the right in seats hung with roseate satin; and Don Diego had the first place preceding the Bishops of Cava, Bitun-

---

[15] Mendoza to Arras, Trent, April 2, 1545, *AIH* II, 155, 156.

tio, and Bertinori, on seats covered with black velvet . . ."[16] And so, for the time being, one problem was solved.

As luck would have it, Massarelli, who always reported faithfully on all pontifical robes and bishops' mantles, never once put down what Don Diego wore or how he looked. But Mendoza must also have worn some sort of clerical garb. In a letter to the Emperor from Rome, May 3, 1547, Mendoza wrote that now he was putting on lay dress.[17] From this and other similar remarks (the reasons for his *not* doing in Rome as the Romans do, will be analyzed below) it appears that up to his arrival in Rome he had done otherwise. Before Trent, when Titian painted him—or when he went into the Ghetto on tender errands—he had not gone around in priest's garments, naturally. Probably only in order to look appropriate at the religious gatherings, he put his sword and feather hat away, dressing the part in Trent in cassock, surplice, and birretta. Or, possibly, he wore a doctor's gown.

It was a cold Easter, with snow on the nearby mountains. The only sign of spring was the appearance on the reverends' breakfast tables of fresh figs from the milder regions of Lake Garda. Now that they had taken each other's measure, both parties knew that their mutual delaying game would take a long time. Realists, they settled down to a period of amiable social living. The cardinals outbid each other in entertainments. "The legates, the ambassador, and the bishops, all went together to the castle [of the Cardinal of Trent, the old fortress on a Roman foundation, Buon Consiglio], where they were served dinner liberally and magnificently, in a gay mood, in the large hall under a golden awning. The meal started at 2 P.M., lasting until about 5, consisting of seventy-four meat and fish courses," wrote Massarelli on April 7. Ten days later, the Cardinal of Trent sent the legates a sixty-pound sturgeon; they claimed only half of it for themselves; the next morning they sent Massarelli to Don Diego with the head, the remaining half for the Spanish bishops. We may assume that the sturgeon's head was still fresh when it came to Mendoza, for Massarelli records on that day that "there was fresh snow on the mountains, and the cold in Trent was strong." It stayed cold until the end of May, and those

[16] Massarelli, *Diaria* I, entries of April 4 and 5, 1545, p. 109.
[17] Mendoza to Charles V, May 3, 1547, in Döllinger, *Beiträge*, I, 53.

present in Trent—all hailing from warmer climes—shivered through an uncomfortable Tyrolean spring.[18]

The summer months passed by, still without official business, the somnolence interrupted only in July with special festivities for the birth of Don Carlos, the Emperor's first grandson. The later most hapless young prince of Spanish history, who was to die mysteriously and tragically, was widely hailed at his start in life as heir to half the world. In Trent, solemn masses in the new Prince's honor were followed by lavish banquets and fireworks. (It was not yet known that meanwhile the new Prince's mother, the young Portuguese Princess, Maria, had died.) On the third day it was Don Diego's turn to entertain all celebrants. "He made fireworks in front of his palace, and in place of the candles usually put in the windows, he had giant torches, most beautiful, which he let burn out entirely."[19]

Eating and jesting with the legates did not close Don Diego's eyes to their intentions. And he was watching from afar the arrival of the Pope's grandson, the young Cardinal Alessandro Farnese, who was on his way from Rome to Worms as a special delegate of his grandfather. Mendoza wrote the Emperor on April 6:

I have heard from Venice that Cardinal Fernes [*sic*] told another Cardinal that the Pope plays a winning game: if the Council does not come to pass, this is what he wants. If, however, it does, he knows how to guide it in such a way that it will do exactly what he desires. Should this fail nevertheless, and Your Majesty will try to apply whatever the Council may decree, you will only antagonize the Lutherans and not achieve anything. In that case the Pope will be satisfied to have done his duty, handing the Council over to Your Majesty. He seems to forget that execution has to start with reform.

The conditions of the Council cannot be worse. Its start shows already that it was never intended to proceed. This is obvious by the short time limit the Pope allowed the [Spanish] prelates to get here [the Spaniards had not yet arrived, missing a deadline, and Don Diego had to make excuses for the technical delay of his countrymen]. He [the Pope] has planned it so that it coincides with the Reichstag, and he slows down the arrival of legates and bishops. Of three legates, one is still absent [Cardinal Reginald Pole, ill], and the Pope is master of the abuses. He is unable to deny that he commits them and that they

---

[18] Massarelli, *Diaria* I, entries of April 7 and 17, 1545.
[19] Ibid., entries of August 7 and 8, 1545.

profit him, so that commonly he is not held to be a good Christian. If he does not need the Council for the soul, certainly he does not need it for the body.[20]

When Cardinal Farnese arrived in Trent, however, Don Diego established warm relations with him. A living symbol of the Pope's nepotism, Alessandro had received the red hat when he was fourteen years old. Yet, brilliantly gifted and educated, he was not unworthy of his privilege. At twenty-five, he was a smooth, efficient representative of Paul III, acting as the old man's right hand. He told those in Trent that the Pope was impatient about the delay of the Council, but advised them to wait all the same until he reported to them about his impending talks with Charles V on his way back. At the moment he was the instrument in a very close game between Pope and Emperor, bringing Paul III's apparent complete surrender to Charles V's wishes. The Pope promised to join in the forthcoming war against the rebellious German Protestants with a contribution of 200,000 ducats, twelve thousand Italian infantry, and five hundred cavalry, as well as part of the income from Spanish churches and monasteries up to some 900,000 ducats.

In return for this massive help from his grandfather, young Farnese had to present the Emperor with a *fait accompli.* Paul III had already taken advantage of the special circumstances in which Charles V now counted on his assistance. The Pope felt especially encouraged to do so in view of the imminent birth of their first common descendant, Margaret of Austria-Farnese's offspring after seven years of marriage. (Twins, born August 27, 1545, of which only Alessandro Farnese grew up, the Pope's great-grandson, the Emperor's grandson, later a famous general and Duke of Parma.) Without waiting for the fellow-ancestor's formal consent, on August 14, in consistory, the Pope conferred the investiture of the duchies of Parma and Piacenza upon his son Pier Luigi Farnese. The territories had passed under the Emperor's control by Clement VII's capitulation after the sack of Rome, but were then returned to the States of the Church by Charles V after the death

---

[20] Mendoza to Charles V, April 6, 1545, Arch. Sim., Est. Ven., book 65, Rose-file.

of the last Sforza. The Pope had no legal right to alienate any part of the territory belonging to the Church. But Charles V could not offend him openly now that both monarchs were about to go to war as allies.

During the time of waiting, Don Diego warned the legates that the question of precedence regarding the actual future Council proceedings was still unsolved; he wished to occupy that seat where the Emperor would sit if he were present at the Council sessions. The legates, disliking his request, referred the problem to the "Urbs." Letters from Rome gave them the ingenious solution of setting up chairs for both the Pope and the Emperor, leaving them vacant. Don Diego would have a place somewhat more honorable than that of other ambassadors, but on the other side of the bishops, separated from legates, cardinals, and all the bishops.[21] This was the best and most fitting that the man, anyway "in a class by himself," could expect.

Mendoza versus De Soto

In the pleasant atmosphere of intellectual pursuits and social gatherings, Don Diego was liked and respected by political adversaries as well as by his own party. The only exception of which we know was one of the Spanish theologians, Fray Domingo de Soto, with whom he feuded over philosophical matters. Four years later, when Mendoza was in Rome, he wrote a long letter to a relative at the Emperor's court, speaking his mind freely about this antagonist. Fray Domingo de Soto was appointed confessor to Charles V in August 1548,[22] and he was then becoming influential in the delicate relationship between Emperor and Pope. No idle courtier's gossip, Don Diego's letter contained crafty political counsel intended to reach Monseigneur de Granvelle, the powerful man next to the Emperor's throne. He advised:

You might tell Monseigneur that the confessor does not like me because in Trent I defended a doctor Herrera whom he had slandered, calling him a heretic in the presence of many bishops. Besides, I refused to let him print at my expense a commentary about Aristotle's *Physics*; and furthermore, in our debates I always upheld against him

21 Massarelli, *Diaria* I, entry of May 3, 1545.
22 V. Beltrán de Heredia, *Domingo de Soto*, p. 211.

and against Saint Thomas the part of Averroës, a thing I would not have done, had I known he would become the confessor. Also, [he dislikes me] because I know more philosophy than he.[23]

The humanist philosopher and the Dominican must have taken up their irreconcilable positions soon after they met. Their encounters would have been interrupted in May, when Don Diego went to Venice for a few weeks. In June and July when he was back at Trent, their controversy was probably at its height.[24] In early August, Mendoza sent the doctor Juan Páez de Castro to Venice to buy the Latin editions of Saint Thomas and Averroës.[25] Don Diego presumably needed the latter only to argue his case against De Soto, who, apparently, knew no Arabic.

But by the middle of August, Mendoza felt poorly. He went for a change of air to the Cardinal of Trent's estate at Bressanone, returning from there severely ill; he and his entire household were stricken with malaria or "quartan" fevers. Wishing to consult his doctor Jacob Mantino, who would not come to Trent where Jews were not allowed (Trent kept alive the legend of a ritual murder supposedly perpetrated there),[26] Mendoza left Trent in mid-September. He remained in Venice all through the opening of the Council in December. On his intended return trip to Trent in March 1546, a relapse forced him to discontinue the journey at Padua, the ancient stronghold of Averroist tradition, where he spent two months. While there, he might have occupied himself on his better days with a renewed study of Averroës.[27] He arrived

---

[23] ". . . sé mas filosofia que el . . . ," Mendoza to a relative at court, May 6, 1549, *AC*, p. 124. The same letter contains subtle directions of Mendoza for removing De Soto eventually from his place of influence: the confessor was to be induced to overreach himself. This advice apparently had the desired effect, because six months after this letter would have reached the Imperial court at Brussels, De Soto resigned from his position. See Beltrán de Heredia, *Domingo de Soto*, p. 231.

[24] Records of Mendoza's movements to and from Trent are found in *Conc. Trid.* I, throughout the *Diaria* I–III by Massarelli. Constancio Gutiérrez, *Los Españoles en Trento* (Cuenca, 1951), worked out his exact schedule (pp. 269, 270).

[25] Páez to Zurita, August 11, 1545, in Dormer, *Progresos*, pp. 464–465.

[26] Massarelli, *Diaria* I, entry of December 28, 1545. H. L. Strack, *Der Blutaberglaube bei Christen und Juden*, p. 119, gives the date of the ritual murder case as 1475.

[27] Mendoza was seldom too ill for his scholarly pursuits, as shown by the re-

back in Trent on May 25, 1546, more than half a year after the Council had been in session. Then he stayed on, with only very short interruptions, until he left for good on December 3. His long absence had not made the two antagonists fonder of each other. As the above-quoted letter from May, 1549, shows, Don Diego challenged De Soto also in 1546. His defense of "the doctor Herrera in Trent," whom De Soto had called a heretic in front of many bishops, can have taken place only in that year, during the actual Council sessions. Herrera, about whom hardly anything is known, spoke in the Council on June 2, September 28, and October 23.[28] When Mendoza imputed De Soto's dislike for him to his refusal to subsidize printing the latter's commentary about Aristotle's *Physics*, he must have referred, however, to the year 1545, as De Soto succeeded in publishing the same work in that year, even without Mendoza's help.[29] If, therefore, De Soto committed his offense against Herrera in the autumn of 1546, and if Mendoza's refusal of financial assistance occurred in the spring of 1545, it appears that the controversy continued throughout nearly two years of their association. Don Diego himself said "always."

De Soto, who chose to quarrel with his two countrymen, Herrera and Mendoza, and who fought almost every speaker in the Council, was the Spanish delegate responsible for the final formulation of the Decree of Justification, the only dogmatic result of that session.[30] He seems to have made himself most unpopular. Al-

---

ports of his doctor Amatus Lusitanus from the time when he was treating the ambassador in Venice in the winter 1545/46 while he was absent from Trent. See Amatus Lusitanus, *Centuriae* I, curatio prima, scholia, p. 31; also, curatio 31, p. 100. Further: Amatus Lusitanus, *In Dioscoridis*, enarratio 119, p. 432, and enarratio 113, p. 530. His stay at Padua might have given Mendoza occasion to renew contacts with the university where Morales says he studied as a young man. See also Baltasar de Zúñiga, introduction to the first edition of *G. de Gr.*

[28] Mendoza's first attendance at any session was on June 4, 1546, according to Massarelli, entry of same date, p. 162. On Herrera, see Massarelli, *Diaria* I, pp. 600–602; and Gutiérrez, *Los Españoles*, p. 408.

[29] "Fray Domingo de Soto publicó sus comentarios a la Dialéctica de Aristóteles (1544), sus Comentarios en los ocho libros de física (1545)," Adolfo de Castro y Rossi, *Obras escogidas de filósofos*, p. xlxi.

[30] See Otto Lehnhoff, *Die Beichtväter Karls V.* p. 71. De Soto was an authority on Canon Law, and a proponent of a system of natural philosophy that defended the right of primitive non-Christians to remain outside the Catholic Church, forbidding all coercion prior to baptism. Born in 1494 in Segovia, edu-

though every participant at the Council was entitled and even encouraged to air his opinions on the formulation of Church dogma quite freely, it soon became apparent that De Soto was intolerant of any thought but his own. One of his antagonists defended the principle of "Double Justification";[31] another defended the opinions of Duns Scotus;[32] another wished to proceed cautiously in applying the label of heresy to every thought uttered;[33] and so on down the line of practically the entire group of Italian prelates, who considerably outnumbered the Spanish churchmen.[34]

Not all the tensions at the Council were of De Soto's making, however. The basic divergence between the Imperial and Papal factions—the former stressing the reform of abuses, the latter insisting on examination of dogma—was almost unbridgeable. But although the "heads" of the Imperial party were only Mendoza[35] and the single Spanish cardinal present, his cousin Pedro Pacheco of Jaén, De Soto assumed the spiritual leadership of the Imperials, imposing it even on the Papals.

There was another, underlying, divergence that cut across national and party lines, as it were. Although there were no Protestant participants at the Council (despite the fact that its basic aim was supposed to be the invitation to Lutherans to work out their

---

cated at the universities of Alcalá and Paris, De Soto taught theology and philosophy at Alcalá in 1520. After entering the Dominican order in 1535, he taught at Burgos, then at Salamanca. He was granted leave of absence from Salamanca to serve as an expert for the Imperial side at the Council.

[31] Jerónimo Seripando; see F. Cereceda, *Diego Láinez en la Europa religiosa de su tiempo*, I, 245, 248 ("Soto Domingo fué el alma de aquella implacable y dura ofensiva . . .").

[32] Bonaventura Costacciaro, the General of the Conventuals; see Valens Heynck, "A Controversy at the Council of Trent concerning the Doctrine of Duns Scotus," *Franciscan Studies* 9, no. 1 (March, 1949): 254.

[33] Ambrosio Catarino, the Franciscan Bishop; see Beltrán de Heredia, *Domingo de Soto*, pp. 202–204.

[34] Twenty-six Spaniards took part in an official capacity. Gutiérrez, *Los Españoles*, p. xiv, describes them as "thirteen *padres* [bishops, with voting rights]; four theologians [advisers]; nine in diverse capacity." The Italian delegation comprised from 64.5 percent to 77.2 percent of the total assembly between December 13, 1545 and January 13, 1547; see Giuseppe Alberigo, *I vescovi italiani al Concilio di Trento*, p. 20.

[35] During Mendoza's illness, Don Francisco de Toledo was sent to Trent, remaining there as Mendoza's associate after the latter's return.

divergence with the Catholics and return to the purified Mother Church), suspicion concerning the presence of "secret Lutherans" reigned among the all-Catholic body.[36] Those wary of any new thought decried every deviation from traditional Catholicism as Lutheran. Although De Soto did not originate this line of suspicious thinking, he made free use of it, denouncing nonconformists as heretics, as a means to beat the members into submission to his doctrine.[37] In the end, despite multiple and diversified antagonisms among the prelates, De Soto's opinion—that is, the Thomistic view —prevailed in the formulation of the Decree of Justification.

At that time the Emperor was already engaged in his war against the Schmalkaldic League (the alliance of Protestant princes). A few of the Protestants supported him against the others, and in his fear to offend his Protestant allies, Charles V did not want the decree published. The Pope's supporters, however, defying the Emperor, proceeded with publication. Ostensibly, therefore, it was *their* victory. But the dogma itself was, thanks to De Soto, a Spanish victory. Consequently, Mendoza gave his approval to De Soto's posture, writing to Charles V: "Yesterday the debates about the article of Justification came to an end, where Fray Domingo de Soto, the Prior of Salamanca, distinguished himself very much, as it was he who guided the business, being the first speaker, and because he is a man of letters of greater experience and reliability than any of the Italians." After commending also the other Spanish theologians present (who doubtless were more sympathetic to him personally), Mendoza finished his report by stating, "I am mentioning them here only in order to fulfill my duty."[38]

If Mendoza then publicly supported his compatriot "out of duty," their private antagonism appears to have been all the sharper. It must have been based on their conflicting views of Aristotle, perhaps even on their competition to establish themselves as commentators of Aristotle. As shown in Mendoza's letter of May, 1549, De Soto had brought with him to Trent his own manuscript of the

---

[36] For example, the Bishop of Fiesole and the Bishop Vergerio of Capo d'Istria; Massarelli, *Diaria* I, entries of January 11 and 25, 1546.

[37] For example, in addition to Francisco Herrera, the abbot Luciano of San Benedetto; Massarelli, *Diaria* I, entry of January 20, 1546.

[38] Mendoza to Charles V, October 28, 1546; excerpt published in *Ciencia Tomista* 65 (1943): 73.

Physics, which he was eager to publish. At the same time Don Diego was working on a paraphrasis of the same book of Aristotle and also on his own translation of the *Mechanica* from Greek into Spanish. He was also writing an introduction to his hispanicized *Mechanica* in the form of a letter supposedly dedicated to the Duke of Alba.[39]

Even had they not already been rivals in their occupation with the Aristotelian texts, De Soto's and Mendoza's differences of opinion would have set in at the point where Averroës and Saint Thomas differ most sharply in their commentaries: the question of the personal immortality of the soul. No doctrine of Averroës was more vehemently denied by Thomas than the Islamic philosopher's teaching—so deeply involved with the question of immortality—of the unity of the intellect. It seems justifiable, therefore, to assume this point to be the kernel of their disagreement.

De Soto, outside of Spain, had gone to school only in Paris, where Averroism, if it had not fully disappeared by the end of the fourteenth century, certainly had not the vogue it enjoyed in parts of Italy.[40] Mendoza, however, having listened to Nifo, Montesdoca, and perhaps even Pomponazzi, must in fact have known "more philosophy," at least of the Averroist kind, than his rival. But the question remains, just what might he have understood to be the teaching of Averroës? What could he have known of "Averroism"? Is it likely that he was able to penetrate to the "real" Averroës, or did he rather share in the legendary Averroës, as he was known in the sixteenth century? Although he had the material at hand to make a fresh translation if he wished,[41] Mendoza was probably not equipped to start an exegesis of Averroës. He may not even have suspected the extent of the difference between the original text and the Latin translation of it. This was not a task for a solitary man to solve, especially since his study of Averroës could have involved only a small part of his time.

[39] The "Paraphrasis," fourteen notebooks written in Mendoza's own hand, survives in El Escorial; see note 9, above. El Escorial has two MS copies of Mendoza's translation of the *Mechanica*; see Appendix.

[40] For a definition of "Averroism" in the sixteenth century, see chapter 2, note 29.

[41] On Arabic manuscripts owned by Mendoza, including MSS of Averroës, see Nemesio Morata, "Un catálogo de los fondos árabes primitivos de El Escorial," *A-A* 2 (1934): 87–181.

If Mendoza had his own personal way of assimilating the supposed Averroist doctrines,[42] we cannot know it. We may safely assume, all the same, that he approached his text, whether Latin or Arabic, according to the traditional interpretation of the so-called Latin Averroists, although his view of Averroës would have been critically tempered by the harsh remarks of Pomponazzi.[43] Without necessarily making a moral judgment, he would have argued from the *soi-disant* Averroist doctrines, that is, the oneness of the passive intellect in all men; the denial of personal immortality to the individual, cogitative soul; the eternity of the world (as opposed to the concepts of Creation and the Last Judgment). He would have argued in the face of De Soto's rocklike conviction that philosophy is nothing but the ancilla of theology and that the principles of Saint Thomas' *Summa contra Gentiles* are irrefutable for a Christian. Whether or not Mendoza believed in any of the theories, he seems to have defended them with some degree of sympathy. One thing is clear: the views of De Soto were anathema to him. "To tell the truth," he says in the same letter where he relates this feud, "wretched as my own conscience is, I would not trade it for his [De Soto's] brains."[44]

On the Threshold of Maturity

At about the time of Mendoza's temporary retirement from Trent because of illness, he still thought of a possible cardinalate for himself. He may have taken the question of precedence in the seating arrangement, being ranked below the cardinals, very much to heart, partly also out of resentment in behalf of the Emperor's dignity. Had he been a cardinal he could have upheld his master's reputation more fittingly. (In 1549, when the time came for Paul III to offer Mendoza the red hat, it was impossible for him to accept—he said he would rather put "yonder *orinal* of red glass on his head"—because the Pope's gesture was expressly meant to

[42] Cf. the three positions as outlined by W. F. Edwards, "The Averroism of Iacopo Zabarella," p. 91; see chapter 2, note 29.

[43] Pomponazzi calls the opinion of Averroës "in se sit falsissima/ vere inintelligibilis & monstruosa/ & ab Aristotele prorsus aliena . . . ," Petri Pomponatii Mantuani, *Tractatus de Immortalitate Animae*, edited by William Henry Hay, II, chapter 4, p. iv.

[44] *AC*, p. 125.

make him desert his Emperor's interest.)[45] On October 19, 1545, Cobos, whose letters to Charles V on behalf of Don Diego usually reflect the latter's own wishes, wrote from his semiretirement:

Your Majesty knows already how Don Diego de Mendoza has served you, and what he deserves for his personality and ability. Since lately such short shrift was made with him [when he did not receive the position vacated through the death of his brother], he is complaining and worrying, thinking that Your Majesty decided not to reward him because of his faults. He sees that Your Majesty has started to recommend other men of his type for cardinalates. I think that in Rome he would do the right service for Your Majesty. I have heard it said that, if Your Majesty would nominate him, His Holiness would be glad to do him this favor of making him cardinal. I beseech Your Majesty to look into this.[46]

The Emperor, as he often did, followed part of the advice. He acknowledged that Don Diego would be an excellent choice for Rome, but he wanted him there as ambassador. The vassal who analyzed the Pope's motives so shrewdly, he knew, would be able to handle his old adversary. But Charles V did not want to send a bishop or cardinal, or anyone in *robba lunga* to Paul III.[47] A cleric would necessarily owe a certain measure of deference to the spiritual head of Christendom. Only a layman could stand up for the Emperor's interest free from any restraint.

Charles V must have replied to Cobos in this vein, because on May 18, 1546, the Comendador suggested to Granvelle that Don Diego be sent to Rome, even though His Majesty did not want a long-robed person in that position.[48] On July 30, 1546, the Venetian ambassador at the Imperial court, Alvise Mocenigo, had already heard that Don Diego was going to Rome as the new ambassador, but that he would go *in other dress* because the Emperor did not wish him to serve the Church.[49]

This is exactly what happened—although Mendoza did not change into lay attire until he appeared in Rome the following

---

[45] Mendoza to Charles V, April 10, 1549, *NB* XI, 777.

[46] GP I, 159, 160.

[47] ". . . il reverendo Don Diego . . .," Mocenigo to Venice, Ratisbon, July 25, 1546, *Ven. Dep.* I, 598–599.

[48] Cobos to Granvelle, Arch. Sim., Est. Castilla, p. 73, Rose-file.

[49] *Ven. Dep.* I, 603.

Easter. For his nomination as ambassador to the Pope he was made to pay with the sacrifice of any aspirations he might ever have had to a high rank in the Church.

It seems that the worst part of Mendoza's "two quartan fevers" was the constant recurrence of his fever attacks. In December, 1545, he had temporarily recovered enough to prepare to go to Trent for the Council's opening on the thirteenth. (In Trent, all through the winter, his Aristotelian academy, nourishing itself on his own books, was carrying on without him.) But then he felt worse and was unable to travel. Luckily, perhaps, he was forced to change doctors at that time. Dr. Jacob Mantino, his physician in Venice, had seen him through three years of grave illnesses but had not really cured him. Yet Mendoza had full confidence in Mantino's art and felt worried when the doctor decided to leave Venice. (A Venetian patrician had invited Dr. Mantino to accompany him to Damascus, and he accepted this offer, although Don Diego tried to dissuade him. Mantino died a few days after he arrived in the East.) As a substitute, Mantino had recommended a doctor of Mendoza's own Salamanca, Amatus Lusitanus, Marrano physician, botanist, and author, who was then teaching medicine at the university in Ferrara. "I went to Venice," reports Amatus, "where I came to Don Diego Mendoza, the Emperor Charles V's most watchful ambassador, who was ill, and I cured him."[50]

It was a slow cure. In March, on his way to Trent, Mendoza had a relapse that forced him to stay in Padua, and periods of fever still recurred during the course of 1546, but gradually he regained more strength than he ever seems to have had. (He had never been so active in his life as he was to be from 1547–1552.)

On December 11, 1545, when Don Diego had to cancel his intended return trip to Trent, missing the formal opening of the Council, he suggested at once to the Emperor that he appoint an associate ambassador as long as he had to remain on sick leave.[51] Charles V nominated Don Francisco de Toledo, a first cousin of the Viceroy of Naples.[52] It was an excellent choice, because Don Francisco's rank as a noble was exactly as high as Mendoza's, while,

50 Amatus Lusitanus, *Centuriae* I, curatio 31, p. 100.
51 December 11, 1545, Arch. Sim., Est., leg. 1318, Rose-file.
52 Massarelli, *Diaria* I, 198.

like most aristocrats, "not a lettered man,"[53] he would not be able to steal Mendoza's limelight. In tightly packed little Trent, where speculation ran wild on why Don Diego did not return, gossip had it that he smarted over the Emperor's choice.[54] But this seems unlikely, since he himself had asked for a "compañero" in this office. An old courtier, Don Francisco had been his friend for many years. He was also a distant relative—though close enough for Don Diego, when Toledo visited him in Padua, to borrow money from him, "although he has not much, either."[55]

That April, Mendoza was at one of the lowest points of his life. He felt miserable and looked it. His mind reached out from Padua to Venice, on the one side, and to Trent on the other, unable to attend to the demands both places required of him. And for some time, the treasury in Milan had stopped all payments—this seems to have been an emergency measure on account of the Emperor's military preparations—so that his personal credit, once so high, had entirely vanished. Also, in his absence "his house in Venice had burned,"[56] and he worried about the future. His sapped strength made him fear a return to the malarial climes of Trent, and he implored the Emperor to send him elsewhere. "The almost seven years I served Your Majesty in Venice have greatly damaged my health. Since that climate, and that of Trent, do not agree with my disposition, I implore Your Majesty to let me serve elsewhere where I can give you better service. I am determined to serve Your Majesty as long as I live, but I must guard my health to be able to do so."[57]

At last Mendoza felt well enough to take on all his duties, and he arrived in Trent on May 25. In June, when he started to attend the sessions, the Council was discussing the problem of "good works," and the connected question, whether "justification" could be attained by faith alone, as Protestantism asserted it could. When he

[53] Mocenigo to Venice, March 23, 1546, *Ven. Dep.* I, 441–443.

[54] Cardinal Jaén, February 4, 1546, Arch. Sim., Est., leg. 1463, Rose-file. See also Massarelli, March 18, 1546, *Diaria* I.

[55] Mendoza to Charles V, April 27, 1546, Arch. Sim., Est., leg. 1463, Rose-file.

[56] Mendoza to Charles V, March 1546, Arch. Sim., Est. Ale. 642, Rose-file.

[57] Mendoza to Charles V, Padua, April 8 and 27, 1546, Arch. Sim., Est., leg. 1463, Rose-file.

left Trent on December 3, after seven months, the Council had not yet finished with the subject.

Although the Spanish-Imperial faction insisted on the discussion of reform, the legates succeeded in achieving a compromise: it was agreed that "dogma" and "abuses" be treated simultaneously by separate committees and be presented in the Council alternately. Paul III was furious about this settlement, but the legates reminded him that they could always lengthen the discussion on dogma so as to receive his opinion on questions of reform that were under consideration at the same time. This gave rise to the saying that "unlike previous Councils when the Holy Spirit used to come from Heaven, in this Council it comes by mail from Rome."[58] Moreover, the "abuses" to be discussed were not those of which the Emperor wanted to hear: the abuses in Rome "to close the mouths of the Protestants."[59] Instead, the Council chose to examine the multiple possession of bishoprics by absent beneficiaries—an abuse the Spaniards themselves were as guilty of as the others. As Don Diego had predicted, the Pope remained the victor in every respect.

Soon the differences between Charles V and Paul III widened still further. With the Emperor's military successes in Germany, his intransigence and haughtiness increased. This, in turn, made the Pope more resentful, especially since the problem of Milan was being revived. The Pope had looked on with restraint when Milan did not come under French rule because of the death of the French prince whose marriage gift it was to have been. He had waited a while after the Marquis of Vasto died in March, 1546. But in April, when the Emperor appointed Ferrante Gonzaga as his new Milanese governor, the Pope's fury rekindled. Until then, Paul III had been nursing hopes that Milan would somehow come to his grandson Ottavio and his and the Emperor's common progeny. Instead, in that coveted place of power he now saw Gonzaga, an enemy of the House of Farnese.

In Germany the Pope's disagreements with Charles V were equally grave. Paul III called the German war a religious war for the suppression of heresy—only under this concept would he be prepared to assist. Yet he feared that the Emperor's success would increase his power. But Charles V, with some of the Lutheran

[58] Mocenigo to Venice, March 29, 1546, *Ven. Dep.* I, 449.
[59] Charles V to Mendoza, June 23, 1546, Arch. Sim., Est. Ale. 642, Rose-file.

princes on his side, tried to avoid all religious references in connection with the war. Though he did not disdain the use of papal money and papal Italian armies, he was intent only on subduing the rebellious German princes under his civil sovereignty. Therefore he still wished to refrain from offending the Protestants when the Papals were planning to do what would offend them most—to move the Council away from Trent.

The papal party was becoming restless in Trent. Prices had inflated; provisions were often difficult to get; troop transports clattered by on the old Brenner road, upsetting the scholarly atmosphere of Trent and making life unpleasant. The climate was notoriously unhealthy, and at last some cases of pestilence were advanced as the official reason for a transfer to Bologna, but this was not to happen until after Don Diego's departure.

While he was there, in the second summer, the demands for a change of locality were already urgent. Cardinal Santa Croce took the lead in arguing for the transfer. In July, some prelates hired barges, had their belongings loaded on board, and were prepared to depart, but the Cardinal of Trent sent the boats away and forbade the prelates to leave. Santa Croce raised a great scandal, accusing the Imperials of wishing to deprive the Council of its freedom. This, he said, now made it decisive for them to move away.[60]

When Charles V heard of this he flew into one of his famous rages. Just as, at the Cortes in Toledo in 1538, he had threatened to throw the leader of the obstinate Spanish grandees down the stairs, he now wrote to Don Diego that the Cardinal ought to be put in a sack and thrown into the Adige.[61] (This method of drowning was the customary punishment for mutineering soldiers on armadas.) Don Diego duly transmitted his Emperor's angry words to the Cardinal, whom he respected as a Greek scholar and to whom he always lent his books. Sarpi records this as if the rage, the idea, and the words were Don Diego's,[62] but it is unlikely that Mendoza

[60] Mendoza and Toledo to Charles V, July 19, 1546, Arch. Sim., Est., leg. 1463, Rose-file.

[61] Holograph memo from Mendoza, November 2, 1546, "that Charles V would order *ensacar* [Santa Croce] *y echar en el rio* . . . ," Arch. Sim., Est., leg. 1463, Rose-file.

[62] Paolo Sarpi, *Istoria del Concilio Tridentino*, II, 322.

shared his master's opinion to the same extent. (The Emperor never forgave the Cardinal, a fact that cost Santa Croce the papacy in 1550.) Mendoza was able to understand the legates' dissatisfaction with Trent, even if he did not admit it to their faces.

In September it was already known that the Emperor was doing well in the German war. His authority sufficed to have the Council for the time being stay where it was, though ill feeling increased on both sides. In October the Emperor received the balance of the papal monetary contribution. Mendoza had gone to Venice, personally taking out the 100,000 gold pieces that Paul III had deposited in a Venetian bank for Charles V; he returned to Trent on October 13 with this load (probably carried on several pack mules) to hand it over to Imperial messengers. Now the Pope bitterly regretted any help he had given. He broke the alliance, recalled his Italian troops from Germany, and made no further contribution to the Emperor's war.

From the moment Don Diego was certain of his new appointment to Rome, his mood improved together with his health. On August 28 he talked with Massarelli about his forthcoming move. They discussed where Mendoza could have a garden in Rome, and once more, even though the Emperor was enraged about Santa Croce, Don Diego gladly lent the scholarly Cardinal seventeen Cyrillic books.[63] On October 30 he wrote to the Bishop of Arras as gaily as he had written to Cobos during his first years in Venice:

I have nothing to write to Monseñor my father nor to you; only that I am well. There is no need to thank you for the favors you are doing me, because I am your creation [*hechura*]; it would be like falling into the error of the jug of Saint Paul: "*Nunquid*" *dicit vas figulo* ["maybe" said the vessel to the potter]. This bit of theology I learned after the theme of justification was discussed. This [discussion] is proceeding so slowly that we have not yet resolved what [Duns] Scotus wanted, because we do not wish to go on without making it known. Incidentally, Cardinal Grimani left for hell the other day, by post. There is nothing else to say.[64]

"Monseñor my father" refers to the Bishop of Arras' father; the Bishop's parents were always "my father and my mother" to Men-

[63] Massarelli, *Diaria* III, August 28, 1546.
[64] *AC*, pp. 112, 113.

doza. In courtesy, Don Diego called himself Arras' "younger broth-er" (although he was about fourteen years older than Arras). The elder Granvelle, in his turn, addressed Don Diego as *mi hijo*.[65] He loved and protected him, and so did his son who substituted for his father during the latter's occasional absences from the court. After Granvelle's death in August 1550, the Bishop of Arras advanced to the first position among the Emperor's ministers. Arras (later to become Cardinal Granvelle) was possibly the most versatile politi-cian of the mid-sixteenth century. His mind formulated and mas-tered the intricate relations within and without the Empire as easi-ly as he spoke and wrote the six principal languages required in the vast domain: French, Latin, Spanish, Italian, German, and Dutch. He proved to be a true friend of Mendoza, even in the times of the latter's greatest adversity. The two Granvelles, as well as Cobos, naturally favored Don Diego's new appointment, although the Emperor did not need much prodding this time. Charles V said that he wished he could divide Don Diego in half, sending one part to Rome and leaving the other in Venice.[66]

There was a last round of social gatherings with the Cardinals of Trent, Del Monte and Santa Croce, including Cardinal Farnese, who had passed through Trent again. Don Diego continued to cul-tivate friendly relations with the latter, whom he considered his most important future link with his grandfather, the Pope. Then Mendoza left Trent for good on December 3, 1546.

On the ninth, looking back at the Council from Venice, he once more described to the Emperor how "furiously" the prelates dealt with the subject of religion, and how greatly they were moved by self-interest.

This is shown by what happened to the article of Justification, and it was obvious already when they were discussing Original Sin, the Con-ception of Our Lady, and the Justification about the certainty of Grace. In each case, so much fury and graft was noticeable, and so little devo-tion where it should have been, that one can easily judge what is going to happen in this Council from what has been going on.

Because in things of religion one has to say what one feels even

---

[65] For example, Granvelle to Mendoza from Brussels, year 1548 (no date), in Arch. Sim., Est., leg. 503, Rose-file.

[66] Charles V to Mendoza, Arch. Sim., Est. Ale. 644, Rose-file.

without being asked, and because I leave the office of the Council to serve Your Majesty elsewhere, I am writing this to relieve my conscience so frankly, wishing to remind you of the troubles likely to occur.[67]

While Don Diego prepared to leave for Rome, no successor to his post had been appointed as yet, but Cobos and Granvelle were urging the Emperor in favor of Mendoza's relative, Don Juan Hurtado de Mendoza, who had served for a year and a half as his assistant. The nomination of Don Juan (a cleric; as a grandson of Don Diego's homonymous Cardinal-uncle he was his second cousin) had been left uncertain for a long time because it was widely known that—though an affable man, now forty, and unusually handsome —he did not measure up to his cousin in ability. In the end, his rank, name (his illegitimate descent was played down), and the wishes of Don Diego and his relatives decided the Emperor in favor of Don Juan, whom he liked as a person.[68] The secretary, Montesa, who had carried on alone very well during Don Diego's absence and who remained in charge until Don Juan would take over later in the year, was a much more experienced official, possessing an excellent, brilliant style not unlike Don Diego's own. But though a noble, his lineage was less illustrious, and so, apparently, unsuited to become an ambassador himself as long as an alternative was available. Montesa continued to work for Don Diego in Rome.

Before Mendoza's departure, he met his brother Don Bernardino in Venice. The admiral was stopping there on his way from Sicily, bringing huge sums of money from that kingdom to court for the war effort. One of his sons, Don Antonio, had come with his father to accompany his uncle and serve him in Rome.

When Don Diego said farewell to the Signoria, he was presented with a parting gift, two thousand ducats. He in turn gave them another warning that they should not accept any offers from the Strozzi and the French. He assured them of the eternal friendship

[67] Mendoza to Charles V, December 9, 1546, Arch. Sim., Est., leg. 1318, fol. 150.

[68] Don Juan's descent is in Luis Vilar y Pascual, *Diccionario* histórico, genealógico *y heráldico de las familias ilustres*, vol. V. On his appearance, Alvise Mocenigo, July 30, 1546, in *Ven. Dep.* I, 602. On his ability, Cobos to Granvelle, May 18, 1546, doubts that Don Juan de Mendoza has ability for the post at Venice. Arch. Sim., Est. Castilla 73, Rose-file.

of his Emperor, and, as was customary for retiring ambassadors, he wrote a comprehensive information about Venice for his master. It is a detailed report about the finances, navy, port conditions, internal politics of Venice, and about its relations with King Ferdinand, France, the Turks, and the Pope. The latter, not surprisingly, gets the worst treatment: "They [the Venetians] take the Pope for a man of bad conscience, utterly untrustworthy, and a miser. He wanted to cheat them twice."[69]

Settling his accounts of the Embassy, he found a balance of 408½ goldpieces left over in favor of the Emperor. Proudly, he added the money bags to Don Bernardino's cargo. He dispatched his staff to Rome ahead of him (probably about a hundred people), equipment, and horses. With only a few companions and an escort of twelve men on horseback, he himself traveled "by post."[70]

Now that he was looking forward to a different life in lay dress, he would have long since discarded all thoughts of gaining the papacy for himself. He expected, however, wider activities, grandeur, titles, and perhaps wealth. It seems that he was no longer satisfied with the prudent middle way that once had appeared so attractive to him when he described his ideal way of life to Don Luis de Avila.[71] He knew for certain that he would now wield great power throughout Italy. Venice, for all its importance, was more peripheral in Imperial interest. Now he would be in the heart of world politics: it was to be a tremendous change. The Republic had been a stable background. He would be transplanted from his field of, largely, contemplation (that he had once praised as the state to be preferred)[72] onto a field of incessant political action. The continu-

---

[69] AC, p. xxv.

[70] GP III, 325, 326.

[71] Speaking about the two extremes of people, phlegmatic or wildly ambitious:
  . . . lo vno y lo otro me parece
  dos estremos que están lexos del medio.
  Tomemos el camino que se offrece,
  ni maderos espesos sin sentido,
  ni fuego que en la llama desuanece . . .
from "Epístola a Don Luis de Avila," in C. Malcolm Batchelor, ed., A tí, Doña Marina, p. 166; this poem dates from 1539/40.

[72] Cf. "Epístola IX, a don Diego Lasso de Castilla," GP III, p. 98.
  Dulce ver es de tierra un bravo viento,
  que levanta la mar alta y hinchada,

ous flow of intra-Italian relationships would cause the very soil under his feet to shift. If, until now, he had kept things stirred up in the tangle of Spanish and French politics, he would now plunge into a never-ending turmoil of the same forces over a much wider area. There would be less time for study. Despite his illnesses, despite his struggle with "poverty," Venice had served him to perfect himself. Ready to step over the threshold, he was now in good health, and all his former debts were paid. (True, he took up a new bank loan of nine thousand escudos in order to pay the Venetian debts and to equip himself to arrive in Rome in style.)[73]

Did it occur to him, by then, that he had really been unable to carry out the ostensible objectives of his different missions? In England, the royal marriages had not come to pass; in Venice, the Republic had not continued in the Turkish war; in Trent, he could not prevent the discussion of dogma, nor had he prevailed into steering the examination of abuses onto the subject of Rome itself. But his master knew that he always ordered him to cope with impossibilities. More often than not, his missions were nothing but feints —these were the core of Imperial service. Mendoza had learned to excel in bluffing; he was a master of delaying tactics; his personal prestige and social grace were unsurpassable; his reports, perspicacious and comprehensive, were incomparable. On December 21, 1546, when he started out on his transfer to Rome, on the way to greater reputation, he was at the summit, but he did not know it then.

sacando las arenas del cimiento.
Entre las altas ondas trabajada,
una pequeña fuste abandonarse,
que en breve será rota o anegada.
Ver sin peligro nuestro menearse
y caminar con fiero continente,
los bravos escuadrones afrontarse.
No porque el mal ajeno te contente,
mas porque en la verdad es dulce cosa
carecer del color que el otro siente . . .

[73] Mendoza to "Monseñor." "I have borrowed six thousand escudos, and three thousand more which I already owed, in order to straighten out my affairs and go to Rome in an appropriate way . . . ," Arch. Sim., Est., leg. 1318, Rose-file.

7. IMPERIALISM IN ACTION, 1547–1549

> You are the Emperor. You have the same
> right to Italy as to Flanders and to Spain
> and consequently to all the world.
> Don Diego to Charles V[1]

The Political Situation in 1547

THE YEAR 1547 was one of great changes. Spanish power and prestige suddenly reached new heights. Charles V defeated his rebellious German subjects at Mühlberg. His life-long antagonist Francis I died, and so did Henry VIII, who was sometimes his friend, more often his foe. The new balance of power in favor of the Emperor drove fear into the hearts of still independent or currently neutral states. Fear gave rise to such countermeasures as the sudden transfer of the Tridentine Council—in defiance of the Emperor's wishes—to Bologna, the attempt at rebellion against Imperial rule by the Fieschi in Genoa and the people of Naples, and the endeavor of the Pope to form a defensive league with Venice and France.

On this pinnacle of Spanish power, exposed to the corresponding rise in anti-Spanish feeling, intrigues, and revolts, Don Diego was now called upon to play a significant part in sustaining his master's unwelcome hegemony over Italy. He was perhaps the most

[1] *BAE* XXI, part one, p. xxii.

outspoken defender of Imperialist aspirations. Charles V was re-emphasizing the power of his crown with the mailed fist. Though his victory proved to be ephemeral, for the moment the Emperor succeeded in forcing the German princes to bow to his will. At the same time, he aimed at putting teeth into the ancient links of vassalage with his Italian feudatories. Feudalism is supposed to have disappeared in the sixteenth century, but Spanish power, that young power just born with the century, in fact revived feudal law. In the hands of the Emperor, for the first time Spanish power was used to provide feudalism with these new teeth. From now on it would be Don Diego's role to show the teeth and, if he thought it advisable, to bite.

A portion of the many changes of this year occurred already during the three months and a half Mendoza spent on the way to Rome. He had been expected there about twenty days after his departure from Venice, but he took his time, remaining for longer or shorter intervals in Mantua, Bologna, Florence, Campiglia Marittima, Piombino, and Pisa, gaining the papal Urbs only by Easter, April 11. The delay occurred because the Emperor had commanded him to effect some rearrangement of Italian geography on his way. The map of Italy showed a far-from-satisfactory face according to the Spanish-Imperial point of view. Charles V, whom Mendoza had scolded a few years earlier for not having added "one stone" to his heritage,[2] now was determined to make up for lost time, and to start, he charged this fervent advocate of his expanding imperialism to contribute to his aggrandizement.

There was little that the Emperor could do—short of war—with the only completely independent states, Venice and the Papal States. That Charles V shared frontiers with both these supposedly neutral entities made for a complex and delicate situation. Suspicion, subversion, inclination toward the French side, caused endless problems, requiring endless watchfulness.

In the rest of fragmented Italy, the Spanish crown so far possessed the Kingdom of Naples, the Kingdom of Sicily, and the Spanish *presidios* (naval bases) along the Tyrrhenian Sea. The State of Milan nominally still an Imperial fief, had been made a crown land of the Spanish heir, Prince Philip; it was currently

2 Ibid.

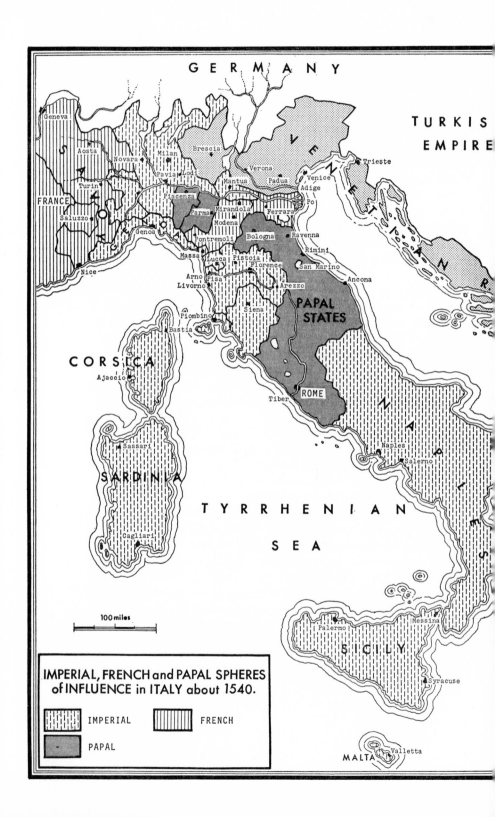

IMPERIAL, FRENCH and PAPAL SPHERES
of INFLUENCE in ITALY about 1540.

IMPERIAL   FRENCH

PAPAL

ruled by Ferrante Gonzaga as Imperial governor. The rulers of a number of still-sovereign states, persuaded of a greater advantage in being on the Imperial side, were loyal allies of the Emperor: Mantua, Genoa, and Florence. In addition, there were still many apparently independent city-states whose status was that of Imperial feudatories without a tie to Spain: the Republic of Siena, the Republic of Lucca, the small principality of Piombino, and scores of other small medieval units—individual hill towns in the possession of fiery clans, but most of them were destined to be flattened under the Spanish-Imperial steamroller.[3]

The focus of French power in Italy was represented by Piedmont, Piacenza and Parma, the duchies of Ferrara and Modena, and Mirandola (midway between Ferrara and Parma). Though inferior numerically, the "French" places were points of great strategic advantage.

But the Imperials were almost ubiquitous; wherever a Spaniard set foot in Italy, a Spanish military base was nearby. Moreover, the Spanish were able to recruit Italian soldiers, any number, as many as they had money to hire. A Spanish-Imperial ambassador, militarily supported in his natural feeling of superiority, moved through Italy as a legitimate ruler of Italian affairs. It did not occur to him that he was an intruder.

On January 3, 1547, Don Diego was in Mantua, being splendidly entertained by the uncles of Mantua's youthful duke, Cardinal Ercole Gonzaga, then regent, and his brother Don Ferrante, when disturbing news from Genoa told of an uprising against Prince Andrea Doria. It was learned that Doria's nephew lost his life.[4] It was not yet known—the news had traveled too fast—that the revolt had ended prematurely through Count Gianluigi Fiesco's accidental death by drowning. Mendoza, fearing that Genoa would be lost, was ready to return to Venice at once in order to forestall any pos-

---

[3] For example, the tiny state of Massa was involved in a civil war between its ruler, the Marchese di Cibo, who leaned to the French side, and the Marchese's mother, of Imperial inclination: this offered Gonzaga, governor of Milan, a pretext to occupy the rock of Massa with Spanish troops.

[4] Captain Giannettino Doria, who had been too ineffectual at Tunis to catch the pirate-king Barbarossa (1535).

sible anti-Imperial alliance between Venice and France[5]—this was the first thought to occur to the Imperial side as a potential consequence, should the French regain Genoa. But as there were no more reverberations at the moment, Don Diego remained for a time with the Gonzagas. Here began his close cooperation with Don Ferrante, which was to last through the coming five years.

Mendoza knew Gonzaga a long time; they were together in Rome at (or before) the time of the sack, in Bologna for the Emperor's coronation, and also in Tunis. Ferrante Gonzaga had entered the service of Charles V in 1523 as a youth of seventeen. In succeeding years he acquired military glory by saving Naples from the French for his master and by beating down the Republic of Florence. His brilliant dash in leading the decisive attack against the Turks before the capture of Tunis had raised Gonzaga's military reputation still higher. When, subsequently, as governor of Sicily, he had shrewdly and ruthlessly overcome the mutiny of the Spanish troops, he made himself ever more appreciated as the Emperor's favorite he was said to have been.[6] He was primarily a soldier—a profession that Don Diego, though no mean captain himself, insisted to be alien to himself. Yet their personalities must have been somewhat akin. They were of the same generation, Gonzaga only two or three years younger. Mendoza addressed him as he did none of his other correspondents, with an equal measure of trust, camaraderie, and respect, but without flattery. He had loved and trusted Cobos, his former protector, but in writing to him, Don Diego always took good care to flatter the older, powerful man. To Arras, in turn, he wrote courteously, ingratiatingly, but here Don Diego was the older; at any rate, his tone toward the young Bishop remained relatively reserved. To the Duke of Alba, friend of his youth, he spoke frivolously, throwing in a dash of derision that smacked of contempt.[7] But to Gonzaga he spoke as plainly as if he were speaking to himself. (Here, even the venerated elder Gran-

---

[5] Mendoza to Charles V, January 5, 1547, Arch. Sim., Est., leg. 1465, Rose-file.

[6] Contemporary historians explained Charles V's unusual predilection for Gonzaga through the almost identical horoscope of both men. See G. Gosellini, *Vita dell illustrissimo . . . Ferrando Gonzaga*, folios 1, 2, and 3.

[7] *AIH* 2 (1911): 537; see also MSS in *Biblioteca Nacional*, MS 10459, Jj-86 (Cartas a diferentes personas), p. 63.

velle was only *el viejo*, and the Bishop of Arras, *el de Arras*.)[8] The fact that Gonzaga was not his patron but only a colleague and that Gonzaga depended, as he himself did, on the court's favor, may have had something to do with this straightforward attitude.

Both, also, were younger sons of princely families: Gonzaga's father, Marquis of Mantua, and his maternal antecedents, the Ferrarese ducal House of Este (his mother was the celebrated Renaissance woman Isabella d'Este), were on a par with the Mendoza and Pacheco. Don Diego did not need to humble himself in front of his peer. By contrast, in a sort of inverted condescension (or false modesty), he never stopped self-deprecating himself, and even his family, when he dealt with the relatively "low-born," Cobos and the Granvelles. And both Don Diego and Gonzaga attained their highest position in the Imperial service at about the same time, "the pair of prancing proconsuls to whom Charles had harnessed his interests in Northern Italy."[9] Gonzaga's predecessor as governor of Milan and commander of the Spanish armies in Italy, the Marquis of Vasto, had been somewhat superior in rank to the erstwhile ambassador in Venice. Don Diego's new location in the hub of Italy was now to give him a status equal in all-Italian affairs with Gonzaga, as also with the Duke Cosimo de' Medici of Florence —the next stop on his trip—and with the Viceroy of Naples, Don Pedro Alvarez de Toledo.

The Imperial "axis," running north-south through Italy, now was to read: Gonzaga in Lombardy, Cosimo in Tuscany, Mendoza in Rome with encroachments into southern Tuscany, and Don Pedro de Toledo in Naples. (Prince Doria and Ambassador Figueroa in Genoa formed a western buttress, but in the "neutral" east, Venice, Ambassador Don Juan de Mendoza was hardly more than an Imperial listening post.) The foursome presented a more or less united front, but it did not take long to fall apart behind the scenes.

Duke Cosimo I de' Medici

On January 30, when Mendoza, accompanied by his nephew Don Antonio, his special guest Martin Pérez de Ayala, a Spanish scholar, and his small escort, arrived in Florence, he seemed to

[8] Mendoza to Gonzaga, March 1550, *AIH* 2 (no. 19); 271–273.

[9] E. Armstrong, *The Emperor Charles V*, II, 173.

have no greater friend in the world than his host. Duke Cosimo and Duchess Eleonora (de Toledo, daughter of the Viceroy of Naples and a distant relative of Don Diego) received him warmly. The Duke gave him the freedom of his possessions—lodgings and feastings at magnificent hilltop castles throughout his part of Tuscany as "though for his own person."[10]

But this charming host was Cosimo I, whom the Emperor's imprudent step had made into a real power; the same Cosimo who had always sent bravi to Mendoza at Venice, reminding him to have the hapless fugitive killed, so that the responsibility for an ignoble deed would fall on Don Diego. At another time, this Duke, so strong and wealthy, had refused Mendoza the simple courtesy of the loan of a book. Once, for his work with the Council, Mendoza wished to consult a rare treatise on heresies from the San Lorenzo Library in Florence, the sort of material needed to elucidate doubtful points. He had not intended to keep the book but only to have two of his scribes copy it.[11] It was a trivial demand, but Cosimo's curt refusal to furnish him with ammunition was significant—although, so far, it was only a question of spiritual ammunition.

This second Duke in the line of Medici rulers is often presented as misunderstood and much maligned. At best, he is talked of as an enigma. Was he the God-fearing, justice-loving, model husband and devoted father he appears to have been by the pens of his apologists? Or was he the tyrant over his people, avenger and murderer not only of his political foes but also of his son and, perhaps, his wife? Eleonora died during an epidemic in 1562, only a few days after the death of two of her sons, young Cardinal Giovanni and Don García. This event gave rise to the popular belief that García, having killed his brother during a hunt, was slain by his enraged father, who may have done away with the Duchess, too; the legend concedes, however, that she might have died of grief.

Cosimo was, in short, held capable of every crime, including incest with his daughters. Modern scholarship, while admitting that he killed one of his servants by his own hand, attempts to trace his

[10] Mendoza to Charles V, February 19, 1547, Arch. Sim., Est., leg. 874, Rose-file.

[11] Mendoza to Cosimo I, December 17, 1544 and January 7, 1545, Arch. Flor., Mediceo 2965, Rose-file.

base reputation to slanders fabricated by Florentine political exiles in Rome.[12] It is more likely that the violence of his access to power lost him the people's confidence. Foreign (Imperial) troops established him, and though he was only seventeen or eighteen, he had as many Florentines of his opposition beheaded as he could reach.

His source of strength was his dukedom in the heart of Italy, the Tuscany he protected, whose grandeur he personified and ever tried to increase. He had come into its possession as much by accident as by the grace of Charles V. The Emperor's troops had defeated the last attempts of Florentine citizens to preserve their republican government; this enabled Charles V to transform the ancient and proud city-state, the Athens of Italy, into a dukedom that was practically a Spanish dependency. In 1532, the Emperor installed Alessandro as first Duke of Florence. Last Medici of the patrician family's main line and illegitimate son of Lorenzo de' Medici, Duke of Urbino, Alessandro was married in 1536 to Charles V's daughter, Margaret of Austria. When Alessandro was murdered in 1537, his cousin Cosimo, scion of a junior branch of the Medici, did not advance automatically to the vacant throne. Without the help of Spanish troops, he would not have had a chance against the anti-Imperial faction of his own realm.

At first Cosimo's foes regarded the young man as a contemptible tool in the hands of a foreign power. The expatriate Florentines (including members of his own family, such as Cardinal Salviati) hated him. Nobles of more ancient rank who had inherited their ducal titles, like the Este of Ferrara, disdained Cosimo for not belonging to the traditional aristocracy. (Cosimo was to quarrel with the Este about precedence until he would succeed, a few years before his death, in being made a *granduca*.) The Venetians snubbed him, tacitly not recognizing Cosimo's dignity as being legitimate; they negotiated with him only through a secretary, never through

---

[12] On the slaying of Cosimo's son, see Aldo Manucci, *Vita di Cosimo I dei Medici Granduca di Toscana*, p. 179. Adulatory views of Cosimo are Lorenzo Cantini, *Vita di Cosimo de' Medici*; Bernardo Segni, *Storie Fiorentine*, II, III; Riguccio Galluzzi, *Storia del Granducato di Toscana*, I, II; Cecily Booth, *Cosimo I*; and the introduction and comments to *Lettere* of Cosimo I de' Medici, ed. G. Spini. Examination of all slanders, based on documents, is in Guglielmo Enrico Saltini, *Tragedie Medicee domestiche*. A more sober view on Cosimo is Edmund G. Gardner, *The Story of Florence*.

a senator.[13] Haughty noble Spaniards, especially one of them, con-
descended to him ("from a fake duke he was made a real duke,"[14]
and "who was angling for tadpoles when Your Majesty made him
duke").[15] But Cosimo proved his own strength and sagacity. He not
only preserved his precarious throne but also grew on it to a power
ultimately respected if not feared by Spanish, French, and Popes
alike—as Mendoza put it, "the vulture of Castile."[16]

In 1547, after ten years of his rule by military dictatorship,
having made himself independent of direct Spanish intervention
and supervision by buying (in 1543) the Spanish fortresses in
Florence, Pisa, and Livorno from the Emperor, Cosimo nevertheless held firmly to the side of Charles V. Until now, his interests—
animosity toward the Farneses, the French, and the Florentine
fuorusciti, and a close alliance with his father-in-law, the Spanish-
Imperial Viceroy of Naples—coincided with the Emperor's. He had
not yet increased his territory, however. Now the first opportunity
to do so was coming his way (so he thought) in the person of Don
Diego, who was bringing in his pocket the proposed rearrangement
of the map of Italy by "the Piombino affair."

The "Piombino Affair"

The small sovereign State of Piombino by the Tyrrhenian Sea,
inhabited by fourteen hundred taxpaying heads of families who
contributed a yearly revenue of eighteen thousand ducats from
their work in the salt mines and alum industries, had been in the
hands of the Appiani family for two hundred years. Their proud
castle rose from crenelated walls on top of the highest cliff of its
splendid sea coast with its natural harbor and gigantic natural
bulwarks.[17]

---

[13] Mendoza to Prince Philip, September 10, 1552, Arch. Sim., Est. Genoa
1382, Rose-file.

[14] ". . . haberle hecho, de duque de burlas, duque de veras . . . ," BAE XXI,
part one, p. xxii.

[15] ". . . su M.t le hallo a el pescando ranas quando le hizieron Duque . . .,"
Mendoza to Arras, May 20, 1551, AC, p. 243.

[16] ". . . y cada dia echa un clauo mas a la deuda, y harasse el açor de Castilla
. . . ," instruction of Mendoza to Ximénez for Charles V, April 14, 1552, AC,
p. 334.

[17] . . . está pegada sobre ella [la muralla] . . . (". . . stuck on the wall . . ."),
Mendoza to Charles V, February 19, 1547, Arch. Sim., Est., leg. 1465, fol. 192–

This tiny state was coveted by the Duke of Florence, who based his claim on services his troops had rendered in Piombino's defense. Piombino owed him fifty thousand ducats for expenses Cosimo had incurred in repairing its decrepit fortifications. Some years back, during the life of Jacopo V of the Appiani (who had married Cosimo's maternal aunt, Elena Salviati), the Duke of Florence had alerted the Emperor to the supposed dangers of Turkish attacks on this poorly defended coast.

The Emperor, liege lord of this "noble and free feudatory," resented its independence. Piombino interrupted the "golden chain" of Spanish-ruled ports and forts from Genoa to Naples.[18] Irritated by Cosimo's warning, Charles V conceived the idea of the *permuta* of Piombino, that is, moving the Appiani to another, strategically less important, Spanish-ruled territory in the Duchy of Milan or the Kingdom of Naples. But the Appiani clung to their possession. After the death of the old Signore in 1545, whose son and heir (Cosimo's first cousin Jacopo VI) was then a boy of thirteen, the Duke began to prod the Emperor once more about Piombino, while Genoa supported the Appiani. The Emperor found that the disagreeable business was becoming increasingly complicated through so much interference; finally the affair turned into a contest of strength between the Emperor and Cosimo on one side, and Cosimo's aunt, Elena, who was determined not to yield an inch, on the other. Charles V hoped now that Mendoza's personal intervention would solve the problem.

This was why Don Diego, on November 8, 1546, when he was still in Trent, received his master's orders to visit Piombino on his way to Rome to persuade the mother of the young Signore of Piombino to give up their state. Surely Don Diego, who with such success had stood firm for the Emperor's interests and prestige in Venice and Trent, would be able "with your customary good judgment, dexterity, and good manner" to cope with one poor old woman—

---

195. Pinturicchio painted this old castle in his fresco in the Libreria Piccolomini of the Siena Cathedral, *Enea Silvio Piccolomini Departs for the Council of Basel.* Piombino was Enea Silvio's (the later Pope Pius II) port of departure. See R. J. Mitchell, *The Laurels and the Tiara*, pp. 51, 52. Anton Henze, *Das grosse Konzilienbuch,* p. 183, in describing this landscape as a "dreamscape" and "unreal" is not aware that Piombino is rendered there quite realistically.

18 *AC*, p. 260.

although the Duke of Florence had already warned him of his aunt's "devilish nature."[19] At once, Mendoza studied all aspects of the problem. He found how indebted the little principality was to the Duke of Florence and advised Charles V (still from Venice) that, on claiming the state, His Majesty should "pretend" (*fingendo*) his intention to pay those debts to Cosimo.[20]

When Cosimo gave his visitor the run of all his realm, praising his work as *amorevole* and *gentile*, telling him that he "loved him,"[21] he was trying to persuade, or thought he had convinced, Don Diego that for the security of the Emperor it was he, Cosimo, to whom Piombino should be ceded. Mendoza left the Duke in this belief. It is unlikely, though, that he was in favor of contributing to an increase in Cosimo's power (according to his opinion of the Duke that we saw above). "Whoever holds Piombino will be master of Rome,"[22] he said on another occasion. At any rate, his powers of persuasion failed him with the Signora de' Appiani, who had to bear his visit in February.

Madonna Elena Salviati de' Appiani twice called all her subjects together on the Piazza, asking them if they would agree to change their lords. The people stood staunchly by her, although every time the Piombinese assembled, Don Diego presumed to address them in behalf of the Emperor.[23] And though he enlisted the help of a Spanish gentlewoman who was lady-in-waiting to the dowager, it was no use.[24] "I am disillusioned now of how little use oratory is," he wrote the Bishop of Arras. "After unpacking all the luggage of Cicero and Aristotle, talking of the spiritual and the temporal, I was unable to persuade an old crone."[25]

---

[19] Cosimo to Mendoza, December 18, 1546, Arch. Flor., Mediceo 9, Rose-file.

[20] Mendoza to Charles V, December 13, 1546, Arch. Sim., Est., leg. 1318, fol. 133.

[21] Cosimo I to Mendoza, February 16 and 21, 1547, Arch. Flor., Mediceo 9, Rose-file.

[22] Mendoza to Arras, February 27, 1547, Biblioteca de Palacio, Madrid (Bibl. Pal.), Rose-file.

[23] Mendoza to Charles V, February 19, 1547, Arch. Sim., Est., leg. 1465, fol. 192–195.

[24] Cosimo I to Mendoza, end of 1546, Arch. Flor., Rose-file.

[25] *AC*, pp. xxvii, 114.

Despite this temporary setback, Mendoza did not dissuade Cosimo from the belief that he was working for his benefit. He returned from Piombino to the Duke's realm, meeting him at Campiglia, Pisa, and other places, where they coordinated their strategy toward the eventual expropriation of the Appiani. The Duke, in turn, preserved toward Don Diego the façade of grateful expectancy, although even then he told his confidant, Don Francisco de Toledo (his wife's uncle and Mendoza's associate from Trent), that "if the matter had been urged more strongly on the Signora of Piombino, a happy outcome might have been gained."[26] And a few months later, when Gonzaga urged the Emperor to send Don Diego as new Imperial governor to rebellious Siena, Cosimo would have preferred someone else.[27] But as soon as he learned that Charles V had confirmed Mendoza's nomination, Cosimo hastened to convey his affection and approval to Don Diego, saying "he has all the necessary qualities to carry out his assignments in Siena."[28]

From the very beginning, then, Cosimo scrutinized Mendoza's every move. He criticized him behind his back—still privately, not yet intriguing at court, as he was to do. He continued to profess friendship for him because, as long as the "Piombino affair" was dragging on, Mendoza remained the only agent through whom he could hope to acquire the state.

Don Diego at first saw no reason to criticize the Duke. The Emperor knew his original opinion of Cosimo—one more reason that he now coordinated both men in his service. It suited Charles V to sow enmity among his vassals; all the better if it already existed between them. From Piombino, Mendoza wrote his master that he had told Cosimo, all that His Majesty wished was "to gratify him, really."[29] This does not mean that either the Emperor or he himself believed their own words.

Soon, Don Diego revealed his view, somewhat guardedly, to Gonzaga. The moment had come when Mendoza was called upon to pacify the Sienese republic. Always in need of Spanish or allied

[26] Francisco de Toledo to Arras, May 22, 1547, Bibl. Pal., Rose-file.

[27] Gonzaga to Charles V, July 22, 1547, Arch. Sim., Est. Milan 1193, Rose-file.

[28] Cosimo I to Mendoza, August 24, 1547, Arch. Flor., Mediceo 10, Rose-file.

[29] Mendoza to Charles V, February 19, 1547, Arch. Sim., Est., leg. 874, Rose-file. See also GP III, 327.

troops to keep those citizens under control, Don Diego was bound to consult with both Gonzaga and Cosimo; the former held the supreme command of all the Spanish armies in Italy; the latter's own troops, theoretically always at the Emperor's disposal, were well prepared, numerous, and close by. Yet, "I do not trust much to the help of the Duke of Florence," Mendoza wrote to Gonzaga on October 26, 1547. "He will not give it when it will be required, and he will let us break our necks. But I believe for sure he acts as a gentleman, without any double-dealing."[30]

Gonzaga agreed but advised Don Diego that "it is necessary to trust in the Duke of Florence, although we may resent it. We even have to disclose His Majesty's plans to him, because his forces are those to help us, since we have no others. You say he will never lend his help graciously: this may well be so, but I believe it would go against his own designs [not to help]." He did not think that Cosimo was as simple a gentleman without double-dealing as Don Diego declared him to be. "I do not believe that he does not understand the Emperor's [Imperialist-annexationist] aims, but, as always, he feigns not to understand. He wishes to appear as though he does not understand, because, if he showed the contrary, he would be unable to refuse to follow the Emperor."

Coming down to practical advice, Gonzaga outlined that "it is necessary to tell him about the general intention of His Majesty, without going into any details, just asking his help. Even though he may give it reluctantly, the main thing is he does give it. We must keep him abreast of happenings and always ask his opinion, not in order to follow it, but so as to be sure of his goodwill until such time as we need it! We will conceal the final strategy from him until you have to tell him. By then he will not be in a position to refuse you assistance."[31]

Dissimulation against dissimulation, within the Emperor's north-south axis! In addition, open differences of opinion were soon to emerge. Even before Mendoza set foot in Siena, Cosimo disapproved of his taking into the Sienese government a certain Milanese, Senator Grasso, disliked by the people of Siena, but favored by Granvelle.[32] Then he thought that Don Diego had made a "weak beginning" of his rule in Siena.[33] A few weeks later, Mendoza left Siena together with the Cardinal of Trent for their combined embassy to the Pope. It was the historic occasion when Charles V summoned Paul III to assist him in offering the Protestants the last chance of coming to the Ecumenical Council (see chapter 9). But Cosimo was not interested in anything outside his own realm. He greatly resented the fact that Don Diego was not instead going to Piombino in his behalf; he went so far as to take Mendoza's trip to the Pope as a personal affront to himself.[34]

In November and December, 1547, Don Diego, in Rome, appeared in dramatic sessions, pleading with Paul III not to obstruct the only remaining opportunity to attempt the reunification of Christendom. On January 23, 1548, he was to deliver the Emperor's great historic "Protest" in the Vatican. But he did his best to satisfy the demands of Cosimo as well. He used the interval of time to return to Piombino, setting out from Rome on December 30. This time he was armed with an ultimatum for the hard-pressed dowager.[35] As soon as Cosimo learned this he adopted his friendliest mien, meeting Don Diego in Volterra on January 10 to discuss the result of his visit with the "old woman."[36]

Almost a year had gone by since all the arguments of Cicero and Aristotle had failed to sway the Signora de' Appiani into abandoning her domain. In the Duke's secret opinion, Mendoza had been too lax. It was said that Don Diego had designs of marrying one of his brother Bernardino's daughters to the young Signore of Piombino. Cosimo might have been the source of this rumor.[37] He himself had once regretted "not having a marriageable relative to give him [the young lord of Piombino]," and Don Diego, perhaps in an impulsive rejoinder, might have said that *he* had a number of

[33] Cosimo I to Francisco de Toledo, October 23, 1547, Arch. Flor., Mediceo 9, Rose-file.

[34] Niccolini to Cosimo I, November 14, 1547, Arch. Flor., Mediceo 1865, Rose-file.

[35] The ultimatum is published in Licurgo Cappelletti, *Storia . . . di Piombino*, pp. 177, 178.

[36] Enclosure from Cosimo I in a letter to the Viceroy of Naples, January 13, 1548, Arch. Flor., Mediceo 9, Rose-file.

[37] See Giambattista Adriani, *Istoria de' suoi tempi*, VI, 381.

nieces.[38] It is true that Don Bernardino had daughters to spare—several of them became nuns—yet this would not have been a reason for Don Diego to be self-seeking in the disagreeable business; he had the strength of character to refuse a cardinalate, marriage with a daughter of the mighty Ascanio Colonna, and other matches endowed with large estates in Italy.[39]

When all former pleas had failed to move the old woman, what means, short of force, could be adopted now? The dowager declared the Imperial determination to be unfair. Anticipating her renewed refusal, Mendoza set her a deadline of twenty days. Within this time she had to deposit the sum of 155,000 ducats as security for the fortifications of Piombino and Elba. (This was over 100,000 more than what Piombino owed the Duke of Florence, but it included the payment of both her late husband's debts and of new works that were declared necessary.) Should the dowager be unable to raise these sums, the Emperor ordered her to state the kind of recompense she would accept in lieu of her property.[40] At the same time, Mendoza ordered Don Diego de Luna, chief of the Spanish garrison at Piombino, to evict the Signora from her castle when the twenty days were over. She was to be forced to reside in the (indefensible) plain.[41]

The dowager remained steadfast. She declared she would rather die poor, but as mistress of Piombino, than live in any other state. But Cosimo now seemed convinced that both the Emperor and Don Diego were coming down to business in his favor. In February, 1548, he wrote to Don Diego as a close, intimate, familiar friend, extremely concerned with his health. He told him domestic incidents of boar hunts and duckshoots and how the family had held solemn funeral services for two of their beloved hounds, the white and the black, and other affectionate messages. With all that, he did not fail to remind Mendoza on the seventh day of February that the twenty-day deadline had now passed, and he urged him to wind up the matter.[42]

[38] Mendoza to Charles V, March 31, 1547, Arch. Sim., Est., leg. 874, Rose-file.

[39] Cf. Mendoza to Arras, September 15, 1551, AC, p. 277.

[40] Agostino Cesaretti, *Istoria del Principato di Piombino*, pp. 126, 127; and Cappelletti, *Storia*, pp. 177, 178.

[41] Riguccio Galluzzi, *Storia del Granducato*, I, 162.

[42] Cosimo I to Mendoza, February 7, 1547, Arch. Flor., Mediceo 9, Rose-file.

Meanwhile the Appiani were offered all the requested sums of money from their Genoese friends (enemies of Cosimo), but the Duke's intriguers at the Imperial court succeeded in counteracting their offer. The pretext, that the neglected estate of Piombino's defenses was an immediate threat to Italy, prevailed. Therefore, one day the Spanish captain presented himself to the Signora. First he urged, then implored her, to get out. "As she did not wish to go unless they forced her, he carried her out together with the chair she sat in."[43]

When this news reached the court, there were immediate repercussions. The Emperor and Granvelle, while still insisting on the takeover of Piombino, did not approve of the lady's eviction.[44] They had hoped that Mendoza would somehow effect a voluntary transfer. In turning the Signora out of her castle he had gone too far: it was bad policy—less so, in the Imperials' opinion, from genuine feelings of chivalry, than from embarrassment in the eyes of other Italian states.

The dowager naturally kept addressing a stream of complaints to the Emperor, so that Don Diego never heard the last of it until she died four years later. More than a year after her eviction, in the face of continuous reproaches, he still had to protect his subordinate's use of force: "He did what I would have done."[45]

Once she was carried out of their ancestral castle, the Signora and her son were reduced, as Piombino's chronicler tells it, to just "two servants," meaning that no more than two visitors (between the ages of six and sixty) were permitted at any time to stay at their palace in the valley with them. Each pair had to leave the premises when another appeared—to prevent the formation of a rebellious group.[46]

It took the Appiani a few months to prepare their next move. The Signora decided to send her son, who was sixteen by now, to the Emperor's court to plead his case in person. Jacopo VI left Piombino in May, sailing to Genoa, where Cosimo's enemies were always ready to assist him. But another visit from Don Diego

[43] Mendoza to Martin Alonso de los Rios, July 15, 1549, *AIH*, II; also Arch. Sim., Est., leg. 1465, Rose-file.

[44] Arch. Flor., C.S. 30, Rose-file.

[45] See note 43, above.

[46] Cappelletti, *Storia*, p. 177; Cesaretti, *Istoria*, p. 128.

would be needed before Madonna Elena herself would leave her territory. By June 8, 1548, Mendoza wrote to Cosimo from Rome that as soon as final orders came from the Emperor he would put Piombino and its castle into the Duke's hands. Mendoza himself would go to carry out the transfer.[47] Cosimo, in his reply of June 10, thought that Don Diego had done the work "divinely."[48]

But before Mendoza could carry out his visit to Piombino, an obstacle arose: the people of Orbetello (the seaport of Siena, seat of a Spanish garrison) revolted, chasing the Spanish out. This was a familiar problem for Imperials; they had learned how to cope with such emergencies. Momentarily, this situation prevented Mendoza from reaching Piombino by sea from Rome, as he had planned. He rearranged his trip to go over land, leaving Rome on June 16, going *por jornada* ("campaign style") until he was halfway, stopping one day in Siena; then he continued *por la bota* by way of Volterra, asking Cosimo to have eight horses ready for him in Volterra, Bibbona, and La Torraccia. At the same time, he sent a Spanish captain with a larger force to Orbetello, who managed to reestablish the Spanish naval base in the wink of an eye.

Between June 18 (still in Siena) and June 24 (back in Siena) Mendoza handled the legal transfer of the State of Piombino to the Duke of Florence. He left its fortresses and government in the hands of Micer Jeronimo Albizis and Lucca Antonio, and he had the Piombinese swear him the oath of fidelity to Cosimo. All in one day (and without our learning any details of his final confrontation with the dowager, who left for exile in Genoa), he finished other matters besides: he rounded up, for example, all the principality's account books, which he carried away with him.[49]

As quid pro quo the Duke had to commit himself to repair Piombino's defenses and to fortify Portoferraio on Elba. But he also had to promise to restore Piombino to the Emperor any time he requested it, provided His Majesty would repay all the sums the Duke had spent and was still spending on the defenses.

[47] Mendoza to Cosimo I, June 8, 1548, Arch. Flor., Mediceo 3095, Milan, Rose-file.

[48] Cosimo I to Mendoza, June 10, 1548, Arch. Flor., Mediceo 11, Milan, Rose-file.

[49] Mendoza to Cosimo I, June 15, 18, and 24, 1548, Arch. Flor., Mediceo 3267 and 1852, Rose-file.

All was well. It seemed that Mendoza had done the greatest possible service to one who might now be his friend forever. Cosimo, at last undisturbed by the obstacles that the dowager had put in his way with the help of the Genoese and also the French, now rushed with enthusiasm into building fortifications. It was then that he created the twin castles on the hills framing Portoferraio on Elba. But although the mills had ground very slowly to afford Cosimo this satisfaction, six to seven years all told, they now started to whirl in mad reverse to deprive him of it. Charles V, who often needed years to make up his mind to follow a certain course, revoked his donation to Cosimo in a matter of days. His confessor Domingo de Soto, who for personal reasons detested the Duke (and, as we know, disliked Don Diego as well),[50] scolded the Emperor for letting Piombino go to the Duke of Florence. The young Lord of Piombino implored Charles V in person.[51] Gonzaga, angered by the entire procedure, considered the transfer of Piombino to Cosimo a mistake.[52] Last but not least, the Genoese offered to repay all of Charles V's debts to Cosimo.

Overwhelmed, the Emperor regretted the entire affair. He hastened to order Don Diego to take everything away from the Duke at once but not to return it to the legal owner. Mendoza himself was told to hold the state in deposit on behalf of Charles V. Never considering that such high-handed treatment might offend the Duke of Florence, the Emperor excused his procedure by declaring that Don Diego, in giving Cosimo possession in the first place, had exceeded his commission.

On July 24, 1548, scarcely four weeks after the takeover, Mendoza's secretary Pedro Ximénez arrived at the Duke's court with the revocation from the Emperor. As was to be expected, Cosimo complained "that he had been put to shame before the world and that his credit had been greatly reduced."[53]

Mendoza now found himself the temporary overlord and governor of Piombino, but this was not, apparently, what he wanted.

[50] Cosimo had expelled De Soto's brethren, the Florentine Dominican friars, who preached against his tyrannical regime, from their convent of San Marco and from San Domenico in Fiesole and elsewhere. On De Soto versus Mendoza, see chapter six.

[51] Galluzzi, *Storia del Granducato*, I, 135–138.

[52] Gonzaga to Charles V, July 18, 1548, Arch. Sim., Est., leg. 1195, Rose-file.

[53] Cosimo I to Mendoza, July 24, 1548, Arch. Flor., Mediceo 11, Rose-file.

At once he asked the Emperor to leave Piombino in Cosimo's hands, and he did his best to reassure the Duke, encouraging him to hope for the success of his intercession. Cosimo's letters continued to be friendly and familiar (as when he advised sweet basil for Mendoza's stomach upsets), and he invited Don Diego to come to Poggio.[54]

Soon, however, the situation required Mendoza to give orders as "superior" to the Duke of Florence.[55] Still, he continued to try to soften the blow to Cosimo's pride. Their correspondence through September and October, 1548, reflects a warm mood. Cosimo was being told that nothing about Piombino was as yet decided, and that it would take some time for the Emperor to make up his mind. Meanwhile Mendoza persisted in his persuasion in favor of the Duke.

During the second half of 1548, Mendoza remained in Siena, where he dealt continually with local unrest, always—rhetorically—asking Cosimo's advice. By the end of the year, the military situation in Tuscany became so unsettled that neither Don Diego nor Cosimo was able to leave his post when every Imperial and their friends in Italy traveled to Genoa to meet Prince Philip. On his first emergence from Spain, the Prince arrived there on his grand tour of the Empire, but the two Lords in Tuscany were conspicuously absent from the welcoming committee.

After almost a year of Imperial procrastination, in June, 1549, there was another crisis regarding Piombino. Apparently, the Emperor, despite financial offers from Genoa (for which he most likely found other use) was unable to provide enough money to repay the Duke. By then, Domingo de Soto, his confessor, continuing to admonish Charles V in behalf of the young Signore of Piombino, had maligned Granvelle, Gonzaga, and Mendoza. Granvelle and Gonzaga now agreed with Mendoza that Piombino must revert to the Duke as long as the Emperor could not pay him back. Mendoza said in Rome, where he had returned in the spring of 1549, that in

---

[54] Cosimo I to Mendoza, August 10, 1548, ibid.

[55] ". . . y esto no se lo hauia rogado sino ordenadoselo como superior, por razon de tener el el puerto y yo el govierno de todo el estado . . . ," Mendoza to Arras, September 15, 1551, *AC*, p. 275.

his opinion the court was keeping Cosimo on tenterhooks purposely in order to get more money out of him in the end.[56]

It appears that, despite their initial mutual distrust, the two Lords in Tuscany had drawn close together during the years of tension and delayed decisions over Piombino. Cosimo must have remained convinced that Mendoza would ultimately enable him to acquire the state. In contrast to his former opinion, he was long since satisfied that Don Diego did not seek the place for himself or his relatives. Their common interest in keeping both the French and the Farneses out of their domains in Italy, as well as their common antipathy to Paul III, still kept their collaboration in harmony.

[56] Don Pedro de Toledo to Cosimo I, June 24, 1549, Arch. Flor., Mediceo 611, Rose-file.

8. ROME, 1547

I am cut out to get into the Popes' hair
Don Diego[1]

First Relations with the Farneses

HAVING TRACED MENDOZA'S PATH so far only as it crossed that of the Duke of Florence, we must return to the year 1547: his arrival in Rome at Easter. By that time Rome had largely recovered from the destruction of the sack of twenty years before. The city had once more become a center for all the refinements of civilization. As far as Don Diego was concerned, there were three different circles among Rome's inhabitants, with cardinals playing leading roles in each.

In the first, the papal court, the reigning House of Farnese, of ancient Roman nobility and always of princely tastes, set a tone more lavish even than that of the luxurious times of the Medici popes.[2] With Michelangelo, at seventy-two, the supreme arbiter of Roman architecture and arts, the city was building, painting, and sculpturing more and better than ever before. The papal court in its magnificence and the courts of several cardinals, almost as sumptuous, patronized literati, scholars, and artists. The cardinals

[1] "Por mi, hecho estoy a andar al pelo con los papas . . . ," Mendoza to Arras, December 14, 1549, *AC*, p. 145.
[2] On Paul III, see Pio Pecchiai, *Roma nel cinquecento*, pp. 49–72; also Carlo Capasso, *Paolo III*.

of the old school, "the rich, old, and dissolute ones" (as Mendoza described them),[3] lived their sybaritic lives as magnates in the world's most profitable business. This was the Rome of gold and purple, of artists and usurers, rich nobles, ambassadors of many nations, and thousands of courtesans. It was the dominant Rome with which Don Diego would deal primarily and whose pretentious standards of luxury he would have to match.[4]

Nestling in the warmth of the first Rome's largesse, tolerated, even overlooked by its carelessness, was the fledgling second Rome of the future Counter Reformation. Ignatius Loyola, the visionary Spaniard, had come there in 1539; he and his companions Láinez and Salmeron had established the Jesuit order in 1540. They agitated, and they watched the increase of their power as the militia for the Holy See. Cardinal Caraffa, like Loyola bent on drastic changes, though not in unison with the Jesuits, had achieved the introduction of the Inquisition in 1542. (Although Caraffa hated the Spaniards and the Emperor ferociously, "Lucifer"—in Don Diego's words[5]—did not mind copying their style of Inquisition.) Several of the younger cardinals, like the Englishman Reginald Pole, and Marcello Cervini (Santa Croce), were of a moral bent, living comparatively saintly lives, aiming at a serious reformation. All were biding their time; none was very loud as yet. A number of them were Spaniards, such as Juan Alvarez de Toledo, Cardinal "Burgos"; occasionally there were fine scholars among them. Don Diego would have individual dealings with these cardinals and Jesuits, but he did not let himself be drawn into the passionate cliques of fierce reformers and fanatical pleasure haters.

[3] Mendoza to Charles V, December 8, 1549, in A. von Druffel, *Briefe und Akten zur Geschichte des 16. Jahrhunderts*, I, no. 355, pp. 313, 314.

[4] Mendoza on Rome: "la plaça de aqui es muy differente de la de las otras partes . . . ," to Arras, May 5, 1551, *AC*, p. 233. "Quiero mas estarme en Granada con miseria perpetua, que tener aqui cierta la verguença en lugar tan señalado . . . ," May 20, 1551, *AC*, p. 245. "No me podiendo sostener sin hazerle [a su majestad] verguença por mi pobreça . . . ," September 15, 1551, *AC*, p. 277. Also, to Don Francisco (de Toledo? unlikely; probably a Mendoza): "la sede vacante me dexo a mi solo sin merced, para que todos [me] mirassen como a bastardo, suplicandole de mi parte que no me tenga por afrentado en la plaza del mundo . . . ," Bibl. Nac., MS 10459, fol. 24.

[5] "[Cardinal Caraffa] . . . es un Lucifer . . . ," *AC*, p. 149; ". . . el diablo," *AC*, p. 162.

The third element in Rome was a conglomeration of all the malcontents in Italy: anti-Spanish exiles from the Kingdom of Naples and the Imperial-minded State of Genoa; anti-Medici and anti-Spanish exiled Florentines; anti-ruling-faction and anti-Spanish Sienese *fuorusciti*. Outlaws all, but since Rome belonged to everyone, their numbers, restless and shifting, kept the city in flux, politics aboil, and peace efforts frustrated. Exiles of all kinds were Don Diego's enemies, because he was colleague and friend of their hated masters. They would keep his life in constant danger, more or less intensely, according to the changing conditions in the various dominions with their intrigues, tensions, rebellions, and wars. Many of these people found protection under the cardinals from their home states (the Florentine exiles, for instance, gathered around the Florentine Cardinals Salviati and Ridolfi), and at this juncture also under the French ambassador and the French cardinals (Tournon, primarily). However, the Imperial-minded Colonna, the greatest Roman family of ancient nobility and Ghibelline tradition, were exiled from the metropolis during the reign of Pope Paul, who had sequestered their estates.

So, when Don Diego took up his post at the Holy See, the pattern of his new surroundings could hardly have been more confused, the general mood toward the Imperials more hostile, nor the dangers lurking at his every step more numerous.

On the advice of his predecessor, Don Juan de Vega, Mendoza tarried on the last part of his way until Easter Monday. He did not want his solemn entry to conflict with the paschal celebrations. Nothing, therefore, detracted attention from his person when he arrived. An ornate procession came to meet him; more than five hundred cavalry, including many cardinals and their households, Cardinal Alessandro Farnese and the Spanish cardinals among them, accompanied him through the streets of Rome to the door of his palazzo facing the Piazza Navona.

The papal city had imagined Don Diego as the cleric in long robes they had heard about when he was in Trent. Now, to everyone's surprise, he appeared in sword, cape, and plumed hat, thoroughly secular, a Spanish knight.[6] The Pope, receiving Mendoza in his first audience on the following day, could hardly conceal his

[6] GP II, 15–18.

annoyance. This change in apparel was immediately understood as the deliberate act of defiance toward Paul III that it was. But His Holiness spoke kind words. He told Don Diego that he had been a friend of his father, the Count of Tendilla, who had held the same position, and that he almost remembered his grandfather who had also come to Rome as Castilian ambassador.[7]

Don Diego was satisfied about the tacit warning that his change of dress gave the Church. The ecclesiastical hierarchy would not humble him, nor would ecclesiastical favor, like perhaps a cardinalate for himself, bribe him away from his exclusive service to Charles V. At the outset, the purpose of his mission had been to prevent the Pope from allying himself with the French, but during the more than three months of his journey, rapid developments had changed the political emphasis. At the time he received his nomination to go to Rome, the Council had not yet moved from Trent, but by his arrival, almost seven or eight months later, it had done so. Now, Mendoza's principal mission was to prevail upon Paul III to let the Council return from Bologna to Trent.

In addition, the general relations between Emperor and Pope were in need of some drastic improvement. The war in Germany had worsened them almost beyond repair, making it advisable to remove Don Juan de Vega. The former ambassador, having borne the brunt of the Pope's anger within the last years, would not be useful in creating a more amiable atmosphere. The Granvelles and Don Diego himself hoped to create a more friendly feeling. Only the Emperor showed himself as nasty as could be to the Nuntius, but he left it to Mendoza's own judgment to set the mood in Rome.[8]

Why had the original alliance between the two potentates faltered? At the beginning of his reign, Paul III had blessed the Emperor's Tunisian campaign. He had contributed to it and had been rewarded by the lock and bolt of the gate of Tunis, the Emperor's gift to "Sanct Peter."[9] He had magnificently received the triumphant crusader on his progression from Sicily to the north of Italy. Since August 27, 1545, Pope and Emperor had been common an-

[7] Mendoza to Charles V, Rome, May 3, 1547, Döllinger, Beiträge, I, 53.

[8] Cf. Charles V to Mendoza, February 11 and March 17, 1547, from Ulm, published by R. Foulché-Delbosc, RH 31 (1914): 133–149.

[9] Ludwig von Pastor, Geschichte der Päpste, V, 161.

cestors to the twin sons—named after each of them, Alessandro
and Carlo—of Ottavio Farnese and Margaret of Austria. And the
old Pope's exertion, in 1538, to effect the Truce of Nice between
Charles V and Francis I, his contribution to the Holy League with
Venice against the Turk, his convocation of the Council of Trent
in 1543 and 1545, as well as his original contribution of men and
money to the war in Germany against the Protestants—all these
were acts of far-sighted politics, of agreement, and of apparently
friendly relations with Charles V.

All would have turned out well had not Paul III shown the ambition of a secular monarch, transgressing into what Charles V held
to be the temporal Empire. One answer to their quarrel is simply:
"Parma and Piacenza"; the wrangle about the possession of these
two city-states was to bring all negotiations between them to nothing. The two contiguous states, in the heart of Italy between Milan
and Bologna, had formed part of the Ecclesiastical States at the
time of the conquest of Rome in 1527, when the Emperor took
them away from Clement VII and added them to the State of Milan,
an Imperial fief, which he let the Duke of Sforza rule as his vassal.
After Sforza died without heirs (1536), Charles V, keeping Milan
for himself from then on, returned the two duchies to the States of
the Church. He did not do so voluntarily, but was prodded by Paul
III, who claimed Parma and Piacenza as former parts of the ancient exarchate of Ravenna. In 1545, however, the Pope took it
upon himself to separate Parma and Piacenza from the Church
States, conferring them as hereditary investitures upon his son Pier
Luigi Farnese. The Emperor was unable and unwilling to condone
this transgression. He had never stopped considering the two states
as possessions of Milan, a fief of the Empire. It was doubtless with
special regard to Paul III's territorial ambition that Charles V now
sent him an envoy who had furiously advised him as early as 1543
to go ahead and strip the Pope of all his secular power.

But despite his dynastic ambitions, Paul III tried to pursue a
true and effective policy of neutrality. He was successful in keeping "the War" from Italy's soil throughout the sixteen years of his
reign, in contrast to the popes who preceded and succeeded him.
(At least, the war resulting from the Imperial murder of Rincon
and Fragoso did not reach further down into Italy than Piedmont.)
But the Imperials refused to understand Paul III's motives. All his

actions touched them in their most sensitive spot, that of their relations with the French. France was the enemy, the basis of Imperial grievances that Mendoza was to lay at the Pope's door.

If his first step, shedding his role as a cleric, was to show Paul III and his court who was his real master, Mendoza's second was to assert the right to recognition of his personal rank. In the protocol of a hierarchically ordered world, precedence was of highest significance. The problem was how close to the Pope was he allowed to sit during religious functions. In clerical habit, his seat would have been with the Governor of Rome. A layman, however, would be treated according to his title, whether duke, marquis, or count. But untitled and not a priest, Don Diego found himself relegated by Rome to the motley group of ambassadors from other states. Losing no time to claim the most honorable seat—at the side of the Pope—Don Diego drew general attention, almost creating a sensation among the diplomatic corps, by not appearing at the first Mass. Yet the scandal was nipped in the bud; Paul III and his close adviser, the young Cardinal Farnese, hastened to humor the newcomer. Against the rules of pontifical etiquette, they granted him the most dignified place. "Be it as it may," Don Diego said, "I have it."[10] Perhaps the Pope's leniency was due to the fact that the Emperor was at the moment so powerful that he did not dare to offend him. Moreover, holding the move of the Council to Bologna as a trump card of his own, Paul III was now satisfied to show himself as kind to his adversary's new envoy. Besides, if Don Diego wanted to, he knew how to make himself irresistible—and so did the Pope.

Then in his eightieth year, Paul III was a living relic of the earlier Renaissance—splendid, corrupt, and pagan—with its mundane, undivided Church. He owed his cardinalate to the Borgia Pope, Alexander VI, who had been his unofficial brother-in-law. When Alessandro Farnese was young, his beautiful sister Giulia was the Borgia Pope's favorite mistress. Now, to be sure, old Farnese's personal debauchery was a thing of the past, hence he was able to pay lip service to the aspirations of the reformers who kept trying to stir his interest. But his real interest belonged to his chil-

10 GP II, 15–18, 59, 60.

dren. Raised in the gentlemanly atmosphere of Italian humanism
—though not a scholar himself—Paul III remained fluent in classical Latin and Greek up to his very last hour. Genuinely courteous
when he wished to be (though, when angry, he had the habit of
"throwing things"), he employed the most cultivated speech, enun-
ciating his well-turned phrases slowly and with measured deliberation. The Pope was no mean antagonist for a Spanish gentleman
who, though two generations younger, was a product of similar
humanist schooling.

In his audiences, Mendoza insisted on bringing up his topic number one, the return of the Council. One of his conversations with
Paul III will serve to illustrate many. At one of their first encounters, Pope and ambassador pledged themselves to tell each other the
whole truth about the reason for their divergent views. Don Diego
named as most compelling his Emperor's promise to the German
people of holding the Council in Trent, a neutral place. The Pope
tried to sidetrack this issue. Emphasizing his great age—"he was
twice as old as Your Majesty, and had fifty-four years of experience in the government of ecclesiastic affairs"—he sought to convince the ambassador of his superior wisdom in Church business.
Admonished to come to the point, he named the "pest" and "famine" as reasons for the transfer, and he belittled the choice of Trent,
since "within two years little or nothing had been achieved there;
nor had any German appeared, whether Catholic or heretic." The
Pope also criticized the fact that Charles V, when he accepted the
surrender of the beaten Protestant princes in Germany, had not
brought up the issue of religion at all, but only that of indemnities,
of hard cash.

Don Diego answered this by explaining that the Emperor's
monetary needs had increased because the Pope had withdrawn
his soldiers from the common enterprise; he also stated repeatedly
that the Germans were lost because they lacked religion. Since the
Pope thought that it was too difficult to conquer them by force,
Mendoza suggested that he do everything else that could be done
to reestablish the Germans in one united religion. Apparently the
Pope, to his own annoyance, was convinced by Mendoza's arguments. Therefore he simply reaffirmed what he said earlier. Then
he proceeded to explain that Bologna was a neutral place because
he, the Pope, was neutral. Don Diego countered this feeble explana-

tion instantly, observing that the Pope's neutrality was between the French King and the Emperor, and not between the Emperor and the Lutherans. At last the Pope offered what he said was his chief reason for the transfer: he felt he could not draw out the Council very much longer because he was old. If he were to die while the Council was in session, it would leave a great schism in the Church. If the Council were sitting in Bologna at such a time, it could be ended quickly there, or the cardinals could make an election on the spot. Don Diego asserted that Trent was just as good for any of such reasons. He reiterated that His Majesty did not consent and did not approve of the transfer, that he objected to any conciliar acts made in Bologna, that the Emperor would hand in a Protest. And since all this seemed to Mendoza himself insufficient new ground, he added a momentary idea of his own: unless the Council returned to Trent, he said, the Germans might call together a separate National Council, and this would mean a schism. With those last words he left the old man, as he reports, in suspense, although the Pope right away said that one could not scare him and would never gain anything from him by trying to do that.

A secondary item concerned the amount of revenue the Pope would allow the Emperor to draw from Spanish churches. Charles V demanded 500,000 ducats. The Pope acted as though the limit were 300,000, but Don Diego succeeded, driving a hard bargain, in raising the amount to 400,000. Cardinal Farnese, who wished to assure the Emperor of his goodwill, assisted him in the financial deal, but advised some softening of his position regarding the Council. Mendoza, relaying everything to Charles V, told his master that it did not seem quite proper to Farnese to treat these two items of business at the same time—on the one hand to ask for money and on the other to oppose the action in Bologna and ask that the Council return to Trent. "They think that, since Your Majesty asks them for money, Your Majesty has to relent somewhat regarding the Council."[11]

Meanwhile the new ambassador was installed in the utmost magnificence within a household that comprised—with embassy staff,

[11] This papal audience and talk with Farnese is in a letter to Charles V, May 3, 1547, Döllinger, *Beiträge*, pp. 53–72.

guests, and servants—about 120 people. The house on Piazza Navona that served him for almost four years as residence and Imperial embassy (at the end of 1551 he moved elsewhere) does not
stand anymore.[12] Piazza Navona is completely changed from its
aspect in the sixteenth century; only its singular shape is the same,
still faintly reminiscent of the elongated horseshoe-pattern of
Dominitian's Stadium. A few landmarks are preserved: the sites,
though not the actual buildings, of Sant'Agnese in Agone and of
the old Spanish Church of San Jacobo (now Church of the Sacred
Heart), and the torso of Pasquin (the famed antique statue to
which the Romans, under cover of darkness, used to affix anonymous lampoons on people "in the news") around the corner. It
was the center of the Spanish colony, and Mendoza's establishment was probably the same that his predecessors had occupied.[13]

Among his first dinner guests was Giovio, who gossiped somewhat superciliously about Mendoza's "militarily Lucullic" cuisine,
with his "half German" cook offering sturgeon, *umbrina*, and *laccia*
with wine sauce; but Mendoza, he adds, was the "most excellent"
host, a man *d'arte di non arte* ("so sophisticated a person as to give
the impression of simplicity"), who "said a thousand bons-mots,
embellishing everything even more than his hangings of gold and
carmoisin did the walls of his second hall."[14]

[12] "La casa de Roma se me hauia acabado y he hecho tomar otra por dos años,
porque en Inglaterra sali de Londres en tomando casa . . . ," Mendoza to Arras,
Siena, January 11, 1552, AC, p. 288.

[13] Cf. Angel González Palencia, *Don Luis de Zúñiga y Avila*, p. 82, where
Avila implies that, in 1539, the ambassador of Charles V, the Marqués de Aguilar, had his house in the vicinity of Pasquin, with "so many people and a tremendous table." In the later sixteenth and seventeenth centuries, the Imperial
and Spanish embassies were still in Piazza Navona (see P. Romano and P. Partini, *Piazza Navona*). Don Diego's walk home from Saint Peter's would take
him by the "Torre di Nona" (still today the Lungotevere *Tordinona*). Gabrielli,
one of the Sienese ambassadors to the person of Mendoza, tells how Don Diego
escorted the tottering old Cardinal of Lorraine, together with the French ambassador, toward the conclave, jokingly remarking: "It is the best possible omen
for the Cardinal to walk along the street between the Imperial and French ambassadors." He then returned with d'Urfé when "together they came to the
Torre di Nona on the usual route to Don Diego's house . . . ," Arch. Siena,
Gabrielli to the magistrate of Siena, dated December 19, 1549 (recte: January 1,
1550, as compared with Dandolo's report of the same event), Rose-file.

[14] Paolo Giovio, *Lettere*, II, 82.

It was perhaps the very day Don Diego had Giovio to dinner, in early May, when the news of Charles V's victory at Mühlberg reached Rome. The Elector of Saxony had been captured, and the Landgrave of Hesse had surrendered. Imperial prestige was at its peak. "Nobody at Your Majesty's court believes that His Holiness would be glad about this news," the young Farnese told Don Diego, "yet he was glad." Paul III made a thanksgiving celebration in Saint Peter's Cathedral. Moreover, the prelates at Bologna, overawed by the victory, postponed their Council sessions until well into September, prepared to await the results of the simultaneous negotiations of Don Diego in Rome, and of the papal nuncio, Cardinal Sfondrato, with Charles V in Germany.[15]

In the same summer, Don Pedro de Toledo, the Spanish Viceroy of Naples, introduced the Inquisition in his kingdom, setting off unrest. From afar, whenever Don Diego had learned of any new trouble in Italy, he usually suspected papal intrigues behind it. But now he did not think Paul III had a hand in the matter. He may have been taken in somewhat by the courtesies of the papal court, where the Pope generously offered the Emperor money to help pacify Naples. That, and his agreement to postpone the sessions at the Council of Bologna for a while, seemed proof of Paul III's uninvolvement.

When, however, some "learned poets" from the court of one of the seditious Neapolitan princes came to the papal court, "singing their zarzuelas there," Mendoza was no longer so sure about Paul III's innocence. He declined the Pope's offer of troops to put down the disturbance in the neighboring kingdom, considering it a hypocritical gesture. He himself set about raising eight thousand infantry for support of Naples. "There will be time later," he wrote to the Emperor. "The Pope can give us money if he wants to. His soldiers we have no need of, we have plenty. It would only be a token help, worth nothing, and we would have to thank them for it."

Despite his suspicions, Mendoza continued to take pains to cultivate an appearance of personal friendship with the Farneses. Noting that the papals made a habit of excusing all previous strain between them and the Emperor by blaming the former Imperial

[15] GP II, 19.

ministers, he was pleased that "they are making a better show with me. It seems we stand to gain by this principle. In truth, I am their friend, as long as it serves the interest of Your Majesty. I should be glad to continue like this. Will Your Majesty please advise me if such an attitude would be harmful for any other thing of which I am not aware?"

Cardinal Farnese, amiable and smooth, was a valuable mediator, although he was probably an even greater liar than politicians usually were. At first, Don Diego did not believe a word he was told "because since I am new I am so suspicious that any word seems false to me." But soon he knew Farnese so well that he could tell by his mien whether he told the truth. It seems that Farnese was not quite untruthful when he professed his devotion to the Emperor. The young Cardinal had common sense enough to know that the reign of his ancestor would not last forever, and, in the event of sudden change, he wished to be on good terms with the Imperial faction as the stronger. "The astrologers say that his grandfather will die this year," Mendoza reports Farnese telling him. Many occasions had presented themselves, Farnese once said, in which the Pope could have "done harm to Your Majesty, and since he had not done so, Your Majesty could see his good intention." Don Diego replied: "If the evil one omits to do were a sign of goodwill, Your Majesty would love the Pope better than anyone, because Your Majesty could have done him more evil than anyone else, but did not do so."[16]

At the same time Mendoza kept watching the movements of other powers in Italy: the forces of Pier Luigi Farnese, the plans of the Venetians, and the Sienese. He also wished to be prepared for the event of a sudden conclave. And he received the first draft of the "Protest." The Emperor wanted to deliver his official and formal Protest to the Council and to the Pope in case a Bolognese session should be opened. Don Diego corrected, amended, and annotated the script; he returned the draft to the Imperial court to have his corrections approved, and told them that there was no hurry. If the Pope were to die, the Protest would never be deliv-

[16] All the foregoing in letters from Mendoza to Charles V, May 3, June 5, June 19, 1547, Döllinger, *Beiträge*, pp. 53–85.

ered; if the Pope should agree to return the Council to Trent—and Don Diego was well on the way to soften his resistance—the Protest would turn out to be unnecessary.[17]

The Emperor persisted, however, in being much less conciliatory than Rome and Mendoza. Nuntius Sfondrato fared badly at the Imperial court. Charles V was even angry with Don Diego for approving, seemingly, of some compromise on Trent. "Since the dispatch from Sfondrato arrived," Don Diego said, "the Pope is worse. If Your Majesty wishes to kill him without murder, this can be done by giving Sfondrato a bad answer."[18]

Madama

Meanwhile, Mendoza noticed a rumor to the effect that the Pope was allying himself with the new King of France and with Venice in a defensive league. This was denied, but the old pontiff made another brilliant move to show the Emperor his professed neutrality: he concluded a marriage contract with Henri II, parallel to that with Charles V ten years before. Orazio, another grandson, brother of Ottavio and the Cardinals Alessandro and Ranuccio Farnese, was to be engaged to the illegitimate daughter of Henri II, Diane of France. (The marriage did not take place before 1552; Diane was only nine years old at the time of her betrothal.) Imperial tongues, not the least Don Diego's, wagged in somewhat bitter irony:

When Farnese asked me what Your Majesty would say to the marriage of Orazio with the King's daughter, I replied that, while Your Majesty was glad that your daughter would get a companion-in-arms, you would not permit him to rob the estate of your daughter's husband. Also, that this manner of keeping neutrality made me laugh. It seems to me he [the Pope] is sinning a little in vanity, more so since, not

[17] On Mendoza's part in drafting the "Protest," see Döllinger, *Beiträge*, pp. 85, 86, 98: "A mi no me contenta el protesto que viene de Trento con todas las respuestas que me ha enviado, especialmente porque fundando V. M. sus platicas con el nuncio sobre que el Papa es ruin Papa, el protesto lo alaba de bueno, con otras cosas, que tambien se yo son de otra manera, y porque no lo oso aqui mostrar a nadie, lo enviare a V. M. apuntado, pues hay tiempo para todo . . .," Mendoza to Charles V, June 19, 1547. Again, June 26 and August 4: "Con esta sera el protesto, como aca parece que debe ser; en la sustancia se muda poco, si bien este es algo mas fuerte, pero no creo que pierde nada por ello. . . ."

[18] Mendoza to Charles V, July 14–16, 1547, *NB* X, 97.

having enough to feed an Emperor's daughter, he now wants to starve to death the daughter of a King of France.[19]

Shortly afterward Don Diego wrote his master:

The wedding of Orazio is said to be concluded soon. I said to Farnese that I find only three drawbacks in it. First, since she is only a child now, once the Pope is dead, they will keep the dowry of 300,000 ducats and dissolve the marriage, giving him old clothes instead. Second, that force is not enough for them to rule with good repute the blood of two kings in one house. Third, that wives who are born enemies, might bring husbands to be enemies, too, so that one will rob the other of his estate and create a noise throughout Italy, and both will lose what they have. There may be other pitfalls on which I cannot dwell now; may they judge them, whenever they occur.[20]

It was not idle irony when Mendoza deplored the fate of the wives in these political marriages. The fate of his own "Madama" aroused his constant sympathy. A pathetic figure in the papal environment, Charles V's daughter Margaret lived a life of service to her father. Her position was at least as arduous as that of any of the Emperor's roving ambassadors and in many aspects worse. Her sense of duty to her father had no limits. He had sent her, a seventeen-year-old widow, into the bed of an evil, unusually repulsive little boy of thirteen. She had despaired, she had rebelled, it had taken her five years to surrender to her marriage duties. But she remained unflaggingly devoted to the Emperor. Just as her aunt, Eleanor, another loyal Habsburg woman, dowager queen of the late Francis I, was still living precariously in France under growing hostility from the new King, her stepson—a sort of hostage of her beloved brother Charles V—so Margaret held up her head in Rome as an outpost of her father, showing an unbounded contempt for "that breed of Farneses."[21] Now, at least, possession of male twin babies was a source of strength for her.

Don Diego knew the Duchess (her husband Ottavio was the Duke of Camerino, later of Parma) from the time, when, eleven years old, she had been brought into Italy, engaged to Pope Clement's nephew, Alessandro, to be educated in the household of the

19 Mendoza to Charles V, May 11, 1547, GP II, 38.
20 Mendoza to Charles V, June 1, 1547, Döllinger, *Beiträge*, pp. 73, 74.
21 Pastor, *Geschichte*, V, 501.

Viceroy of Naples. On her way to Milan to meet the Viceroy's wife, the little Princess had stopped at Vigevano, where Charles V enjoyed a spell of hunting, to see the Emperor and his party (January, 1533).[22] The next time Mendoza saw Margaret was in Naples, early in 1536, when her wedding there gave occasion to great celebrations. Now he tried to assist her where he could, but usually he had nothing cheerful to report. Ottavio had taken the armies of his grandfather to Germany and had not yet returned from the Emperor's court when Mendoza came to Rome. "The Duke of Camerino is soon expected here," Don Diego wrote on June 5, "and since he is Your Majesty's son-in-law, I do not know how the precedence question should be handled. Your Majesty please advise, as I do not wish these clerics to interfere with me. . . ."

Later on, Mendoza wrote to the Emperor:

I understand that Duke Ottavio will try to come straight over here without detaining himself in Piacenza. Madama knows about the [syphilitic] boils he has, and she cries about it every day. They say that a symptom of this disease is the enjoyment of giving it to one's partner. Your Majesty may please advise what should be done. It may not be possible to delay him until then [until the Emperor's orders arrive]. Although he broadcasts that he is healed, I have heard that he is not, and Madama does not know this. It will be up to Lope de Guzman and Doña Maria de Mendoza [governors of Ottavio Farnese's household] to do their duty, as I understand they have always done it in other things. I will take their advice.[23]

The duty of the majordomo and his wife would consist in preventing the ill-matched couple from sleeping together, just as their predecessors, Don Lope Hurtado de Mendoza and his wife, had the more difficult duty to effect the approach between the two when Ottavio had not reached manhood.

Madama, Don Diego felt, was not always treated with fitting deference by the Farneses, although to his face the Pope, when his mood was agreeable, praised her to the skies. On the occasion of a ceremony (the marriage by proxy of the Pope's granddaughter Victoria to the Duke of Urbino), Mendoza watched, reporting with indignation:

22 Pedro Girón, *Crónica del Emperador Carlos V*, p. 30.
23 Mendoza to Charles V, June 5 and 19, 1547, Döllinger, *Beiträge*, pp. 76–80, 85.

It was the day of Saint Peter. The Pope sat on his chair, the cardinals to both sides of him, and all the women of Rome knelt among uncounted people. A very significant spectacle on a significant day. They treated Madama very wretchedly, leaving for the wedding without her, I do not know if on purpose, or because the instant of 19¾ hours had passed [and proud Madama was not on time?]. They did not give her a chair, as they used to do, but a cushion, as to all the others. Although these are unimportant details, they are tokens of a not very good intention, though afterwards they made many excuses.[24]

Maybe "they" did not treat Margaret too respectfully because she did not hide her opinion of the Pope? The old pontiff, who sometimes said her little finger was worth more than all of himself, was perhaps unaware of this.[25] But others knew. "I heard," Don Diego wrote on June 26, "that Cardinal Farnese spoke to Madama, telling her that Your Majesty should give Siena to Ottavio or to herself as a ruler. She told him they [the Farneses] had rendered no services to Your Majesty that would make you feel obliged to do such a thing. Farnese answered her that the Pope could give 200,000 escudos [for Siena]. Madama replied to this that, unless His Holiness deserved it for his merits, he could not buy it, but the Pope had treated Your Majesty in such a way that all that remained of his life, since he is so old, would not suffice to make up for it."[26]

In at least one respect, the efforts of Margaret's mentors were successful: she kept Ottavio at arm's length for at least a year after this date. On May 26, 1548, King Ferdinand's ambassador in Rome, Diego Lasso, reports to his master:

Right now His Holiness is dealing with Madama to induce her to sleep with the Duke, her husband, and he has therefore sent doctors who certify as to his health. Madama holds him off as long as she can. They say she has done so ever since the Duke came from there [the Imperial court] with the ailment. They also say he still has something of it in his throat, and there are malicious people who believe that His Holiness would not be very sad if he gave it to his wife.[27]

[24] Mendoza to Charles V, July 14, 1547, *NB* X, 97.
[25] Mendoza to Charles V, May 3, 1547, Döllinger, *Beiträge*, pp. 53–60.
[26] Ibid., p. 86.
[27] Druffel, *Briefe*, I, no. 162, pp. 114, 115.

By the middle of August, 1547, when Naples had somewhat calmed down, Don Diego received the Emperor's commission to go to Siena at the head of a new Imperial garrison to deal with the unrest there. The Pope had been suspected as a source of the trouble in Siena. But when Mendoza paid his farewell visit to him, Paul III denied any complicity; he professed the purest intentions toward Charles V, again offering all possible help for Naples. Then the Pope quickly left Rome even before Don Diego's departure, his destination a secret.

"The Pope who had intended to leave on the second of September," Mendoza wrote on August 27, "left already on the twenty-fifth, at eighteen hours. The reason was because in that hour there was a conjunction of Jupiter with the moon. This became known because the astrological design was on the memorandum sheet that he gave the Governor of Rome with the list of all the things he has to do during his absence."

Despite the astrological precaution, Paul III had been careless. He left Cardinal Alessandro behind in a sulking mood. He had just given an abbey this grandson wanted for himself to Alessandro's brother Ranuccio, the young Cardinal of Naples. Farnese, resentful at his grandfather, blurted out the Pope's real intention to Don Diego. "He told me that the Pope wished to make his brother "French" because it did not please him that he [Alessandro] was Imperial." And Farnese revealed that the Pope was on his way to Bologna, "determined to send English bishops to Bologna to raise their number to a hundred, and the thirteen French bishops were already in Turin, arriving in Bologna on the sixth of next month, where the Council would be continued. It would be ended by Christmas, with His Holiness making a reformation all by himself that would leave nothing to be desired."[28]

Mendoza was alarmed. Now he understood that the Pope, going to Bologna, intended to interfere in the question of the Council unfavorably for the Emperor. Paul III's presence would mean the actual opening of the first Bolognese session of the Council, an action to upset the unusually friendly atmosphere Mendoza thought to have achieved with the old Pope. Don Diego set out as

[28] Mendoza to Charles V, August 27, 1547, *NB* X, 107–108.

fast as he could get away, and he caught up with the Pope in Perugia. Once more displaying all his charm, deftly intermingled with threats, he succeeded in swaying the old man, persuading him to a further postponement of such an irrevocable act. Besides, he exacted a solemn promise from Paul III to notify him fourteen days in advance before the next session of the Council would be called (so as to allow the Imperials to deliver the "Protest" in time). The Pope was put in such a pleasant mood by this unexpected visit with Don Diego in Perugia that he told him—this was September 10—he considered himself a most fortunate man, comparing himself with the Emperor Tiberius.

The Pier Luigi Farnese Case

At approximately the same hour of Paul III's conversation with Don Diego, Pier Luigi, Duke of Castro, was murdered in his castle at Piacenza, the state (belonging to the Church) with which his father, the Pope, had unlawfully invested him. Although Don Diego was not a party to the assassination, the event would reverberate until the last day of his stay in Italy on all subsequent events concerning him.

The outline of that fatal deed, briefly, was this: In 1545, when the Pope invested Pier Luigi with the duchies of Parma and Piacenza, the Emperor had grudgingly acquiesced. His preoccupation with the Schmalkaldic War and the assistance Paul III was giving him (on the advice of Pier Luigi, incidentally), let Charles V put his plans for revenge in abeyance. Moreover, expecting the octogenarian to die any day, he hoped the situation would clear up by itself. In that case he would have a free hand to chase the Pope's son from the territories he had usurped. Pier Luigi's powerful neighbor in Milan, the Marquis of Vasto—a mild man, actually, despite his fame as a soldier and his clumsy deed against Rincon— even affected friendly relations with the unwelcome upstart (Pier Luigi was an unsavory character, accused of debauchery and perversion, and regarded as a would-be Cesare Borgia).[29] When, in 1546, Vasto died, however, while the old Pope lived on with undiminished mental powers, Charles V changed his strategy. He appointed Ferrante Gonzaga, one of his most aggressive ministers, to

[29] Cf. Ireneo Affò, *Vita di Pierluigi Farnese*, p. 70.

succeed Vasto, entrusting him from the beginning with the task of chasing Pier Luigi from Parma and Piacenza at the earliest opportunity. In February, 1547, Charles V told Gonzaga to go ahead, if an occasion should arise, "without waiting for a *sede vacante*, to attack either Parma or Piacenza, as long as you can make it appear to come from your own head, without any order from Us."[30] On July 31, Gonzaga wrote the Emperor about Pier Luigi's part in the conspiracy of Genoa, discussing ways and means for murdering him in Piacenza. Gonzaga urged immediate assassination. Less than six weeks later it was done—this was fast work in the 1540s. Four noblemen from Parma, whom Pier Luigi had offended, had conspired under Gonzaga's auspices and with full knowledge of Charles V. The deed was accomplished on September 10 while Pier Luigi sat at dinner; the conspirators took his citadel and cut him down, spilling his brains on the floor tiles, and flinging his body out of the window into the ditch. Ferrante Gonzaga and his Spanish soldiers arrived in Piacenza the next morning, occupying the town in the name of the Emperor.[31]

No one on the Imperial side felt any qualms. The Imperial alibi was considered foolproof. Why should the Emperor wish to murder a Duke whose heritage would anyway go to his own son-in-law (and the victim's son as well), Ottavio Farnese, and to his grandsons? The deed appeared to be too purposeless to be ascribed to Charles V. When Don Diego heard of it, he was as astonished as the Farneses themselves. "I told Farnese what I deemed convenient, despite the fact that I have received no advice. These people are so lost and beside themselves; they don't know their head from their feet."[32]

Possibly because Mendoza usually urged moderation and conciliation, he had not been informed in advance. This time, neither the Emperor nor Gonzaga wanted any restraint. They had decided to

[30] Charles V to Gonzaga, February 11, 1547, Arch. Sim., Est., leg. 1194, fol. 359–361, Rose-file. See also Giuseppe de Leva, *Storia documentata di Carlo V*, IV, 355–367. De Leva gives examples of how Gonzaga, over the summer of 1547, kept the Emperor steadily informed of all plans as they matured, and about all contingencies to be reckoned with, including the anticipated death of Pier Luigi.

[31] Affò, *Vita*, pp. 179–185.

[32] Mendoza to Charles V, September 18, 1547, Döllinger, *Beiträge*, pp. 114–118.

risk this ugly offense against the Pope for the simple, utilitarian reason that they wanted to catch Pier Luigi off guard while his protector was still alive. Now it had been, militarily, child's play to get at him. After the Pope's death, Pier Luigi would have entrenched himself.[33]

The old Pope was generally expected to succumb under the blow. "His Holiness is so done in that his life is in doubt. Will Your Majesty please send me orders about the pontificate? I must know what to do in case the Pope dies."[34] But Paul III, well aware that the Imperials meant to hit him and his son *uno ictu*, said that God, having granted him such an old age, had also given him the strength to bear it.[35] And while he did not disguise his anger against Ferrante Gonzaga, the Pope wished to convey the impression that he considered the Emperor guiltless. Mendoza explained that he understood the Pope's double-talk. Paul III's professed disbelief in Charles V's connivance, he said, had the purpose of preparing his revenge without detection.

I hold the Pope, as I have written at other times, to be timid when he is shown strength, but foolhardy when he suspects your guard is down. He is master of dissimulation and delaying tactics. Some think he has little faith and little conscience. [Don Diego usually concealed his own opinion behind unnamed "others" or "some" when he cast doubt on the piety of the Pope.] Several times I have seen him praising Your Majesty, and after launching an attack on Your Majesty, then again he returns to praise. His art seems to consist in denying what he really wishes, and concealing what he fears. In truth, he fears nothing else of this Council but the reform [of abuses]. Your Majesty holds him in your hands as long as he fears that.[36]

Notwithstanding his pretended ignorance as to the real culprit, the Pope was unable to suppress his justified suspicions. The first Imperial representatives who came to Perugia to offer condolences were Madama's majordomo in behalf of his mistress, and Abbot Brizeño in the name of Don Diego. The Pope was giving them to

---

[33] Affò, *Vita*, p. 145.
[34] See note 32, above.
[35] GP III, 341, 342.
[36] See note 32, above.

understand "that Don Fernando hatched the death of Pier Luigi and that Your Majesty knew about it."[37] And "Don Fernando" was not the only one the Pope did not trust: "The soldiers that [the Farneses] recruited here are 2,500 infantry and 150 cavalry," Mendoza wrote the Emperor, "and they have lodged two companies of soldiers next to my house, so that I retire and arise to the sound of drums. I am not making any demonstration." (Naturally, he did not. He could not, when more or less subtly he had been put under surveillance!) At the same time he was "detained from going to Siena because of this novelty from Piacenza and because the Pope and Farnese asked me to delay my going."[38] Unable to depart, he became concerned about his personal safety—in the wake of an Imperial murder, the situation started to resemble the cloak-and-dagger picture in Venice. Pending the Emperor's approval, he ordered a guard of a hundred men to protect his person and his house, especially because of the constant danger from recently exiled Neapolitans who swarmed on the loose in Rome.[39]

"The friendship between the Cardinal Farnese and myself cannot last very long," he wrote Charles V more than a month after the murder of the Cardinal's father. And he reported that the Pope suspected "I had orders from Your Majesty to steal the Castle of Sant'Angelo with the money—not a difficult feat, incidentally, if the times were not so full of suspicion—and they make it appear as though there were some basis to such rumors because His Holiness put up two companies of soldiers to the left and right of my house, reinforcing also the guard of the Castle; and wherever I go, two spies draw up behind me, following me night and day. I let them."[40]

The Pope, in trying to conceal his thoughts of revenge from the Emperor, did so mainly out of his concern for the Farnese dynasty. He needed Charles V to achieve his ambitions, hoping the Emperor

---

[37] Mendoza to Charles V, September 22, 1547, Döllinger, *Beiträge*, pp. 119–121.

[38] Mendoza to Charles V, October 5, 1547, Döllinger, *Beiträge*, pp. 128–130; also October 16, 1547, *NB* X, 576.

[39] Mendoza to Charles V, October 16, 1547, *NB* X, 572.

[40] Ibid., p. 591.

would now let Ottavio have Piacenza in addition to Parma, which he already held. He dispatched Ottavio to the Imperial court in Germany to ask in person for Piacenza. "I have tried to prevent his going," wrote Mendoza, "to spare Your Majesty such trouble, but I have been unable to stop him."[41]

[41] Mendoza to Charles V, October 5, 1547, Döllinger, *Beiträge*, pp. 128–130.

9. SPIRITUAL WAR, 1547–1548

> I could have created a lot of noise in
> the time of Pope Paul when His Majesty
> ordered me to fire off the protests, which
> I softened as much as possible . . .
>
> Don Diego[1]

The Last Chance

CHARLES V NOW CONSIDERED HIMSELF the most powerful monarch in the world. Surrounded by his Spanish and Italian troops, he opened the "harnessed Diet" in Augsburg on September 1, 1547. In deep humility, the seven electors and almost all the temporal and spiritual princes of the Empire promised in the name of the German nation to submit to the decisions of an Ecumenical Council in Trent. (They were not prepared to go to Bologna, even now, because Charles V had at the outset promised them a German site for the Council.)[2]

This was the last chance to attempt a reunification of the Church. At this critical moment, Mendoza should have had the opportunity to obtain the Pope's agreement to let the Council return to Trent. Don Diego had so far been successful in making the Council at Bologna ineffectual: Paul III had agreed to postpone its opening indefinitely. Nothing had disturbed the friendly atmosphere Men-

---

[1] *AC*, pp. 343, 344.
[2] Ludwig von Pastor, *Geschichte der Päpste*, V, 631–639; particularly p. 632.

doza had created between himself and the Farneses. It was only a
matter of time, he hoped, until the Pope would agree to return the
Council to Trent. But just then the Imperials would hurt the Pope
mortally! Moreover, Charles V was not willing—even after his
henchmen had assassinated the Pope's son—to remedy the situation as far as it might have been still possible. Paul III would still
have been tractable if the Emperor had let Piacenza go to Duke
Ottavio. But Charles V did not wish to give the Pope any concession for the favor he now imperiously requested from him. As will
be seen, unless Gonzaga and the Emperor expected the Pope and
his son to die at the same time, the murder of Pier Luigi was an
incredible political blunder.

Far from thinking so, in his supremacy, Charles V dramatized
this extraordinary opportunity for a try at conciliation within
Christendom by entrusting Cardinal Madruzzo of Trent with new
and urgent instructions for the Pope. "Trento," with a foot in each
camp, seemed a fit instrument for this purpose. As a Prince of the
Empire, he had participated in the "harnessed Diet"; as a Cardinal
he had the right to speak in consistory, a privilege as a rule denied
to ambassadors.

On his way to Rome, Madruzzo arrived in Siena on November
21 with a splendid train. He was usually accompanied by sixty
mounted nobles in his service, all dressed from boots to hat in red
and saffron; forty halberdiers in the same colors marched ahead of
them, while six fellows, also in red and saffron, opened the procession with drums, cornets, and pipes.[3] Don Diego, who awaited him
in Siena, was ordered to accompany Madruzzo as associate in this
special embassy to the Pope.

There must have been a reason why Mendoza would describe the
Cardinal of Trent some time later as an "indiscreet fool."[4] Perhaps,
affected by his own "poverty," he resented the swiftness with
which Madruzzo, so ostentatiously wealthy, moved out of his
(Mendoza's) house the day after their arrival in Rome to accept
instead the hospitality of Cardinal Chamberlain Guidascanio Santa
Fiore, one of the Pope's grandsons. Still, it seems that Madruzzo

[3] Feliciano Cereceda, *Diego Láinez*, I, 241.
[4] *AC*, p. 134.

did well enough on this futile mission. He spared no effort in urging Paul III to send the Council back to Trent and to stop involving Church politics with his family affairs.[5]

But the Pope, who gave both him and Mendoza private interviews, had all his ammunition ready—evasion, counterarguments, and side-stepping proposals prepared (in Don Diego's words) by "the principal corrupter of the spoiled mind of the Pope," Cardinal Marcello Cervini ("Santa Cruz"), and delivered by another of Paul III's advisers, the Cardinal of Trani, Giovanni Domenico de' Cupis ("Trana"), Dean of the College of Cardinals. Paul III was also influenced by opinions of the French, which decided him not to consider removing the Council from Bologna without the consent of the prelates in Bologna themselves. To this end, much time was consumed with messages between Rome and Bologna. "Santa Cruz, with his accustomed malice and fraud" (as Don Diego said), drafted a letter to Cardinal del Monte (who still presided as legate in Bologna) in which he not only put the questions to him but also furnished all the sophisticated arguments that would serve Del Monte to write his answer.

In the meantime, the Cardinal of Trent and Mendoza resolved to move their plea from the private scene to the wider public of a consistory. Madruzzo exerted himself to prepare the ground for Don Diego's admission to the consistory. It would be the first time the Emperor's case would be presented to all the cardinals; so far, the few close advisers of the Pope were the only ones informed. The Pope was unable to prevent the Cardinal of Trent from addressing his peers, but he did not want to allow Mendoza's appearance. He was uncomfortable enough during Madruzzo's first public address. While "Trento" was speaking, the Pope was observed to change color. When Trent was praising the Emperor and his high purposes, His Holiness shook from head to foot—in fact, his right foot, which protruded from below his robes, did not stop trembling. Several times he tried to interrupt the speaker, and despite the

[5] This, and the following information up to p. 205 (including the quotation from Serristori, p. 201), is taken from Gottfried Buschbell, "Die Instruktion der kaiserlichen Bevollmächtigten in Rom für Aurelio Cattaneo" (based on joint letters to the Emperor by Madruzzo and Mendoza from November 23 and December 17, 1547), in *Quellen und Forschungen aus italienischen Archiven und Bibliotheken* (1931–1932), XXIII, 218–241, 255–266.

clarity of Madruzzo's exposition, he professed not to know what he was driving at.

Madruzzo spared no pains reiterating the importance of his mission. "Now is the time, and this is the moment to reunite Christendom," he reminded the assembly. Therefore the Emperor had sent him. He had come gladly enough, as a Cardinal, as a faithful servant of the Pope, and as a Prince of the Empire, expecting to bring both wholesome and desired news. Should the Emperor's request be refused, he warned, he predicted a number of difficulties for the papacy. "These Don Diego will discuss when His Holiness may see fit to allow him to enter the consistory, as I had urged shortly before."

Don Diego followed up Madruzzo's preparation in a private audience with the Pope. He stressed the fact that it was his legitimate business to negotiate the details of the Emperor's instructions. Paul III told him plainly that he did not believe in the Germans' submission. "I replied that the proof of German submission was Your Majesty's signature and the testimony of the Cardinal of Trent, a German Prince and an eyewitness." As for the details, the consistory had answered Madruzzo that a return of the Council to Trent needed the agreement of all the nations and princes. This implied that, because of French opposition, there could be no such agreement. Mendoza answered this new evasion: "Since it is Germany which is in danger," he told the Pope, "Germany must necessarily consent to the request. And she has done so, and has offered to come to the Council in Trent. As for the other provinces and princes, their opinion is no reason to deny spiritual aid to Germany just because Spain or France or some other nation might dissent, inasmuch as it is not their affair. The delay would be great and the danger obvious of applying the cure when it is too late." Finally, he begged the Pope directly to allow him to set forth in consistory "the good intention of the Emperor and to discharge the part that the Cardinal of Trent has assigned to me."

The Pope still opposed his request. It was not customary for ambassadors to speak in consistory on spiritual matters. If he wished to inform the cardinals, he told Don Diego, he was free to visit each of them privately and to talk to them in their homes. No ambassador had entered the consistory except twice in Paul III's experience —once in the case of a Queen of Bohemia and once in the English controversy. Mendoza reminded him of the case of the Duke of Lorraine, when Juan de Vega (Mendoza's predecessor) and the French ambassador had spoken in the consistory, and he insisted that the case at hand was a spiritual one. He had to ask remedy for the souls of Germany and could do this anywhere. "This present case is more important than any other Your Holiness has mentioned. Therefore, there is more reason for my being heard on it in consistory, and even if Your Holiness denied me the right, I should not fail to be knocking at the door."

Upon reflection and consultation with Cardinal Farnese, the Pope at last ceded to Mendoza's request under two conditions: the ambassadors of all the other princes were also to be present, and any one of them might answer him; also, he could not expect any answer from His Holiness on that occasion; this would come later. Even so, Farnese tried his utmost to win Madruzzo over to some other arrangement to avert the confrontation of Don Diego with all the cardinals—a sign to what extent the Curia must have feared Mendoza's powers of persuasion. But the Cardinal of Trent did not falter in sponsoring Mendoza's request, and Don Diego was heard by the Sacred College on December 14.

"This morning," wrote Serristori, Cosimo I's ambassador, on that day, "a consistory was called at which all the ambassadors were present except the one from Urbino, who was indisposed or otherwise impeded from coming. After the doors were closed, the signor Don Diego knelt for an eighth of an hour at the feet of His Holiness. [The Pope must have failed to give Mendoza the sign to rise, and deliberately so—as will be clear from the following.] Then he returned to his place, and with much modesty and reverence gave the Sacred College an address that was as prudent as it was lengthy."

Mendoza started out by noting all that the Cardinal of Trent had already told them about the Emperor. Then he appealed to the Pope: "I beg Your Holiness, as universal father, with the reverence and humility of an obedient son, by the passion and blood of Christ, to order the prelates in Bologna to return to Trent for the cure of religion in Germany, for union against the Turk, and for reformation of the abuses." He had begun his speech in Castilian, but the Pope and Trani interrupted him, asking the meaning of certain words, and telling him to speak louder. Suspecting that they intended only to upset him, he switched at once to Italian. He argued that the failure of returning the Council to Trent would give rise to three difficulties:

One. In Germany are Protestants, undecided persons, and Catholics. If obstacles were put in the way of the continuance of the Council in Trent, or if its actions were delayed, the Protestants would harden their beliefs, and we would lose all hope of bringing them back into the fold. The indeterminates would be lost. With the Catholics, religion would lose prestige and the papacy would suffer in the eyes of all the people. Both sides would attribute it to negligence or carelessness in Your Holiness or even to something worse. This would not be pleasing to God, nor would it be expected of Your Holiness: you are a prince of such piety, prudence, and honesty.

The second difficulty is that generally in all the provinces each prince in his own way resists the opinions of the wayward who are slowly working their way in. [He indicated particularly what the princes of the ambassadors there present—naming each one, presumably France, Portugal, Ferrara, Venice, Florence, and Lucca—were doing to combat this evil.] The evil will continue to grow if they see that Your Holiness declines to cure Germany by not returning the Council to Trent, and this is unimaginable.

At this point the Pope interrupted him, stressing that the Council was ecumenical and general, not national, and that it should look to universal benefit. To save one province, others should not be abandoned. But Mendoza, once almost a papal aspirant himself, knew how to defeat the Pope in his own field. "Christ sought the one sheep," he said. "I fail to see how making Germany Christian means abandoning the other provinces."

At this, His Holiness appeared much disturbed, saying: "Ah, you don't see it [*Non lo vedite vui*]?" "No, Holy Father," replied Don Diego. "Basta," said the Pope, motioning him to go on.

The third, but not the least, difficulty to which Mendoza then alluded was simply a reminder to the Pope and Cardinals of the many tribulations brought into the world by former dissensions between popes and emperors. "You must be aware," he told the assembly, "of what evil might be the result if in punishment of our sins there should be discord between Your Holiness and His Majesty."

"What discord? What discord?" cried the Pope.

Thinking that the Pope wished to disturb him and take him off his guard, Mendoza replied, "Discord—as Your Holiness says. God will not permit that there be any; nor will it [discord] be the fault of His Majesty, because Your Holiness will be willing, as the universal father of Christendom, to return the Council to Trent during your own lifetime."

Again, as in the private audience, Paul III asked Mendoza what evidence he had of the submission of the Germans, and how he knew that they would come to the Council; he interrupted him twice with the same argument. Don Diego answered that he had the signature of His Majesty and the Cardinal of Trent, a Prince of the Empire, who had been present, and whom His Majesty and the King of the Romans in the name of the German states had sent to inform His Holiness of it. There were no individual signatures from these states—because when the head signed, there was no need for the subjects to sign as well. "Your Holiness knows this well from your *breves*," Mendoza pointed out, "which are not signed by the cardinals because they bear the phrase *de consensu fratrum*."

Driven to anger by Don Diego's irrefutable logic, the Pope turned with a contemptuous laugh to Cardinal Trani: "How can he be so certain that the Germans would come to Trent?"

"*Nolens volens* they would do so," countered Mendoza, "of their own free will, if Your Holiness were willing to return the Council to Trent, or [they would go] under compulsion, if it seemed wise to force them."

"What security have you that they will come?" the Pope asked again. Mendoza told him what had been done in the recesses of the other German Diets and begged him to have the patience to listen a little longer. With that he began to remind the Pope of how in the days of Leo and Clement and in the early days of his own pontificate His Majesty had always sought and urged the Council.

Paul III answered that, on the contrary, he himself had always been the proponent since the beginning of his pontificate. "Whether Your Holiness was the instigator or the instigated is of no importance in the present discussion," he began, but the Pope cut him short. Mendoza had planned to enumerate the many steps the Pope had done to thwart the Council, such as his premature publication of the Decree of Justification and the transfer to Bologna, but when he saw that the Pope was close to losing his temper, he reverted to his plea for the return to Trent. "If an unbeliever—a Turk—should come requesting Your Holiness for baptism on condition that it be given him at the font of Saint Peter's and not at that of Saint John Lateran's," he said, "Your Holiness would be acting contrary to your office if you did not comply. And this is all the more true of a province that expects the same thing."

"Where are these people who are coming to be baptized?" asked the Pope. "Let them come, and then the Council can return to Trent."

"Your Holiness should remember," Mendoza told him, "that Christ and the apostles had sought out in their houses those who wished to be converted and had not waited to be sought out, and that our Redeemer stands with open arms, shedding his blood to redeem sinners." He followed this up by warning Paul III that further delay would be prejudicial to the cause, only to hear the Pope say that delay had usually come from the Imperial side.

"Yes!" exclaimed Don Diego. "His Majesty has taken up arms as a means of reaching this end, and God has granted him victory. By victory and negotiation, God has inspired the Germans in their deliberations, and the time is beginning when something of profit can be done in Trent. Therefore from now on delay would be most pernicious."

When he finally stopped, after the Pope had told him several times to finish, he announced that he would deliver the rest of his discourse another time in the same place. "You said all you had to say," remarked the Pope. "I will say whatever is necessary," Don Diego replied, walking out.

A moment later the Pope called him back in the presence of the ambassadors. He told Don Diego that if he had spoken to him privately, he would have replied; but since he had spoken in consistory, he was, to comply with the rules, ordering his secretary Blosio to reply to him. The secretary drew a Latin paper from his bosom and, turning to Don Diego, read it. The substance was that His Holiness, having heard Don Diego, it being a serious matter for deep consideration and consultation with the most reverend cardinals, would order that Mendoza be answered in the next consistory in the presence of the same ambassadors and notaries, whom he

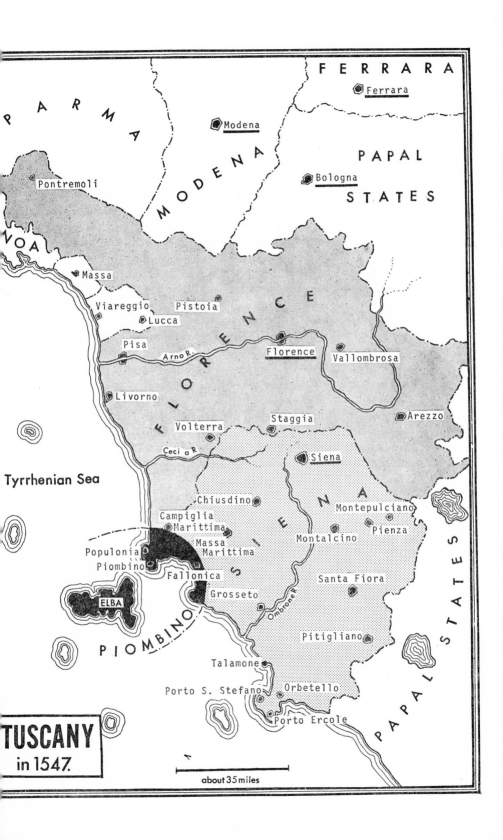

FERRARA

◉ Ferrara

P A R M A

◉ Modena

M O D E N A

PAPAL

Pontremoli

◉ Bologna

S T A T E S

NOA

◉ Massa

Viareggio   Pistoia

◉ Lucca

F L O R E N C E

Pisa

Arno R.

Florence   Vallombrosa

◉ Livorno

F
L
O
R
E
N
C
E

Volterra   Staggia

Ceci a R.

◉ Siena

Tyrrhenian Sea

Chiusdino   Montepulciano

Campiglia
Marittima   Pienza

Massa   Montalcino
Marittima

S
I
E
N
A

Populonia
Piombino

Fallonica   Santa Fiora

ELBA   Grosseto

P
I
O
M
B
I
N
O

Ombrone R.

P
A
P
A
L

Pitigliano

Talamone

S
T
A
T
E
S

Porto S. Stefano   Orbetello

TUSCANY
in 1547.

Porto Ercole

about 35 miles

warned not to say anything of what had passed until the reply was given.

Madruzzo and Mendoza sent a joint letter to the Emperor, describing their audiences, and Mendoza wrote: "It is impossible to judge where this business will lead. The Pope complains about the way I negotiated with him. He thinks I did it all to delay him until the time of a resolution of Germany. He says that I, Don Diego, have acted like a gypsy and like a Venetian 'meriol,' which means 'pickpocket.' I do not resent it, because he has called others by this name, too."[6]

The Pope's reply to the Emperor was promised for the next consistory, but it was learned beforehand that it would be negative, or at least evasive. When Cardinal Madruzzo understood that his mission was unsuccessful, he did not wait for the reply. Don Diego remained to receive it, but "Trento" departed quickly, not wishing to get involved in this papal-Imperial quarrel.

The Pope, hardened into irreconcilability, spoiled the Emperor's last and only opportunity to combine his military victory over the Lutherans with a Council they could not have refused to attend. Gonzaga's ill-timed deed had blocked Mendoza's impending diplomatic success. No one can now assert whether any power in the world could have healed the split in Christendom then and there, but the obstinacy of one offended old man frustrated even the last attempt.

The Protest

Aware that the Emperor's cause was lost and the delivery of the Protest now unavoidable, Mendoza saw fit to show the Pope his utmost disdain. But Paul III anticipated him. On Christmas Day, when Don Diego appeared in the Sistine Chapel for Mass, he found his customary seat (the first beside the raised throne of the Pope) occupied by Orazio, the fiancé of the French King's daughter. The Marquis d'Aumales, brother of Cardinal Guise, sat next to Orazio. Mendoza squeezed past the two young men, leaned against the chair of the Pope, and signaled the ambassador of France to come to his side. The master of ceremonies bustled up and told him that

6 GP II, 58.

Drawing of Mendoza by J. L. Engurdas from an engraving by Navia.
In the Museum Casa de los Tiros, Granada. (Photo by José Choin
Castro.)

General view of the Jardines del Partal, located on the grounds of the palace of Tendilla.

View of the remaining brick foundations of the Count of Tendilla's palace. In the background is the Church of Santa María (erected 1581–1618) on the site of the ancient royal Mezquita, which was demolished in 1576.

View of the oblong pool in the Count of Tendilla's palace. In the foreground are remains of the ancient walls of Don Diego's birthplace.

Another view of the oblong pool, from the former house of the Count of
Tendilla.

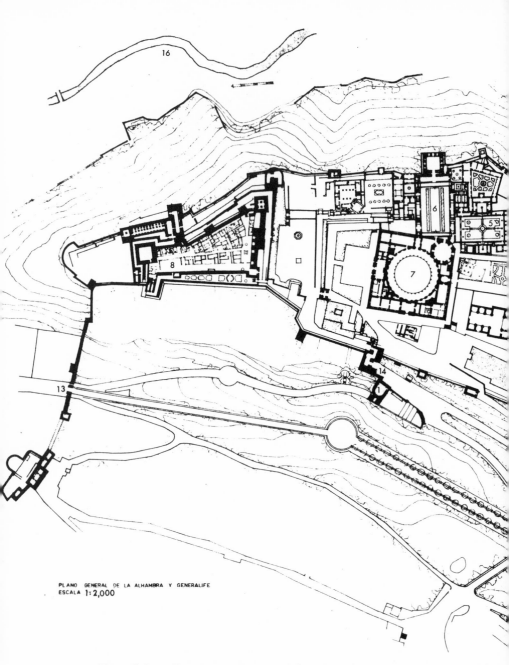

Plan of the Alhambra and Generalife. (Courtesy of Don Jesús Bermúdez Pareja, Director del Museo Nacional de Arte Hispanomusulmán, Alhambra de Granada.)

1. Large basin, center of the Palace of Tendilla
2. Remains of the tower and wings of the vanished palace
3. Remains of the baths of the palace
4. Frontyards, entrance of the Tendilla palace
5. The famous Court of Lions of the Royal Palace of the Alhambra
6. The Court of Myrtles of the Royal Palace

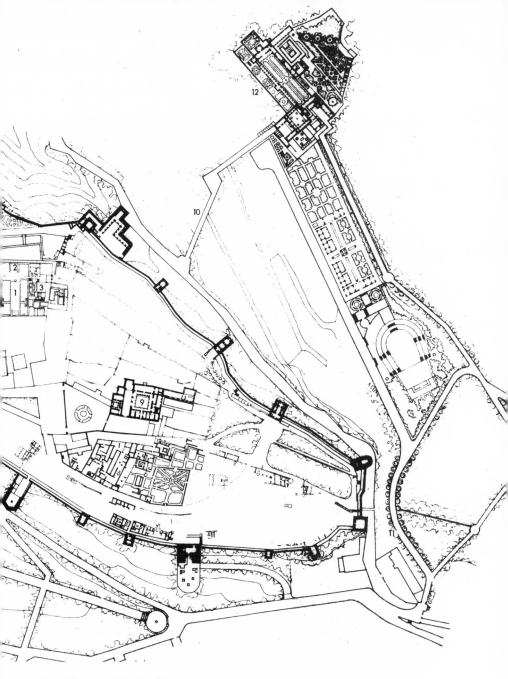

The Mendoza coat of arms, sculptured in stone on the wall of the "Fountain of Charles V" at the Alhambra. Shown are the diagonal stripes and the legend AVE MARIA, GRATIA PLENA.

Panorama showing the brick-wall remains of Tendilla's palace across the gardens of the Alhambra. In the background are the Sacromonte, *left*, the "Torre de los Picos," *lower right*, and part of the Generalife, *far right*.

Portrait of the second Count of Tendilla, Don Iñigo López de Mendoza, father of Don Diego. The Count wears the armor of a captain-general, one hand holding his insignia of commander, the other holding a pomegranate, symbol of Granada. (Reproduced by permission of the Patronato de la Alhambra y Generalife; photo by José Choin Castro.)

Last page of Mendoza's letter to Charles V, May 30, 1552. Arch. Sim., Est. 878, fol. 62:

Guarde nuestro señor y ensalçe la S.C.C. persona de V. Magd. con mas acrecentamiento de Reynos y estados. En Roma, a XXX de Mayo 1552.

El Piguino ha quatro dias que vino y hoy lo ha publicado, o, ha de publicar en Consistorio su Santidad por Cardenal.

Humil vasallo y criado de vuestra magestad
Don Diego Hurtado de Mendoça/rubricado/.

this place was for the dukes, not the ambassadors; Mendoza ought to concede it to the signor Orazio who was Duke of Castro (the title of his murdered father).

Don Diego curtly replied that he did not understand such language and turned his back on the official. Alarmed, the Cardinals "Paris" and Ridolfi, who sat nearby, started to persuade him to give way. "I do not understand the ceremonies of the chapel," Don Diego told them. "I am in the same place where I have been at other times."

The Pope pretended not to notice what was going on below and around him. He asked Cardinal Ridolfi what was the matter, and then he said in a loud voice: "I shall tell him!" Then, as Don Diego reports:

Turning to me with much fury, he told me that we did not consider Orazio a duke, but that he was one, and that I as Caballero had to give way to the dukes. I replied that I took Orazio for a duke, and if His Holiness wished it, I would give it to him in writing, signed by my hand; it is quite true I am not a duke, but if I were, I would not be the second in my house. I was there as ambassador of His Majesty and in the place where the other ambassadors had been, and I myself at other times, from where nobody would remove me alive [*vibo*].

The Pope started to wring his hands, bumping around [*nalgueando*] in his chair with very little decorum. The ambassador of France left at the Evangelium, and Orazio and the other Marquis left at the Preface . . . I remained behind alone without competition until the end of Mass. And without awaiting the Blessing of His Holiness, nor wishing to wait to escort him out [as was the custom], I left, so that he had no ambassador to accompany him. Ridolfo [Cardinal Ridolfi] told me when I was leaving that I should wait for the blessing. I replied that it was not important and I did not care much. They say the Pope says I am already a Lutheran because I did not wait for the Benediction, and that the blessing of God would desert me because I do not want the Pope's. I understand it all the other way around."[7]

The consistory in which Don Diego was to receive the official reply was scheduled for December 27. At the first consistory, when he had still hoped for success, his mien had been comparatively

---

[7] Mendoza to Charles V, December 27, 1547, *NB* X, 616; GP III, 377, 378. Cf. Mendoza's insistence on his seat with the almost identical behavior of his grandfather, the first Count of Tendilla, at the Congress of Mantua (chapter one).

modest, his appeal to the Pope heartfelt and warm, although he had not been able to suppress his argumentative spirit completely. Now he went to the Sacred Assembly carrying the Protest in his hand. There was no more use in trying to be conciliatory; instead he intended to announce that he would deliver the Protest at the earliest opportunity. While he waited in an antechamber together with all the other ambassadors and diplomatic agents, the Pope let him languish there for more than two hours. Apparently moved by the desire to prevent Mendoza from opening his mouth during the assembly (although he should have known this to be a vain endeavor), the Pope sent several Cardinals out to him at intervals to make Mendoza agreeable to a number of suggestions. First appeared Cardinal Trani, then Farnese, and later "Coria." They asked Don Diego to accept the reply of the prelates from Bologna without comment and send it just as it was to the Emperor. The legates in Bologna, they assured him, would dispatch no official business within the next twenty days (the time the Emperor's reply would take to arrive). The Pope, they told him, desired that judgment be rendered as to whether the move from Trent to Bologna had been good and legitimate. Mendoza should consent to let the Pope himself, as head of the Church, be the arbiter of that.[8]

Don Diego answered that he would gladly receive the reply from Bologna and forward it to the Emperor on condition that it contain nothing that would oblige him to protest—otherwise he would have to do so. But he explained he had no authority from the Emperor to refer to the Pope the judgment about the legitimacy of the transfer. Although the Cardinals urged him to accept the proposals without further ado, and end the matter, he stood by his words. He was finally summoned in together with his usual suite of Montesa, Ximénez, ambassador Diego Lasso, and all the other ambassadors and notaries. Before he made the customary prostration in front of His Holiness, Mendoza, either vengeful for having been made to wait such a long time or in accord with a persistent line of action to challenge the Pope's authority, staged another of his incidents. In the face of the entire Sacred College, ignoring the Pope on his throne, Don Diego went up to each of the three Cardinals who had

[8] This paragraph and the following until p. 209, based on *AHE* I, 170–173; also GP II, 61–65.

talked to him outside and made each of them, singly, give him his solemn word that he would keep the twenty-day limit of which he had spoken before. Unconcerned about the visible consternation of the assembly, Mendoza then paid his obeisance to the Pope and asked in formal words for the reply he had come to receive.

The Pope still hoped to prevent any discussion. He asked Secretary Blosio to read aloud the reply from the prelates in Bologna, and Blosio did so, kneeling. The substance, as was to be expected, was that the prelates raised so many obstacles that they were virtually refusing to return to Trent.[9] As soon as Don Diego had heard the reply out, he began to speak. The Pope interrupted, saying Mendoza had heard the reply and would receive a copy of it, so there was no reason for him to talk. If he spoke, he would have to be answered; then there would be a dispute, and they would never come to an end.

I humbly begged His Holiness to hear me because it was necessary and advisable that I say a few words. His Holiness was silent. I said that I had heard the answer, and since in the present situation and necessity delay was most prejudicial to Germany and the health of its souls, I begged His Holiness to specify quickly a suitable cure. Also, in the reply, the "Council of Bologna" was mentioned many times. Although I had not contradicted or replied during the reading, I did not wish it implied that I approved of such an appellation; nor did I approve of the delay the remedy would suffer. The Pope said: "Then you protest?" I replied that I was not protesting but merely making a declaration, or, if the opportunity were lost, the fault would be laid at the Emperor's door. His Holiness replied that everyone understood we

---

[9] In the reply from Bologna, the Bolognese *patres* declared themselves willing to return to Trent, if this could be arranged without general harm to Christendom; for this it would be essential, first, that those who had all this time remained in Trent should now come to Bologna; second, as the German nation had promised only to submit to a Council that was to be held in Trent, it must be made clear that the decrees about questions of faith already legally published were irrevocable and could not be subjected to a new examination; third, security must be given that nothing new would come up for examination in the Council; fourth, if they had to go back to Trent, it would be necessary that the entire assembly and each individual member would be assured of complete freedom to remain there or to leave; fifth, it must be recognized that the *patres* had the right to transfer or end the Council. GP II, 61–65.

did this in order to pin him down as negligent in an indirect way, but we would not catch him.

I said it was done only to show the good intentions of Your Majesties [Charles V and King Ferdinand], who would not be guilty in case some inconvenience should result from the delay. He replied angrily that I knew well how many times I had asked him for delay in behalf of Your Majesty, including the last time in Perugia. I answered with all reverence that it was not so, and then His Holiness told me to admit the truth. I said that Your Majesty never wanted to consent to a suspension nor a vacation nor a delay of the Council, and that Cardinal Farnese and Cardinal Crescencio and His Holiness himself knew that I had always said so at the negotiations and the last time in Perugia, and that I had talked then not as Your Majesty's man, but as Don Diego.

To this he replied that my identity had nothing to do with him when he dealt with matters of state. Only as ambassador of Your Majesty would he listen to me. Since it seemed to me that the substance of the business was more important than what concerned me personally [these words imply that he felt personally insulted all the same], I said I may be who I may be; but this had never been requested nor consented to on Your Majesty's behalf and the Cardinal Farnese knew it. The Pope then asked Farnese to speak. Some cardinals rose to their feet, and the Cardinal Farnese claimed I told the truth and was right.

This admission from his grandson made the Pope lose his temper. Several cardinals tried to stop Mendoza, but he continued challenging Paul III until the old man got up and left.

Reporting in more detail, Mendoza notes that the Duke of "Malfa" (Amalfi) and Lope de Guzmán had also been in his entourage as witnesses on that occasion "because they are qualified persons." He notes also how the Cardinals from the Imperial side had behaved: "Cardinal Coria [Francisco de Mendoza y Bobadilla, his relative] spoke very religiously, honorably, learnedly, and to everyone's great satisfaction; and Cardinal De la Cueva was all right. Burgos [Juan Alvarez de Toledo] and Carpi were not present as they were ill, and Farnese did not behave badly."

Don Diego's mind leaped ahead to the possible consequences of this spiritual war. He ended his letter to the Emperor by advising him to request all Spaniards, vassals, and priests to leave Rome and return to Spain. "This would be a lance thrust at His Holiness. The

Catholic Kings and the Bishop of Cuenca of the time of Pope Julius [II] provide an example for such procedure. . . ."[10]

During the twenty days of "grace," Mendoza went to Piombino (as we saw above) to deliver an ultimatum to the dowager Appiani. In view of these and other Imperial activities that disturbed the peace in Italy, the Pope tried to contract a defensive league with France and Venice.[11] And on January 16, 1548, somewhat hurriedly anticipating the deadline of those twenty days, the Council opened in Bologna under the presidency of Cardinal del Monte.

The Emperor's two lawyers, Vargas and Doctor Velasco, had been ready for the Council, staying in Bologna since the previous November. They lost no time in appearing at this first session. Accompanied by the required number of notaries and witnesses, they delivered the formal Protest. (Don Diego, then in Rome, had already held the duplicate of the Protest in his hand at the last consistory and was now to read it to Paul III in person.) In an uninterrupted session lasting six hours, Del Monte listened to the address and formally replied by denying every point of it.

As soon as the news of this event reached the Urbs, the Pope fled, shutting himself up in one of his country estates. He hoped to escape the delivery of the Protest, but forgot to reckon on Mendoza's persistence. Don Diego, in his pursuit of Paul III, was intercepted on the road by Cardinal Farnese. In a friendly conversation held right on a meadow, Farnese finally succeeded in getting rid of Mendoza by promising to take his grandfather back to Rome the next day and to hold another consistory soon.[12]

Monday, January 23, 1548, Mendoza and his large suite of companions arrived outside the assembly hall before the Pope showed himself. Among Mendoza's escort, besides a notary, were, as witnesses, the Duke of Amalfi, Senator Grasso, Don Diego Lasso, Abbot Brizeño, Don Diego's nephew Don Antonio de Mendoza, the secretaries Montesa and Ximénez, Doctor Velasco, who had come

[10] Arch Sim., Est., leg. 875, fol. 3; also GP II, 66; NB X, 623.
[11] Mendoza to Charles V, Rome, February 2, 1548, Döllinger, Beiträge, pp. 134–143.
[12] Ibid.

from Bologna, and the Sienese ambassador, Nicodemo Fartegueri. As at Don Diego's former appearances in the same place, all other ambassadors had been invited. With the exception of the envoys from France and Venice, the entire diplomatic corps was present.

As soon as Don Diego appeared, the Cardinals Trani and Farnese made an appeal to prevent him from delivering the Protest. But Mendoza realized they were only trying to delay him, and he saw no reason to withdraw. When this decision was reported to the Pope in his private chambers, he sent the Spanish Cardinals "Burgos" and "Coria" out to Mendoza with a last-minute offer. The Pope proposed to let the prelates from Bologna meet in Vicenza with those from Trent, with full freedom for all those assembled there, to determine if the original transfer had been legitimate. They could then return to Trent with every assurance that no Council act would be made in Bologna.

It was a desperate proposal, a bargain to save the Pope's reputation at least halfway, and the Spanish Cardinals urged Mendoza earnestly to heed it. There is no doubt that it was in Mendoza's power to postpone and even suspend the delivery of the Protest. While he answered the Cardinals that he was not authorized by the Emperor to accept any offer except that of returning the Council directly to Trent, he might have submitted the Pope's face-saving proposal to His Majesty's judgment. But having gone so far, he refused to let himself be talked out of his purpose.

When he and his suite filed into the hall, the Cardinals had already taken their seats. The Pope, dressed in white, with a scarlet cape over his shoulders, wearing a red "birretta," walked in vigorously, mounted the two steps to the pontifical throne, and sat down. At His Holiness' appearance, everybody knelt on the ground for a moment, and all remained bareheaded until the end, with the exception of the Pope himself—and Don Diego. Standing in the same place where he had addressed the Sacred College before, Mendoza started to speak, but the Pope interrupted him, calling out very loudly: "On your knees, and thus remain!" (*Genibus flexis et non aliter.*) Startled, Mendoza looked around for a moment, and then, hesitantly, went down on his knees. His entire entourage, including the ambassadors Diego Lasso and Fartegueri, loyally followed suit, while the ambassadors of the other nations, among them those of Urbino, Ferrara, and Florence, remained standing.

After Don Diego's opening remarks in Spanish, introducing the lawyer Doctor Velasco, who had come from Bologna to do the actual reading of the Protest, the Pope and Cardinal Trani interrupted him again, asking for the Emperor's authorization to let Mendoza make the Protest. Don Diego ordered his secretary Ximénez to exhibit the "power" (a customary parchment with its red tassel, plumb, and seal) and to read its text aloud. Then Doctor Velasco proceeded to read the lengthy Protest in Latin. He was listened to in silence. The Pope gave no sign except at one point, where it said: "His Majesty, singly, ended the war." Here the Pope laughed sarcastically. When it was over, he commented that it sounded like an invective rather than a protest, but he would reply to every point.

Still on his knees, Mendoza proceeded to ask the notary and six or seven of his witnesses to give testimony of the action; then, a prepared letter from the Pope, also in Latin, was read to all. It said that His Holiness and the Sacred College had heard what was read and that answer would be made in the next consistory. Meanwhile, all ambassadors and witnesses were ordered to remain in Rome until the Protest had been answered, and no notary was allowed to give notice of the Protest prior to the response.

Don Diego at once took exception to this, saying that he had no authority to receive a reply. The Pope, very angry, asked how he could have authorization for one thing and not for another? Don Diego, as usual, had the last word. He proposed to listen to the answer not as Imperial ambassador, but as a private citizen.[13]

On the same day, Maffei, the papal secretary, wrote Cardinal Santa Croce: "The revenge we have taken was to make the signor Don Diego and all his company stay on their knees while the Protest was being read."[14]

"It seemed to go over well," wrote Don Diego to the Emperor, referring to the delivery of the Protest. "It moved the minds of all the Cardinals to some extent. . . . His Holiness took it as a threat. In the beginning he was very brave, but furious. He did not say a word because his people had admonished him to be quiet. I am told

[13] Ibid.; see also GP II, 70–75. The content of the Protest is summed up by Pastor, *Geschichte*, V, 642.

[14] GP II, 74.

that after I went out His Holiness and the Cardinals were silent for a while, and quite bewildered."[15]

The Pope's reply was written carefully and cleverly by Cardinal Reginald Pole, who used the finest points of diplomacy. In order to avert a complete break with the Emperor, the papals made Don Diego responsible for the Protest. He was accused of having exceeded the order of his master, with the soothing qualification that Mendoza must have felt pain in delivering words that hurt the Pope so deeply. The reply also offered a new proposal: Paul III himself would judge the legality of the Bologna Council (instead of leaving this judgment, as he had done until then, up to the members of the Council). For this he would consult four Cardinals from different nations—Du Bellay from France, Alvarez de Toledo from Spain, Crescenzi from Italy, and Pole from England. For the immediate welfare of the German souls, His Holiness proposed to send three legates to Germany, and to avert a sudden schism, the Pope ordered a suspension of the Council. The reply did not change Don Diego's attitude. He persisted in the Protest and said he would continue to protest until the Day of Judgment, and even later if need be.[16]

Although the general tension had been dissolved in a sort of spiritual truce, Mendoza again shouldered the entire burden of, and blame for, his master's policies. (He insisted having "moderated the Emperor's fire," he could have gone much further.)[17] Rome stood in awe of his intrepidity. "Don Diego will soon leave for Siena, and it is believed that, before he departs, he will do something else that is perhaps even worse than the Protest," wrote the ambassador of Lucca on February 5.[18]

But it did not come to that. The formal meeting was followed a few days later by an informal audience with the Pope, where he and Mendoza went through every point of the Emperor's complaints. "In the midst of it he dropped off in a nap," reports Don

[15] Döllinger, Beiträge, pp. 134–143.

[16] About the reply, and Mendoza's reception of it, Nicodemo Fartegueri to the Dieci of Siena, February 1, 1548, Archivio di Stato, Siena (Arch. Siena), Dieci Cons., vol. 18.

[17] AC, p. 343.

[18] Pastor, Geschichte, V, 646, n. 1.

Diego, "and seeing he did this to show me how little all this matters to him, I stayed there until he awoke. Then he replied to what I had read to him while he slept. Very annoyed I told him I would read it to him once more, but he said he had understood it well and reflected on it. With this I took my leave."[19]

Freedom of Conscience

In the four months following the Protest, affairs of Siena kept Mendoza away from Rome. As soon as he was outside the papal court (where he suspected the papals of prying into his mails) he described the Pope in franker terms. With Paul III now allied with France and Venice, Mendoza wrote: "I remind Your Majesty of the nature of the Pope. [He tries] to make foes for Your Majesty in Italy, where he persecutes and destroys your servants but favors those of France. He harmed many [of them] as long as they were under your protection, but as they passed under the French King's protection, he favored and helped them."[20]

During 1548, conditions in Europe were again changing drastically. The German Protestants, recently so browbeaten, recovered quickly and soon showed their former intransigence. The moment for an attempt at religious unification could not be recaptured. And France, after the sudden vacuum resulting from the change of kings, was once more on the warpath; Henri II continued the policies of his father. In Rome, the Pope still demurred about the Council, at the same time insisting on his claim to Piacenza.

In the first half of that year, Charles V's theologians in Germany (several Spanish and German Catholics, and a few Protestants) prepared the "Interim." This declaration of faith in twenty-six chapters was to substitute for the nonexistent Council. The Emperor hoped it would pacify the religious quarrels that by then were a generation old. All chapters of the Interim corresponded to Catholic dogma, but in a mild and vague form. Mention of Purgatory was omitted; and there was no clear pronouncement on Justification or on the Holy Mass. Most articles were open to varying interpretation. Aimed at easing the Protestants back into the old Church,

[19] GP II, 77, 78.
[20] Mendoza to Charles V, Milan, April 9, 1548, Döllinger, *Beiträge*, pp. 144–150.

this collection of articles was to serve as a compromise between the faiths until (the Emperor hoped) the Council would be reconvened to make the final decision on the questions of the sacraments and articles of faith. Although the Pope, much to his chagrin, had not been consulted before the publication of the Interim ("this Interim has given His Holiness a great blow"[21]), the Emperor requested Paul III to send him certain powers in order to have his Interim applied successfully. By one of these powers the Pope was expected to give the German people a general dispensation so that they could take communion in both kinds.[22] The Pope refused.

Concerning this dispensation, Mendoza made a comment that discloses his attitude toward religious, political, and philosophical matters. On September 1, 1548, writing to the Bishop of Arras from Rome, he analyzed and criticized item by item the powers of faculty that the Pope had worded and sent in reply to the Emperor. Referring to Paul III's insistence that each individual confess and do penance before he could receive the dispensation, Don Diego observes:

As regards [the powers of faculty] it seems to me, frankly, that they are only so much air. They [the papals] wish to give us some empty straw [because] they do not give powers for general dispensation but only for the particular individual. Everyone wishing to confess his error [has] to go and do penance and [receive] dispensation from the said legates. But it is impossible to force individuals because if I, an individual person, do not wish to go to the house of the legate, and [if] another and another [refuse also], the police ought not to go from house to house to force me to do so. The Emperor may thus issue a general dispensation for all, and the Pope can give general absolution; but they cannot force anyone, nor is it possible in thousands of years to absolve individuals this way. And this I say as a philosopher and as Moor of Granada, or as a Marrano, as even today the Inquisition has more to do in Spain than on its first day.[23]

Apparently Don Diego's personally conditioned view of Spain with its three still-existing faiths colored his equally personal pro-

[21] Mendoza to Arras, May 25, 1548, *AIH* II (1911): 184.

[22] Druffel, *Briefe* I, no. 180, p. 131.

[23] Mendoza to Arras, September 1, 1548, *AC*, pp. 119–120. See E. Spivakovsky, "Diego Hurtado de Mendoza and Averroism," *JHI* 26, no. 3 (1965): 307–326, particularly pp. 317–320.

posal for a solution to the confessional split in Germany. He thought the Spanish attitude could serve as a model for the Germans. He saw his own country as a reasonable place, where adherents of the most divergent beliefs (Moor, Marrano, philosopher— as he distinguishes the most obvious ones) could live side by side with Catholics so long as everyone conformed outwardly, without running afoul of the Inquisition. This institution, which had been introduced into Castile a full generation before his birth, Mendoza apparently accepted as another of the political realities one simply had to live with.

It is significant not only that the conditions Don Diego described corresponded to the reality of 1548, but also that this state of outward conformity and inner freedom appeared perfectly reasonable to him. Counseling others to compromise with the Church, he must have practiced what he preached. Naturally unaware at that time (near the end of Spain's splendid half-century of transitory enlightenment) that Spain would soon succumb to deep reaction and intellectual stagnation, he found its prevailing laissez-faire condition so exemplary as to recommend it to the Teutons! If only the Pope would show a bit of good will and grant a general pardon to those who had publicly repudiated Catholicism, the German Protestants would, in Mendoza's opinion, be quite content to worship as Lutherans in the privacy of their homes. No need for all those bitter quarrels, so long as appearances could be saved! Since he knew no other atmosphere of religious liberty, such a compliance with unavoidable circumstances must have appeared to Don Diego to be the only possible existence for the individual.[24]

However ill advised it may have been for Charles V to recommend this particular kind of "Marranism" to the religious dissidents in Germany, Mendoza's peculiar interpretation of the papal rejection of the Emperor's demand shows how precious an inviolate private conscience was to him. By this, he did not advocate concealment or lip service. Besides, he spoke from political experience; he dealt similarly with the people of Siena to whom, as their absolute, autocratic ruler, he left their freedom of speech. "Let them grum-

---

[24] His attitude may be difficult to imagine for a citizen of a democracy who takes his liberty of conscience for granted, but anyone who has lived under a government exacting conformity, or even a smaller pressure group, might find it far from strange.

ble," he said, "as long as they let me do what I have to do!"[25] He simply recommended that as long as the people went through the motions of obedience, the Church should shut an eye and leave a certain leeway for the individuals' mental reservations. "In things concerning the conscience and the soul, I will always say what I feel," he had said in Trent.[26]

Meanwhile Paul III agreed to send the Legates with the proper powers, though with strictly Catholic measures, to Germany. But again it was too late. Religious tension in Germany had worsened, the Interim had not helped, and the Emperor still resisted the Pope in the questions of Trent and Piacenza.[27]

[25] "Yo los he siempre dexado dezir a su plazer y ellos a mi hazer el mio ...," Mendoza to Prince Philip, Rome, October 14, 1550, GP III, 358.
[26] Don Diego to Vargas, December 16, 1546, GP III, 325–326.
[27] Pastor, *Geschichte*, V, 664–668.

10. CHANGE IN THE PAPACY, 1549–1550

The most beautiful, most perfect, and most
important business in the world. . . .
. . . devils in Judas' cauldron . . .

Don Diego[1]

The Death of Pope Paul III

MENDOZA SPENT THE LATTER PART OF 1548 and the first three months of 1549 in Siena. When he returned to Rome in April, 1549, the Emperor had given him a somewhat gentler commission than formerly—or so it seemed on the surface.[2] This improved mood must have been the reason for Mendoza's broadcasting, before his arrival, that Ottavio Farnese would probably receive Piacenza soon.[3] As this did not at all correspond to Charles V's intentions, Don Diego must have invented it. The papals, grasping at the slightest indication of hope, responded with great affection. At this juncture the papal secretary Dandino brought Mendoza Paul III's offer of a cardinalate, only to be haughtily rebuffed.[4]

Perhaps Don Diego said this canard about Piacenza only because

---

[1] "el mas hermoso negotio i mas hecho i mas importante del mundo," Mendoza to Arras, December 31, 1549, *AC*, p. 159; "los diablos en la caldera de Judas," Mendoza to Arras, February 3, 1550, *AC*, p. 183.

[2] Mendoza to Cosimo I, March 31, 1549, Arch. Flor., Mediceo 3268, Rose-file.

[3] GP II, 111, n. 2.

[4] GP II, 115.

the Pope's death was expected daily. A year earlier, on July 30, 1548, Mendoza had written to Charles V that the astrologers were convinced "the Pope will die this year. [The astrologer] in whom he believes most and who predicted the pontificate to him, after much begging by His Holiness, granted him life until next May."[5] During Mendoza's stay in Siena, Montesa had reported to him on the Pope's health, and Mendoza passed the news on to the Emperor: "The secret illness of the Pope is true . . . the surgeon says he is going." Early in January, 1549, Mendoza reports: "The Pope continues in his indisposition. For three days he has been eating privately, not wishing to see anyone, nor does he wish to be seen, because he looks so bad that the *albayade* [white powder-paint] does not do him any good."[6]

Yet Paul III pulled through once more. For Don Diego's reception after his absence of half a year, the Pope ordered honors as lavish as though he were a new ambassador. When he greeted Mendoza personally, with much ceremony, he again praised Mendoza's father and grandfather "who had served in this same business at the Apostolic See."[7]

On their side, the papals thought they were making progress in the territorial question of Parma and Piacenza by producing ancient original documents that proved ecclesiastical rights to the disputed lands. As long as these parchments were searched for, and before they had been examined at the Emperor's court, the improved mood held.

Don Diego ingratiated himself particularly at this time by trying to cure the Pope of his superstition. Throughout his life Paul III had let himself be guided by soothsayers; astrologers chose the days and set the hours of his every audience, consistory, or journey. Now the old man still believed he would die in May, and Mendoza told him not to fear the astrologers, demonstrating to him that they were liars. He advised the Pope so persuasively to settle his disputes with the Emperor on account of his age and illness that he endeared himself even more. Paul III "offered me his house and the

5 *NB* XI, 669, 670.
6 GP II, 127.
7 *NB* XI, 771.

pontificate, and in such a way that it seems to me I have never seen him so beside himself."[8]

The Farneses' temporary affection for Don Diego increased when he conceded that some documents they showed him seemed authentic to him. To be sure, the papals let him look only hurriedly at the parchments: "Now you see it—now you don't."[9] But when these documents reached the Emperor's court, they were studied more leisurely. There, they read quite differently from what the Curia said and revealed that neither the Apostolic See nor anyone invested by a Pope had a right to Piacenza or to Parma. Consequently, instead of giving back Piacenza, Charles V now also asked for Parma. But to keep up negotiations, the Emperor proposed to give Ottavio Farnese another estate for Parma within the Kingdom of Naples, "not as a recompensation but as a mercy."[10]

This was a blow to the improved mood in Rome. Again rebuffed by the Emperor, but having happily survived the fearful month of May, the Pope's manner toward Mendoza cooled visibly. Don Diego took the first opportunity to return Paul III's slights.

The day of Saint Peter had come. It was the Spanish ambassador's duty to function in an age-old ceremony on behalf of the Viceroy of Naples. From the beginning of the eleventh century, Naples, as a bishopric, sent an annual contribution to the papacy. To be delivered on Saint Peter's Day, it consisted of "a beautiful white caparisoned *hacanea* [hackney steed] together with the annual tribute of six or seven thousand ducats."[11] Don Diego, as in former years, had to select a magnificent horse (for which the Viceroy had sent him a thousand escudos). He was to present it to the Pope the morning of the feast day, after Mass, as soon as His Holiness emerged from the chapel. The Spaniards used this occasion to display their forces and alliances. Their ambassador and his colleagues, the ambassadors of Savoy, Florence, and Siena among them, all in festive robes of red damask, would ride behind a caval-

---

[8] *NB* XI, 780; also GP II, 116.

[9] "a veote y no te veo, sin dexarlas leer . . .," Mendoza to Arras, April, 1549, *AIH* II, (1911).

[10] Ludwig von Pastor, *Geschichte der Päpste*, V, 669.

[11] *AC*, p. 128, n. 1; also GP II, 119, 120; *NB* XI, 305, 801.

cade of a thousand gentlemen and in front of fifty bishops. The gift horse would be led ahead of the procession, together with another horse on which would ride a festively liveried page of the ambassador, who was to carry a crimson purse with the seven thousand gold ducats.

But both Don Diego and the Pope believed rumors that the other was planning some mischief in connection with this ceremony; such was the current mood of Imperial-papal relations. Apprehensive of a possible slight to himself, Don Diego carefully prepared some mischief of his own. To begin with, instead of purchasing the finest horse in Rome, he bought a cheap old steed that the Pontiff had once received in a similar ceremony and given to his granddaughter Francesca, daughter of the Count of Santa Fiore, as a wedding present thirteen years before. Although Mendoza assured the Emperor he had adorned the hackney "better than usual," the Florentine ambassador, for one, reported that it was caparisoned rather poorly. So far so good. But when Don Diego with the gift-bearing procession arrived at the door of the chapel, among an expectant crowd that filled Saint Peter's Square, the Pope, who had ended Mass much earlier than usual, was gone. At the door stood the Cardinal Chamberlain Santa Fiore (brother, incidentally, of the horse's former owner) to receive the steed in his grandfather's behalf. Santa Fiore blamed Mendoza for being late, but Mendoza reminded him that the Pope had ended the service early. The Pope may have planned to avoid Mendoza simply because the identity of the horse—an affront if ever there was one—was perhaps disclosed to him by his relatives; but if he thought he could escape Don Diego he had reckoned once again without the latter's resources. Don Diego had no intention of sparing the Pope a personal encounter. He sent word to His Holiness to show himself at the *baranda* so that he could present the hackney to him from below, but the Pope, who had gone to his dinner, did not condescend to reply.

"And so I decided to go upstairs with my hackney, right into the Pope's chamber," wrote Don Diego. He was made to stand (together with four workmen who had carried the horse upstairs for him, and with people of his entourage) in a narrow passage outside the Pope's dining room. He waited patiently as long as His Holiness sat at dinner, but let it be known that, unless the Pope received the horse personally from his hands, he would leave and take it back to his own house. In that case the papal See would forfeit the tribute from Naples forever.

Paul III was within earshot of the clatter and commotion in the corridor, where his bewildered table stewards, coming and going with tureens, platters, and jugs, jostled Don Diego's frolicking party. The Pope consulted with his advisers as to whether he could refuse to see Mendoza if he let a minister act in his stead. Cardinals Santa Croce, Farnese, Crescenzi, Caraffa, and the Count of Pitigliano, pondered; but Crescenzi apparently was the only one in that group whose historical knowledge matched Don Diego's. He convinced the irate Pope that Mendoza acted correctly within the feudal law.

When Don Diego was finally called in by the papal chamberlain, he first pretended to hesitate, remarking, with the most serious face, that now that the Pope had eaten he should take his customary nap. He went in, however. The Pope showed him his anger. "So, this is the second act of the comedy in the chapel!" he told Mendoza, taking the reins of the horse from him. "Why didn't you want to give it to my grandson?" As Mendoza had just taught His Holiness a vivid lesson in feudatory law, he preferred to remain silent and presented the tribute with the appropriate ceremony.[12]

Cosimo's ambassadorial assistant in Rome, Buonanni, who always regarded and judged Don Diego with a jaundiced eye in order to please his master, reports this story with every detail. He adds that "Don Diego has laughed with many people about it, under a pretense of grace and pleasantry."[13]

However much of a practical joke it was, Mendoza himself writes of it to the Emperor with a straight face, never mentioning that the steed was old, cheaply bought and shabbily outfitted.

Some time later Mendoza asked his secretary, Pedro Ximénez, who had gone to the Emperor's court with this letter, to tell him what they said over there "about my bringing the hackney to His Holiness in the chamber."[14]

[12] All details of this episode are in GP II, 119, 120; *NB* XI, 305, 801.

[13] Benedetto Buonanni to Cosimo I, June 29, 1549. Pastor, *Geschichte*, V, 862, app. no. 82.

[14] July, 1549, *AIH* II (1911), no. 34, pp. 558–561. The letter there is erroneously dated 1552.

Annoyance over the question of Parma and Piacenza continued, and Don Diego was blamed for it even by some of his own faction. He kept defending himself. By now, successful in his two outstanding posts, and possibly not a little arrogant in consequence, he had made many enemies among his own Spaniards and Imperials, and he knew it. "Please tell Monseñor [the elder Granvelle]," he told Ximénez in July 1549, "that Burgos, Carpi and the Pope are in league against me. They want nothing better than to trip me so that I should stumble and have to be thrown out of Rome."[15]

But he remained in Rome, alert to the possibility of sudden change. Conditions in Siena were stagnant at the time; the "Piombino affair" was still unsettled; the Duke of Florence kept waiting. The territorial dispute between Pope and Emperor remained stalled over the summer, too, and so did the problem of the Council. When the Pope started some maneuvering about a single-handed reformation that he wished to undertake (a pretext whereby he tried to recall the Imperial bishops still holding out in Trent), the Emperor threatened with a schism. At last, swayed by Mendoza, Paul III yielded all the plans he had hatched about his Council in Bologna. On September 17 he ordered the bishops still present there to disband.

At the same time, the Pope also decided to end the problem of Parma and Piacenza. Suddenly he changed his mind about enriching all his descendants. To the consternation of the Imperial faction, he decided to return both states to the Church, promising to compensate Ottavio by the small duchy of Camerino, in addition to money, but intending to shift Parma into the hands of Orazio and the French.[16] Despite the protests of Madama, Ottavio, and Cardinal Farnese, Paul III sent Camillo Orsini to take possession of Parma for the Holy See.[17]

The old man's action drove his grandsons Ottavio and Alessandro to despair. Don Diego seized the opportunity to advise them to come to terms with the Emperor. In a clever coup to save themselves from the sinking ship, under Mendoza's instigation, Ottavio Farnese left Rome secretly on October 20, hurrying to Parma in order to reoccupy it. Camillo Orsini would not let him enter unless

15 Ibid.
16 Giuseppe de Leva, "La elezione di Papa Giulio III," *Riv. St. It.* I, 21–36.
17 Pastor, *Geschichte*, V, 673.

the Pope had ordered it, but the Pope did not give this permit; instead he ordered Ottavio to return to Rome at once.

Ottavio now applied for support to Ferrante Gonzaga, the enemy of his House. Gonzaga was prepared to assist him if Ottavio would hand over Parma in exchange for compensation or hold it as Imperial fief. When Ottavio agreed to these conditions, Gonzaga proceeded to conquer Parma.

The news of these events reached Rome on the evening of November 5. The following day it was Cardinal Farnese's painful duty to read the latest letter from his brother to the Pope. Ottavio declared that he did not intend to give up Parma; he boasted he had no lack of friends, among them the Cardinal Madruzzo of Trent, who had already given him ten thousand crowns, and Don Ferrante Gonzaga, "a good honest man who had promised him assistance."

When the Pope heard this—that Ottavio, his grandson, had sold out to the murderer of his own father and was rebelling against his grandfather—he started up in a sudden rage. He tore the cardinal's cap from Farnese's head and threw it on the floor and then he collapsed. He died a few days later, on November 10, 1549.[18]

The Conclave

The great international event of electing Paul III's successor was to boil down to a contest of strength between Mendoza and the Duke of Florence, deepening any former antagonism between the two Lords in Tuscany. How could an event of such incomparable importance come to depend upon just these two worldly men, persons who had no functions whatsoever within the system of the Roman Church? Their wishes would seem to have had little relevance in a game of chance for the highest stakes in the world.

Doubtless, no other European event would be as consequential as the conclave in the Sistine Chapel. Neither the death of an emperor nor of a king of France could signify such an upset. At that time of hereditary monarchies, the pontificate was a rare instance of a government subject to the chance of choice. While the Doge of Venice was elected from among the senators, his peers, he was only

18 Dandolo to Signory of Venice, November 9, 10, and 13, 1549, *Cal. St. P.*, Ven. V, 241–247.

a figurehead; the body of the Senate retained all the executive power, leaving the contest entirely devoid of excitement. Also the citizens of Siena used to elect their magistrates, but this was a small provincial matter (although it happened to concern Don Diego, in his function as Sienese governor, in particular. Incidentally, he had put an end to that last semblance of republican government in Siena). The papacy depended on the election of one of the cardinals by a two-thirds majority vote of the cardinals of the Sacred College. There were about forty possibilities at this conclave where forty-seven cardinals assisted. No other election could have had the same importance. The person of the Pope, in theory the greatest prince of universal Christendom, and in reality still a monarch commanding a large part of Italian territory, intimately affected every human being wherever Christian influence prevailed. The new Pope's favor, if given either to Spain or France, might make one of them the greatest power on earth, probably dragging all of Italy back into endless wars. No wonder the outcome was watched as anxiously by the mightiest monarchs of Europe (who meddled recklessly in the secret proceedings) as by the Roman populace who were powerless to interfere, but who were kept in frantic suspense.

From the closely concerned point of view of Mendoza, the possibilities of grave trouble were endless. Instantaneously he would have to deal with whatever dangers the future might bring. But much worse, the Emperor, as he knew only too well, would hold him responsible for the outcome. If a French cardinal were elected, probably the Spaniards would be driven from Italy; also, no attempt would then be made to heal the religious split in Germany, where many Spaniards still hoped to bring the Lutherans back into the fold by reviving the General Council in Trent. All Italy would turn "French." But he knew that a Frenchman had as little chance as a Spaniard, because the Italians held together much more firmly these days. Cardinal Farnese had told him that "they have so many lords [of small sovereign principalities] in Italy that it is an intolerable situation; it would not do for them to bring new [foreign] lords in. . . ."[19]

To Mendoza a choice almost as evil as a French candidate would

[19] Mendoza to Arras, January 12, 1550, *AC*, pp. 166–167.

be an Italian subservient to France, such as Clement VII. Rome had been punished for that Pope's anti-Imperial policy by the sack. And "French," in Don Diego's view, had been the late Pope, too, despite his profession of neutrality. Therefore he had to do everything possible to promote those who would let themselves be dictated to by the Emperor. The first difficulty confronting him here was the fact that the old Pope's hold on the Sacred College, as well as on Rome, did not vanish immediately after his death.

Since about three-fourths of all the cardinals had been elevated to the purple by Paul III, the new Pope was likely to be one of his own "creatures," obliged out of gratitude not to touch the properties of his benefactor's progeny—precisely the disputed states of Parma and Piacenza, the recent major cause of disunity between Emperor and Pope. And the weight of the three Farnese cardinals alone, Paul III's grandsons, Alessandro and Ranuccio Farnese, and their cousin Guidascanio Sforza, Cardinal of Santa Fiore, could be decisive in swaying the election. Since the Imperial faction needed the Farnese group to outvote the French party, Mendoza at the very beginning made a deal with Cardinal Farnese that would, though indirectly, determine the outcome of the election.

It was the supreme moment of Don Diego's life; never again would he hold such power. But he was not in the best condition to face the crisis that he had been expecting every day for the past three years. In his house, his favorite nephew and invaluable assistant, Don Antonio, son of Don Bernardino, lay fatally ill with tertian fever; before the year was over Don Diego would be mourning his untimely death. He himself, often somewhat rheumatic, suddenly was unable to move one of his arms.[20] Moreover, he had received no instruction from the Emperor to guide his immediate actions. Even so he deemed it his duty to protect the peace of the city, and he lost no time in making himself the temporary master of Rome.

In the precarious times of *sede vacante*—while a late Pope was being mourned, or, as the case might be, derided,[21] and while all

---

20 *AC*, p. 140.

21 Cf. Carlo Capasso, *La politica di Papa Paulo III e l'Ialia*, I, 1: ". . . In uno scoppio d'ira i Romani giugevano a scoperchiare il recente sepolcro [of Clement VII] e a insozzarlo repetutamente. . . ."

the cardinals were confined in conclave in the Vatican—murder, robbery, and absolute lawlessness was the usual order of the day. But not so after the long and strong reign of Paul III, who was solemnly mourned. The people had venerated him, not, perhaps, as the saint they knew he was not, but for his wisdom and grandeur. Even on the last day of his life, the late Pontiff had had the foresight to order Rome occupied by five thousand protection troops. It seemed as though from the grave he could still prevent the Imperials from asserting their superiority. While his grandfather was still breathing, Orazio Farnese, the fiancé of the French King's daughter, had closed all the gates of Rome. Outgoing mail—even Mendoza's—was prevented from leaving without Orazio's permission, and his troops also guarded the Castle Sant'Angelo, which held the papal moneybags.

But while the hand of the dead Pope could still annoy the Imperial ambassador, it had not been able to direct him while he lived and could not do so now. The grandsons, for all their cardinalates, dukedoms, and royal marriages, never impressed Don Diego even during Paul III's life. Now, there was no one in Rome superior to himself. At once he sent messengers to the three other members of the Imperial "axis," Gonzaga, the Duke of Florence, and the Viceroy of Naples, requesting their troops as well as, humbly, their "advice," although he acted exclusively by his own counsel. At the same time he had his own lieutenants recruit troops in Rome, and he issued proclamations throughout the city and state for every Spanish and Sienese subject to assemble on the Piazza in front of his house—a sea of people, ready to bear arms for the Emperor.

The College of Cardinals, shocked by Don Diego's sudden seizure and display of power, which was without precedent, warned him not to exceed any measure he might take legitimately for protecting just his own person.[22] But they had to acquiesce in the "protection" he graciously proffered on them. They acceded to his request that they assume the responsibility for all the papal fortresses and troops (by these measures he diminished Orazio's authority), giving Mendoza the final authority over all of them. His troops succeeded in preventing possible civil battles between the "Ghibelline" Colonna and the "Guelf" Orsini, the two principal Roman families

[22] Dandolo to Venice, November 13, 1549, Arch. Ven., Despatches of Dandolo, Rose-file.

who had been in "desperate conflict" already in the early 1300s.[23] He did not even need all the help quickly offered by his "axis" partners. The Duke of Florence was willing to send ten thousand infantry under a captain and command a further fifteen thousand himself if needed. All the Florentines in Rome were ordered to be at Don Diego's disposal, and Cosimo offered also 300,000 escudos toward their equipment and pay. The Viceroy of Naples sent four *banderas* of infantry to the border and promised to send all the troops of his kingdom, if necessary, raising even more.[24] From Don Ferrante Gonzaga came his son-in-law, Fabrizio Colonna, with six hundred cavalry.

Paul III had deprived Fabrizio's father, Ascanio Colonna, of his estates and exiled him as a rebel. Don Diego at once invited the Imperial-minded Roman to return to his properties and to Rome. (Colonna's formal restitution had to await the signature of the new Pope.) Others of the same family, most of whom had resided during the Farnese rule in the kingdom of Naples, followed the call, so that Colonna troops joined the Imperials, recovering castles sequestered years ago by their enemies, while the leaders, at one time numbering four members of their clan, were all lodged in Mendoza's house. "It is as safe in Rome as in Valladolid," Mendoza wrote the Emperor proudly; and to Arras he wrote, "In Rome, which I have kept so quiet for you—all the Colonna and Orsini are like sheep."[25]

The French ambassador, Claude d'Urfé, also equal to his task, forestalled the quick election of an Imperial Pope before the arrival of the six or seven cardinals who lived in France. (His partisan, the Cardinal of Ferrara, succeeded in delaying the Pope's funeral until November 21, and according to age-old custom, the conclave could not start before another eight days had passed.)[26] While not attempting to oppose the overwhelming Imperial forces, d'Urfé

[23] Henri Pirenne, *A History of Europe*, p. 452.

[24] On Cosimo's offer, see Mendoza to the Viceroy of Naples, November 15, 1549; on the Viceroy's offer, see "Instructions of Viceroy of Naples to Comendador Ulloa for Mendoza," November 10, 1549, Arch. Sim., Est. Napoli 1038, Rose-file.

[25] To Charles V, December 8, 1549, Druffel, *Briefe* I, 313; to Arras, December 8, 1549, *AC*, p. 142.

[26] De Leva, "La elezione," pp. 26, 27.

thus managed by negotiation to postpone the opening of the conclave until the evening of November 29.

At the opening ceremony in the Sistine Chapel, the entire diplomatic corps, as well as the leading great lords presently in Rome, were invited to swear a solemn oath to keep the conclave inviolate, "Mendoza the first to swear the oath, then the French ambassador d'Urfé, then the Venetian ambassador Dandolo, followed by all the others according to rank." Don Diego, who had so often assumed to address the Sacred College (to the annoyance of the late Pope), seized this last opportunity to speak to them while they were as yet without a head that could prevent him. Letting everyone else file out (except Dandolo who, fortunately, remained to report everything), while he and his entourage of eight or ten "barons," including the Duke of Amalfi and Fabrizio Colonna, stepped behind the altar (since Mendoza preceded all those present, the other ambassadors could not have left otherwise, presumably), he emerged with his group, giving the cardinals the gist, as it were, of his nearly three years of frustrated negotiations with the last Pope, and of his hopes for the next. He wanted them to acknowledge that the transfer of the Council from Trent to Bologna had not been valid and would not be so under any Pope who might be elected. Savoring the moment of being the head of Rome, he talked straightforward Italian to the cardinals, dispensing with the formality of an interpreter whom he sometimes used on official occasions. In the name of His Majesty, he bade them to "elect a Pope who should be a just man and a good pastor."

Assuring Mendoza that they were already inclined to do so, but that a Pope must be elected before anything else, including a Council, could even be mentioned, the Dean of Cardinals suggested that Don Diego pray for the election of a wise new Pope. Praying was a business of theirs, retorted the ambassador—his was only to make them understand the invalidity of the transfer in the eyes of the Emperor![27]

He must have felt the full magnificence of his position when he forced the cardinals' attention on what he considered the deepest concern of his master and therefore his own. But Charles V, when

[27] Dandolo to Venice, November 30, 1549, Arch. Ven., Rose-file.

he learned of this, did not approve of the address in his behalf. (By
that time, malevolent tongues at court had already been trying to
turn the Emperor against Don Diego. Besides, Charles V was not
particularly inclined toward gratitude, as most of his vassals would
learn sooner or later. In Don Diego's case he seems to have been
quite unable to appreciate fully the deep fidelity of this Spanish
hidalgo who worked for the glory of the Emperor mainly because
he happened to be his Spanish King.) Don Diego thought he knew
his Emperor's mind so well that he could anticipate even the instructions he had not yet received. In his experience, Charles V had
never hesitated to offend the last Pope, even mortally; and during
the last three years he had belabored Mendoza incessantly to talk
of practically nothing but the Council. But now the Emperor re-
buked him for bringing the matter up on this occasion, chiding his
vassal for "exceeding his commission" by mentioning the problem
of the Council at a time when it might offend the as yet unknown
person of the new Pope.[28]

Knowing he had to guide the election indirectly, Mendoza started to cut his own trail, unguided, through what was from the outset a jungle of intrigues, ambitions, and wild guesses. Trying to
evaluate from his own knowledge and experience which candidate
might be acceptable to Charles V, he saw that there were very few
men agreeable to the policies of the Imperium who would be
"good" human beings as well. Many of the candidates were of a
type already outmoded in a time that cried out for reform—the
"rich, old, and dissolute cardinals [as Mendoza described them]
who contradicted the election of all good men proposed to them,
giving as objections the very reasons for which they [the good
men] ought to be popes."[29] Others were hardly more than boys;
the Cardinal of Guise was twenty-three, the most prominent of the
Farnese grandsons just thirty. (Yet Alessandro Farnese, aware of
the power of his family, imagined he could be chosen, inheriting
the papacy, as it were. He lost no time in imparting this unusual
idea to his sister-in-law, Madama, urging her to persuade Don

---

28 Charles V to Mendoza, January 4, 1550, Brussels, Arch. Sim., Est., leg.
875, Rose-file.
29 Mendoza to Charles V, December 4, 1549, Druffel, *Briefe* I, no. 352, p. 307.

Diego in his favor. Mendoza dismissed Farnese's pretensions as "chimera" and "fantasia.")[30]

The ideal candidate, then, was supposed to be neither too old nor too young. He must lead a religious life and be interested in reforming the abuses of the Church, without, however, being a fanatic like "Teatino" (the later Paul IV), abhorred by Charles V, who in his turn called the Emperor in open assembly "a false deceiver, Jewish whorseson and other virtues . . ." (as Don Diego wrote to Arras).[31] He ought to have no sons, unlike the last Pope and several of the cardinals, some of whom, in Don Diego's words, had "a calendar of sons,"[32] and no hangers-on, though without being monkish. He should have no selfish territorial ambitions, without being low-born and miserly, but withal have enough personal stature to command the respect of all men. Such a paragon also had to be frail enough to prevent too long a reign. So the Imperial choice was narrow.

Such requirements made Don Diego's sarcasm all the sharper when, after almost two months of conclave, he put his head through the small window provided for the admission of supplies and suggested that the delay in the election was probably due to the fact that "there are so many excellent candidates among the cardinals." He made this remark at one of the several occasions when he had to assure the cardinals that, contrary to the rumors current in Rome, the Emperor was not dead.[33]

In fact, Mendoza's private choice had boiled down to two: Jacopo Salviati, Cardinal of Florence, and Reginald Pole, Cardinal of England. Just as exemplary a man was, as he well knew, "Santa Croce," the future Marcello II, who would be Pope only two weeks. But his anti-Imperial inclination made him unacceptable from the outset. Ercole Gonzaga, the Cardinal of Mantua, who was as devoted to the Emperor as was his brother Don Ferrante, was a close friend of Salviati and desired to see him Pope. Eight or nine months earlier, when the old Pope looked very frail, a three-way secret correspondence had joined the Granvelles, Gonzaga, and Mendoza

---

[30] Mendoza to Charles V, December 13, 1549, Druffel, *Briefe* I, no. 358, p. 322, 323.

[31] Mendoza to Arras, December 13, 1549, *AC*, pp. 142–144.

[32] Mendoza to Charles V (see note 30); "calendario de hijos . . ."

[33] Dandolo to Venice, January 25, 1550, Arch. Ven., Rose-file.

in an informal deliberation to prepare the ground for Salviati's candidacy. This communication was detected and reported to the Duke of Florence and Paul III by Averardo Serristori, Cosimo's ambassador in Rome.[34] Gonzaga had been the prime mover, Don Diego remaining only at the listening end, as the affair had not concerned him personally.

While Don Diego had known Salviati from his youth, he was not, it seems, one of his intimates. In his young years, Mendoza had been introduced into the service of Clement VII by Salviati's father; hence he felt a certain obligation toward the son, apart from the fact that Salviati seemed to be in his opinion an excellent choice, "because he [Salviati] has not that malevolence, nor obstinacy, nor that animosity and bestiality."[35] Apparently, the absence of bad qualities was enough of a sign of distinction, the best that could be hoped for, human nature being what it is.

A nephew of Leo X, Salviati had been named a cardinal by his uncle more than thirty years back. At the Cortes of Toledo in 1525 he had come to the young, victorious Emperor's court as the papal nuncio. Mendoza knew him to have led a not quite saintly life in his younger years, but he never believed the rumor that the Cardinal had sons,[36] judging him always to have been "a virtuous caballero." Politically, Salviati was so well liked by the governors of northern Italy, that the Emperor's policies, under the Gonzagas, would be sure to prosper under his papacy. As beloved uncle of the present Queen of France, Catherine de' Medici, he had, moreover, unlike any other Italian cardinal, equal weight in both opposing camps. If any one man with good will and without self-interest could bring the Emperor and the French King together, it would perhaps be Salviati, because no one else (except Reginald Pole) was likely to stand above the factions. (Salviati was at odds with the Farneses, though, but Mendoza was confident that a compromise with them was possible.)

Only one thing stood against this beautiful setup: Cosimo's secret but unabated enmity. Salviati was Cosimo's maternal uncle, broth-

34 Averardo Serristori, April 13, 1549, in De Leva, "La elezione," *Riv. St. It.* I, 24.

35 Mendoza to Arras, mid-December, 1549, *AC*, p. 149.

36 May 6, 1549, *AC*, p. 130.

er of the hapless dowager of Piombino, whom he always supported in her defiance of the Emperor and Cosimo. If he became Pope, the state would of course revert to his nephew Jacopo Appiano, the rightful heir. For political reasons the Duke was officially reconciled with Salviati, but he never forgave his uncle's former partisanship with the Florentine exiles, as well as his endeavor, at the start of Cosimo's rule, to dissuade him from accepting the throne of Florence as a tyrant under Spanish auspices. How could Cosimo govern a people, Salviati had said, "where there are few about you who love you?"[37]

The Duke left no stone unturned to intrigue at the Emperor's court against this powerful uncle of his, promoting instead, to the exclusion of almost every other candidate, his wife's uncle, the Spanish Cardinal of Burgos, Juan Alvarez de Toledo. Immediately after the Pope's death, before the Emperor's wishes were known (but the possibility existed that Salviati might be one of his choices), Cosimo sent his brother-in-law Pedro de Toledo to Rome. Ostensibly, Don Pedro brought generous offers of troops and money to Don Diego, but surreptitiously he was to test Mendoza's mind. One of the first things Don Pedro did was to thank Don Diego, in the name of the Duke, for the goodwill he was showing toward the affairs of Salviati.[38]

Don Diego did not fall into this trap. In reply he explained that the Imperial cardinals were not strong enough in number to elect a Pope by themselves, but that the Farneses would never agree on Salviati, and that therefore his case looked bad. Don Pedro agreed that Salviati's prospects were poor. Then he alerted Mendoza to the fact that Cosimo would always be grateful to him for favoring Burgos (if Salviati had no chances), whereupon Don Diego was quick to assure him that he had been working for three years to make Burgos Pope, although his case did not seem hopeful either.

Cosimo himself carried on a loving correspondence with the uncle and even for the uncle whose chances he was destroying, urging Salviati to keep him informed of Mendoza's efforts in his behalf, so that Cosimo might be of still further service to Salviati! He

[37] Cecily Booth, *Cosimo I, Duke of Florence*, p. 73.
[38] Pedro de Toledo to Cosimo I, November 16, 1549, Arch. Flor., Mediceo 611, Rose-file.

added, just in case, a request for Salviati's help for Burgos, should his own chances fail.[39]

A few days later, Don Pedro de Toledo wrote the Duke of Florence that Mendoza would have completely followed the wishes of Cardinal Gonzaga if he, Don Pedro, had not told him to wait for the Emperor's instructions to Cosimo. In this way, proceeding from Serristori's earlier denunciation, Don Pedro added to the slander. The truth was that Don Diego was waiting anyway for the Emperor's response before plunging into any action that might later compromise him. Watching Mendoza with the malevolence displayed by all reporters to the Duke, Don Pedro describes him here as "the man whom Your Excellency knows: changeable and subject to influence from Mantua [i.e., Gonzaga], but what we truly believe of him is that he is afraid of what His Majesty will resolve and of what he suspects Your Excellency has written [to Charles V]."[40]

But it soon appeared that even Don Pedro could not avoid reporting, truthfully enough, that Mendoza had already prepared the ground for the eventual elimination of Salviati. He wrote that Don Diego, in preliminary talks with Farnese, obtained a pledge to remove both Santa Croce (Farnese favorite and logical "heir" to the Farnese papacy) and Salviati (least liked by Farnese) from the list of eligibles. This was the aforesaid "deal" that was to determine the entire course of the election and should have been credited exclusively to Don Diego by the Emperor as well as Cosimo. All other evidence shows that, whatever his private sympathies might have been, Mendoza had refused to commit himself, despite Gonzaga's urgings to promote Salviati. "Neither don Fernando nor Christ can make me do what I should not do."[41]

The Emperor's instruction finally arrived on December 1, the second day of the conclave, too late, apparently, to convey the news to the sealed-in assembly. Outside interference with the sacred, secret election process was a grave sin, punishable by excom-

[39] Cosimo I to Cardinal Salviati, November 18, 1549, Arch. Flor., Mediceo 13, Rose-file.

[40] Pedro de Toledo to Cosimo I, November 25, 1549, Arch. Flor., Mediceo 611, Rose-file.

[41] Mendoza to Arras, December 1, 1549, AC, p. 136.

munication. Besides, the ambassadors had sworn not to interfere. But Charles V, while withholding his own name from messages to the cardinals in conclave,[42] expected his vassals to risk even the salvation of their souls in his behalf. Mendoza was prepared for this. He reasoned, "If I offend against the rules and censures, I am doing it only as an instrument, and all [sin] will be charged to those of you whose orders I follow. Although I have few scruples . . . I still cling to this support, but since this is the papacy, I hold on to this rein. . . ."[43]

But he was not prepared for the capricious wishes of Charles V. To his disappointment, the Emperor objected to Salviati. While he and his master concurred in disliking Santa Croce, Ridolfi, Capo di Ferro, and Veraldo, "against whom you have to do the utmost you can so that they should not be elected,"[44] this was small consolation for having to fight Salviati, the candidate with the largest following. Just as bad, at the head of the Emperor's list of favored candidates stood Pio, the Cardinal of Carpi. In Mendoza's eyes this was a dangerous intriguer who had tried to drive Don Diego out of Rome in the time of the late Pope. While he agreed with Charles V's second, third, and fourth choices—Pole, Morone, and Sfondrato—his master's decision to favor Carpi was a great blow.

Fortunately, mainly because Don Diego had suspected Cosimo's intentions, he had not yet acted on Salviati's behalf. On the contrary, the foundation for Salviati's defeat had already been laid through Mendoza's "deal" with Farnese. (He could have revoked this agreement at any time, had it become necessary to do so.) Since the "deal" canceled out both Santa Croce and Salviati, Don Diego could say to Arras: "Thank God I succeeded in three parts out of four to guide myself according to the Emperor's instruction in everything I have done until now, without neglecting to dot an i. . . ."[45] The controversial fourth part concerned Carpi, whom he would not promote under any circumstances. Consequently, Carpi never came near a candidacy, a sign of how effective Mendoza's own wishes were—if only negatively. Elsewhere Don Diego relates

[42] Charles V to Mendoza, December 24, 1549, Druffel, *Briefe* I, no. 369, p. 336.

[43] Mendoza to Arras, December 8, 1549, *AC*, pp. 141–142.

[44] Charles V to Mendoza, November 20, 1549, GP II, 131.

[45] Mendoza to Arras, December 1, 1549, *AC*, pp. 136, 137.

the delicate process of blacklisting or favoring candidates without revealing the Emperor's personal likes or dislikes.[46]

To destroy Salviati's chances was, however, a disagreeable business to Mendoza, yet he would do so, because "when I shall be promoting the persons I already named—Burgos, England, and Sfondrato—any of them can only be helped by destroying Salviati. He had many votes, and I had to employ great artifice to lower them. . . ." Detailing all his maneuvers, including the "deal" with Farnese, he says that "with all this, much remains to be done to block Salviati. The way Farnese and Carpi spoke out against him resembled more a squabble of washerwomen or tavern-wenches than anything serious. . . ."[47]

He had, then, in fact, done nothing to which the Duke of Florence had reason to object. Yet Cosimo I and his relatives did their best to undermine the Emperor's confidence in Mendoza. They found their task greatly eased because at court a new situation had developed, unfavorable to Don Diego, through the absence of Monseigneur Granvelle, who was spending the last months of his fatal illness in his private domain in Burgundy. Although his work was carried on by his brilliant son, the Bishop of Arras, the younger man could not mold the Emperor's opinions in quite the same way. Instead, the older Granvelle's influence on Charles V was presently replaced to a large extent by the Duke of Alba, another relative of the Duchess of Florence, nephew of Cardinal Burgos. True, Alba was a most intimate friend of Don Diego's youth; yet his interests were directed primarily toward the aggrandizement of the Toledo clan. That the Emperor now advised Don Diego so firmly to eliminate Salviati, in whom he was in fact not much interested one way or another (Charles V's *bête noire* was Santa Croce), was chiefly due to the pincer movement of Alba's advice at his ear and the letters from the Duke of Florence and the Viceroy of Naples from abroad.

In such a climate at court, slanderous rumors about Mendoza's activities spread unchecked. On January 1, 1550, the Venetian ambassador to Charles V, Marin Cavalli, reports to the Signory of Venice that "Don Fernando, the *Duke of Florence* [my italics] and

---

[46] Mendoza to Charles V, December 20, 1549, Bibl. Pal., Rose-file.
[47] *AC*, p. 138.

Don Diego, with their letters, have twice given the greatest assistance to Cardinal Salviati for the pontificate. They have promised that, if Salviati is elected Pope, the Emperor can have anything he wants from Rome . . . and that the Toledos consider that their support for Salviati is the reason why Burgos, their relative, has not been elected."[48] Ironically, in this Venetian's report, Cosimo's bluffing letters in apparent favor of Salviati, written for public consumption, are lumped together with "the family Toledo's" disgust about those very letters—again including Cosimo.

In the meantime, the climactic near-election of Reginald Pole, the other candidate whom Don Diego esteemed personally, had come and gone.[49] Pole needs hardly any introduction for the English-speaking reader. He was of the royal blood of the Plantagenets; at first he was protected by Henry VIII, who sponsored his university studies at Padua where he developed into a notable classical scholar. Later, at odds with the English King because of his divorce, Pole returned to live in Italy in exile, favored by Paul III, who made him a Cardinal in 1536. Born in 1500, he was near in age to Mendoza, who probably knew the fellow humanist from his earliest student years in Italy. In Trent, Pole and Mendoza had met only fleetingly. Pole had served as one of Paul III's legates to the Council, but, being of frail health, he had had to curtail his stay, departing from the Council as early as June 1546, only shortly after Don Diego's return from his own sick leave. As a papal candidate, Pole compensated for his relatively young years with his poor health. Few other cardinals could equal him in his unassuming, ascetic life of a scholar, in his mild and equable disposition, or, most important, in his complete disinterest in the Italian serpents' nest of personal intrigues. To Don Diego he was "a subject free of blemish, most worthy of the papacy. . . . One can see that the blemishes they [his opponents, notably 'Teatino'] accuse Pole of—that he is spiritual, that he will upset the Apostolic See in order to reduce England [forcing England back into Catholicism,

---

[48] Arch. Ven., Anali Marin Cavalli, Rose-file.

[49] Because Pole, at Trent, had explained the Lutheran point of view for the sake of argument, Caraffa accused him of being a heretic. Cf. Pastor, *Geschichte*, VI, 12–15.

if need be, by war], that he will not live in Rome until he has achieved that enterprise—every single one is reason enough to qualify him for the pontificate."[50]

The Imperial faction was in fact rushing to elect Pole by acclamation (the actual counting had left him short by just one vote) in the opening days of the conclave—before the arrival of the French cardinals. But the Cardinal, in his humility, would not let himself be elected this way.

After that came the brief but ineffectual flurry in behalf of Burgos, the Spaniard, for whose defeat the Toledos would blame Mendoza. When the news about Burgos' dwindling chances arrived at the court in Brussels at year's end, the Duke of Alba, the Duke of Florence, and the Viceroy of Naples denounced Don Diego. Mendoza gave, however, a thorough explanation for the reasons for Burgos' defeat—apart from the obvious one that a Spaniard was distinctly unwelcome. One of the reasons was that "his relatives helped him too openly, while he personally showed his eagerness and ambition for the papacy; also, the Duke [Cosimo] helped him. . . ."[51]

Mendoza's involuntary involvement in this situation of others was becoming an insoluble dilemma for himself because "for two years these people [the Toledos and Cardinal Carpi] think of nothing else but how to get rid of me here. . . ."[52] "They will keep on harping, eating away little by little like a cancer, if I do not put out the fire. My position is so great, and therefore so envied, that it brings a man honor with a flaw in it. . . ." "Please, try to understand my position in case Salviati should become Pope after all—a thing that could happen without any fault or sin of mine. If you knew all the rascalities and machinations that went on here, and are still going on, . . . you would be shocked, because it concerns all of us. . . ."[53] (This probably refers to the disclosure by Cosimo's agents of the old, compromising, correspondence between the Granvelles, Gonzaga, and Mendoza, mentioned above.)

---

[50] Mendoza to Charles V, December 12–13, 1549, Druffel, *Briefe* I, no. 358, p. 321.
[51] Mendoza to Arras, December 31, 1549, *AC*, p. 158.
[52] *AC*, p. 159.
[53] Ibid., p. 160.

Communication between the "secret" convention and outsiders operated quite smoothly. To be sure, the ambassadors of Spain, France, and Venice, each in turn, guarded the door to the conclave day and night, but not so much, obviously, to protect its secrecy as its safety.[54] Many notes, hidden and unhidden, passed in and out of the little window, and in several places the walls had been pierced by speaking holes. One of Mendoza's secretaries, serving Cardinal Pacheco as "conclavist," reported to his master: "A note was found today, covered with tin foil, and stuck in the wing of a capon coming out from inside the conclave to be cleared away. . . ."[55] Having placed this young man and a few other embassy assistants in the conclave, Mendoza had an excellent channel of communication, and his friends inside were well aware of his difficulties.

The Cardinal of Jaén (Pacheco, Mendoza's first cousin) took up his pen to defend Mendoza against the lying gossip. Don Diego, Jaén wrote to Arras, was being accused of two things: that he had not urged the election of Burgos as strongly as he should have, and that he had supported Salviati much too strongly. Both these accusations, said Jaén, were utterly false. Burgos, as a Spaniard, had no chance anyway, "no more than a Turk." He assured Arras that Mendoza had been as active in blacklisting Salviati as he had been in supporting Pole and Burgos. Those who persisted in this accusation were moved, Jaén concluded, by "passion" and "personal interest."[56]

Jaén's good letter did not reach the court before February 8, the day after the election. Before that, other rumors and bad feelings had ample time to spread, especially the news about the obsolete three-way letter in support of Salviati that was now constantly broadcast by the Cosimo clique. Yet all the evidence shows that Don Diego as well as the Cardinal of Mantua (Salviati's original supporter) were disregarding their former understanding entirely. Both were executing the Emperor's orders loyally. But the poison had been spread, and Marin Cavalli wrote to Venice: "The Em-

[54] Dandolo to Venice, December 1, 1549, Arch. Ven., Rose-file.

[55] Mendoza to Charles V, December 3–5, 1549, Druffel, *Briefe* I, no. 352, p. 307.

[56] Cardinal Jaén to Arras, January 5, 1550, Bibl. Pal., Cartas del Obispo de Arras, Rose-file.

peror believes that if it had not been for the favor shown by his ministers to Salviati, Burgos would now be Pope. The Emperor of course is furious and can see no good in anyone who interfered with Burgos' election."[57]

The French cardinals entered the conclave on December 13, bringing the number of participating cardinals to forty-seven. They took up their positions (Santa Croce was among their preferences), while the Emperor remained inflexible in his preference for Burgos or Pole, so that the assembly continued week after week in a stalemate. The year 1550 dawned over those fixed positions, with no new head of Christendom in sight. It was the start of a jubilee year, looked forward to by thousands of pilgrims intending to come to Rome to receive absolution. But without a Pope the jubilee could not be inaugurated.

While the Imperial-French split appeared to remain unbridgeable, the papal treasury was being drained, paying for five thousand protection troops. The people of Rome were becoming restless; noisily they demanded a new Pope. The pious marched daily in processions, praying to God for help in the decision. Inside, "there was such smoke from candles and torches, such dust, and such stench from the urinals and buckets, that gradually most feared truly they would get sick." By and by a number of the cardinals succumbed to the discomfort, many fell ill, several of them died.[58]

When they entered the eighth week of their ordeal, they exerted themselves to bring about a little reform. An attempt was finally made to get rid of some of the nearly four-hundred cooped-up persons—secretaries, spies, valets, brothers, and cousins of cardinals, as well as physicians. They expelled about eighty superfluous assistants, holes in the wall were boarded up, and a turnstyle was introduced for the first time, serving to control the passage of objects through the little window. Festive banquets whereby many cardinals had eased their tedium had previously been forbidden, and now meals were limited to one dish. By such measures the closure, hitherto disregarded so shamelessly, was tightened some-

---

[57] Marin Cavalli to Venice, January 23, 1550, Arch. Ven., Rose-file.
[58] Pastor, *Geschichte*, VI, 24, n. 2.

what, so that d'Urfé, the French ambassador, had to creep with ladders over the roofs to confer with the Cardinal of Guise.[59] It is not reported whether Mendoza went into similar acrobatics, although a Pasquinade mocked him as a *mal gatto* who kept watch day and night around the conclave. Apparently, he also showed himself there when his colleagues stood watch. He spent much of his time leaning against the door of the conclave, writing long epistles.

Throughout this time Don Diego continued his struggle against the intimation that he had favored Salviati. "I knew that the dust of Salviati was not laid, but now I see it whirled up again. . . . What annoys me is that they think I have a personal interest in it. If Salviati does not emerge as Pope, they will think it just so happened by itself, but if he does, then it's my fault. . . . Salviati cannot be Pope, naturally, and I am the reason. If His Majesty inclines to believe what they write him, I hope he also will disbelieve when they accuse me falsely. I can write the truth only. Salviati had and has a large following; to write something else would be to deceive the Emperor. . . . If His Majesty does not wish to know the truth, that it is impossible [to elect his favorites], we will have to tell him only what he would like to hear. . . ."[60] The good thing is that Salviati will not be Pope, he will not be Pope, and he will not be Pope, naturally. . . ."[61]

"I do not know what to do, except to leave it to God and curse the Cardinals of Burgos and Salviati, who have been the cause of the ruin of Christendom and perhaps of the Church of God, because without them things would have gone the usual way. . . ."[62] "I do not exert myself in anything any more, because of fear. I'll only see to it that Salviati does not emerge as Pope. . . . It may as well be the devil, for if it were the latter, I would be punished; but if the former were chosen, I would be called a traitor. . . . This is what they have done to me, and what I have done to the conclave, because the thing has gone so far that now I object to him only to

[59] Ibid., p. 28.
[60] Cf. the *Escudero* in *Lazarillo de Tormes*: "Nunca decille [the master] cosa que le pesase, aunque mucho le cumpliese . . .," as discussed by E. Spivakovsky, "The *Lazarillo de Tormes* and Mendoza," *Symposium* 15 (1961): 280.
[61] Mendoza to Arras, January 24, 1550, *AC*, pp. 174–179.
[62] Mendoza to Arras, February 3, 1550, *AC*, p. 188.

save my own skin from such great malevolence, and not for the Emperor's sake. . . ."[63]

During the more than nine weeks that the conclave lasted, Mendoza dispatched fifteen "special deliveries" to the Emperor; with this, and his military efforts, the *sede vacante* cost him seven thousand escudos.[64] Yet the inevitable slowness of these communications with Brussels let the accusations against him stand unchallenged for so long that his apologies and explanations, however truthful, limped behind, of little avail in their lateness. "A sharp reproof has been given to Don Diego," wrote the Venetian ambassador at court. "He is told that he has his own personal interest more at heart than the service of His Imperial Majesty; this proceeded from the Duke of Alba and the whole Toledo family who are extremely dissatisfied with him."[65]

In the end a "dark horse," Giovan Maria del Monte (1487–1555), was elected to become Julius III. This was a compromise instigated by the Duke of Florence, whose efforts in behalf of Del Monte resulted in the election of the ambitious Cosimo's second choice (after his Spanish uncle)—a weak and self-indulgent Pope from a Tuscan family who, as Cosimo's "creature," would be bound to him in life-long gratitude.[66]

At first this news seemed annihilating to Don Diego. He had regarded Del Monte as most obnoxious toward the Emperor's interests. On December 21, 1549, he wrote:

I cannot stand Monte because of his intention [supposed to be anti-Council and antireform] which I can prove; please, tell the Emperor if he should wish to promote him because the Duke of Florence wants him to, may he send someone else to do it. As vassal of His Majesty and by my duty to God, I can never in good conscience support one so detrimental to the service of God, the public benefit, and His Majesty. I do not say this from personal dislike, because [Del Monte] is my friend. I am moved by honest zeal. I do not wish to see the ruin of Christianity and be instrumental in it. . . . Santa Cruz [Santa Croce] is not as bad, but the same holds good for him, too.[67]

[63] Mendoza to Arras, February 7, 1550, *AC*, pp. 189–193.
[64] Mendoza's instruction to Ximénez, April 14, 1552, *AC*, p. 352.
[65] M. Cavalli, January 12, 1550, *Cal. St. P.*, Ven. no. 626.
[66] De Leva, "La elezione," *Riv. Stor. It.* I, 37, n. 3.
[67] Mendoza to Arras, December 21, 1549, *AC*, pp. 155, 156.

The Emperor resented Del Monte because as papal legate he had seconded Santa Croce in the transfer of the Council to Bologna. When Mendoza reminded him of Del Monte in the early days of the conclave, Charles V at once sent orders to blacklist him. On second thought, Mendoza had not acted on this Imperial order; possibly he kept it in his pocket to prevent an open break with Cosimo. (But he shared the information with the most Imperial of the cardinals, Trent, Jaén, Mantua, and De la Cueva.)[68] Afterwards, the Emperor was to praise him for this precaution.[69] But "on the night of the Pope's election, [Don Diego] did not appear very joyful," wrote Dandolo to the Signory of Venice.

The following morning, presumably after one of the worst nights of his life, desiring to be done with his duty of greeting the new Pope, Mendoza went to the Vatican so early that "he [the Pope] was still dressing, and immediately, seeing him enter the chapel, [Julius III] exclaimed: 'Ecco Don Diego!' " Apparently, Don Diego's face and manner still bore signs of shock and contrition, for the Pope laughed and said, "Non tanta paura, Signor Don Diego!" "When Don Diego tried to kiss his feet, His Holiness would not allow it, saying it was neither the time nor the place, but embraced him and made him rise. . . ." Julius III's kindness restored Mendoza's self-confidence at once. He joked in the Pontiff's presence, saying—possibly in an aside—that the Pope had better accept his homage now, as he was not at all sure whether he would kiss His Holiness's foot officially (in token of the Emperor's acknowledgment of this election).[70]

"The consent was so general, unexpected and sudden that, although the cardinals are very tired, the election is nevertheless considered miraculous by everybody," continued Dandolo, expressing the opinion of the day. The Venetian ambassador did not know then, nor did anyone else, that the greatest "miracle,"—the revela-

---

[68] De Leva, "La elezione," p. 38.
[69] Charles V to Mendoza, March 18, 1550, Arch. Sim., Est., leg. 875, Rose-file.
[70] Dandolo to Venice, February 8 and 9, 1550, *Cal. St. P.*, Ven. no. 642, p. 309. Also in Eugenio Alberi, "Relazione di Roma di Matteo Dandolo," vol. III, series I of *Relazioni degli ambasciatori veneti al Senato*, p. 347. Here, Dandolo recalls that he met Don Diego on the morning before the election and was told by him that under orders of the Emperor he was holding out in favor of England [Pole], so that, when Dandolo heard on the same evening shouts of "Monte, Monte," he did not believe them, but only a single voice exclaiming "England."

tion of the unknown qualities (or lack of qualities) and inclinations of the new Pope—was yet to come.

Without the interference of both Mendoza and the Duke of Florence, Santa Croce, who was to win the next election five years later, would probably have been the new Pope already. So, the first contest of wills between the two Lords in Tuscany was over, but neither of them was down. While Burgos' defeat somewhat marred Cosimo's victory (his personal advantage through Del Monte's election would appear at a later time), Don Diego could take credit for the defeat of Santa Croce, Salviati, and all the other cardinals blacklisted by the Emperor. Though Mendoza had felt the strength of his personal enemies most disagreeably, he suffered no obvious impairment in the Emperor's good graces. When all the facts were assembled, Charles V accepted his explanations, withdrawing his earlier criticism; he continued to require Don Diego's services in the center of Italy where events were now rapidly moving again.

The New Pope Astonishes

On November 10, 1549, immediately after the death of Paul III, the bankers of Rome had placed their highest bet on Del Monte as his successor. If the electors had listened to the vox populi, they would have saved themselves much trouble. Farnese's reign had been so long, Rome's way of life was so much set in the most sumptuous, sybaritic, splendid style, that the bankers instinctively knew a sudden reversal to be impossible. Rome had already once tried the experiment of contrasting a luxury-loving era with a period of contrition, but the mistake of an Adrian VI could not happen twice. The future might hold some change; the number of "reform" cardinals, of those who, as Don Diego said, lived "not as a cardinal did, but were religious men,"[71] was growing. The "dissolute and rich" were old. But Paul III's character had been so regal and magnificent that one of his satellites would yet be swept into power on the last Pope's skirts. The old regime, so strongly entrenched, decried, and doomed as it might be, would disappear only gradually. And the bankers of Rome had the right hunch; one of them, thanks to it, made twenty thousand crowns.[72]

When the new Pope told Don Diego not to be so scared, the poor

---

[71] "ha hecho siempre vida mas de religioso que de cardenal . . .," *AC*, p. 149.
[72] Dandolo to Venice, February 12, 1550, *Cal. St. P.*, Ven. no. 644.

ambassador had been shaken by more than the bad surprise, although the unexpectedness of this compromise choice was considerable. Rather, his own bad conscience made him tremble. He had fought hardest against Salviati, hard against Santa Croce, but he had regarded them as honorable opponents. He did not need to regret his fights, for he had only followed orders. Personally, he esteemed these candidates, even regretting the exclusion he had had to impose on them. But for Del Monte he had shown only disdain, so much so as to have almost completely disregarded him as a possibility. Only near the end, to be on the safe side, he had effected a little scheme of exacting Farnese's promise not to help Del Monte, and Mantua's not to help Trani.[73]

But it did not take him long to discover that he had been mistaken all along. Could he have been blind before—or was Julius III, by God's grace, quite a different person from the Giovan Maria Ciocchi del Monte whom he had known for years? Yet there was really no error: Cardinal del Monte had in fact offended the Emperor continually as far back as Don Diego could remember. Anyone could have seen that. But no one stopped to question how many of Del Monte's actions had had their origins in his own apparently well-versed and clever head. Neither Don Diego nor anyone else could have known that Del Monte was only a faithful instrument of Pope Paul, and that, in truth, he did not care at all one way or the other. His skillful anti-Imperial maneuvering during the Council of Trent, his wilful obstruction of Charles V's wishes by heading the anti-Council of Bologna where he had still resided at the time of Paul III's death—these offenses of Cardinal del Monte against the Emperor, which Don Diego found to be unforgivable, and, worse, ineradicable, had been nothing but emanations of the late Pope's iron will. The Cardinal, who in contrast to his late master had a vacillating nature, may have believed in the old Farnese's policies, making them his own. But once his mentor was gone, his own self emerged.

If the new Pope did not precisely repeat the famous words of Leo X, "since God has given Us the papacy, let Us enjoy it," he acted as if this were his credo. Having followed his predecessor's anti-Imperial policies faithfully, he had also seen what trouble

73 *AC*, pp. 185, 186.

their obstinacy had invited. During the sack of Rome, Del Monte, then a man of forty, had almost lost his life as hostage for Clement VII. Imperial soldiers had exposed him to all kinds of indignities. Later he had seen Paul III suffer endless aggravations from the same side. Julius III, sixty-three and not in good health, would stay out of trouble. The best way to do that was to acquiesce to the Emperor. No, Don Diego need not be scared! The Pope, whose revenge he reasonably feared, did not exist at all. The accession had made a changed man of Cardinal del Monte, and Don Diego understood soon why this was so, writing Prince Philip on March 18: "He [the Pope] knows that the Popes do not always fare well if they get into His Majesty's hair."[74]

The new Pope, whose origin was middle class compared to the princely background of his predecessors,[75] wasted no time in swinging himself up to the level of aristocratic pretense. With full hands he distributed the considerable bounties he still found in the papal treasury (much depleted by the long conclave). He won the people's heart by abolishing the flour tax; he gave generous presents and gifts of money and benefices to all cardinals, including former antagonists like the Imperials Mantua and Trent, who had not participated in his "adoration." He returned the duchy of Parma to Ottavio Farnese. At the same time he made a large donation to Camillo Orsini, who had prevented Parma from falling back into Ottavio's hands. He fully forgave the Colonnas, sanctioning the restitution they had carried out, de facto, while Don Diego was presiding over the "peace of Rome." And last but not least, he sent special embassies to the Emperor, promising to convoke a new Council in Trent; and he thanked the French King for his support in the conclave. It looked like a new era of peace.

Don Diego recognized the situation promptly. "If the Pope proceeds as he says," he wrote to Arras three days after the election, "all of us have deceived ourselves and we have a good Pope." Much of the success, he warned, would depend on favorable treatment by the Emperor. And he suggested caution regarding the Curia: "I

[74] Mendoza to Philip, March 18, 1550, Arch. Sim., Est., leg. 876, folio 54, Rose-file; also GP II, 147.

[75] Vincenzo del Monte, the Pope's father, was a Roman lawyer of Tuscan descent; his mother, Cristofara Saraceni, belonged to a good Sienese family.

fear that, if he retains the ministers of Pope Paul, his own trans-
parency and their opaqueness might result in a worse cross section
—according to Aristotle's saying that an upward motion and a
downward motion result in a diagonal. We shall soon see."[76] Three
days later he said: "The Pope shows himself with better intentions
each day. . . ." But in a postscript he pronounced one of his uncanny prophecies: "I am afraid it will be said of this Pontiff,
promittet multa, faciet pauca."[77]

[76] *AC*, p. 198.
[77] *AC*, p. 203.

11. THE CASTLE OF SIENA, 1547–1551

> Peoples have to be either forced or deceived.
>
> Don Diego[1]

WITH THE ELECTION RESULTS favorable both to Cosimo I and the Emperor, how did the Duke of Florence now feel toward Mendoza? Were the two Lords of Tuscany where they had been before the conclave? In view of their mutually revealed enmity, this was impossible. If each deceived the other formerly, their dissimulation had no limits now. Don Diego knew that the Duke regarded him as an obstacle in his push for still greater power. Analyzing the recent *sede vacante*, he commented to Gonzaga on the desire of Cosimo and his relatives to oust him from Siena and Rome, where the Toledos wished to replace him with Don Francisco de Toledo or another member of their family: "Wouldn't they enjoy joining Milan with Florence, Siena, Rome, and Naples into one 'highway of Toledo' like that of Santiago?"[2]

On the surface, Cosimo's and Mendoza's correspondence continued to show them as pleasant friends. In fact, Cosimo did not mind supporting Don Diego in a matter of policy when Mendoza was at cross-purposes with the Viceroy of Naples, Cosimo's father-in-law

---

[1] "Los pueblos o han de ser forçados o engañados," Mendoza to Arras, May 20, 1551, *AC*, p. 242.

[2] Mendoza to Gonzaga, March, 1550, *AIH* 2 (1911): 271–273.

and true ally.[3] Much of the Duke's reluctance to show his real feelings to Mendoza was due to the fact that the "Piombino affair" was still unsolved, and, as he wrote Don Diego in September 1550, all his hopes for a favorable final decision on Piombino rested with him.[4]

To be sure, since Charles V still owed the Duke a great deal of money, while Piombino urgently needed defenses Cosimo was in the best position to provide, Mendoza no longer had any objection toward ceding him the territory. With the new Pope agreeable and malleable, the balance of power had changed so much in favor of the Imperials that they might now tolerate a minor increase in Duke Cosimo's power—as long as the Imperials were able to increase their own. And this they set out to do in the new papal era, Don Diego in the forefront. In the summer of 1550 he made preparations to build an Imperial fortress on top of the hills of Siena, and he proceeded to repair the existing fortifications of the Sienese ports Orbetello and Porto Ercole. Cosimo had three citadels, and soon Mendoza would add a third to the two in Sienese territory. This was a new factor that once more was to upset the situation between the two Lords in Tuscany, but, still hoping that he would soon acquire Piombino, the Duke of Florence had been cooperative enough to tolerate the building of the new castle in Siena. (In the beginning of Don Diego's enterprise only Don Francisco de Toledo, always Cosimo's confidant, knew that the Duke did not approve of the castle at all.)[5]

---

[3] Mendoza to Cosimo I, August 13, 1550. The Viceroy had requested Don Diego to send him troops stationed in Siena, and Don Diego expressed his delight that Cosimo agreed with him about the impossibility of removing any troops from Siena at that time. Cosimo was also readily prepared to sign an agreement between Piombino and Florence to the effect that he would send to the galleys all those escaping into Tuscany from under the rule of Piombino's Spanish garrison who were apprehended in his territory. "The galleys of Xerxes," says Mendoza, "would not be enough to carry away all the rascals of this realm." Arch. Flor., Mediceo 1852, Rose-file.

[4] Arch. Flor., Mediceo 15, Universale, Rose-file.

[5] Don Francisco de Toledo to Cosimo I, September 9, 1550. Don Francisco reminded Cosimo that, if he wished to attain his ends in Piombino, he must support the Emperor's ends in Siena; on November 7, 1550, Don Diego told the Sienese that the castle was not being built to subdue *them*, but to hold the Duke of Florence in check. Don Francisco advised the Duke not to mind Don Diego's

In addition to his embassy in Rome, Mendoza had been holding the governorship of Siena since the autumn of 1547, a position for which Ferrante Gonzaga had recommended him to the Emperor. Siena, a prosperous trading and banking town on the road across Tuscany linking France and Rome, was a fief of the Holy Roman Empire ever since Frederick Barbarossa granted it freedom in 1186.[6] In the early Middle Ages it was the focus of Ghibelline-Guelf clashes (Imperial versus papal partisans); usually its own citizens were at each other's throats in a primitive class struggle between the very rich, the middling well-to-do, and the small traders. Each time one party got the upper hand, the temporarily vanquished exiled themselves until they made their next onslaught, and prosperity returned overnight. In each such short breathing spell, the city enjoyed itself deliriously. In the beginning of the sixteenth century, Siena was subjected to the tyrannical rule of one of its own citizens, but in April, 1525, in the wake of Charles V's triumph at Pavia, Siena had declared itself once more a free republic under the Emperor's protection (which he sold them for fifteen thousand ducats). The following summer, when the "League of Cognac" (the French, Pope Clement VII, and a number of small Italian states) combined in a desperate (and fruitless) effort to drive the Imperials out of Italy, Siena triumphed over the papal forces that had attacked the city with cannon. The citizens, in a solemn procession, presented the keys of their city to their Madonna del Voto, as was their custom in an emergency, and their patroness gave them a glorious victory. After that a strong Spanish garrison had to come in lest the Sienese, in their inflamed passion, destroy each other.

At first a Sienese noble, Alfonso Piccolomini d'Aragona, Duke of Amalfi, served as captain-general of the Spanish forces in Siena, but he was soon replaced by a Spanish governor. One way or the

---

words, as those were his own, not the Emperor's. He asked if Cosimo did not know Don Diego well enough by this time, and his extravagant way of speaking without foundation. He said Cosimo ought to forget these words of Mendoza as idle talk; rather he ought to remember that, regarding Piombino, Don Diego had done him a very good service in the past. Arch Flor., Mediceo 611, Rose-file.

[6] "Freedom" meant the right to elect their own consuls, coin their own money, and administer justice in town and country.

other, the periods of peaceful government never lasted long. New civic tumults required a repeated change of command, so that sooner or later every distinguished man in the Emperor's inner circle came to rule this unusually restless city-state for a while. The names of Imperial governors between 1529 and 1545 read like a *Who's Who* in the Empire: Don Lope de Soria, Don Ferrante Gonzaga, the Marquis of Vasto, Monseigneur Granvelle, and Don Juan de Luna. Since the Imperials invariably favored the Sienese Noveschi, that is, the wealthy, aristocratic faction, they were periodically chased out by the Popolani, the popular party. This happened once again early in 1546 when all the Spanish soldiers, Don Juan de Luna, and the Noveschi were driven out together.

The two years following were a sort of interregnum. The Sienese had the illusion that they were ruling themselves as a free republic, although in fact they lay defenseless, as open prey. Pope Paul III and Ottavio Farnese (who in 1543 had vainly bargained with Charles V to buy Siena) still hoped to acquire the city-state; Duke Cosimo patiently waited for his chances to ripen toward eventual conquest; and Ferrante Gonzaga directed its immediate destinies from Milan through two Imperial-minded civilian appointees (the Milanese Senator Grasso, and the Sienese Girolamo Muzio), each of whom was disliked by the people.

In such a complex state of affairs, the choice of Mendoza as the new Imperial overlord of Siena seemed unusually fortunate. He was already on the spot in Rome, watching any possible machinations of Paul III against Sienese liberty. He was an old friend of the Sienese; memories of his carefree younger days of studies and pleasures were still alive, while his current international reputation was great. Honoring the Sienese with his nomination, as it were, the Imperials succeeded in 1547 in slyly foisting an unwanted new Spanish garrison on them. Siena would now have no reason to complain, because such a garrison was to be regarded as only the minimal soldierly company of an illustrious captain.

Don Diego's first entry, on October 20, 1547,[7] as governor, into the beautiful city on its three hills—this Gothic gem amid vineyards, silvery olive woods, and golden cornfields—equaled the tri-

---

[7] Senator Grasso to Charles V, October 21, 1547, says he reached Siena with Mendoza "yesterday." Arch. Sim., Est., leg. 1465, Rose-file.

umph of a monarch. Festive delegations of Sienese patricians met him at the border of the republic, carrying presents of marzipan and cheese. "In the city the shops closed as a sign of joy and so it was continued for three days . . . the bells chimed in glory, and at night the towers of the city shone with flares and torches. . . ."[8]

But Mendoza, who knew he could not trust the Sienese, was not taken in by these demonstrations.[9] Before he went to Siena, Gonzaga had presented him with a plan for the construction of a fortress "which shall dominate Siena in such a fashion that no one henceforward can think of revolt as in the past."[10] Yet at first Don Diego thought to dispense with such strong measures. He relied rather on his crafty plan of sowing even more discord among the citizens themselves, preventing the Noveschi from getting the upper hand again (he wanted them "neither superior nor inferior"). He intended, gradually, to "lower the ones and the others . . . because, even though those who rule may be the rich—in the end, all of them being rascals, all will finish up being poor."[11]

In this respect he did not see eye to eye with Gonzaga. Shortly after Mendoza arrived in Siena, Don Ferrante had written the Emperor: "Mendoza wants to follow the opinion of the people now in power, the poor and the criminal, while I want to hand it over to the rich and innocent."[12] However, Mendoza's pretended tolerance of the leaders of the Popolani in power was no more successful than the previous rule of the Noveschi. Intermittent unrest and revolts kept him and the various puppet governments he had installed in such a precarious situation that, after little more than a year, he agreed to Gonzaga's plan for a castle.

Yet during the life of Paul III the execution of this project was left in abeyance. The old Pope, in his frustrated wish to add Siena

[8] See A. Liberati, "Onoranze rese a Don Diego di Mendoza nella sua venuta a Siena," *Bullettino Senese di Storia Patria (Bull. Sen.)* 18: 364–368.

[9] ". . . procurare de entretenellos haciendo del ladron fiel y cansallos o engañallos . . .," Mendoza to Charles V, November 3, 1547, GP II, 160.

[10] Instructions (1547) from Gonzaga to Juan Gallego for Mendoza, Arch. Sim., Est., leg. 1193, Rose-file.

[11] ". . . Bien es que sean ricos los que gobernaren, porque al cabo segun son bellacos, todos vendran a ser pobres . . .," Mendoza to Gonzaga, October 26, 1547, GP II, 165.

[12] Instructions for Charles V from Gonzaga, November 4, 1547, Arch. Sim., Est., leg. 1193, Rose-file.

to the house of Farnese, had already looked askance at Mendoza's position as governor of the city-state; he would have made too many words about such an undertaking. But shortly after his death, during the stagnant days of the conclave, Don Diego came back to the idea of building the fortress. In a letter to Arras of January 12, 1550, he urged the Emperor to proceed at once: "It will have to be done as soon as we have a new Pope, while the iron is hot, before he can possibly become aware of it."[13]

With the usual delays it was August, 1550, before the Emperor gave Don Diego the starting signal. "We have resolved in all points that the said castle shall soon be made," Charles V wrote him, trusting in Mendoza's "quickness, prudence and experience" to carry his order into effect. Charles V told Gonzaga to provide Mendoza with twenty thousand escudos, but deplored that the latter had already asked the Duke of Florence for fifteen thousand escudos "as We are aware that We already owe him a great sum, as you know, feeling pain at not having been able to repay him."[14] Don Diego did not approve of the Emperor's delicacy. "I cannot understand," he wrote to Prince Philip, "why His Majesty did not approve of my borrowing fifteen thousand ducats from Florence. Every bit of money one does not extract from Italy is lost. . . ."[15]

Charles V was confident that the entire sum to be invested in the castle "will be reimbursed to Us by lo ["that"—that is, all the income] from the State of Siena," for this was exactly what Don Diego had promised his master: he had pledged his honor that the entire undertaking, carried out by himself alone, would not cost the Emperor "one maravedi."[16] His imagination was at a higher pitch than ever. He felt and acted the absolute, independent ruler of Siena. A glance at the notes he wrote the Sienese magistrate from Rome—curt, commanding, hasty, and always in Spanish (their content usually a request of favors and privileges for individual postulants)—shows the imperious way he lorded it over them.[17]

[13] Mendoza to Arras, January 12, 1550, *AC*, p. 172.

[14] Charles V to Mendoza, August 22–27, 1550, *RH* 31 (1914): 141–151.

[15] ". . . tanto dinero pierde hombre quanto dexa de sacar en Italia . . .," September 1, 1550, Arch. Sim., Est., leg. 1466, folio 177.

[16] ". . . Yo tengo dada la fee al Emperador que el castillo no le costara un maravedi de principal ni de interes . . .," Mendoza to Francisco de Toledo (dated erroneously January, 1548), *AIH* 2 (1911): 176, letter no. 9.

[17] Archivio di Stato, Siena, has over a hundred of them; Filza 722, and others.

But he knew his rule to be temporary; he was not enriching himself there—he was no Borgia, nor even a Cosimo. He wished to prove himself by enriching his King. By incorporating Siena into the Spanish crown's possessions, adding it to the other Spanish crownlands in Italy (Naples, Sicily, and Milan), he would raise his self-esteem to the level of Charles V, who recently had overlooked him in his distribution of rewards. (When the Emperor distributed thank-you gifts, such as bishoprics and other income-producing benefices, to friendly cardinals and conclavists serving him during the election of Julius III, Don Diego was passed over with the explanation that he had been rewarded formerly, and, anyway, was living extravagantly).[18] "In these parts the Emperor is not my superior," he said, "nor my master, but only a gentleman like myself."[19] He would become his royal master's benefactor, the pinnacle of a Spaniard's proverbial pride.

Throughout the summer of 1550 Don Diego busied himself with preparations. Engineers were hired, different sites studied, lime, bricks, stone, and instruments assembled. Purchasing was a complex operation; to insure secrecy, all was done through agents who concealed the destination of the vast amounts of material required to supply the construction.[20] And he clung to his astonishing impression that the citizens were resigned to the idea of a fortress. Since at the core of the Sienese' unhappiness was the presence of the garrison among them (the Spanish soldiers, of whom Don Diego had brought in a thousand more since the start of his rule, used the beautiful Church of San Domenico as their barracks), Don Diego had promised the citizens shortly to remove the entire garrison from there to a location outside the walls of Siena—a plan which delighted the Sienese. But in return Mendoza suggested they

---

[18] "la verguenza que me ha hecho en no hacermela en esta coyuntura," Mendoza to Arras, May 24, 1551, *AC*, pp. 247, 344, and elsewhere. Also, Jaén hears that the *consulta* had been finished and that Mendoza had received no favor of any kind; Jaén is very sorry. Mendoza is trying to hide his disappointment and finds it difficult to maintain his prestige. Jaén to Arras, May 23, 1551, Bibl. Pal., vol. 2315, Rose-file.

[19] Mendoza to Arras, July 16, 1551, *AC*, p. 254.

[20] Document dated July 9, 1559, Arch. Sim., Contaduría Mayor, Rose-file.

allow him to provide accommodations for his men outside the city limits, and this the citizens found impossible to deny.[21]

By picturing the future fortress as a substitute for the present barracks while he deplored the sacrilege his soldiers were committing by using the church for such a purpose, Mendoza had prodded the Sienese puppet government to ask for the erection of the citadel themselves: the oxen had been taught to beg for their yokes. But they were far from resigned. The fact was that many of the Sienese, disgusted, went into exile, others died of grief, and the government, though powerless and spineless under Mendoza's rule, continued to dispatch petitions to the Emperor. They served him with an appeal signed by more than a thousand Sienese citizens,[22] imploring him to revoke the order and annoying Charles V greatly. Yet Don Diego professed that he found them acquiescent. "They are taking the castle for granted, without being suspicious or getting excited about it; only in my absence . . . they speak out more freely, but I always let them do their talking at their pleasure, and they let me do mine. . . ."[23]

In January, 1551, excavations began on a square mile of the hill of San Prospero, a hillside with many medieval towered buildings, then looking something like San Gimignano today. (The site is now La Lizza, a public park.) Don Diego had to defend himself against reproaches that he was sequestering landed properties. He was accused of demolishing many houses, particularly the towers, but he assured Arras that no more than ten houses had been involved.[24] Yet he admitted another time that "the Sienese have not resented the castle so much as the demolition of the towers."[25] Still later, when he prepared his expense accounts for the Emperor, he admitted the unforeseen consequence of his procedure more openly: "We have taken hereditary possessions to clear the land for the castle and roads. We have demolished some houses, although few; and the owners, relatives, dependents and friends are therefore our ene-

---

[21] Mendoza first informed Arras of this plan during the conclave, detailing the entire procedure on January 12, 1550. *AC*, p. 172.

[22] Charles V to Mendoza, November 30, 1550, Arch. Sim., Est., leg. 875, Rosefile.

[23] Mendoza to Philip, October 14, 1550, GP III, 358.

[24] Mendoza to Arras, October 10, 1551, *AC*, pp. 280–283.

[25] Mendoza to Arras, September 15, 1551, *AC*, pp. 273–277.

mies because they have not been compensated, nor is it possible presently to pay them, and these people are dragging the larger part of the city behind them. . . ."[26] Once the project was started, he vowed to carry it through against all difficulties. Soon he fought against famine, bad weather, lack of money, and, worst of all, an inadequate work force consisting of forced labor, with women and children working in the summer to free the men for agricultural work.[27] During harvest time he had 150 women working on the castle, finding "they do much better than the men."[28]

Still, the excavations yielded him great treasures; the foundations were dug so deep that he discovered artifacts from Roman, Etruscan, and prehistoric times. Apparently he was entitled to appropriate whatever he found in the earth—it seems such things had no market value at the time. Nothing prevented him from adding a small museum of antique sculpture to his collection of books, manuscripts, coins, and paintings. He lavishly distributed gifts to those of his friends who shared his interests, such as the Bishop of Arras, and his cousin Doña Mencía de Mendoza, Duchess of Calabria (she was the Marchioness de Cenete, granddaughter of the Gran Cardenal of Spain, and one of the richest, fattest, and most cultured women).[29] He chided both of his friends for their interest in *antiguallas*, "laughing about your folly," yet he retained the lion's share. "The *antiguallas* for her [the Duchess] of Calabria have not been dispatched yet; so I will retain half a dozen of those dilapidated and smoke-stained ones, among them [a sculpture] of Marco Marcello which is said to be the only one in existence; to you and to Her Excellency I will send the new ones which you will like better; I do not care for one or the other. . . ."[30]

He did care a great deal, of course, for later he had dozens and dozens of antique sculptures in his possession. Among those he kept were busts or half and full figures of Venus, Vespasian, Hadrian, Augustus, Commodus, Julius Caesar, Domitian, Trajan; heads and busts of Homer and Aristotle, and many others. Some of them he

---

26 Mendoza's second instruction to Ximénez, April 14, 1552, *AC*, p. 333.
27 Mendoza to Charles V, June 27, 1551, Arch. Sim., Est., leg. 1468, Rose-file.
28 Mendoza to Arras, June 19 and 24, 1551, Bibl. Pal., vol. 2315, Rose-file.
29 Cf. Bataillon, *Erasmo y España* (Mexican edition), II, 71.
30 ". . . me rio de vuestra locura . . .," *AC*, p. 266.

might have come by in Rome; in his bedroom in Rome, in fact, was a statue of Commodus that he had taken at first to be the likeness of "Messer Fatio, my landlord."[31] In Etruscan graves he found cameos and gold rings: "The other day we found in a sepulchre two rings and a glass with writing on it, a marvelous thing, in pyramid shape. . . ." And reaching back into past ages when the site of Siena was sea bottom: "In this mountain one finds also snails and mussels and animals of land and water that were once soft earth and have turned into stone. . . . I have looked up Aristotle again and begun to write about the reason for this. . . ."[32]

But while such priceless bounties fell into his lap, the Sienese population suffered in passive resistance to his military government. (Passive they were because he had already disarmed them in the latter months of 1548.) The sullen peasants purposely neglected the usually so fertile countryside. As a result of dwindling yields and poor harvests, his construction gang was often plagued by famine.

The mood of the people was reflected in, and further incited by, the wild rantings of a certain hermit, called the "Prophet Brandano," who once had accurately predicted the sack of Rome and now predicted Mendoza would never finish his structure. "Except the Lord build the house, they labor in vain that build it," he sang and shouted, stoning a red-coated Spanish officer on the construction site whom he took for Don Diego.[33] Sending the old fool back to his hermitage, Mendoza gave his whole mind to the enterprise, appearing every day at the site to hurry it along. Another bad omen appeared: an iron ball was found in the depths of the excavations, inscribed: "Nel Giardino Delicato la fortezza si farà, e poco tempo durerà." [A fortress will be built in the Lovely Garden, and it will not last long.] In past times, Don Diego was told, the hill of San Prospero had been called Giardino Delicato.[34]

[31] ". . . soy tan ruin maestro de conocer antiguallas, que tengo una sobre la puerta de mi cámara dos años ha, la qual me dicen es de Comodo, y la mejor que hay en Roma, y siempre he pensado que era un retrato de messer Fatio, que fue patron de la casa donde moro . . .," Mendoza to Arras, Rome, November 9, 1551, AIH 2: 545.
[32] AC, p. 271.
[33] GP II, 187, 188.
[34] Bernardo Segni, Storie Fiorentine, III, 28, 29.

The actual work was to take twenty months, and all the time Mendoza knew that the Spanish and French were gliding step by step into a new war in Italy.[35] This situation would bring new danger to the exposed, poorly fortified coast of Piombino, for which he was also responsible. The French and "rebellious Italians," he feared, might overrun Siena before his defenses were ready, a thought driving him back to renewed concentration on the structure, for he was ever mindful of the fact that almost all former Spanish governors had been forcibly expelled by the Sienese in times of general unrest. "I do not want the Sienese to chase me out with sticks one day," he said, "as they usually do their friends. . . ."[36]

At first the work proceeded so rapidly that, in a state of euphoria, he declared: "It will be one of the strongest and best prepared and most beautiful and finest built and least costly [of fortresses] in all of Christendom." With the rising ramparts, his feeling of self-assurance increased: "There is no one who could make the castle so easily, nor arrange the [Sienese puppet] government as I." In his interdependence with the Emperor he would never feel better than now, believing that he was doing him a unique service:

Personally, for me, there is little gain in ruling Siena, since I am poor, and all I do is spending my property or that of the Emperor, and work, and living in danger to my person . . . [The "Prophet's" was by no means the only attentat against him; already in 1548 a group of disgruntled Sienese intended to slay Mendoza at mass on Christmas Day, and another time assassins fired on him but killed only the horse on which he was riding.] But I take much more pride than I would in seven embassies in Rome in the fact that I have served the Emperor for twenty years without having made a mistake, in my opinion. On top of this, I have done him this service of lime and stone, founding a state which will be as princely as Milan for him and for his own to enjoy.[37]

His sense of accomplishment might have made him triumph over sickness, difficult terrain and working conditions, over the discon-

[35] His own role in committing Julius III into this war on secret orders of Charles V is discussed in the next chapter.

[36] "No quiero que . . . cavando cavando me carguen un dia de palo como lo suelen estos seneses hacer a sus amigos . . .," Mendoza to Philip, February 19, 1551, Arch. Sim., Est., leg. 876, Rose-file.

[37] Murder plan of 1548, *AC*, p. 126; remainder of paragraph, Mendoza to Arras, March 1, March 14, and June 7, 1551, *AC*, pp. 210, 214, 253.

tent of the people, and even over assaults on his person. But one obstacle managed to cast too large a shadow over his enterprise to be ignored: the Duke of Florence. Forced to watch his nearest neighbor growing like a noxious weed into another tyrant in his Tuscany, Cosimo was angered by the "castle," and Don Diego knew it. "The Duke is like a poison, seeing the castle being made," he wrote to Arras, ". . . above all because I appear to wish to hold on to Piombino. . . ."[38]

The Emperor had already decided in May, 1551, to retain Piombino for himself, once more promising the Signore of Piombino an equivalent recompense.[39] Consequently, Don Diego had stopped trying to persuade his master in Cosimo's favor, ostensibly so, because the Duke had haughtily declared his intention to wash his hands of it entirely. But in fact the growing success of Mendoza's fortress was what led him to believe it feasible to dispense with the Duke's help in the future. He and Gonzaga contemplated the eventual possibility of combining Siena, Piombino, and even Parma (about which the current war was being waged) into one new Spanish state. Cosimo had suspected Gonzaga and Mendoza of such an intention all along, yet he had still hoped it might turn out otherwise.[40]

Out of consideration for the Duke of Florence, Charles V advised Mendoza not to publish the affair now, but Don Diego was to inform the young Signore of Piombino, his mother, and Cardinal Salviati about his decision. Cosimo would be repaid all the Emperor owed him.[41] As late as June 23, 1551, Cosimo was still unaware of the fact that the Emperor had made up his mind, and he enlisted his friend, Pope Julius, to work in his favor.[42] When Julius III sent Cardinal Dandino as special nuncio to Charles V to negotiate the affair of Parma with him, Dandino tried to alert the Emperor to the "dangerous weakness of Piombino—either the French or the Turk can occupy it," suggesting that Charles V, taking over the state, pass it on to the Duke of Florence. But the Emperor declared

[38] Mendoza to Arras, September 1, 1551, AC, p. 269.

[39] Charles V to Mendoza, May 16, 1551, Arch. Sim., Est., leg. 646, Rose-file; also Charles V to the Viceroy of Sicily, ibid.

[40] Av. Serristori to Cosimo I, GP II, 221–222.

[41] Charles V to Mendoza, May 16, 1551, Arch. Sim., Est., leg. 646, Rose-file.

[42] Cosimo I to Francisco de Toledo, June 23, 1551, Arch. Flor., Rose-file.

it was not his policy to take property from one man and give it to another.[43]

Shortly afterward Cosimo learned of the decision against him. Giving full rein to all his real feelings about Don Diego, he denounced him to Arras in reviling terms,[44] raising the tension between the two Lords of Tuscany to such a pitch that Arras felt compelled to step in. The Bishop tried to work toward their reconciliation, advising Don Diego, of whose personal irresistibility he was convinced, to thresh it all out with Cosimo in person.

On one of his forthcoming journeys to Rome, Don Diego went out of his way to visit with the Duke and Duchess at Poggio a Caiano. But he, rather than the dissimulating Duke, gained from this encounter renewed trust in his neighbor.[45] He tried to analyze the reasons for the Duke's ill humor, doing his best to reassure him. First, he attempted to convince the ducal couple that in the business of Piombino, contrary to what they might have heard from the court, everything had been the Emperor's own decision. Once Charles V had made up his mind and the Duke had told him that he did not want Piombino any more, Don Diego had simply stopped trying to persuade the Emperor to revoke his decision. (This was true, though in view of the ulterior motive of the great new Spanish state-to-be, it was but a half-truth.) Second, Don Diego straightened out some minor differences. These had resulted from conflicts in command within Piombino and Elba when Don Diego, as governor of the entire state, had given the Duke administrative orders as his superior (enough of a fact to antagonize the vainglorious Duke for life!). But third and most important, "He [Cosimo] would like to make the Emperor understand that no

[43] Document from 1551, undated, but it must be from April–May, the time of Dandino's interview. Arch. Sim., Est., leg. 876, Rose-file.

[44] Cosimo I to Arras, August 5, 1551, Bibl. Pal., Cartas del Obispo de Arras, Rose-file.

[45] Several months before, when the question of Piombino was still undecided, Don Diego had announced a friendly visit to the Duke at which the latter was astonished: Cosimo professed not to understand why Mendoza should want to accompany Don Francisco de Toledo, but said that if he did come he would not fail to listen to him. Cosimo said he would wink at Don Diego's bits of treachery and deceit and would receive him warmly as a minister of the Emperor and not as if he were Don Diego de Mendoza. Cosimo to Francisco de Toledo, April 6, 1551, Arch. Flor., Mediceo 17, Universale, Rose-file.

armaments but his own should be built up in Tuscany, yet now he sees the making of a castle in Siena, as well as the fortification of two important places [Orbetello and Porto Ercole], and who knows whether we will not fortify a third? So, for all he knows, we may found a state between his own and that of the Church where with one hand one can knock at Saint Peter's door in Rome, and with the other at Saint John's in Florence."

It was true, Mendoza admitted, that the turn of affairs, the growing might of Siena and of Don Diego as the author of it, was very painful for the Duke. But since there was no remedy for it (Mendoza took this for granted!), he believed he had convinced Cosimo to adjust to this irrevocable situation:

We are on good terms—friends, so to speak—and he is satisfied about all the rest. Both of us have done all we could to come to this term: I, because it truly is required in the service and authority of the Emperor, and because, to tell you my mind frankly, I have much love for him. I think he is a very virtuous man who conducts himself well; he, because it is as important to him as his own life, for his reputation at home and abroad, that we ministers of the Emperor should . . . acknowledge his authority and meet him warmly, especially I, as I am in the heart of his state and of the business. This is my book of the Duke of Florence.[46]

Arras was further away from any personal charm that the Duke and his household may have exerted on Don Diego. When Cosimo wrote him again after Mendoza's visit, by no means withdrawing his earlier invective,[47] Arras warned Don Diego: "I should be glad if the friendship with Florence were as firm as you write, but I fear that the Duke does not understand it so. . . . You will have great trouble curing this evil by the root, because it depends upon Piombino, which His Majesty is still very anxious to keep for himself. . . ."[48] (Not even Arras, from his position of eminence that let him survey all the happenings in the Empire, could see at that time that Cosimo I aspired to no less than the possession of Siena.) In reply, Don Diego promised Arras: "I shall try as best I can to assure the

[46] Mendoza to Arras, September 15, 1551, AC, pp. 273–277.

[47] As reported in a letter by Cosimo to Francisco de Toledo, Arch. Flor., Mediceo 18, Rose-file.

[48] Arras to Mendoza, from Schwatz, October 28, 1551. Revista de Archivos, Bibliotecas y Museos (RABM), 1899, pp. 615–618.

Duke."[49] Then he continued with his fortress, unperturbed by the real sentiments of his "friend, so to speak," and unaware of a conspiracy of the Sienese with the French.

Almost from the day he had begun the construction, a group of Sienese patriots started to work for the liberation of Siena. The group contained persons in whom Mendoza placed great trust. They repaid his confidence in them by calling the unsuspecting governor-philosopher "Aristotle" in their secret code.[50] "Aristotle" did not know that he was on the way of falling victim to his own hubris.

Why should Mendoza have entered a path that would lead him irrevocably toward his own political destruction? Why should this scholar and poet, this fair-minded Aristotelian, have developed into a potential tyrant, dictator, and usurper of other peoples' liberties, lives, and property? "Potential," yes, although in the histories of Siena, Tuscany, and Piombino he lives on in infamy as though he had been all those things.

But despite all the havoc he created and the animosity he incited toward himself, he did not want to be a tyrant. It is true that, in his present frenzy to complete the fortress while trampling on the people's rights, he seemed to have little similarity to the man who seven or eight years before (in the letter of Busseto) had pleaded with his Emperor to respect the freedom of the unfortunate republic:

Your conscience would not allow it, invincible Prince, you would have no reason according to the laws of gratitude and humanity, to rob that republic of its liberty and give it to your enemy [Pope Paul III]. Does Your Majesty not remember the great faith, the true spirit of those citizens? When all the world conspired against you, look, they alone remained faithful to you [the League of Cognac]. Such loyal vassals, proven loyal friends, most excellent servants, should you repay their services now with unfaithfulness? With damage? Neither goodness, nor reason, nor virtue, nor religion would permit this. . . ."[51]

---

49 Mendoza to Arras, November 9, 1551, *RABM*, 1899, no. 30, p. 546.
50 Cf. Alessandro Sozzini, "Diario delle cose avvenute in Siena dai 20 Luglio 1550 ai 28 Giugno 1555," *Arch. Stor. Ital.* 2 (1842): 492.
51 *BAE* XXI, part I, p. xxiv.

Could this be the same man who now pledged the Emperor that the money for the works would be reimbursed to him from the revenues of the oppressed state, not within three years as calculated in the beginning, but, better by far, within the next six months? "When the Sienese have one foot in the grave, so to speak—if the Emperor provides me with enough money to finish the construction by October, I shall start to repay fat sums of his money [much sooner than he expects] by January, 1552."[52] Did his present actions correspond to the notions of "goodness, reason, virtue, and religion" of the adviser who had loved the liberty of Siena? In Mendoza's mind, apparently, they did. The Republic of Siena had, in fact, "one foot in the grave," yet, by his own definition, he did not wish to kill its liberty. Although he was helping the Emperor and his heir "to remain secure, and to perpetuate themselves [in their hold on Siena]," he affirmed (July 16, 1551) that "His Majesty must know that I would never help either him or his son to become tyrants."[53]

In a letter to Gonzaga of November, 1550, before the ground for the castle was broken, Don Diego revealed another view of the same enterprise, calculating its negative aspects, a knowledge he shared only with Gonzaga, the coauthor of the fortress. According to that he knew from the beginning that the enterprise was a colossal mistake. Outlining three difficulties, he says:

The smallest [difficulty] concerns the Emperor's plans that call for a stronghold of such enormous proportions as would remain unfinished for ten generations. . . . Worse is the fact that the official to carry out the work [himself, as it turned out to be] must be a tyrant as well as a stand-in for another man [the Emperor or his son]. . . . Worst of all, the King listens to persons who do not like us [the clan of Toledos, primarily], and since this is a violent business which will offend many people, everyone will listen to those slanderers, and they will keep on hammering it into the Emperor in a way that would give the lie to Saint John's Gospel, while making that of Nicodemus true; and since the Emperor has some conscience occasionally, disliking hypocrisy, they will find him more than willing to listen. . . .[54]

52 Mendoza to Arras, June 7, 1551, AC, p. 253.
53 Mendoza to Arras, July 16, 1551, AC, p. 260.
54 Mendoza to Gonzaga, AIH 2, no. 35, 561–563.

This lets it appear than Don Diego's disagreeable stance as a tyrant toward the Sienese was little more than a mask that hardly fitted him and therefore failed to protect him. He made a practical demonstration, as we have seen, of trying to show the Sienese that he was no tyrant by inducing them to "accept" the citadel, promising them that, as soon as it would be finished, he would remove the Spanish garrison from San Domenico. When the fortress was half-ready, he lived up to his pledge, reducing the garrison by four companies. "I made a great experiment," he wrote to Arras, "because this confidence I showed them sent a chill down their spines; it [the withdrawal of the companies] was broadcast throughout the city as proof that the castle is not being made for their disloyalty or any distrust we might have of them, and, consequently, their spirits have quieted down considerably."[55]

While he thought to impress the Sienese with such fairmindedness, the practical result was that he, the philosopher, only weakened his own defenses. At the same time, by inference from his words of explanation, he angered the Duke of Florence, who complained of being openly threatened by Mendoza's words to the Sienese about the ulterior purpose of the castle.

In the lights of the standards of his time, Mendoza ought not, perhaps, to be blamed for what seems to us most objectionable, namely, that he saw no basic injustice in his meddling in a foreign people's destiny. Since the Emperor was legally the overlord of Italy, the premise of his actions was, in Mendoza's eyes, indisputably honest. After all, Naples and other parts of the peninsula, no less Italian than Siena, were, and continued to be, Spanish-ruled for centuries (and the entire Grand Duchy of Tuscany would belong to Austria in the dark future). But because inwardly he showed contrition for the means necessarily to be employed—he was honest enough to admit to "punishing the Sienese"—he rationalized his aims to justify these means: "I call 'punishing the public' making a castle for them, taking their revenues away from the power of those who tyrannize over them, giving them into the hands of just persons who dispense them as they should. . . ."

"Is it really 'punishing,' " he asks further, "if we take away the arbitrary, sinister government, self-interest-ridden and passionate,

55 Mendoza to Arras, July 29, 1551, AC, pp. 262–263.

putting up, instead, a 'Vicar' for them? [By "Vicar" he meant the future King of Spain.] In his [the "Vicar's"] place will be a person of authority who directs them and guides them toward the good without offending their liberty, only repressing their license. . . ."[56]

With "Aristotle's" head continually in the clouds, the conspirators against his rule were weaving an indestructible net, in full daylight, as it were. One of them, Amerigo Amerighi, even served as Sienese ambassador of the puppet government to his own "magnificence" when he was in Rome. The conspirators went so far as to deliver into Mendoza's hands—with regret, but, to protect their secret machinations, without mercy—another Sienese patriot who, singlehanded, had also started to work with the French. Don Diego fumingly arrested, prosecuted, tortured this Cesare Vaiari, who even under "exquisite application" was unable to reveal anything of substance, because he knew nothing incriminating about the other Sienese. The other, clever ones worked openly as Imperial vassals and secretly with the French in Rome, continuing their game without detection.[57]

Meanwhile, Mendoza raced the work of his construction ahead against the impending lack of money as well as the unforeseeable result of the War of Parma. At the same time he prepared the legal ground for the "vicariate," as he called the intended absorption of Siena into the Spanish crown. Artfully he set one faction of the Sienese against the other, flattering himself in having made the Sienese so dissatisfied with themselves, that they would come clamoring for permanent Spanish rule.[58] "I asked them," he wrote to Prince Philip, "that they should voluntarily beg His Majesty for the protection of Your Highness and the House of Spain. . . . I have the business in such a good shape that I am certain they will do it. . . ."

Satisfied in having fulfilled his promise to the Emperor, hoping he could soon retire from these parts of the world with his and Philip's permission, he added that "the castle, where the walls are now being built, will be in such a state by the end of June [1552],

---

[56] Ibid.
[57] Sozzini, "Diario," p. 492.
[58] Mendoza to Charles V, February 1552, GP III, 392–395.

so God will, that one can defend oneself against the whole world within that edifice of brick and earth."[59]

In reality, though, he was now near the point he had envisioned a few months earlier, when he wrote: "Either I will finish it, or it will finish me. . . ."[60]

[59] Mendoza to Philip, January 29, 1552, GP III, 390–391. Cf. Walter Friedensburg, *Kaiser Karl V und Papst Paul III*, pp. 25, 26. When Paul III in 1536 wanted Siena, the Emperor said, "Siena gehöre zum Reich, so dass er nur mit Zustimmung der deutschen Kurfürsten darüber verfügen könne." But Mendoza produced historical examples, enabling the Emperor to circumvent the German electors. See E. Spivakovsky, "El 'Vicariato de Siena,' Correspondencia de Felipe II, Príncipe, con Diego Hurtado de Mendoza y Ferrante Gonzaga," *Hispania* 26 (Madrid, 1966): 583–596.

[60] ". . . o yo tengo de acaballe o el a mi . . .," Mendoza to Arras, August 28, 1551, *AC*, p. 264.

12. THE WAR OF PARMA, 1550–1552

The war was not of my invention nor persuasion.

Don Diego[1]

THE KING OF FRANCE and d'Urfé, his ambassador in Rome, whose support in the conclave had led to Del Monte's election, took the new Pope's friendship for granted and relaxed their zeal. Not so the Imperials. Working fast to remove any unfavorable impression of himself lingering in the Pope's mind, Mendoza now made it his policy to honor Julius III extravagantly. After the election he must have ordered himself a magnificent new mantle of gold cloth, for, on February 22, the day of the papal coronation, it seems that he alone was dressed in gold. The French ambassador was not, "because he had not heard of Don Diego's dress until the evening before."[2] Also, the Emperor, King Ferdinand, and Prince

---

[1] *AC*, p. 348.

[2] Dandolo to Venice, February 22, 1550, Arch. Ven., Rose-file. A new festive dress for the ambassador implied new finery for his numerous escort and liveries for his pages. The following shows how Don Diego raised money to pay for such extravagance: "Mendoza has borrowed six thousand escudos from the Altovisi, on condition that he gives security here in Rome. He has bound himself to repay them within four months, and also to repay two thousand escudos, a bill that he has run up for cloth and silk." Bernardo Buonanni, secretary of the Florentine ambassador Serristori, to Pagni, April 28, 1551, Arch. Flor., Mediceo 3270, Rose-file.

Philip followed Mendoza's urgent advice to court the new Pope; each of them dispatched special envoys to Rome, bearing congratulations on the accession. Henri II, still under the impression that Julius III was naturally his partisan, did not hasten to pay him special respects.

But when King Henri learned that special ambassadors from the three Habsburgs were approaching Rome, he charged d'Urfé to pay His Holiness a congratulatory visit at once. On March 26, accordingly, d'Urfé, by then dressed "in a robe of silver cloth with a French overcoat of gold cloth, lined in gold and silver," accompanied by the entire French party in Rome led by Orazio Farnese, went in procession to the Vatican. During the ensuing ceremony, Don Diego sat next to Julius III and "busied himself with chasing flies off His Holiness with his bonnet."[3] The Pope delivered a polite speech of gratitude to the French and then apologized for his words in an aside to Mendoza. "Turning to me as I sat beside him, he told me the French were so jealous of the demonstrations he had made toward Your Majesty that it was necessary for him to say these words to them. . . ."[4]

This was the pontiff's attempt to regain a balance that already had been upset by his inclination toward the Emperor. The courtesy of Charles V and Don Diego, contrasting with the thoughtlessness of the French King, may have helped to turn the formerly "French" Cardinal del Monte into an "Imperial" Pope, for he was always afraid of being slighted. Now he was naively enjoying his princely status, and the Imperials understood how to make use of his weakness. In Brussels, Prince Philip gave a sumptuous feast in Julius's honor. "His Holiness is very pleased and grateful," wrote Don Diego, "about the demonstration Your Highness made of your satisfaction in his election. Neither he nor his own people ever stop telling everybody that Your Highness spent twenty thousand escudos on a feast honoring his election. This is the first time anyone did such a thing in honor of the papacy."[5]

In his gratitude to the Farneses, whose support had been decisive in giving him the papacy, Julius III was at first so kind to Cardinal

3 Lucien Romier, *Les origines politiques des guerres de Religion*, I, 223.
4 Mendoza to Charles V, April 1, 1550, A. von Druffel, *Briefe* I, no. 402, p. 385.
5 Mendoza to Philip, March 18, 1550, GP III, 382–383.

Alessandro and his brothers that "until now Alessandro has hardly noticed the absence of his papal grandfather," reports King Ferdinand's Ambassador Lasso. "But this will not last very long," Lasso continues, "because the Pope has his own relatives and [has] feelings for them. He shows himself no less a friend of his own [relatives] than Pope Paul was, nor does he cover up his sensuality any longer. About three days ago, a concubine of [the Pope's] brother came here with her three-year-old son. Escorted by more than four hundred cavalry, they proceeded through the center of Rome to Saint Peter's, and I am told they lodged there. This causes great scandal and much talk. Some say that this infant is a 'nephew of the Pope,' as sons of clerics are called."[6]

The Pope's real nepotism emerged only gradually, however. The first blow came when he nominated as Cardinal the seventeen-year-old Innocenzo, the "Prevostino" (Little Provost) on May 31. The origin of the boy was not then divulged, and historians usually profess ignorance, while making rather scandalous insinuations. But according to Massarelli this "former keeper of the apes" was Julius III's son.[7] The Imperials extended their courtesy to the Pope's protégé. Mendoza induced the Emperor to give Innocenzo an annual pension; the Cardinal of Trent sent the "Prevostino," as well as the little "nephew" mentioned above, a pony each, addressed "to my most illustrious, most serene lordships."[8] (In private, to Arras, Don Diego permitted himself to call the Little Provost "half a cardinal" and a "little ape.")[9] Don Diego must have given the Pope or his relatives some princely present himself, because on April 26, Giovanni Battista del Monte, son of Julius III's brother, gave Don Diego a horse, "a beautiful and beautifully adorned ginetto. That day, the Imperial ambassador, wearing a black velvet cloak over a white satin doublet, rode [this horse] in a procession to receive an ambassador from the Duke of Florence."[10]

While the Pope's own relatives were waiting in the wings to supplant the Farnese family, the Imperials started to move heaven

[6] Lasso to King Ferdinand, March 21, 1550, Druffel, Briefe I, 375.
[7] Cf. Ludwig von Pastor, Geschichte der Päpste, VI, 54, 55; Dandolo, Cal. St. P. Ven. no. 662, p. 355; Massarelli, Diaria I, entry of April 20, 1545, p. 177.
[8] Lasso to King Ferdinand, May 24, 1550, Druffel, Briefe I, 398, 399.
[9] Mendoza to Arras, May 4, 1551, AC, pp. 225–232.
[10] Buonanni to Cosimo I, April 26, 1550, Arch. Flor., Mediceo 3269, Rose-file.

and earth to undermine Julius III's initial kindness to them. Although Gonzaga had been prepared to reconquer Parma, ostensibly to help Ottavio against his grandfather, his actual aim was to hold it for the Emperor. The new Pope did not suspect any Imperial scheming. He confirmed the restoration of Parma in good faith, inviting Ottavio to Rome to be invested formally with that duchy as a fief of the Church. (The ceremony was scheduled for the end of April, but it had to be delayed until May 21 because the Pope was ill.) This confirmed Ottavio's right in perpetuity to keep the coveted territory of Parma that adjoined the Imperial lands ruled by Gonzaga, Milan and Piacenza. While neither the Emperor nor Gonzaga approved of this development, they did not deem it wise to endanger their own relations with Julius III by reopening the old, disreputable negotiations. Instead, their game of politics now resorted to intrigues, Imperial strategy working to make the new Pope fall out directly with Ottavio Farnese.

This was Don Diego's newest task. It was fraught with danger of war, for which his enemies later called him a warmonger. Ordered to set a trap for the Pope, he had to postpone even his long-delayed return to Siena. From the outset he knew Julius III's character to perfection: "He is excitable and choleric, also restless. He does not seem foolhardy to me, but rather timid. He is open to advice. [Cardinal] Crescenzio rules him, naturally, as he [the Pope] has had little experience of things of state. He is most liberal and seems a good Christian. He likes to provide for his family, and although he says he has only moderate aspirations for them, apparently he is reasonable in this respect. He loves to be praised and is vain. He is given to making fast decisions because business tires him. I believe he will shift it all to Crescenzio."[11]

A man as tractable as that now found himself exposed to the bottomless reservoir of Imperial guile. The late Pope had been the match of the Imperials. Don Diego, studying the tortuous ways of Paul III's scheming mind, had in fact learned much political trickery in Rome. Now he used his skill to sway the simpler, though by no means simple-minded Julius to go to war for Parma against Ottavio Farnese.

Mendoza himself, by meddling in Italian affairs, was more and more guided by Gonzaga's ideas. "He is changeable and influenced

[11] Mendoza to Arras, May, 1550, *AIH* 2, no. 22.

by Mantua," as Don Pedro de Toledo had said of Don Diego, not inaccurately.[12] Don Diego's life in that whirlpool of intrigues was grooming him to be receptive to them. In the first year of his stay in Rome and Siena, he had still advised a gentler policy than had Gonzaga, who always reached for the sword at once. Also, until the second year he insisted on being able to handle the Sienese without building a castle over their heads. He had also tried, though unsuccessfully, to conciliate the divergent policies of the late Pope with those of the Emperor. Now, conditioned in the poisonous Roman atmosphere, he listened to Gonzaga's ideas with greater sympathy. In addition, he was propelled by the Emperor's orders (according to Cosimo I, "Mendoza tells everyone that Charles V's intention is to take possession of everything upon which he can lay his hands"), and possibly also by his growing feeling of defiance toward the clan of Toledo. Knowing that his rivals, particularly the Duke of Florence, wished to drive him out, he felt forced to prove what he could do. Such motives do not evoke the best side of a man, and what he now proceeded to do was not a noble thing for the philosopher who, in younger years, had favored and understood the Venetians' withdrawal from the very war he had been ordered to prolong.

In preparing for his grand strategy, Don Diego won the Pope's trust so completely that the latter confided his secret ambition to him: "Yesterday he [the Pope] spoke at length to me of his aims for the House of Monte. He started with moderate plans, but ended up by contemplating a marriage between a daughter of the Duke of Florence and [the Pope's] three-year-old nephew. Between his teeth he mumbled something about a daughter of the King of the Romans. . . ."[13] Rewarding himself for his patient ear, Don Diego used every opportunity to incite the Pope against the Farneses. One occasion to influence Julius III arose when the Pope received Ottavio for the swearing of his feudatory oath. It seems that some of Ottavio's troops had on their march made disturbances in Rome or in territories of the Church, with the result that Julius III ordered one of Ottavio's captains to be hanged. Three days after the ceremonies of the oath, Diego Lasso commented to King Ferdinand:

[12] Pedro de Toledo to Cosimo I, November 16, 1549, Arch. Flor., Mediceo 611, Rose-file.
[13] See note 11, above.

"The Pope is starting to leave off being so intimate with the Farneses."[14] Pouring oil into the fire, Don Diego built up the apparent affront that had angered the Pope against Ottavio. He goaded Julius III into asserting his power to declare Ottavio a rebel against the Church and excommunicate him, promising him the Emperor's support in case Ottavio should dare to take up arms. Ideas that he started to plant so early would take about a year to sprout. "It seems to me," he wrote to Gonzaga, "that the Pope would like to break the heads of these Farneses even more than you do, and, confidentially, I have admonished him to do so."[15]

Not suspecting, or at least not worrying, that such sinister schemes were being concocted under his own eyes, the Pope made the most of the papacy, as much as his poor health would permit. Parties, feasts, banquets, women, playboys, were the rule. Many cardinals feasted with him. Only the sour, brooding "Teatino" (Caraffa), and some others who represented the severe reform party, kept away from the frivolous life that was already outmoded.

At that time the Counter Reformation was gaining influence. Ironically, it did so in a Rome, where life was still being celebrated in the carefree style of the Farneses, because the late Pope, in his liberality, had let the Jesuit order and the Inquisition establish themselves there. These two institutions, together (although not in concert) with Cardinal Caraffa, fought the old habits of sloth, luxury, and religious indifference. And since Julius III cared even less than Paul III about what was going on, not investigating what he signed (as he shied from uncomfortable decisions), the reformers made him sign the first censorship bull in literature, which Caraffa had prepared years before.[16] After April 29, 1550, the reading and owning of "heretical," "Lutheran," or other infidel or suspicious books was forbidden. By June 3, a great burning of heretic books was celebrated in the papal metropolis (three years later, Roman bonfires were to include the Talmud of the Jews), while the Pope himself, one of the most tolerant people in the world, trusted his gout- and catarrh-ridden body to the care of Jewish doctors, among

---

[14] "Con los Frenesis [sic] comienza a descompadrar . . .," Lasso to King Ferdinand, May 24, 1550, Druffel, Briefe I, 398, 399.

[15] Mendoza to Gonzaga, May 1550, AIH 2, no. 23.

[16] Pastor, Geschichte, VI, 159.

them the Marrano Amatus Lusitanus, who had established his
famous practice in papal Ancona and was called to attend Julius
III in the still-liberal Rome.[17]

Although the Pope regarded Parma as a fief of the Church, the
Emperor still insisted it was a fief of the Imperium, and he retained
Piacenza under the same pretension. Gonzaga pressed with Imperial troops on the confines of the duchy; within Parma, Imperial
partisans fomented unrest; and Don Diego worked hard to convince
the Pope of the folly of offending Charles V. Julius III was becoming uncomfortable under these pressures. Mendoza had succeeded
in making him distrust the Farneses. The Pope had long since regretted his imprudence in having helped Ottavio so generously,
but unwittingly, to a usurpation wrought with evil consequences
for himself. When Ottavio, as vassal of the Church, asked for the
Pope's protection and assistance against Gonzaga's machinations,
he met with a cold reception. Despairing of Rome's attitude, Ottavio applied in December for aid from Henri II of France, who
was always willing to go to war against Charles V.

When Mendoza later maintained that he had not intended to
lead the Pope into war, he told the truth about his personal inclination. Early in 1551 he proposed an agreement to Julius III that
could have averted the War of Parma. The Pope, he advised, should
bestow the fiefs of Piacenza and Parma on the Emperor, the latter
paying tribute to the Church as well as a compensation to Duke
Ottavio. But by that time the Pope was no longer so malleable.
Averse to being pushed to extremes, his policy guided by the efficient negotiator Dandino, he did not wish to humiliate himself by
revoking his own investiture of Ottavio. He offered to invest and
infeud His Majesty with Piacenza if Charles V would give a compensation for it to Ottavio; but he asked the Emperor to renounce
all pretensions to Parma. Don Diego attributed this proposition to
the still existing influence of the Farneses. "Regarding Parma," he
wrote to Arras, "the Farneses are fencing so as to make us stumble.
The Emperor could now make a very big deal at their expense.
The Pope is tired, and his nephews do not like the Farneses. If they
enter into a war with us, it will cost the Pope ten times as much.
But since Farnese has to make common cause with France, it will

17 Marini, *Degli Archiatri Pontifici*, I, 414–417.

come to the worst anyway, with or without his consent. So, if we just wait, the business will have to drop into our lap."[18]

Even this does not mean that Mendoza wanted the war, now apparently inevitable, to come in the approaching spring. Its outbreak would disturb the other Imperial project, the new Council of Trent, which was scheduled to open in May. If there was to be a war over Parma, the Council would have to wait. No one knew this better than Mendoza, who had plodded to Trent over snow-covered roads, all for nothing, and later had sat there in vain for months. He was annoyed, therefore, when Ottavio Farnese, driven to transgression in his exasperation with the inflexibility of the Emperor, began some military adventures. On February 7, 1551, Ottavio marched against an Imperial stronghold within the State of Parma, the estate of Colorno, and occupied it. Militarily, then, Ottavio started the war. Yet Mendoza still said: "This affair of Parma has to be considered carefully, because, as I say, it involves the Council. In my opinion—although it does not count for much—any violent use of force should be suspended until the conclusion of the Council, unless the blow could be strong enough to tear Parma out by the roots right out of their power with the very first attack. Until then I deem it better to treat the Farneses with good excuses, because if we attack, and then fail, the Council goes head over heels."[19] (Precisely what was to happen. In April, 1552, Julius III suspended the Council for "lack of attendance by French and Lutherans.")[20]

Once again a prophet, Don Diego suspected that the war would not be conducted in the grand manner. He dreaded long, inconclusive, niggardly involvements. But the forces now set in motion did not any more allow for alternatives. It became generally known that Ottavio was allied with the French, though at first Don Diego was not much perturbed by this. He belittled the ominous development that would draw the French back into Italy. To keep Julius III favorably inclined, he alerted the Emperor toward bribing the Pope's three (real) nephews, Giovanni Battista del Monte, Vicenzo de' Nobili, Ascanio della Corgnia.[21] But by March the progress to-

---

[18] Mendoza to Arras, January 31 and February 20, 1551, *AC*, pp. 204–206, 207–208.

[19] Ibid.

[20] Romier, *Les origines*, I, 289.

[21] Mendoza to Arras, March 1, 1551, *AC*, pp. 209–211.

ward war was impossible to arrest. Then, Mendoza wrote one of his long, professorial letters to the Pope, admonishing him to take up arms against Ottavio and fast.[22]

With the coming of spring, Pope Julius had to take time out from his round of diversions to formulate a decision. His pride and self-confidence had received a strong blow from the actions of Ottavio, his supposed vassal. Contrary to the Pope's warning, Ottavio had not only allied himself with the French King, but had also induced the French to raise troops in the heart of Italy. Troops in French pay had stationed themselves in Mirandola, ready to fight any attackers on Parma. In his pride, which was the Pope's predominant characteristic, nothing was left the supreme pontiff but to counter such a defiance with a *monitorium poenale* against Ottavio. This ultimatum left only two possibilities: Ottavio could either surrender to it or disregard it. In the latter case, now inevitable, the Pope would have to honor his word and go to war against this "rebel of the Church."[23]

Mendoza hastened from Siena to Rome in time to help the Pope reach this decision, promising all the necessary assistance from Charles V's side. But he had not the smoothest sailing because, as usual, his opposite number, the French ambassador, was also on the spot. The French had sent a new envoy, Monseigneur de Termes, a large military leader whose sumptuous appearance, surrounded by a great armed escort, went very much against Mendoza's grain at that time. The Emperor's finances had been dwindling again in expectation of the new war, and Don Diego felt the consequences. From Siena he had already been imploring Arras for reimbursement of his expenses (he drew no salary for his post in Siena), "especially because Monseñor de Termes is coming with such a large escort and commission to spend money, while I, being so poor, unless I get paid, shall hardly be able to sustain myself. It will not look good if I have to go through the streets ragged and alone."[24]

Termes had arrived just in time to belabor the other ear of the Pope. "He warns that if His Holiness goes to war against Parma, the King will convoke a National Council, threatening to withdraw

[22] Mendoza to Julius III, March, 1551, *AIH* 2, no. 24.
[23] Lasso to King Ferdinand, April 6, 1551, Druffel, *Briefe* I, 608, 609.
[24] Mendoza to Arras, March 14, 1551, *AC*, p. 215.

his obedience [from Rome]," wrote Diego Lasso. But the Pope remained deaf to the entreaties of the French. He disregarded also the subtle resistance that Dandolo, the Venetian ambassador, and the Florentine ambassador tried to exert on him. While his attitude was largely due to Don Diego's persuasion, the influence of the papal nephews helped. According to Lasso, "they [the nephews] incite him much, seeing that the destruction of these Farneses would be to their own best advantage."[25]

But why had the Emperor let things come to such a turn that, under the transparent disguise of intervening as "protector of the Holy See," he should wage war against his son-in-law? (Ironically, in this period of their generally stormy marriage, the couple was living in domestic peace. Madama Margaret had moved to Parma with Ottavio and their remaining son.) Not even the Emperor's greed for more Italian territory could have been the reason: he was certain Parma would become his grandson's. Oddly, Charles V was only trying to use the passions of Ottavio and the Pope in order to acquire complete domination over the latter. In a secret instruction from Charles V to Mendoza, dated April 20, 1551, the Emperor told him that his true motive in the Parma proceedings was really to attach the Pope to his own policy: "Do your best to keep the Pope incensed about the King of France and Ottavio. Always persist in stirring things up. Make him stay enraged against these two, so that We can make use of what might be necessary in the future." Translated into ordinary speech, this "Imperialese" euphemism means: "Persuade the Pope to make war against Ottavio, so that His Holiness will be tied up in a war of his own and will be dependent on me later on when I will have an open war with the French."[26]

Expecting the outbreak of these artificially instigated hostilities, Charles V set out for Innsbruck, establishing his court there in order to be near Trent for the opening of the Council. Here he would also be near the theater of war. But, less logical than Mendoza, the

[25] Lasso to King Ferdinand, April 19 and April 6, 1551, Druffel, *Briefe* I, 609.
[26] Charles V to Mendoza, April 19 and 20, 1551, *AC*, p. 347, n. 1. See also Druffel, *Briefe* I, 622; K. Lanz, *Correspondenz des Kaisers Karl V*, I, 177; *Cal. St. P.*, Span. 1550–52, ed. Gayangos, p. 277; Pastor, *Geschichte* VI, 97. On this War of Parma, see G. de Leva, in *Riv. Stor. Ital.* 1: 632–680 and 8 (1891): 713.

Emperor did not foresee that he would not be able to have the
Council and the war going at the same time.

Papal and Imperial policies now seemed to be in harmony, yet
Don Diego's actual situation in Rome was becoming less pleasant.
His life was again in danger. Acting against the Farnese as he had
been doing for over a year, he had brought new mortal enemies on
himself. The road between Siena and Rome ran through territory
belonging to the Farneses, and he had to keep his eyes open along
the way, requiring a heavy escort. Foreseeing the inevitable deterioration of his standing if the war should have a disappointing outcome, he wished to leave Rome for good.

My resolution is to quit Rome while the sun shines. I believe for certain that although His Majesty and His Holiness will try to preserve
their friendship if possible, all things have periods of growth, leveling,
and decline. If at any time that friendship should diminish—although
now one sees no trace of that—it would be the greatest rupture that
ever existed between Pope and Emperor. I would not like to put myself
into that danger, should it happen during my time. I am the Pope's
servant, and I love him like my own life, which I owe him, incidentally. [Why, we do not know.]

To Madrid once came a friar from Preste Juan of the Indies, [he
pursues his idea the next day] where it is said that the land is irri-
gated because it never rains. He asked Cardinal Fray Francisco Ximenez how wheat was harvested in Spain, and the Cardinal told him
that, first, it rains, then the sun shines, then it rains again, then it
snows and freezes, and the sun shines again, and there is the north
wind, and later there is drought. The Indian grew thoughtful, and
after a long time, shaking his head, he said: "Spain cannot last!" It
seemed to him that the world would come to an end in Spain, because
we cannot eat bread without having so many cares. And although I
differ with that friar, since I believe no clouds can come between the
Pope and Emperor because both are truly good men—yet I should be
glad to leave while the sun is shining.[27]

Although Mendoza denied the imminence of clouds, he saw them
clearly enough. Later in the month he reports to the Emperor:

His Holiness becomes more lukewarm every day. The French are talking a lot. The Cardinal del Monte secretly goes to the house of Cardi-

[27] Mendoza to Arras, May 4 and 5, 1551, *AC*, pp. 225–242.

nal Ferrara at night, which makes me think this diligence of the French has some truth behind it. They want to make His Holiness suspicious of Your Majesty, and the Cardinal del Monte wishes to have the glory of concerting this business for good or bad. His Holiness has so tender a spot for this Cardinal that he might agree to this concert. It seems to me he no longer enjoys discussing business with me. Rather, he talks of other things, as a friend. I doubt that he will finally declare himself, even if we give him troops and money. I think we will have to drag him along, and with great force."[28]

As late as May 20, regardless of all his manipulations and persuasions that had pushed the Pope into the Emperor's camp, Don Diego hoped Charles V would decide to avert the war: "As I said before, the Emperor can count only on his own forces and not on those of the Pope."[29] But his master continued to pursue his design. Although, hypocritically, the Spanish-French peace treaty of Crépy was still being upheld, Charles V made a new (unofficial) Spanish-French war on Italian soil, with Italy's men. It was one of those wars arising out of medieval ambitions—that of Charles V to hold on to the Imperial fiefs as feudatory lord, and of the Pope, similarly, to preserve the spiritual and temporal fiefs of the Church.

The House of Farnese was a strong antagonist in the center of Italy. With the duchy of Castro (close to Rome) belonging to Orazio, Urbino's Duchess being Vittoria Farnese, and the Duke of Ferrara taking the French part, the Ecclesiastical States were oppressed by the enemy on several sides. Sitting on the sidelines, although professedly Imperial, was Cosimo I, waiting to reap the fruits that would come his way, because of his favorable location, whoever would be the loser.

In June, 1551, the Pope appointed Ferrante Gonzaga as general commander of the entire expedition against Parma, sending the papal troops under his nephew Giovanni Battista del Monte to join in the occupation of that "spiritual and temporal fief." Don Diego continued at his post until the end of June, watching the developments, propping the Pope up whenever the latter showed signs of vacillation. This happened several times during audiences the Pope gave an extraordinary ambassador of the French King, Monseigneur de Montluc. Don Diego remained at the Pope's side, "sweet as

28 Mendoza to Charles V, May, 1551, Arch. Sim., Est., Rose-file.
29 Mendoza to Arras, May 20, 1551, AC, pp. 242–245.

a lamb, and always a hand at his bonnet, with the mien of hypocrite."[30]

The war lasted about a year, with indecisive results for all sides. Parma withstood a siege of Imperial and papal troops for many months. The intention was to starve Parma out, with one exception: Gonzaga, the besieger, daily sent fresh provisions through the blockade to Madama. For a time, though, Margaret's regular income failed to get through to her. She wrote her father: "I cannot remain like this; I have suffered and will continue to suffer everything possible in the service of Your Majesty as your most devoted servant, but I regret that I cannot live without eating."[31]

Julius III, who would not have taken Ottavio Farnese's offenses seriously unless the Emperor had seen to it that he did, soon rued the day he had been inveigled into this adventure.[32] He became disheartened at needlessly losing money, prestige, and lives—including that of his nephew, Captain Giovanni Battista del Monte; although, according to Don Diego, the Pope did not feel his nephew's death any more deeply than if he had lost a calf, a statement corroborated by Cardinal Jaén. This nephew, it was said, had been a source of great anxiety to the Pope; within the two years of his uncle's papacy he had run through more than 100,000 ducats.[33]

When it became apparent that the Pope wished for peace, Mendoza, who had spent the summer building his castle in Siena, returned to Rome and stayed there in October and November. As long as he remained in Rome, the Pope could not make any progress with the peace deal he really desired. While this did not make much difference in the current situation, all warfare being held up

[30] Du Thiers to Cardinal de Guise, July 4, 1551, Romier, *Les origines*, I, 246.

[31] "Cosi non posso stare: Io ho patito, et so per patire qual si voglia cosa possibile per servitio di V. Mta. come serva devotissima che io li sono, et mi dole non potere vivere senza mangiare . . .," Margaret of Austria to Charles V, Arch. Sim., Est., leg. 1468, folio 117.

[32] "Preti, frati, monachi e monache e tutto il mondo ci grida in le orecchie: 'pace pace!' . . . Havemo ricevuta una lettera di don Fernando, nella qual mostra di credere, o di voler far credere a noi, che le cose della guerra, cosi di Parma come della Mirandola, siano ben proviste; non è vero, non è vero, non è vero." Julius III to Fano, October 8, 1551, Druffel, *Briefe* I, note to no. 768, p. 760.

[33] Mendoza to Gonzaga, April 19, 1552, Arch. Sim., Est., leg. 878; and Jaén to Arras, April 21, 1552, Bibl. Pal. vol. 2322, both in Rose-file.

in the winter, Julius III resented the powerlessness that made him dependent on the Emperor. He showed this by lashing out in the area where he had his own say, the making of cardinals. Out of eight candidates presented to him in the name of the Emperor, he gave the hat to only four.[34] And he did not conceal his ill mood from Don Diego. "Every time we talk to His Holiness and tell him what is going on, he replies to me I am talking subtleties," Mendoza wrote Arras in October. "To Don Juan he says that he does not understand Spanish."[35] (Don Juan Manrique de Lara had come to Rome as special ambassador bringing the list of Charles V's candidates for the cardinalates.)

"It occurs to me," Don Diego wrote, coming back to his wish to leave Rome, "that, since he thinks I am subtle, and since he is possibly overly diffident, I do not please him much. With the opinion he now holds of me, negotiations might suffer. I am letting you know this so that His Majesty can do what he pleases and what might suit him better. It is really all the same to me." Farnese had written the Pope, Mendoza said further on, that "His Holiness was ruling through me and Don Fernando de Gonzaga who are his [Farnese's] enemies."[36]

The Pope also expressed his displeasure about the despoilment of the "poor señor of Piombino," and about the castle in Siena, which he called "the clearest possible indication of Siena's servitude."[37] "This castle has made me little liked hereabouts," said Don Diego.[38] He now saw that Cosimo was not the only Italian prince who was disturbed by his great venture in Siena.

When the sieges of the fortresses of Parma and Mirandola had lasted nine or ten months, even Charles V became thoroughly weary of the war. By then, too, the Emperor had many other problems to cope with. His letters now ordered Mendoza to get him out of the war as inconspicuously as he had entered it. Someone had to be blamed, however, for the war was a reality. Who would be the perfect scapegoat but the Emperor's ambassador? Don Diego would

[34] G. Adriani, *Istoria de' suoi tempi*, III, 193.

[35] Mendoza to Arras, October 10, 1551, *AC*, pp. 283–285.

[36] Mendoza to Arras, November 23, 1551, *RABM* 3 (1899): 612–622.

[37] Dandolo to Venice, December 20, 1550, Arch. Ven., Rose-file.

[38] See note 36, above.

be the one to blame, not only by public opinion of the day, and most of the historians since, but by the Emperor himself as well. By the time the overexpanded edifice of Imperial grandeur was starting to crumble and tumble down from all sides, Charles V seemed to have forgotten how this war against his eldest child's husband had come about. In the spring of 1552 he scolded Don Diego for having talked him into it.[39]

After thirteen years of service in Italy, Mendoza had accumulated so many grievances against his master that he sent his secretary Ximénez to court with a list of explanations and complaints long enough to fill a book. Bristling from the accusation about the War of Parma, he said in one of the instructions to Ximénez to be read verbatim, and shown, to the Emperor:

I declare that it never entered my thought—nor will it ever occur to me—to persuade His Majesty to this or to another war. If it will please His Majesty to look into my letters, he will find the exact opposite to be true. I declare also with all fitting humility and veneration, that His Majesty bears the guilt that he imputes to me. He wrote me that it was essential to bring the Pope to declare himself [for the war], because otherwise the King of France would set foot in Parma, and it would be right to prepare an excuse for His Majesty's part in it [i.e., for Imperial participation without a declaration of war], entering it under the pretext of being protector of the Church. This was very expressly [ordered], and not only once, but each time I received letters in this business, His Majesty was of the same mind. He ordered me to offer the Pope help, and his person[-al commitment], and his money, once and twice and thrice, and that I should persuade him to take [Parma] away from Ottavio and put Farnese in prison. I did my best to achieve this end with His Holiness on orders of His Majesty, from whom I expected to earn great thanks and rewards. The reason I do not get any is that I do not make a show of my services, and dislike doing so.[40]

For the benefit of the Emperor's prime minister, the Bishop of Arras, Don Diego adds: "Understand, Sir, that it [the war] has not been my brainchild, nor have I persuded him [the Emperor] to go to war, but rather the contrary."[41]

[39] *AC*, p. 291, including footnote 1, p. 292.
[40] *AC*, pp. 345–346.
[41] Ibid., pp. 348–349.

With all that, it was not enough for the Emperor that he had tired of the war and now wanted to quit. He even pretended that he did not wish the Pope to make peace in Italy. Again, Charles V made the ambassador his instrument, letting Don Diego drag him into the peace as if it were against his master's will, so that "with either God or the devil I have to free Caesar from the bother of Parma and Mirandola."[42]

Mendoza undertook this new, devious commission. He also shouldered the blame for the origin of the war, at least in the public eye, and for a long time to come in history. These matters did not worry him unduly as long as he knew his own conscience to be clear. For him, it was satisfaction enough, in this case, that his master himself knew the truth. When his good friend Arras spoke up for him, reminding the Emperor of his injustice in blaming the War of Parma on Don Diego, the latter was only amused: "I have laughed a lot over the fact that you took my part so tenderly when His Majesty spoke to you."[43] He reassured Arras: "By the life of the Emperor, by yours and mine, I swear that I was not at all disturbed by the opinion His Majesty has of me in this case. . . . It is certainly not true, and I am so used to hearing complaints and reprehensions instead of getting remuneration, that I do not care. . . ."[44] But in the end he reiterates: "The war was not of my invention nor persuasion. Indeed, in the beginning of the thing I tried to avert the break; and in the midst of it, and at the end, I advised His Majesty of the little that could be expected of the zero forces and easygoing nature of the Pope."[45]

[42] Mendoza to Arras, April 13, 1552, *AC*, p. 310.
[43] *AC*, p. 295.
[44] Ibid., p. 300.
[45] Ibid., pp. 348, 349.

13. THE DEBACLE, 1552

We lost a kingdom within two days . . .
Don Diego[1]

Too Little — and Too Late

By February, 1552, the developments in Europe were so unfavorable to Charles V that Mendoza seemed to be the only Spaniard still thinking an increase in Spanish power possible. Dreaming of transferring the suzerainty of Siena to the Spanish crown as a heritage of Prince Philip, he now took steps to conclude the legal transfer of the republic. To this effect, Don Diego had the *balia* of Siena, his puppet magistrate, send a fully "empowered" Sienese delegate, Orlando Mariscotti, to court. The delegate was to present Charles V with the *balia*'s "voluntary" request to transform their government into a vicariate under the authority of the Spanish crown. Siena literally begged Charles V to hand their republic over to Philip and to his successors in perpetuity.

But joined with this request (of Mendoza's inspiration and fabrication), the delegate was to submit also a list of his people's genuine desire for improving their situation: the Sienese wanted a confirmation that the castle was not being built on account of any lack of faith in their loyalty to the Emperor; they asked to be relieved of the duty of lodging soldiers and of paying taxes, and most urgently they requested indemnification for the properties seques-

---

[1] "Se que avemos perdido un reino en dos dias . . .," Mendoza to Gonzaga, August 5, 1552, Arch. Sim., Est., leg. 1201, folio 48.

tered for the castle and all other damages they had suffered in its construction. They also asked the Emperor to confirm the city's liberty in his name and that of his successors; they begged him to see to it that they would receive no injury from the "Vicar," that is, the person who would supposedly succeed Mendoza and in the future would reside in Siena in the name of the Emperor and his heirs.[2]

While Mariscotti, a man "of devotion [to the Imperials], experience, and wit,"[3] was carrying the list of requests to Innsbruck, Mendoza wrote to the Emperor and Arras, suggesting answers for them to give him: the Sienese ought to be impressed with the fact that the only reason for the construction of the castle was to maintain peace in the city and to protect it from the outside. They could be told they would be asked to lodge troops only in emergencies. Mendoza suggested that relieving them of taxes would not be possible at present, but that they should be given fair words and fair promises. As for indemnities, it would be a good thing to appoint appraisers first. In the meantime, Mendoza proposed, pay them 7 percent interest on their claimed losses. As for their liberty, he said they would certainly have their liberty granted to them. They should be assured that their overlord, in command of the castle, seaport, and all armaments, would see to it that they had their liberty![4]

When Mendoza was on his way to Rome a short while later, he advised his superiors to detain the Sienese delegate at court until he himself could return to Siena, so that he would be present at Mariscotti's return to supervise the "transfer." But together with all his grandiose plans, he had to tell the court also that all his resources were exhausted. He implored them to give him new funds to finish the castle and pay his soldiers, who had not been paid for several months and were becoming unruly.[5]

Mendoza had conceived establishing a "vicariate" as early as May, 1551. It seemed to him and to Gonzaga the only means of

---

[2] Mendoza, probably to Gonzaga, February 10, 552, Arch. Sim., Est., leg. 1470, Rose-file.

[3] Mendoza to Arras, February 16, 1552, Bibl. Pal., Cartas del Obispo de Arras, Rose-file.

[4] See note 2, above.

[5] Mendoza to Arras, March 10, 1552, from Viterbo, AC, pp. 295, 296.

effecting the "legal" alienation of Siena from the German Imperium.[6] Earlier still, Charles V had considered it impossible to transfer one of the fiefs of the Holy Roman Empire to his own Spanish crown. In 1536, when Paul III wished to acquire Siena for his son Pier Luigi, the Emperor said that Siena, belonging to the Imperium, could not be disposed of without the approval of the German electors.[7] But when Don Diego took on the project of Siena he looked for precedents in history, finding that "for six hundred years emperors, until the successor of Charles IV" had created vicariates. Therefore it was not necessary to consult either the electors of the Empire or even the citizens themselves.[8] (But he also warned that the creation of a "vicariate" might not augur well—"they [vicariates] never lasted long under that name. . . .")[9] Charles V, who guided himself willingly by the examples of his medieval predecessors, made no more objections to the plan; Prince Philip was delighted with it,[10] and so were Arras and Gonzaga.

But when the Sienese delegate came to the Emperor to complete the legal process, Charles V changed his mind again. This, he said, was not the time even to discuss the "vicariate." Moreover, Charles V suddenly disapproved of the legal subterfuge to be employed. He called the intended transfer an act of "deprivation"; he would not subject the Sienese to it unless they had shown him a lack of faith that could be used as a reason to punish them. The Sienese had many documents in which the Emperor praised them for their loyalty. He could not now contradict himself in writing, and, in the absence of any pretext to accuse them of disloyalty, any of his successors to the Empire would legally have the right to revoke the vicariate that favored Spain—and they would certainly do so. If his ministers wished to proceed in their designs, they would have to provide Charles V with a different approach and with unobjectionable documents.[11]

The Emperor's change of heart was a blow to Mendoza. His

[6] Mendoza to Arras, May 27, 1551, AC, p. 251.

[7] Walter Friedensburg, *Kaiser Karl V und Papst Paul III*, pp. 25, 26.

[8] Mendoza to Gonzaga, July 26, 1551, Arch. Sim. (no number), Rose-file.

[9] Mendoza to Arras, May 5, 1551, AC, p. 234.

[10] Cf. E. Spivakovsky, "El 'Vicariato,'" *Hispania* 26 (1966): 583–596.

[11] Memo of letters from Charles V to Gonzaga, March 18, 1552, Arch. Sim., Est., Milano 1200, Rose-file; also Arras to Gonzaga and to Mendoza, with copy to Prince Philip, March 19, 1552, Arch. Sim., Est., leg. 1469, Rose-file.

cherished project—the basis and justification of all his work in Siena—would not be accomplished. No more was said about the "vicariate." Mariscotti, one of the few truly "Imperial" Sienese (despised by his people), returned in the beginning of May to Don Diego as ambassador to his person from the *balia*. Mendoza continued to honor him, lodging the Sienese in his house in Rome.[12] But though his own prestige, career, and perhaps his life, depended on the preservation of his government of Siena, the light had gone out of his enterprise with the vanishing of his quixotic dream—that he, single-handed, would aggrandize the power of the crown of Spain. It seems that from then on he no longer gave Siena his whole mind and soul.

In the spring, the War of Parma drew to its end in what the Imperials considered a stalemate, although the French claimed they had won total (political and moral) victory. It had been impossible to dislodge the French from any place. In Mirandola it could hardly be denied that Gonzaga and his Spaniards had suffered outright defeat; the French moved into the fortresses that the Imperials had been forced to abandon, and now they were apt to strike wherever they pleased, in unexpected Imperial regions.[13] Duke Cosimo, alert to the danger to his own state, advised the Emperor to send new, substantial infantry and cavalry into Italy, "otherwise *those* might play Your Majesty some notable trick."[14] At the same time Don Diego requested new funds and men for Siena.

But Charles V had reached the bottom of his finances and his luck.[15] Remarkably, the rumors that the King of France had aligned himself against Charles with the Emperor's friends, Prince Maurice of Saxony and Duke Albert of Brandenburg (a secret treaty

---

[12] Orlando Mariscotti to the Balia of Siena, May 4, 1552, Arch. Siena (no identification number), Rose-file.

[13] Lucien Romier, *Les origines politiques des guerres de Religion*, I, 290.

[14] "gli sara fatta qualche burla notabile da costoro . . .," Cosimo I to Paddolfino, February 17, 1552. Abel Desjardins, *Négociations diplomatiques de la France avec la Toscane*, III, 299.

[15] Cf. Charles V to Queen Marie, Innsbruck, January 28, 1552: "Ceste guerre de Parme, que au diable soit elle! donne ma ruine, car tout l'argent venu des Indes avec se qu'il s'en est payé est casi au bout, et je ne voys de quoy draper . . .," Druffel, *Briefe* II, no. 944, p. 71.

had already been concluded in October, 1551), did not perturb him. Charles V did not believe it, just as Don Diego, still concerned about the blind-alley case of the "traitor" Cesare Vaiari in Siena, did not believe himself threatened by the news of a real conspiracy against his rule by the Sienese and the French. Don Diego continued his trust in the brothers Amerighi, leaders of the Sienese conspiracy; but, then, whatever information he received formed only a part of countless confusing rumors—it was impossible to believe anything.

In March, 1552, Maurice of Saxony dropped his mask and marched against Charles V, his former ally. By April, while the French started to exercise control in Italy, the Imperials in Italy were becoming concerned about their master's difficulties in addition to their own. On April 23, Mendoza even offered the Emperor troops—an astonishing gesture when he was at the same time requesting German troops from the Emperor![16] But he was then raising troops in the territory of Siena in support of the Viceroy of Sicily, who needed reinforcements against the Turks. (Mendoza sent three companies of infantry to Juan de Vega in Sicily, "a large part of the troublemakers" among them.) He could easily draw off more of those fellows for service in Germany—but he could not use them for his own purposes. One of the secrets of Imperial rule was to get local men out of the subjected territory, for an exchange of foreign troops. Italian recruits, Mendoza had found out, were deserting "three by three and four by four" as soon as they received their pay, if they were near their homes.[17] For the same reason, the Viceroys of Naples and Sicily also preferred troops from outside to the local.

But Mendoza's offer of troops could not prevent the once mighty Emperor from fleeing in humiliation from Innsbruck to Villach to escape the advancing Maurice of Saxony just in time to avoid arrest (May 19). Charles V's flight, incompatible with the Imperial dream of gaining domination over more Italian feudatories, was referred to by the Imperials simply as a "departure" of the court from one city to another. A few days later the Emperor wrote

16 Mendoza to Charles V, April 23, 1552, Rome, Arch. Sim., Est., leg. 878, Rose-file.

17 Mendoza to Charles V, quoting a letter from Montesa, November 28, 1551, Arch. Sim., Est., leg. 1468, folio 74.

Mendoza that he was "pursuing" Prince Maurice.[18] Yet no euphe-
mistic choice of words could conceal Imperial embarrassment: the
real news of May 19 traveled to Italy with horses' speed; by June
4 it arrived in Siena through some "red-haired German students
with excellent information," who broadcast the Emperor's flight to
the now barely masked delight of the Sienese people.[19]

In the face of this weakening Imperial power, Mendoza and
Gonzaga strove to hold on to their friends in Italy—and to buy new
ones. They urged the Emperor to buy up a number of small, independent lords. The suspect neighbors of Siena, the Counts of Santa
Fiore and Pitigliano, could be secured, they estimated, with a thousand escudos of "pension" each, and many smaller signori might
be had with pensions ranging from four hundred to eight hundred
escudos annually.[20] "I think we are losing the Count of Santa Fiore;
would to God that Pitigliano does not go as well; their pensions are
not paid on time. They must not become a 'tiny little Maurice and
Albert'. . . ."[21] By giving a man his thousand ducats three months
too late, it will cost us 100,000 [through losing him]. . . ."[22] Gonzaga, whose counsel in Italian affairs the Emperor had willingly
accepted for years, had tried to prevail on Charles V to make peace
in Germany shortly before Maurice's pressure on Innsbruck. He
wanted the Emperor to throw all his resources into a war in Italy.
It was much cheaper to wage war in Italy than in Germany. A
good strong war there for a whole year would secure the Emperor's
position as well as an inheritance for his successor to the throne of
Spain.[23]

But even in the best of times, the Emperor's finances never sufficed to carry on an extended war in Italy or to buy up Italy piece-
meal by hiring all remaining small "independent" Italian lords

[18] For the "departure" from Innsbruck, see Charles V to Mendoza, Villach,
June 18, Arch. Sim., Est. Ale. 647, Rose-file. For the "pursuit" of Prince Maurice, Charles V to Mendoza, May 23, 1552, Arch. Sim., Est. Ale. 648, Rose-file.

[19] "como su magestad yva huyendo . . .," Don Francés de Álaba to Mendoza
in copy, the original going to Secretary Vargas at the Imperial court to show
it to His Majesty, June 4, 1552, Arch. Sim., Est., leg. 878, folio 181.

[20] Gonzaga to Charles V, spring of 1552, Arch. Sim., Est., leg. 1469, Rose-file.

[21] Mendoza to Arras, April 13, 1552, Rome, AC, pp. 310, 311.

[22] Mendoza to Arras, April 29, 1552, Rome, AC, p. 369.

[23] See note 20, above.

—though Charles V attempted to do as much as he could in this respect.

The disastrous (for the Imperials) events were crowding each other from the beginning of March, when Mendoza went to Rome. He was called there to assist the Pope with the peace negotiations (or, as the Sienese said, "disturb the negotiations between the [French] Cardinal and the Pope").[24] On the way Mendoza fell very ill. In Buon Convento he had eaten some "little fish with eggs" that gave him a violent stomach upset (he thought at first someone had given him "herbs" to poison him), and he did not arrive in Rome until mid-March, in a weakened condition.[25] The few times he was well enough to seek audience with the Pope, he was on the old, companionable terms with Julius III, whom so often in the past he had entertained for hours on end with his witty conversation.[26] It embarrassed Don Diego that the Emperor still wished to preserve the impression that he did not want peace; he urged his master to drop this dissimulation and be less secretive with His Holiness "whom we have not taken as serf, but as companion, as they say in the marriage service."[27] Mendoza's health continued to be poor. With sciatic pains in one leg, in addition to his always rheumatic arm, "one-armed and lame," he claimed he understood why the Pope, who was plagued by gout, should be so desirous of peace.[28]

But Mendoza had to do his utmost to prevent the Pope from giving in to the Farneses. A special Imperial aim was to prevent Julius III from returning the State of Castro (buffer state between Siena and Rome) to them, and so the Pope, who wished for complete reconciliation with the Farneses, became more and more annoyed with Don Diego. Mendoza had no one to support him in this com-

---

24 "per sturbare i negozii che il Cardinale trattava con il Papa . . .," Alessandro Sozzini, "Diario delle cose avvenute in Siena dai 20 Luglio 1550 ai 28 Giugno 1550," *Arch. Stor. Ital.* 2, serie I (1842).

25 Mendoza to Arras, Viterbo, March 10, 1552, *AC*, pp. 294, 295; from Rome, March 14, 1552, *AC*, p. 298.

26 E.g., Dandolo to Venice, April 25, 1551, Arch. Ven., Rose-file.

27 "No por siervo sino por compañero, como dizen en los matrimonios . . .," Mendoza to Arras, Rome, March 19, 1552, *AC*, p. 299.

28 Mendoza to Arras, April 4, 1552, Rome, *AC*, p. 302.

mission of his master. Even his relative, Cardinal Mendoza—the former "Coria," now "Burgos"—advised friendliness toward the Farneses.[29] And against Mendoza's advice Julius III suspended the Council at Trent: "The Pope does not tolerate contradiction. He shouts, and often it looks as though he were coming to blows. . . .[30] According to my judgment, His Holiness would like to have peace but let His Majesty stay in the war, because the Popes' sausage is to see Emperor and King at war and themselves at peace, so that the Pope can be the true boss of the Council."[31]

As the talks proceeded, the Pope cooled perceptibly. Before, he had sent for Mendoza almost every day. But in May, when the ambassador was in bed for a week with a high fever and kidney trouble, the Holy Father did not even inquire about him.[32] Yet finally a truce was concluded. It was a suspension of arms for two years between the Pope and Ottavio Farnese, a separate agreement between Pope and Emperor on one side, and Pope and French King on the other. Nothing was contracted between the Emperor and the King, but on May 16, after a consistory, Julius III kept both parties with him to celebrate the truce: the French Cardinal Tournon, Don Diego, and Cardinal Jaén joined the Pope at dinner, and Cardinal Carpi (one of the Imperials) came in later.[33]

When Mendoza had been called to Rome, he left his task in Siena unfinished, and this at a time when the construction was in worse shape than it had been earlier: "The castle is at such a critical stage. While eight months ago it could have been defended, subsequent construction [opening it up toward the side of the city, prior to making the gates] has made it indefensible. Yet with proper

---

[29] On difficulties regarding Farneses, see Mendoza's instructions to Pedro Ximénez for His Majesty, April 14, 1552, Rome, *AC*, pp. 312–322. The former "Burgos," Cardinal Juan Alvarez de Toledo, had advanced to the Archbishopric of Santiago and was now called "Santiago" by Mendoza; Cardinal Mendoza y Bobadilla then was moved up from the bishopric of Coria to the see of Burgos. On the new "Burgos' " critical attitude toward Mendoza's policy regarding the Farneses, Burgos to Diego de Vargas, secretary of Charles V, July 13, 1552, Arch. Sim., Est., leg. 878, folio 131.

[30] *AC*, p. 313.

[31] *AC*, p. 319.

[32] Mendoza to Arras, May 11, 1552, Rome, *AC*, p. 366.

[33] Jaén to Arras, May 16, 1552, Bibl. Pal., vol. 2322, Rose-file.

provisions it could be finished in such a way that Your Majesty and the King of France and the Turk together would not be able to take it, and this is the truth."

The Sienese puppet government sought to benefit from this impasse, offering to buy the unfinished fortress from Charles V. They would pay the Emperor for all he had spent on it, if he gave them his permission to tear the castle down. But Mendoza disapproved. He proposed to hold out; he continued to request more money to finish the construction, and set about raising funds himself.[34]

Having left the Sienese works in charge of his lieutenant, Don Francés de Álava (a gentleman of manners so delicate that the Sienese nicknamed him *la donzella* ["the Maiden"]),[35] Mendoza was however fully aware of the desperate situation he and his Spaniards were in. Now he acknowledged that the Sienese sabotaged him on every occasion: they prevented the collection of tithes (a tax laid on them for the fortification of the ports); they prevented carloads of grain from reaching the city, and the raising, locally, of moneys and other provisions; they helped the surrounding towns resist the Spanish garrison; and they did nothing to arrest Corsican marauders who roamed the coasts of the Siena state, ravaging the countryside, making the roads unsafe, and lying in wait to assault Don Diego himself. At the same time, his famished Spanish garrison in Siena, already grumbling in their cramped lodgings, were now without pay for three or four months. Many sold their weapons secretly, sometimes just for food. The disarmed Sienese had gladly bought fifteen hundred harquebuses from them by April, helping the deserters escape to Florence. And even the rich Sienese, the landowners, did not deliver their grain to town; "to force them to do so would offend their liberty (although it is license, rather); this we can do only when the castle is connected up with the city walls. . . ."[36]

Yet despite all these drawbacks, Mendoza continued to believe in pulling Siena through, chiefly because he relied on the Duke of Florence, whose interests he believed identical with the Imperials' in their common danger from the French. Mendoza often asserted that the Duke had promised his military help in case of a real

---

[34] Mendoza to Charles V, May 20, 1552, Arch. Sim., Est., leg. 878, Rose-file.

[35] Sozzini, "Diario," p. 88 et passim.

[36] From one of the instructions to Ximénez, *AC*, pp. 325, 326.

emergency. He did not, however, allow Cosimo's soldiers to be stationed in Siena, because, as he said, the Sienese hated the Florentines so much.[37]

By the end of April, things in Siena deteriorated to such a degree that Don Francés was forced to sell the provisions for the castle to raise some cash for continuing the construction work.[38] In growing despair, Don Diego solicited loans from literally anyone. In Rome the Spanish cardinals came forth quite generously after Cardinal Burgos helped Mendoza prod them.[39] Don Diego appealed also to his colleagues—Gonzaga, the Viceroy of Naples, the Imperial ambassador in Genoa, but none of them was in a position to help him, nor was, or pretended to be, Cosimo, the richest of his "friends." Despite an earlier frown of Charles V, who did not want him to ask the Duke of Florence for money again, Mendoza did so,[40] and the Emperor, disregarding his own scruples, himself approached Cosimo (vainly) for 200,000 ducats.[41] Yet with some 8,000 ducats he succeeded in raising elsewhere on his personal pledge, Mendoza kept the construction going past several earlier deadlines.[42]

Don Francés' messages daily became more harassed. Although he assured Mendoza by the end of May that the Spanish garrison subsisted very well "on cherries and lettuce," the Sienese irritated him increasingly. The Arte della Lana (the wool-workers' guild) assembled outside the city limits and staged a comedy in which they mocked the Spaniards (especially Mendoza and Álava) and their habits in front of four thousand Sienese, three thousand of whom were carrying arms. Denouncing their "scandalous" derision, Don Francés had all the principal actors locked up in the tower. Then Brandano came back to town, the "prophet," the holy fool who had intended to kill Don Diego on the site of the castle. Brandano, who had an uncanny reputation ever since he predicted in 1527 the disaster of Rome in the presence of the Pope, had an enormous hold on the superstitious people. Now he addressed a crowd in the

[37] *AC*, p. 332.

[38] Mendoza to Arras, May 11, 1552, Rome, *AC*, p. 369.

[39] Burgos to Vargas, see note 29, above.

[40] Cosimo I to Mendoza, May 30, 1552, Arch. Flor., Mediceo 20, Rose-file.

[41] Secretary Vargas to Prince Philip, June 10, 1552, Arch. Sim., Est., leg. 648, Rose-file.

[42] Mendoza to Arras, May 16, 1552, *AC*, p. 373.

great *Duòmo*—packed to overflowing—reassuring the Sienese that, just as he had told them a year ago, the castle would never be finished. Don Francés now could not afford to be as magnanimous as Don Diego had been when things were more secure. Afraid that the "prophet" might have been in touch with the underground, Don Francés arrested him, too, and had him tortured, though no admission could be wrung from the stoical old hermit other than that the Holy Spirit and the Virgin Mary had sent him.

Hardly had that been taken care of, when a friar who once had served Don Diego in Venice but had since gambled his clerical garb away, showed up in Siena on his way to Rome to ask Mendoza for help. He came to Don Francés and reported what talk he had picked up among troops in the surrounding country about plans to free Siena. In the taverns of Castro and Buon Convento he had listened to murder plans against Don Diego and Don Francés; people also said that Cosimo would never help the Spanish because he was more aggravated by the castle than anyone else in Italy.

Another of Don Francés' worries was the newly strange behavior of those apparently loyal citizens, the Amerighis. Captain Pero Maria Amerighi was not returning from the spa where he had gone for a cure, though the baths had since been closed, and Don Francés had sent for him four or five times![43] But however hysterical the "Maiden" was becoming, he was a strict taskmaster, and he brought the castle "almost" into a state of defense by June 10.[44]

In Rome, Mendoza's confidence in his Sienese enterprise, and his mood, kept vacillating with the ever-shifting prospects. During April, while the Pope shouted at his unwelcome counsel, Don Diego was writing up a report on his services to the Emperor, on his lack of rewards, and on the whole complexity of the political and military situation in Italy, in which he and his master were so inextricably enmeshed.[45] Here, he energetically refuted the accusa-

---

[43] On "çereças e lechugas," Brandano, disrobed friar, and Amerighi, Don Francés de Álaba's letter of June 4, 1552 (note 19, above). On the comedy by *Arte della Lana*, Don Francés to Mendoza, May 20, 1552, Arch. Sim., Est., leg. 878, folio 57.

[44] Mendoza to Eraso, June 10, 1552, Arch. Sim., Contaduría, periodo 1420, Rose-file.

[45] Mendoza's four instructions to Ximénez, April 14, 1552; (1.) to read to His

tion that he had started the War of Parma. "On the contrary," he declared, "I am almost an heretic in being the only one always in favor of peace."[46] He figured out his income and expenses in the fifteen years of foreign service since London, finding out that "no one else has served in so many different parts, with so much work, so much expense, and himself owning so little property, and no one has received less *merced* ("rewards") and less recompense for expenses."[47]

Mendoza's secretary, Pedro Ximénez, weighted down with written and verbal instructions (and with complaints and assurances not to blame Mendoza in case of a catastrophe in Siena), traveled to the court in Innsbruck to talk to the Emperor, Arras, and the royal accountants. Ximénez arrived there at an untimely moment; he had to join Charles V in his precipitated "departure" in night and fog, and it took months before Mendoza's accounts could be cleared.[48] But as soon as Ximénez had left Rome, carrying the depressing reports away with him, Mendoza bounced out of a temporary bitterness. "I am now nine thousand escudos in debt," he remarked, "but I am alive, which is not little!"[49] Life was becoming precious to one who had survived various plots and direct attempts against his person. (When the Emperor complained about Mendoza's heavy expenses for armed escort, Mendoza countered: "I don't

Majesty, or show him, on matters of Roma, *AC*, pp. 312–322; (2.) on the State of Siena, the construction, Piombino, and "my private affairs in regard to public office," *AC*, pp. 323–338; (3.) in reply to a letter by the Bishop of Arras, to read to the Emperor in order to defend Mendoza, *AC*, pp. 339–349; (4.) for you, Secretary Pedro Ximénez, to confer with His Majesty about my private affairs, *AC*, pp. 349–353.

[46] *AC*, p. 343.

[47] Ibid., p. 352.

[48] Apart from these unfortunate circumstances, the lack of attention given Mendoza's claims was due also to sloth, and, apparently, intrigues at court. In 1563, Granvelle (the former Bishop of Arras, now Cardinal) wrote to Gonzalo Pérez that Eraso, who handled Charles V's financial matters, was to blame for keeping "the Abbot Ximénez so long [at court] that, losing while playing for ain, *we* lost Siena . . ." (que por haber detenido tanto tiempo el abad Ximenez, mientras se jugava a la gana pierde, perdimos Sena). Brussels, July 25, 1563, in Granvelle, *Papiers d'état du Cardinal de Granvelle*, VII, 159–170, edited by C. Weiss.

[49] "ando biuo, que no es poco," Mendoza to Arras, April 18, 1552, *AC*, p. 358.

have to let myself be beaten up or assaulted on the road. . . .")[50]

With the load of his personal affairs temporarily lifted off his mind, he now reconsidered the Sienese situation from all angles, estimating that he would be safe from all possible dangers with an additional two hundred cavalry and one thousand *Tudescos* (German *Landsknechte*), as well as a sum of thirty thousand escudos, He had requested this in February, reiterated the request with Ximénez's mission in mid-April, and set himself to waiting. Even three months later he was still waiting for the German soldiers and the money (he engaged a hundred cavalry himself) and had not lost patience ("si no, paçientia . . .").[51]

Yet he was not unaware of the conspiracies. Already at the papal "truce" dinner with Cardinal Tournon, he had known of the French Cardinal's secret dealings with the Sienese. In May he wrote repeatedly to the court that this Cardinal was involved with them, and that he suspected Cardinal Farnese as well.[52] At that time Sienese patriots, especially the five brothers Amerighi, worked out their final plans with Cardinals Tournon and Farnese, with the Francophile Cardinal of Ferrara, the Counts of Pitigliano and Santa Fiore (Siena's independent neighbors, supposedly in Charles V's pay—which was not arriving punctually), and Enea Piccolomini, leader of the Sienese exiles.

Mendoza suspected that something was going on, but he did not know what was being done or precisely who was doing it. He gave sweeping counsel to the Emperor: through the puppet government His Majesty should order the return of such self-exiled Sienese to the city as Mendoza might indicate, under pain of loss of their estates. Many such men of importance had left town when the work on the castle began and were now among the troublemakers. And, Mendoza advised, the Emperor should remove the Archbishop of Siena (who was all the time inimical to Don Diego, once having masterminded a murder plot against him) by calling him to the Imperial court under some pretext to keep him out of mischief. (Charles V followed Don Diego's advice to the letter.) At the same

---

[50] Mendoza to Arras, July 7, 1552, *AC*, p. 380.

[51] *AC*, p. 379.

[52] "Relación" of letters from Mendoza to Arras, May 11, 16, and 30, 1552, Arch. Sim., Est., leg. 878, Rose-file.

time Mendoza suggested that Charles V reward the Amerighis, "though they are rascals, too," in order to encourage loyalty in others.[53]

While Don Diego remained but half-aware of the conspiracy as long as the rumors were vague and self-contradictory, Cosimo I alerted him on June 8 to a conference the conspirators held in Ferrara. French ministers were meeting there with many exiled Sienese whose aim was to raise money to drive the Spaniards out, set the city free, and blow up the fortress.[54] In view of this growing insecurity, Mendoza provided himself in mid-June with two companies of horsemen, fifty in each, hoping, though they served him in Rome, to charge their expense to the Sienese government.[55] But by the end of June, the conspirators spread rumors throughout Italy that the French, together with various exiles, were aiming at attacking the Kingdom of Naples.[56] The Imperials believed them— though it was only a blind to divert their suspicions from the real target, Siena. Then, from July 15 to 20, Cosimo was informed of a conference at Chioggia, where an attack on Naples was discarded while Milan and Siena remained "possibilities." (In fact, the fate of Siena was decided at that meeting in Chioggia.)[57]

Having made it a habit to discount most rumors, Don Diego was not only unalarmed, but on July 7 he estimated he could have the castle in Siena in a state of defense by the end of the month. He thought Siena was safe now, relying on the promise of the Duke of Florence's support; and he remained optimistic despite the fact that he was still waiting for the funds and troops he had requested from the Emperor in February.[58] Everything would arrive too late because Charles V was not able to attend to Mendoza's appeal before the end of June; only then did he send a sum of 20,000 escudos,

[53] Mendoza to Arras, May 10 or 11, 1552, Rome, Bibl. Pal., vol. 2322, Rose-file; also *AC*, pp. 370, 371. On the Emperor's following Mendoza's advice, see Charles V to Balia of Siena, June 28, 1552, Arch. Sim., Est. Ale. 647, Rose-file.

[54] Cosimo I to Mendoza, June 8, 1552, Arch. Flor., Mediceo 20, Rose-file.

[55] Mendoza to Charles V, June 13, 1552, Arch. Sim., Est., leg. 878, Rose-file.

[56] Cosimo I to Mendoza, June 28, 1552, Arch. Flor., Mediceo 20, Rose-file. Cosimo I to Pandolfino, June 30, 1552, Desjardins, *Négociations*, III, 307.

[57] Cosimo I to Pandolfino, July 15–20, 1552, Desjardins, *Négociations*, III, 315–316.

[58] See notes 50 and 51, above.

dispatching the thousand German troops by way of Gonzaga. He also sent a hundred light cavalry to augment the forces Don Diego already had, advising him "to do the best you can with these troops," and "look after yourself as you so often assured Us you can do." The Emperor also reminded the Duke of Florence to cooperate with Mendoza in Siena as well as Piombino, as "Don Diego is in charge of both places."[59]

Mendoza's general optimism was apparently not even disturbed by the fact that he was in poor health throughout this spring and summer, and that the Pope was becoming ever curter toward him, "as long as His Majesty is as weak as now, one discovers the Pope's true nature more and more."[60] One aspect of that true nature showed itself in the Pope's permitting the Cardinals Farnese to return to Rome and "treating them so well that Cardinal [Alessandro] Farnese is displaying here all the authority and company he had in the time of his grandfather."[61] Another aspect was revealed when Mendoza sought to talk to the Pope about the creation of new cardinals. He reminded him of the Emperor's wishes, and of the Pope's promise to give Charles V some numerical advantage in the nomination of Imperial and French partisans. Julius III, while condescendingly promising to look at the Emperor's list, told Mendoza: "A cricket by the window does sing well."[62]

After he had achieved his truce, the Pope, unconcerned about the growing intrigues between the Imperials and the French around him, had reverted at once to making the most of the apparent tranquility of the times: "All he does is engage in banquets, garden parties, games. . . ."[63] But by mid-July, even he took notice, and despite his scant sympathy for Don Diego at this time, the Pope notified him that the French were planning something serious against both Piombino and Siena. The French at the papal court,

[59] Charles V to Mendoza, June 28, 1552, from Villach, and July 18, 1552, from Linz, Arch. Sim., Est., Contaduría Mayor 1420.

[60] Mendoza to Arras, July 12, 1552, Rome, *AC*, p. 381.

[61] Diego Lasso to King Ferdinand, July 3, 1552. Rome, Druffel, *Briefe* II, no. 1626, pp. 661–662.

[62] Mendoza to Charles V, May 20, 1552, Arch. Sim., Est., leg. 878, Rose-file. "Dixo que cantaua bien un grillo que estaua en la ventana," Mendoza to Arras, July 12, 1552, *AC*, p. 382.

[63] Lasso to King Ferdinand, July 13, 1552, Druffel, *Briefe* II, 676.

he let Mendoza know, were now expressing themselves in terms similar to those they had used before the actions of Maurice of Saxony had come out into the open.[64]

The Pope's counsel alarmed Don Diego—but only in part. He discounted the French designs on Siena, thinking they aimed for Naples. As late as two weeks before the catastrophe he recommended for duty in Naples one of the several Roman captains who was serving him. This was the Pope's nephew, Ascanio della Corgnia. It had been a minor Imperial triumph to hire Ascanio. While most Italians were now openly or clandestinely—as the Count of Pitigliano—deserting Charles V's camp, Don Diego had lured Ascanio by higher pay (a pension of two thousand ducats) away from his service to the French King. To Mendoza's (relatively) good fortune, Ascanio did not then go to Naples. But Mendoza was strangely deluded in proposing to let Ascanio serve in Naples at this time.[65]

It seems he took to heart from the Pope's warning only the part about Piombino. This problem worried him continually more than all the others.

Mendoza was still the supreme commander of Piombino, but holding his four jobs: Rome, Siena, the castle, and Piombino, he had known, helplessly, from the outset that one job would have to suffer from his involvement with the others.[66] Charles V himself had authorized him to throw all resources into the completion of the castle in Siena and the two fortresses of Orbetello and Porto Ercole. Meanwhile Piombino had fallen into ruins. After Mendoza had put three thousand to four thousand escudos into its fortifications, there was no more money, and there were no men to spare to make the stricken state secure.

The dowager lady had died at the beginning of 1552 in her Genoese exile. This removed one of the irritating voices from whatever negotiations about Piombino's fate might still occur.[67] Gonzaga

64 Mendoza to Charles V, July 15, 1552, Arch. Sim., Est., leg. 878, folio 96.

65 Mendoza to Charles V, April 15, 1552, Arch. Sim., Est., leg. 878, Rose-file. Mendoza to Arras, July 18, 1552, AC, p. 384.

66 Mendoza to Charles V, April 15, 1552, Arch. Sim., Est., leg. 878, Rose-file.

67 The death of the lady of Piombino is mentioned without further details by Agostino Cesaretti, *Istoria del Principato di Piombino*, p. 143; Licurgo Cappelletti, *Storia della città è stato di Piombino*, p. 193; Mendoza, instruction to

(who had been so ineffectual in the siege of Parma and Mirandola), wishing to insure future support against the French, then
suggested to the Emperor that this would be a good time to hand
Piombino over to Cosimo. "If we can control the Duke of Florence,
we will have important friends and money behind us."[68] Perhaps
the Emperor and Don Diego had also been keeping the Duke of
Florence in the back of their minds, holding the bait in readiness
for an emergency. In the meantime the bait had fouled, however,
and Cosimo did not even want it anymore; at least, he was able to
pretend not to want Piombino in its present deteriorated state.

But Mendoza could not reconcile himself to the weakening of
Piombino and the loss of prestige if the enemy took it. He offered
to go there himself and either to keep it for the Emperor or die in
the effort "to save the reputation of Your Majesty. No one should
say it [Piombino] was taken from the Signore because he was unable to keep it up and we let it perish ourselves."[69]

When the Pope now warned him that the French were planning
to make Piombino a base for action against Siena and Florence,
while reports came in also that the Turkish fleet was being sighted
near Salerno, Mendoza tried to guess the enemies' plans. He pondered the potential appearance of a French fleet with several thousands of troops on the insufficiently guarded coast of Piombino,
and the support they might be getting from the Turks.

There might be, he imagined, four possible results from these
eventualities: one, the enemy would not attack after all—thereby
the French would lose hope of future help from the Turks; two, if
the French attacked, they would be routed; three, the citizens (of
Siena) would have been taught a severe lesson; they would never
again cause trouble in the future; and four, since the French fleet
was on the way to France at present, it could not return with troops
before August 10 at the earliest. But in the canal of Piombino, the

---

Ximénez, April 14, 1552, "siendo la madre muerta y el señor hombre y no
mentecato," *AC*, p. 334.

[68] Possibly the dowager's death (see preceding note) moved Gonzaga to this
advice. From Gonzaga's instructions to Antonio Vivero, April 9, 1552, Arch.
Sim., Est. Milan 1200, Rose-file; also Arch. Sim., Est., leg. 1468, Rose-file.

[69] Mendoza to Charles V, July 16, 1552, Arch. Sim., Est., leg. 878, folios 100–
102.

weather would be bad by August 15, and there is no harbor (in stormy weather, a landing on Piombino's steep cliffs was impossible) therefore, after that date the danger would have passed, and the Emperor would be saved the expense of a guard.[70]

But apparently Mendoza did not conceive of a fifth possibility: Imperial defeat. And he failed to consider the fact that the French already had many troops in Italy, although he knew it. Therefore his theoretical evaluation, which implied a preliminary shuttle service of the French fleet, bringing troops from Marseille into Tuscany, seems unrealistic, the more so, because the potential attack on Piombino was one of the many feints of the enemy—the actual event was not to come by way of Piombino at all.

For weeks on end, Duke Cosimo's voice had sounded reassuringly in the background: his person, all his armed might, his entire state, was ready any moment to succor His Majesty in the case of danger. On July 13, Mendoza sent Don Francés de Álava to Florence to "reduce those generalities of the Duke to the particular."[71] He wished Cosimo to draw up a workable plan for Siena's defense in case of an enemy attack—but the Duke stuck by his generalities. Cosimo sought to impress the young Spanish marshal, parading his well-trained lancers, harquebusiers, and other troops before him; and he talked with him for four hours, assuring Don Francés that there was no danger by sea or land. Reaffirming that he was entirely at Charles V's service and a great friend of Mendoza, the Duke promised that he would come running with his person and his forces to help Siena or any other part that concerned the service of the Emperor.[72] As for immediate help, he suggested to Don Francés that he station one or two thousand of the Duke's infantry right in Siena—Cosimo would provide them with rations, but no pay. This offer alarmed the "Maiden"—it was Don Diego's policy not to let the Duke's troops come in; besides, the Spaniards had no money to pay their own troops, which numbered hardly three hundred at that time; to accede to Cosimo's proposition was equal

70 Mendoza to Charles V, July 18, 1552, Arch. Sim., Est., leg. 878, folio 103.

71 Mendoza to Arras, July 12, 1552, *AC*, p. 382.

72 Don Francés de Álava to Mendoza, July 14, 1552, Arch. Sim., Est., leg. 878, folio 102.

to letting him occupy the State of Siena. Both Mendoza in Rome and Don Francés, back in Siena, wrote the Duke that it would be enough if Cosimo stationed his troops nearby on the border, at Staggia, so that Don Francés could summon them as soon as the emergency drew closer.[73]

In the face of the growing threat against Siena, with irritating news coming to him from all sides, Don Diego lost his customary composure. On July 17, a Roman *bargello* (police officer) arrested one of his messengers who was taking Mendoza's secret mail to Cardinal Burgos for dispatch to the Viceroy of Naples. (The fellow carried a sword—an offense against the current papal law under the truce stipulations.) Mendoza, on confronting the *bargello* to berate him for his mistake, forgot himself and punched him in the nose, pulling a tuft out of his beard besides. The *bargello* threw himself at the Pope's feet to complain, and this incident enraged His Holiness even more than Don Diego's importunate voice in the truce negotiations had done. The Pope was quick and expressive with his pen; he tossed off a letter to the Emperor, bitterly accusing Mendoza. For several days he refused to see the ambassador. All diplomats stationed in Rome at the time sent colorful versions of the scandal into the world. Don Diego could not forgive himself for having lost his temper in such unfavorable circumstances—the last thing he wished to do was to annoy this Pope.[74]

Mendoza's correspondence with Don Pedro Alvarez de Toledo, the Viceroy of Naples, was beset by great strain even without an interference from outside. Throughout this uneasy summer, Don Pedro had been at odds with him about the disposition of Imperial troops. The Viceroy, whose kingdom was threatened by the Turkish armada, wanted all the men for the protection of Naples. Arguing against Mendoza's wishes to protect Siena, he countermanded military appointments made by Don Diego; and by his letters to

---

[73] Cosimo I to Concino, December 1, 1552, Arch. Sim., Est. Tusc. 1441, Rose-file.

[74] Mendoza to Arras, July 18, 1552, *AC*, pp. 382–385; also Montesa to Arras, July 28 (recte: 18), 1552, Bibl. Pal., vol. 2322, Rose-file; Adriani, *Istoria*, IX, 595; Lasso to King Ferdinand, July 23, 1552, Druffel, *Briefe* II, no. 1675, pp. 699–700; Jaén to Prince Philip, November 12, 1552, Arch. Sim., Est., leg. 877, Rose-file.

the Emperor and the Imperial cardinals, the Viceroy (a personage about whom no sympathetic word can be found in the records; he was universally disliked) did all he could to undermine confidence in Mendoza.[75]

On July 23, the Pope, though still offended by the incident with his *bargello*, warned Don Diego of impending trouble in Siena. At the same time, Don Francés wrote of his fear that the Sienese were on the point of rising. He had found an ominous paper nailed to the door of Don Diego's house in Siena: a halved coin was attached to the paper on which an anonymous writer related how the Count of Pitigliano had secretly switched to the French and was about to march with three thousand Italian troops against the Spaniards in Siena. The informer said he kept the other half of the coin so that he would be able later on to prove his identity as the one who had brought this timely warning. Now, at last, Mendoza decided to go to Siena—secretly.[76]

It had long become a puzzle why Mendoza should not have returned to Siena in over four and a half months—and the question is puzzling still. For, no matter what he heard, Don Diego did not budge from Rome in all that time. True, he had exhausted his credit; he waited vainly for the Emperor's money to arrive; only with new funds would he have been able to satisfy his creditors to whom he had had to pledge his presence in Rome. Ultimately, when he despaired of receiving the Imperial court's money in good time, he had sent an urgent appeal to Prince Philip in Spain. The Prince responded at once, sending him an authorization to draw twenty thousand escudos—but it took six weeks to arrive in Italy.

---

[75] On Mendoza's conflict with the Viceroy of Naples: Mendoza to Charles V, July 15, 1552, Arch. Sim., Est., leg. 878, folio 96; Viceroy of Naples to Cardinal Burgos, July 19, 1552, Arch. Sim., Est. Nap. 1042, Rose-file; Viceroy of Naples to Mendoza, July 19, 1552, and to Charles V, July 21, 1552, Arch. Sim., Est., leg. 1043, Rose-file. For general dislike of this Viceroy, see Jaén to Arras, February 25, 1552: the Pope asked Jaén in confidence how Charles V could continue to keep the Viceroy there when everybody detests him so heartily. Bibl. Pal., Rose-file.

[76] On the Pope, and Mendoza's secret departure, Mendoza to Charles V, July 23, 1552, Rome (no identification number), Rose-file; on letter found by Don Francés, see D. Francés to Mendoza, July 25, 1552, Rose-file (no identification number); and Sandoval, *Historia*, book 29, pp. 402, 403.

By then it was too late to be of use to Mendoza.[77] At last, on July 24, the Emperor's twenty thousand escudos, so long en route, were being transported from Genoa to Siena, but not yet the promised German troops, which did not arrive in time. Without troops on whom he could rely against the rebellious Sienese, without funds—until the very last moment—to pay his Spanish soldiers, the workers on the castle, and new troops, Mendoza must have felt that his presence in Siena would not achieve more than his lieutenant Álava was doing in his name—except that he would perhaps uselessly expose his life to all the hatred he knew he had engendered there.

Perhaps to defend his continuous absence he tried, as was his habit, to minimize in public the impression of the seriousness of the situation. Just before mid-July, in his letter to the Emperor, his view of the situation in Siena had in fact been tinged with euphoria.[78] Earlier, when the gap in his fortress had still been open, the trouble had seemed greater to him. Afterwards he had rationalized the extent of the danger away; another time his explanation was: "I cannot leave Rome because my creditors will excommunicate me."[79] As late as July 18 he wrote to Arras: "It is impossible to leave Rome though all be lost, because I am paralyzed."[80] That was a day or two after he had been flexible enough to assail the *bargello* —his own shock and contrition must have brought on one of his recurrent attacks of rheumatic immobility, in addition to his legal and financial paralysis.

Cosimo I, who had often expressed concern about Mendoza's absence from Siena, professed on July 26 to be in a state of great anxiety about Siena. He felt that many things could still be corrected by Don Diego's presence there.[81] On the 27th, Serristori, Cosimo's ambassador in Rome, replied to the Duke that Mendoza had disregarded all warnings of trouble in Siena, and had even ridiculed the

[77] Mendoza to Prince Philip, June 26, 1552, Arch. Sim., Guerra 47, Rose-file.
[78] Mendoza to Charles V, July 12, 1552. Arch. Sim., Est., leg. 877, Rose-file. At that date Mendoza still expected the thousand Germans from the Emperor to arrive in time; therefore he considered Siena's safety assured.
[79] "Relación" of letter of Mendoza (to the Imperial court), July 12, 1552 (no identification number), Rose-file.
[80] Mendoza to Arras, July 18, 1552, *AC*, p. 385.
[81] Cosimo I to Mendoza, July 26, 1552, Arch. Flor., Mediceo 21, Rose-file.

possibility of trouble.[82] But by this time, unknown to Serristori, Mendoza had left Rome.

On July 24 the Pope received Mendoza again. The Cardinal of Jaén was present, relating that Julius III entirely forgave the ambassador. He refused to hear any further apology, but did not show Mendoza quite the same familiarity as formerly; though later he told Jaén that he was very fond of Mendoza.[83]

On July 26, when Mendoza "had his foot in the stirrup," his messenger to Don Francés returned to the embassy: he had been unable to reach Siena because all the roads were blocked with enemy troops. (The courier had given the letter to a Genoese, though, who carried other dispatches and somehow had means to get through.)[84] Meanwhile, Mendoza had conducted his preparations for leaving so secretly that people in his own household were unaware of it.[85] It seems that besides Don Diego's Roman captains, Ascanio della Corgnia and Giulio Orsino, only Montesa and Cardinal Jaén were kept informed of his plans. But a Roman goldsmith must have wondered on the same day why the ambassador should suddenly have been selling him his table silver for ready cash.

Escaping his creditors, trusting his books and collections of antiques and other treasures to the mercy of his friends, and leaving faithful Montesa in charge of everything, Mendoza stole out of Rome "by post" before dawn on the 27th—without so much as a final good-by to those who were still his friends, or to the Pope. (Montesa and Cardinal Jaén excused him later in the day in papal audience, explaining that Mendoza could not disturb His Holiness in the night.)[86] But Mendoza did not know at the time that he would never return.

Though hurriedly prepared, his flight must have been well organized, for he managed to join the Captains Ascanio and Giulio

[82] Desjardins, *Négociations*, III, 340.

[83] Jaén to Arras, July 28, 1552, Bibl. Pal., vol. 2322, Rose-file.

[84] "El pie en el estrivo me tomo el aviso," Mendoza to Charles V, July 26, 1552, Arch. Sim., Est., leg. 1442, Rose-file.

[85] Don Juan de Rojas to Arras, August 10, 1552, Bibl. Pal., Rose-file.

[86] Jaén to Philip, July 27, 1552, Arch. Sim., Est., leg. 877, Rose-file; Montesa to Cosimo I, July 27, 1552, Arch. Sim., Est. Tusc. 1441, Rose-file.

with their troops. That very night, or the day before, Ascanio had caught some bandits who had planned to assassinate Don Diego in Rome—the deed being intended as one of the signals of the Sienese uprising.[87] When Mendoza now rode into the golden summer morning at the head of his new (if yet small) army, drums beating, and Imperial banners flying—the first time in almost five months that he left the confining walls of Rome behind him—action buoyed up his spirit. The thousand Germans and one hundred extra cavalry had never come, but the assurance that the Emperor's money had arrived in Genoa and was on the way to the castle in Siena, must have made it possible for him to gather new Italian troops on the strength of justified new promises. And once again he had foiled a murder plot against his person—surely, his life was charmed!

The Cassian Way from Rome to Siena that he sometimes had crossed in furious haste in seventeen hours in the saddle, was now blocked, but he chose the road through the Ecclesiastical States to Perugia, territory under Ascanio's command.[88] Confidently, Mendoza sent new messengers ahead with one of his typical, curt, peremptory Spanish notes to the *balia*, his puppets. He ordered the Sienese magistrate to prepare lodgings for his troops near the gate of Camollia, which he expected to enter the next day. Remarkably, that letter, and two others the following day (preserved in the Siena archives), somehow got through to his still-functioning bureaucracy.[89] But perhaps his couriers had used disguise or similar means to smuggle the letters in, because it was not possible for Mendoza or his companions to reach his goal. They fought their way, taking minor strongholds, one after the other: Chiusi, Foligno, and Castel della Pieve. Marching 140 and more miles without a rest in twenty-three hours, they advanced toward Perugia, and Ascanio's infantry of three hundred men put to flight four companies under French command; during the night they combed all the hostelries along the highway, surprising and capturing the enemy

---

[87] Marcantonio Damula to Venice, August 17, 1552, *Ven. Dep.* II, 544.

[88] See note 84, above.

[89] Mendoza to the *balia* of Siena, from Foligno, July 27, 1552; from Castel della Pieve, July 28, Arch. Siena, Balia 215, Rose-file.

captains there resting, drunk, or asleep. The captured troops swelled their own to three thousand.[90]

From Castel della Pieve Mendoza wrote again to his magistrate in Siena. It was July 28, late at night, and he did not yet know that Siena was already lost, his house there sacked, and his Spanish garrison driven into the dungeons of his unfinished, wretched castle. Unaware of the dimensions of the catastrophe, he dashed off another command to his supposed subjects, warning them that he and his two thousand troops were coming from Rome with all speed! He still wanted lodgings prepared for his troops, and provisions arranged—his men would be tired when they arrived.

Yes, he was coming, and he still felt confident. His friend was in the background, the mighty Duke of Florence, an honest man, the Emperor's creature and ally—Cosimo with his 8,000 troops, the best in Italy, who could raise 25,000 men altogether at a moment's notice—with such a protector, what had Spanish Siena to fear? Still, uncertainty nagged him all the while.

The news of the accomplished uprising in Siena reached him the next day. The blow had fallen. Had he not dreaded it all the time? He had feared precisely these events—but, no! He never quite believed they could happen. Foreboding and hope had conflicted in his soul. On learning the news he wrote to Gonzaga: "I always feared exactly what has happened." But to Arras he wrote: "I regreat having made such a bad guess."[91]

A Fair-Weather Friend

The group of conspirators for Siena's liberty was liberally financed by the French King. With many French troops still in fighting trim available in Italy and fresh Italian troops brought into the enterprise by individual leaders, they concealed their target almost up to the last minute by simulating interest in preparing an attack on Naples or even Milan. On July 26 they sent an army of about eight thousand men toward Siena.[92]

---

[90] Ascanio della Corgnia to Pagni, August 5, 1552, from Chiusi, Arch. Flor., Mediceo 3271, Rose-file.

[91] Mendoza to Gonzaga, July 29, 1552, Arch. Sim., Rose-file; to Arras, same date, *AC*, p. 386.

[92] The story of the conspiracy and *cacciata* of the Spaniards from Siena is told

Don Francés de Álava had little more than three hundred men in his Spanish garrison, but his troops guarded all the gates of Siena well. On July 26, when he learned that the enemy was approaching, he requested a reinforcement of a thousand men from Cosimo, to which appeal the Duke responded by letting about four hundred men ("wretched troops") stationed at Valdielsa, the nearest point, move into Siena under Otto da Montauto.[93] The Florentines arrived in the following night on the Campo—the public square of Siena—where all the Spanish soldiers were gathered, and, by the light of the lanterns hanging on the wall of Fonte Gaia (the "Gay Fountain," at the top center of the Campo), each soldier was counted and given his pay.[94] The Spanish entrenched themselves all the way up to San Domenico and their fortress; most of the Florentines were left in position right on the Campo, the rest stationed themselves to guard the gate of Camollia—the door to Florence by which they had come. Theirs was only a token force; anxiously Don Francés sent message after message to the Duke, asking him to send as many reinforcements as he could.

But no armies appeared to challenge the many thousands of Siena's besiegers, and during the same night of July 27/28—almost coinstantaneously with the entry of the four hundred Florentines—the French burned down one of the opposite gates and, taking advantage of that diversion, broke elsewhere through the wall; about four thousand men stormed into the city, greeted by the Sienese people with cries of "liberty!" They dislodged the outnumbered Florentines from the Campo almost as soon as those "wretched" troops had taken up their position. But the Spaniards, entrenched behind barricades from the Campo to the fortress, succeeded in slowing down the attack until morning. Still no reinforcements appeared.

On July 28, fighting proceeded from house to house. Eventually, the Spaniards had to yield San Domenico, and the Florentines the gate of Camollia, and both forces withdrew into the fortress. The

by Nerino Bartoli, *Le congiure di Siena e la cacciata degli spagnoli del 1552*; and in "La cacciata della guardia spagnola da Siena (1552)" by an unknown author, *Arch. Stor. Ital.* 2, serie I (1842): 481–524.

[93] Don Francés de Álava to Duke of Florence, and the latter's reply, July 27, 1552, Arch. Sim., Est. Tusc. 1441, Rose-file. Also Cosimo I to Mendoza, July 28, 1552, Arch. Flor., Mediceo 21, Rose-file.

[94] Sozzini, "Diario," p. 78.

victorious French, aided by the liberated Sienese population, laid siege to the castle where the inmates huddled in unfinished subterranean quarters. According to the Duke of Florence, there were no supplies in the castle except for some bread rations for only three or four days; but Don Francés said later there was enough to hold out for forty days—a statement supported by Mendoza, who in his time had put in enough for such an emergency.[95] That, however, was before Don Francés had sold most of the provisions, without being able to replenish everything in time.

While Don Francés and the Spaniards, Cosimo's lieutenant, Otto da Montauto, and the Florentines were holding out in Don Diego's besieged castle, the Duke of Florence was trying to decide (if his protestations can be believed) whether or not to send reinforcements—a move expected of him as ally of Charles V by friend and foe alike. But in fact Cosimo had already decided on July 20 that his help would consist of only "good advice."[96] Immediately after their successful coup, the Sienese sent him a delegation to propose negotiations. They proclaimed "their unchanged devotion to the Emperor." Their only grievance, they professed, was "Don Diego and the fortress."[97] Simultaneously, the Pope sent the Duke word to think twice before he acted against Sienese liberty.[98] And un-

[95] "Three or four days": Cosimo I to Charles V, August, 1552, Arch. Flor., Mediceo 22, Rose-file; Don Francés on "forty days": Bishop of Palencia to Prince Philip, from Pavia, August 17, 1552, Arch. Sim., Est. Milan 1198, Rose-file. (The bishop to whom Don Francés told the story when he passed through Pavia on his way to the Emperor's court may have exaggerated, because elsewhere Don Francés estimated the supplies to last for only twelve to fifteen days. Retrospectively the situation may have looked better to Don Francés himself.) Mendoza's estimate in a letter, presumably from Mendoza, to the Duke of Florence, a copy forwarded to Prince Philip, August 4, 1552, Arch. Sim., Est., leg. 877, Rose-file. The transcript of this document is unsigned, but its content reveals Mendoza's point of view, especially the writer's urging Cosimo I to reconsider his refusal to reconquer Siena: "Princes, in their resolutions, should give great weight to their reputation. . . ."

[96] Cosimo I to Pandolfino, July 20, 1552, Desjardins, *Négociations*, III, 318.

[97] Cosimo I to Charles V, summary of memos in July and August, 1552, Arch. Flor., Mediceo 22, Rose-file.

[98] Serristori to Cosimo I, July 27, 1552, Desjardins, *Négociations*, III, 339–341; Lasso to King Ferdinand, August 13, 1552, Druffel, *Briefe* II, no. 1720, p. 735; Cardinal Alessandro Farnese to his agent, from Valentino, August 1, 1552, Arch. Sim., Est., leg. 878, Rose-file.

known to anyone else, Cosimo, no lover of the French, yet fearing for his state in the midst of an overwhelming Imperial debacle, was just then committing himself to a secret agreement with the French King, whereby he promised not to assist the Spaniards.[99]

Officially the Duke excused himself for his inaction on the grounds that the fortress was insufficiently provisioned. If he delayed his decision any longer, he feared the lives of the Florentine and Spanish soldiers now within it would be endangered (he refused to agree to Don Diego's urgent proposal to take more victuals to the fortress). For a local disturbance, the Duke declared, his help would have been ready, but this was much worse. The presence of the French army changed the situation; the rebels' forces were increasing all the time, and his interference now would provide the basis for a general war.[100] "Despairing of being able to relieve the castle and regain the city that had been lost, and therefore judging that it was best to take any means that might keep it under the protection of the Emperor rather than drive it into the arms of the French," Cosimo de' Medici made his decision to abandon his ally.[101]

By that time Mendoza had not yet seen the Duke. Still on the road, he expected Cosimo to come forward with his might, and he expected his fortress to hold out for at least two more months, allowing enough time for recovery of the city. But before Mendoza reached Florence, Cosimo's agreement to negotiate with the rebellious Sienese was brought to him. It was, as Mendoza said, a "tolerable" agreement that the Duke let him see at that time. But by August 4, a few days after he had come to the Duke's court, the Sienese, with permission of their French liberators, had concluded a separate treaty with the Duke of Florence, which was, in contrast to the one shown Mendoza, a "shameful" agreement.[102] The only favorable clause in it provided for those besieged in the fortress to come out "with drums beating and flags flying." The troops were

---

[99] E. Palandri, *Les négociations entre la France et la Toscane*, III, pp. 78, 321, 325.

[100] Cosimo I to Gonzaga, July 30, 1552, Arch. Sim., Est. Milan 1201, Rose-file.

[101] Cosimo I to Pandolfino, August 3, 1552, Arch. Flor., C.S. 72, Rose-file.

[102] Mendoza to Philip, September 10, 1552, Arch. Sim., Est. Genoa 1382, Rose-file.

allowed to carry all their belongings, which included the bags with the Emperor's 20,000 escudos earmarked for the final work and provision of the castle, and which had arrived just one day before the upset. Otto da Montauto and his troops, whose uselessness in the short fight was topped only by the importunity of their presence in the castle with its scant supplies, emerged first from the dungeon; Don Francés, who had done his best, "eating only oats and drinking water," came out reluctantly as the last to leave his master's dream citadel.[103]

As the Spaniards and Florentines marched off to Florence, "on the side toward San Domenico, the Sienese came in to tear the castle down. . . . Lanssac [the French commander and "natural" half brother of the French King] entered with the principal citizens of the city who had been watching the enemy's departure from the Camollia gate. Lanssac addressed them, saying that the object of the King of France had been to set Siena free and that now they should decide whether they wished the castle to remain or wished it torn down." Immediately the Sienese set to, demolishing the castle, women and children taking part in the destruction. "It took them one hour to destroy what could not be built in four months!" Resentful Sienese also vented their anger on the cage of eagles, the heraldic birds of the Empire, that their city, as Imperial fief, looked after—they killed all the living symbols of their oppressor; and tearing the eagle banner from the poles, they raised the French lilies in its stead.[104]

This, then, was the end of "the castle," but in Cosimo's eyes it was also the "end of Don Diego." "In an unfortunate hour Don Diego arrived here," the Duke wrote in identical words to Don Francisco de Toledo at the Imperial court and his father-in-law, the Viceroy of Naples.

According to the nature of this *galantuomo*, now that he has ruined Siena, he wants to light the fire all over Tuscany and put Florence in

103 Cosimo I to an ambassador, August 3, 1552, Arch. Sim., Est. Genoa 1382, Rose-file.

104 "Relación" for Prince Philip of the tumult in Siena, Arch. Sim., Est., leg. 877, Rose-file; a report, Arch. Sim., Est. Genoa 1382, Rose-file; Sozzini, "Diario," p. 90.

danger. I know that, with his usual chimeras, he will say that the castle can still be saved. . . . But this will be the end of Don Diego. Therefore I do not wish to share in his negligence. He has expressed himself here in front of myself and others in terms that would have turned Saint Francis into a devil. How could the servant closest to His Majesty become such a great enemy [of Cosimo]? But I know him, and from what he told me I have seen that he is a desperate man and must not be taken into account. . . . You may be certain that we will have no dealings with him whatsoever, as we know his evil nature and his intense desire to injure us.

In the Duke's opinion, Mendoza could do little to relieve the castle and still less to recover the city, "although we are certain that he, to excuse his mistakes, will not fail to write the contrary, as is his custom. . . ."[105]

With Siena wrenched from his grasp, Mendoza was still the supreme commander over Piombino, Orbetello, and other Sienese fortresses. But meanwhile he had received orders from Charles V, authorizing him to hand these places over to Cosimo under certain conditions. Duke Cosimo did not avert his eyes from the defenseless state, although only recently he had still professed indifference toward its fate. Now he waited for it to fall into his lap—and here was his unwelcome guest, once more with the apparently unwelcome gift of Piombino in his pocket. On August 3, the Duke made out a receipt to Mendoza, agreeing to all the conditions stipulated by the Emperor, but Don Diego was still consulting by letter with Gonzaga before conceding the final transfer.[106]

Meanwhile Don Diego was still Cosimo's guest. Following the ancient custom that to tell a man the truth you should seek him out in his own house, Mendoza did not spare his host any words of what he thought of him. He called Cosimo to his face "a Frenchman" and a "poor servant" (desservidor) of Charles V, a "doublecrosser of the Emperor," and he added that the Duke of Florence

---

[105] "Questo sara il fine di Don Diego . . .," Cosimo I to Don Francisco de Toledo, Arch. Flor., Mediceo 20, Rose-file; Cosimo I to Pandolfino, August 2, 1552, Arch. Flor., C.S. 72, Rose-file; published in Bull. Sen., n.s. I (1930).

[106] Cosimo I, August 3, 1552, Arch. Flor., Mediceo 20. Rose-file; Mendoza to Gonzaga, August 4, 1552, Arch. Sim., Est. Milan 1201, Rose-file; and August 5, 1552, Arch. Sim., Est., leg. 1201, folio 48.

would be "chased out of his own state as an ally of the French."[107] He suspected his treacherous host of detaining the couriers he sent to the Emperor.[108]

On August 6 or 7 (the dates on the documents differ slightly), Cosimo and Don Diego signed the new agreement on Piombino. It provided, besides the surrender of Piombino, for the surrender of many places in its neighborhood with land fortresses, such as Soverito, Scarlino, Suriano, and Populonia, as well as places on the island of Elba. Cosimo promised (once again) to return all the places to Don Diego on order of the Emperor when the present emergency passed.[109]

At the same time that Cosimo's affairs were beginning to prosper beyond all expectations, the Imperials started to recover from their reverses. The Emperor concluded the Peace of Passau (August 2; the news reached Italy about a week later). Cosimo expressed his delight, writing Charles V to send his troops into Italy where they were sorely needed. By August 12, he hastened to revoke his secret treaty with the French King. Once more he declared himself entirely for the Emperor.[110] Fear for his state had motivated his defection to the French. He returned to the Emperor's side as soon as he could believe in his power again.

But, as usual, events, news, and results of news did not synchronize between the absent Emperor and his ministers in Italy. On August 20 Charles V was still under the impression that Cosimo had refused to accept Piombino. He saw no reason to disbelieve the sour-grapes pretext the Duke had advanced earlier in the month. Since Cosimo obviously did not want to take Piombino, the Emperor wrote, Mendoza could after all hand it over to him without any condition other than defending it from attack. At the same time, remembering the infelicitous, short-lived donation to Cosimo in 1548, he ordered Don Diego not to exceed his instruction. Before

---

[107] Cosimo I to Charles V, August 30, 1552, Arch. Flor., Rose-file; and Cosimo I to Concino, December 1, 1552, Arch. Sim., Est. Tusc. 1441, Rose-file.

[108] Mendoza to Philip, September 10, 1552, Arch. Sim., Est. Genoa 1382, Rose-file.

[109] Cosimo I to Don Francisco de Toledo, August 6, 1552, Arch. Flor., C.S. 86, Rose-file.

[110] Desjardins, *Négociations*, III, 321, 325.

the Emperor sealed the letter, however, Don Francés de Álava reached the court with the latest news.[111]

It was a good thing that Don Francés arrived, because the Duke's eyewitnesses were already there, Hippolito da Correggio among them, "defending vociferously the Duke of Florence for not going to the help of the Spaniards in Siena."[112] There was also the strong faction permanently at the court that guarded the Duke's interest: the Duke of Alba, Don Francisco de Toledo, and Pandolfino. The Emperor, though, did not like to listen to the explanations pro or con. "Say what you will, I have lost Siena," he complained, blaming them all.[113]

After Charles V had received Don Francés in audience, he added a postscript to his letter to Mendoza: since Piombino was already in Cosimo's hands, nothing more was to be said. But Don Diego was still to preserve Orbetello, and the Emperor expected the Duke of Florence to help him in that undertaking.[114]

On August 28 Don Diego left Florence, taking the rest of his Spanish veterans from Siena to sustain the Spanish *presidio* of Orbetello. One wonders that not only Charles V, so far away, but even Mendoza himself still believed that the Duke would not obstruct this last order from the Emperor. Neither *amo* nor *criado* was able, each in his natural haughtiness, it seems, to believe in the possibility of wilful noncompliance. After all that Cosimo had done to contribute to his downfall, Don Diego made the reasonable request that the Duke let him use the artillery that was still available in Piombino for the campaign of Orbetello. But Cosimo refused point-blank. As a pretext he adduced his agreement with Siena. He had pledged to the Sienese that from his territory no help would be forthcoming for the Spaniards in Siena, and now he stretched his interpretation to include his new territory of Piombino as well as the Sienese possession of Orbetello. Besides, he predicted that Mendoza's undertaking in Orbetello would lead to no good results any-

[111] Charles V to Mendoza, August 20, 1552, Arch. Sim., Cont. Mayor 1420, Rose-file.

[112] Damula to Venice, August 17, 1552, *Ven. Dep.*, II, 544.

[113] Dom Alfonso de Castro, Comendador Mor, to the King of Portugal, October 16, 1552, *Cap. Dipl. Port.* VII, 181–182, Rose-file.

[114] See note 111, above.

way. All he would do in "service" to the Emperor would be to ask Prince Doria to let Don Diego have "two heavy pieces and two medium heavy" from Doria's galleys, and he, Cosimo, would replace them for the Admiral from his own arsenal.[115]

In vain Don Diego pointed out to the Duke that the Emperor counted on his assistance. Cosimo, repeating his refusal, regretted it particularly because of Don Diego's information that the Emperor himself had written Mendoza to use his favor in these circumstances. Cosimo himself, however, had not seen such a special order from the Emperor—adding insult to injury by hinting that he did not believe Mendoza's assertion.[116]

Never at a loss for arguments, Mendoza criticized Cosimo's reason for refusing to lend Piombino's artillery for use in Orbetello: "It does not go against your treaty with the Sienese because the state [Piombino] does not belong to you. You only have it in deposit at present."[117]

Despite the obstacles laid in his way by Cosimo (Doria's rusty old guns were not usable, either), Don Diego succeeded in the campaign of Orbetello. "It is reported from Orbetello that Don Diego entered last Sunday morning with three hundred Spanish troops and that he went back to the fleet again in the evening, leaving the Spaniards there, so that there are now in Orbetello between four hundred to five hundred infantry."[118] "The news was received in Siena with great sorrow. Termes [the new French governor of Siena, formerly the French ambassador in Rome, and Don Diego's rival in more than one way] felt so badly about it that he would not eat on that day."[119]

The Duke begrudged Don Diego even this minor success. He wrote to Pandolfino on September 8, explaining Don Diego's success in securing Orbetello—disregarding the fact that the Emperor had ordered it—as turning the Sienese closer to the French, "the result of the relief of Orbetello is that the Sienese who had disunited

[115] August 28, 1552, Arch. Flor., Mediceo 22, Rose-file.

[116] Cosimo I to Mendoza, August 30, 1552, Arch. Flor., Mediceo 22, Rose-file.

[117] Mendoza to Cosimo I, August 31, 1552, Livorno, Arch. Flor., Mediceo 3271, Rose-file.

[118] Ricasoli to Cosimo I, from Siena, September 7, 1552, Arch. Flor., Mediceo 1851, Rose-file.

[119] "Avisos de Siena," September 7, 1552, Arch. Sim., Est. Tusc. 1441, Rose-file.

and were quarreling among themselves, have become united. We have received *no thanks for our good offices in his behalf* [italics added] with Prince Doria. . . ." Cosimo interpreted the entire action of Orbetello solely as "Don Diego's desire to injure us, and offend us in whatever way he can. . . . He regards us as his greatest and most odious enemy in the world, and as the Emperor's greatest enemy, too."[120]

On the same day, Cosimo wrote a letter full of invectives to Don Francisco de Toledo maligning Don Diego's reputation at court. In his attempt to justify his own temporary desertion of the Imperial cause, afraid of what the report of his activities would be in places that mattered, the Duke of Florence now spared no effort in trying to blame all he could on Don Diego.[121]

On the first leg of his journey to the Imperial court, Don Diego embarked at Orbetello in a frigate of Prince Doria. Andrea Doria had also assisted very poorly during the fracas. He refused to send German troops (when he had four thousand of them on board his galleys as close by as Livorno) on the very day of the attack on Siena. The Germans were earmarked for Naples, it is true, and Doria lost seven galleys with many of the new troops in a sea battle with the Turks shortly after the Siena debacle, another Imperial defeat. The Emperor, however, when he dispatched those troops, had told his ministers to use the Germans where they were most needed; doubtless, they would have been more needed in Siena in the week of July 26–30 than in any other place. At the height of the emergency, not only Don Diego, but also the Duke of Florence had asked Doria for the Germans.[122] (The often-mentioned one thousand Germans especially allotted to Mendoza were a separate force; they had been marching overland through Lombardy and barely reached Bologna by August 12.)[123]

The Admiral now refused Mendoza a galley that would have taken him in company of his Spanish captains and sailors all the

[120] Cosimo I to Pandolfino, September 8, 1552, Arch. Flor., C.S. 72, Rose-file.

[121] G. Spini, ed., *Lettere di Cosimo I*, p. 118; also Cosimo I to Prince Philip, September 6, 1552, Arch. Sim., Est. Tusc. 1441, Rose-file.

[122] Summary for Prince Philip, August 31, 1552, Arch. Sim., Est. Genoa 1382, Rose-file.

[123] Cosimo I to Pandolfino, August 12, 1552, Arch. Flor., C.S. 72, Rose-file.

way to Genoa, his first destination on the way to court. To take a
smaller craft, he had to leave his men behind. The frigate must
have run into a storm, because he lost the rest of his papers from
Italy at sea, and could make it no further on the small vessel than
the fifty miles to Piombino.[124] From there he took the post to Genoa
and then visited Gonzaga in Milan. He spent three days with Gonzaga, who was convalescing from a long illness. One of the many
factors contributing to the Imperial debacle in Italy was that Gonzaga, at a decisive time, had been incapacitated so that he could not
lend his energetic support and alert advice. The two "prancing proconsuls" had seen better hours together than now, when they sat
formulating ambitious plans to reconquer Siena.[125]

From Milan, Mendoza went to Basel, where he embarked on a
rivercraft on the Rhine that brought him to the court at Speier by
October 3.[126] "Don Diego arrived at court," Pandolfino wrote the
Duke of Florence, who must have been furious when he learned
that "Arras went out to meet him on horseback and brought him
to his lodgings, receiving him with the greatest affection. . . . Many
people are astonished at such a demonstration," he continued.
"They say that he could not have been received with greater affection if he had come bringing his Majesty news of a conquest."[127]

124 Çafarello to Arras, from Rome, September 8, 1552, Arch. Sim., Est., leg.
875, folio 161, tells of a frigate so small that he himself and others were unable
to accompany Don Diego on it; hence this group of captains went instead to
Rome.

125 Mendoza to Philip, September 10, 1552, Arch. Sim., Est. Genoa 1382, and
Gonzaga's instructions to an envoy for Philip, November 7, 1552, Milan, Arch.
Sim., Est. Milan 1199, both in Rose-file.

126 *Ven. Dep.* II, 566.

127 Arch. Flor., C.S. 82, Rose-file.

14. HONOR SAVED, 1553

> I have sacrificed my reputation and risked
> my honor to preserve Your Majesty's repu-
> tation in wretched times. . . .
>
> Don Diego to Charles V[1]

"Hidalgo de España" and His King

IN THE LATE AUTUMN OF 1552 Mendoza moved westward through Germany with the Emperor's court, against the French who had entrenched themselves in Metz—a disastrous campaign that extended into the winter and brought Imperial losses of thirty thousand men. For a long time he found himself unable to gain his master's ear in a long private audience he desired. Charles V was becoming less and less accessible to anyone except the Bishop of Arras, the Duke of Alba, and his most intimate servants. Morose, plagued by illness and disappointment, if not yet despair and resignation, the Emperor did not want to hear from Don Diego. The last time he had seen Mendoza, almost ten years earlier at Busseto when he had his meeting with Paul III, Mendoza's advice

NOTE: A portion of this chapter originally appeared in *Hispania* 53 (May 1970).

[1] From a letter to Prince Philip, "Lo que paso á Don Diego de Mendoza con el Emperador dandole quenta al Rey D. Felipe el segundo siendo Príncipe," ed. Cristóbal Pérez Pastor, *MRAE* 10 (1911): 221–225; no date, but presumably during March, 1553. The original is said to be in Biblioteca de El Escorial, Don Diego de Mendoza, *Epistolas*; also published in GP II, 284–289.

and his explanation of the world-wide powers inherent in the Imperial dignity had been valuable to him. But with all his great ideas, this man had obviously been miscast in his role in Italy. Besides, Charles V was becoming tired of his Imperial dignity. The Imperial House was crashing down around him; his crown was a burden. The financial balance of his reign showed that he never could afford the campaigns, the wars, the very trappings that he thought commensurate with his pretensions to an Emperor's power.

The Imperial dream might be dispelled, but this was no reason for Mendoza, a most loyal hidalgo, to lose his honor. His master was his rightful King, the King of Spain. Serving his King was honorable in victory or in disaster, and it was the duty of his master to vindicate his vassal from the slander of his enemies.

By the beginning of 1553, the Emperor had raised the siege of Metz. He attributed his defeat to nothing but his "old age."[2] Perturbed and confused, the Imperial court, Don Diego with them, went to Brussels, where they arrived on February 6.[3] Charles V, fatigued and disappointed, now gave in to a long illness. When he recovered, Mendoza once more approached him for a private audience, but the Emperor again wished to postpone the interview. He sent Mendoza word to unburden all he had to say to the Bishop of Arras, who would report it to His Majesty. But by now, Don Diego's patience was at an end. He refused to answer any of the Bishop's questions. At last he told him, "It is not customary for hidalgos in Spain to confess to others what they have to say to their King."[4] In the last instance, no one must stand between *amo y criado*.

"I sent the Bishop of Arras to him," Don Diego wrote Prince Philip, "imploring His Majesty, seeing I had reason to feel offended, that he should agree to listen to me as King of Spain." According to the old law of *primus inter pares*, his King could not refuse seeing a Spanish noble with a grievance, "his good vassal of loyal lineage that never had had a traitor nor enemy of their King." His

---

[2] "Fortune is a woman, forsaking the old men to smile at the young," quoted in M. Van Durme, *El Cardenal Granvela*, p. 148.

[3] Sir Andrew Dudley and Sir Richard Morysine from Brussels, February 12, 1553, *Cal. St. P.*, foreign, 1547–1553, pp. 244–245.

[4] "Yo dige que no era costumbre de hidalgos en España confesarse con otros lo que habian de decir a su Rey." From the letter referred to in note 1, above.

purpose was to show the Emperor "how little cause there was for others to slander me with so much craftiness out of self-interest."

"I have sacrificed my reputation and risked my honor to preserve Your Majesty's reputation in wretched times," he told Charles V when finally he stood before His Majesty in private audience. "I knew that the malice of others harmed me, as well as the situation in which Your Majesty found yourself, and the times and circumstances that I need not enumerate."

The Emperor replied that he had Mendoza's case investigated, finding that the imputations against him were partly false; a part were retracted by those who had made them, and the rest were nothing but suspicions without basis or reason. But he could do no more than regret what had happened. Mendoza would have to look out for his honor as best he could, and the Emperor concluded: "People usually think that they can do many things at which in the end they do not succeed."[5]

That was not the tone to take with an hidalgo of Spain, and Mendoza did not spare his King the truth. Except for his service in Rome—for whatever else he had done for the Emperor in Italy, "his Majesty is my debtor and will always remain in my debt." He continued:

And if their accusations of me are false, I have all the more reason to complain of His Majesty, for he condemned me without cause, acting only upon the meddling opinion of my enemies. . . . What I resent most is that, some time ago, when they slandered me falsely, saying they would drive me out of Rome and throw me out of Italy, they found favor with His Majesty against me. His Majesty did not stand up for his *criado* as is his duty. . . . So he now obliges me to vindicate my honor. . . . Since His Majesty knowingly hurt me, I have no means of defense other than that of women who find themselves overpowered and scream and complain. This is what I shall do wherever and whenever the occasion calls for it, good vassal that I am, of loyal lineage. . . .[6]

He outlined to his master that the only way to repair his honor in the face of the *vulgo* would be to honor and reward him. The Emperor referred him to the Bishop of Arras, who would take care "of the one and the other." "I said, regarding my reputation which

<hr />

[5] "Que los hombres pensaban de si muchas cosas que al cabo no les salian, como yo podria hacer al presente, debiendo contentarme." GP II, 286.

[6] GP II, 287.

is what is most important to me, Ras [*sic*, the Bishop of Arras] had nothing to do with it. And regarding the other point [rewards] I did not wish to broach the subject with him. He [the Bishop] should come to me if His Majesty decides to do something about it."

Long wearied of this importunate vassal, so eloquent, turbulent, and indefatigable in his bitterness, the Emperor nodded his agreement. "He replied it was all right with him and would be done."[7]

The first offer that Arras brought him, a small annual rent, was unsatisfactory. "I told him I am not used to renting out my honor for a price." When Arras and Eraso, the Emperor's Spanish secretary, continued to "seek me out, repeatedly, telling me, unless I accepted the mercy of His Majesty, I would destroy my own House, for that was the way things were now—I did not reply." A few days later the Bishop came again, offering him an honorable nomination as *caballero de Alcántara*, in a chivalric order, "La encomienda de las Casas," together with a lump sum of money. Don Diego accepted without a word, as the least that was his due.[8]

In a letter to Prince Philip he regained his voice: "I will live perpetually offended and aggrieved as long as His Majesty and I live, since he is not properly vindicating my reputation. Because all His Majesty gave me is barely enough to free himself from the blame, in the face of the world, of having been unfair to me who am proven innocent."[9]

What Don Diego resented most was the Emperor's failure to conform to the feudal law of master and man that every Castilian noble had in his blood. Although Mendoza had lived up to his part, serving to the best of his ability, he had never been servile, never having sacrificed his customary frankness and bluntness. He had not hesitated to contradict Charles V, claiming his right to *libero arbitrio* ("free judgment"), a privilege of which he seems to have made uncommon use.[10] In his own opinion, he had failed through circumstances, not through his own fault. (Who, indeed, can judge whether another man might have done better in the same situation?) And he felt that the Emperor had not reacted spontaneously

---

[7] ". . . Respondio que de buena gana, que asi se haria . . . ," GP II, 288.
[8] GP II, 288.
[9] GP II, 289.
[10] Mendoza to Charles V, July 29, 1551, Arch. Sim., Est., leg. 1467, Rose-file.

as, according to the feudal law, he should have. Instead of coming forward to rescue the honor of his noble vassal, he had behaved as the new-style, autocratic, absolute monarch that he was. But by taking the matter in his own hands, jolting and inveigling the master into some feeble performance of his duties, Mendoza had succeeded in converting his downfall into a sort of personal triumph, although the *vulgo* did not quite see it so. The French ambassador, for instance, spoke of him as *desfavorisé*.[11]

Mendoza understood well enough that he had disappointed the Emperor. But for a considerable time he refused to believe that he had lost his favor permanently. At first, following his audience, the Emperor was still ailing and all business at a standstill. Mendoza had to wait seven or eight weeks before Charles V was ready to grant him the benefices on which he insisted. The *vulgo*, the world, meanwhile thought he was waiting for another commission in the foreign service, or, at least, for a renewal of his appointment in Rome, but this was not the case. Years earlier he had wished to leave Rome when he might have done so in good graces. Why should he want to return there now? There is no indication that he expected a new high office, although it is uncertain whether the Emperor had decided not to employ him further. He did not appoint another ambassador in Rome for over a year, and during that time Don Diego's Roman embassy was kept going in his name, with the faithful Montesa in charge and in continuous correspondence with him.[12] Pope Julius had long ago forgiven him and wanted him to come back.[13] Also, one of Mendoza's worst enemies in Italy, the Viceroy of Naples, had died.

Under such outwardly favorable conditions, he probably could have received a new commission, but perhaps Don Diego himself had no desire to return to Rome. Intentions like that could not be stated outright; they were handled by implication, through mediation, mostly by the Bishop of Arras, Mendoza's indefatigable spokesman. Evidently, he stayed on in Brussels long enough to get the maximum in grants, privileges, and back pay that he could

[11] Noailles from London, September 7, 1553, *Ambassades de M. de Noailles en Angleterre* (1763), II, 146, Rose-file.

[12] Montesa's letters to Mendoza of that year in Arch. Sim., Est., leg. 878.

[13] Montesa to Mendoza, Rome, November 16, 1552, Arch. Sim., Est., leg. 878, folio 127.

expect. As soon as these affairs were settled, by August, 1553, he felt ready to return to Spain.

The Emperor still owed him a fortune; Mendoza's expense accounts presented to him covered the time from July 25, 1539, until April 14, 1552, for his services in Venice, Trent, Rome, and Siena.[14]

On behalf of Charles V, Don Diego had spent 27,000 ducats, 643 escudos, and one Julio, in addition to interest charges of 1,924 escudos on loans he had been forced to raise. (He had drawn part of that money over the years, the back pay he now claimed and received was 12,987 ducats.) The accounts had been prepared partly from oral statements that Mendoza submitted under oath to the royal accountants in Brussels, his papers being incomplete because he had lost the material pertaining to Siena.[15] In addition to his retroactive salary and expense-account compensation, he was now assured of the annual revenue going with the habit of a *caballero de Alcántara*; of two estates, and 10,000 escudos in cash.[16] Together with a few other benefices that he held for many years since, he now had enough income to leave the Emperor's service without hardship, and he was satisfied doing so "as long," as Charles V wrote to Philip, "as his removal does not injure his honor."[17]

To feel his own honor fully reestablished, Mendoza still needed a master who looked upon him with pleasure, and he hoped to find such a man in Philip. He knew his Prince as a child, and quite possibly he preferred him as a person to his father, the Emperor. He approached him with great self-confidence, although it seems astonishing that Mendoza was so unpolitic as to complain about

[14] Charles V to Cardinal Jaén, Brussels; Charles V to Figueroa, July 7, 1553, Arch. Sim., Est., leg. 505 and 1383, Rose-file.

[15] These accounts were not challenged as long as Siena remained under French rule and during the ensuing war. But from 1559 on, just when Duke Cosimo had established his firm hold of the state, Mendoza was persecuted on account of his handling of Siena's finances. Cosimo, who had already denounced Mendoza's expenditures in Siena ("a large sum of this money has gone up in smoke . . . ," Cosimo I to Arras, August 5, 1551, Poggio, Bibl. Pal., Rose-file). perhaps had a hand in casting suspicion on Mendoza six years after the royal treasury in Brussels had cleared his accounts. From 1559 on, the "Crown of Spain" sued and harassed Mendoza until his death.

[16] Damula to Venice, Brussels, April 29, 1553. *Ven. Dep.* II, 601, n. 1.

[17] Charles V (through Secretary Vargas) to Philip, Brussels, April 3, 1553, Arch. Sim., Est. Flandes 505, Rose-file.

the father to the son. The tone in which he narrated his interview with Charles V in his letter to the Prince was angry and challenging. Regardless of consequences, he vented his annoyance with Philip's idolized father. Philip, as is well known, was an exemplary son who not only followed the Emperor's orders obediently during his father's life, but later venerated his memory. In his treatment of people, in other affairs, in politics, he tried to follow the directions and inclinations of Charles V as long as he himself lived. If the Emperor had shown disfavor to Don Diego, might not Philip have done the same? Perhaps so, had not Mendoza had a special claim on Philip's gratitude.

In his attempt to make the Spanish crown absorb Siena, Mendoza (together with Gonzaga) had been the first to cultivate the young man's own dignity independently of that of his august father.[18] Philip knew and appreciated the fact that both these ministers had contrived their plan of the "vicariate" of Siena with his rather than Charles V's benefit in mind. Though the entire enterprise ended in failure, Philip, apparently took the good intention for the deed.[19] He had witnessed that Mendoza used the best years of his life, wrecking his own career, in his futile effort for Philip's crown. For a long time his behavior to Mendoza indicates that he felt indebted to him; he seemed pleased to live up to his obligation. No matter what his great father now thought of Mendoza, Philip extended his "grace" to this unruly and self-willed "servant" for nearly two more decades.

On his first return trip to Spain in fourteen years, Don Diego was able to do his young master a complimentary service. Crossing over from Antwerp to London by September, 1553, he prepared the ground for the famous marriage of "Philip and Mary." Usually, Simon Renard, the Imperial ambassador then in England, gets the credit for having put forward to Queen Mary Tudor his Emperor's proposal of marriage with his son, but Don Diego was in fact the

[18] See E. Spivakovsky, "El 'Vicariato de Siena,'" *Hispania* 26 (Madrid, 1966): 583–596.

[19] Charles V revived the concept of "vicar" in 1554 when he and Cosimo I waged war against Siena and the French, naming Philip "perpetual Vicar" of the Imperium over Siena. It remained an empty title because Philip was forced to cede Siena to Cosimo. *Ven. Dep.* III, 159, n. 3; p. 297, n. 3.

first to broach this subject to the Queen. While Mendoza was still in Brussels, Edward VI, the young King of England, died on July 6, 1553. (Mendoza then recalled that he had been the first to kiss the hand of Edward VI immediately after his birth.) As soon as Mary Tudor was firmly on the throne, Charles V pursued his dynamic and dynastic imperialism, claiming the faded and rather pitiable spinster (once his own fiancée) now for Philip, her nephew and eleven years her junior.

Just as Mendoza had started his diplomatic service almost eighteen years before as a would-be matchmaker for Princess Mary, he now rounded out the unfinished business by making the first step toward its belated fulfillment. The new Queen received both him and his traveling companion Don Diego de Acevedo, Prince Philip's current majordomo. Nothing so gross was done during that audience as to mention the intended marriage. Instead, Mendoza set the whole plan down in a Latin letter addressed to the Queen, but he handed it to Madame Clarentius, the Queen's Mistress of the Robes. During the six days he spent in England, he conferred several times with this lady in the house of a London alderman. Madame Clarentius duly submitted Don Diego's letter to Mary, though possibly not before the visitors had left.[20]

After a good crossing in a rapid, small, two-masted vessel (a *zabra*), Don Diego landed in Spain on an autumn day in 1553. He looked after his new estates and met his brothers; in the second week of November he was in Valladolid, where the court then resided. Prince Philip received the future *caballero de Alcántara* well. But Mendoza did not stay long at court. He was to take up residence in a monastery where he would prepare himself for the ecclesiastic dignity he had desired.[21]

[20] *Cal. St. P.* 12 (1554): 179, 180.
[21] The time of Mendoza's residence at the convent might be inferred from the dates of his correspondence. On March 12, 1554, Arras, in Brussels, replies to several letters of Don Diego that had reached him all at once, belatedly, dated October 9, November 10 and 11, 1553, and January 7, 1554; *Bibl. Pal.*, vol. 2318, Rose-file. In November he was still at Philip's court, "making love to the dowagers of Valladolid as he had to the ones in Flanders" (Francisco de Mendoza to Arras, November 10, 1553, Bibl. Pal., vol. 2318, Rose-file). On February 16, 1554, Don Diego wrote to Arras again from Valladolid (Mendoza to Arras, February 16, 1554, ibid., Rose-file).

Renunciation of Fame

The knighthood of the Order of Calatrava was the reward Mendoza appreciated most highly as saving his honor. But to comply with the rules it entailed—unwritten rules perhaps, but apparently a *conditio sine qua non* for attaining the "habit" at this late stage in his life—he found himself forced to condemn all of his literary work to oblivion. While he was waiting in Brussels to learn which of the order's estates would be assigned to him, he must have made the decision to renounce literary fame. At the time, it seems he did so light-heartedly, for after his anger with the Emperor subsided, his characteristic good humor reasserted itself quickly—so much so that his merriment at the table of the Duke of Alba scandalized the ambassador of the Duke of Florence.[22]

Yet he made up his mind not to publish any work (nor to acknowledge any work printed anonymously) that he had written, be it scholarly (e.g., his "Paraphrasis" of Aristotle), satirical (e.g., the "Dialogue between Charon and the soul of Pier Luigi Farnese"), historical (e.g., his report of the campaign of Tunis), or, especially, poetical.[23] There exists, for example, a collection of his poems, written at least in large part during his stay in Venice, which he had bound into a manuscript book, a sort of "Cancionero," "prepared as though to create the impression of an elaborately printed work."[24] One of the poems contained in this autograph, the "Fábula de Adonis y Hippómanes," found its way into print—anonymously—at the time Mendoza must have made this decision, August, 1553.[25] Simultaneously another anonymous work appeared that has been ascribed to Mendoza for more than three hundred years—the *Lazarillo de Tormes*.[26]

[22] Pandolfino reports having been to see the Duke of Alba, staying to lunch. Don Diego was there, "in capo della tavola," the constant table companion of the Duke; Mendoza was cracking jokes all the time . . . behaving in a fashion quite unseemly for one who holds his high position. Pandolfino to Cosimo I, Brussels, February 12, 1553, Arch. Flor., Mediceo 4314, Rose-file.

[23] See Appendix.

[24] C. Malcolm Batchelor, ed., *A tí, Doña Marina: The Poetry of Don Diego Hurtado de Mendoza,* p. 71.

[25] *Las Obras de Boscán, y algunas de Garcilaso de la Vega* (Venice: Gabriel Gilito, 1553), ed. by Alonso de Ulloa; the volume contains a "Fábula de Adonis, la qual nuevamente se ha añadido a este libro . . ."

[26] For arguments in behalf of Mendoza's authorship, see E. Spivakovsky, "The

Publishing he had foresworn, but not writing, and no sooner had he entered the monastery than he wrote another work, a long rhymed epistle in which he laments his decision. His mood was volatile, as his enemies had always maintained, and once in his new surroundings he regretted the step that now was irrevocable.[27]

The dates of his residence at Alcántara are somewhat conjectural, although it is a fact that he visited his encomienda soon after his arrival in Spain, even digging up antiquities there. He seems to have started his time of probation—one of the prerequisites to attaining the "habit"—at the end of November, 1553.

The great Spanish religious-military Orders of Calatrava, Santiago, and Alcántara were founded in the twelfth and thirteenth centuries in imitation of chivalrous Muslim brotherhoods, with the object of fighting the Moors, then all powerful. In the sixteenth century, many parts of Spain were still covered with the orders' castles, monasteries, and whole townships. Corporations of huge vested financial interests, the orders belonged nominally to the crown of Spain. When their original purpose no longer obtained after the eclipse of the Moors, the revenues from these landed properties provided the King with an inexhaustible fund for endowing the greater nobles among his veteran ministers. Prospective members had to prove that they were descended from at least three generations of nobility and were free of Jewish and Moorish blood. Don Diego, although a grandson of the famous "Maestre of Santiago" of the fifteenth century, Juan Pacheco, of noted *converso* descent, easily passed the test. Several persons, sixty-six to eighty years old, were found who could testify to having known some or all four of his grandparents. One witness of seventy-five even professed to remember his maternal grandmother, Doña Beatriz (María, rather) Portocarrero, who in 1553 had been dead for about seventy-two years. All agreed that he was of legitimate and noble birth.[28]

Lazarillo de Tormes and Mendoza," *Symposium* 15, no. 4 (1961): 271–285; "¿Valdés o Mendoza?," *Hispanófila* 12 (1961): 15–23; and "New Arguments in Favor of Mendoza's Authorship of the *Lazarillo de Tormes*," *Symposium*, Spring 1970. The date 1553 of a possible first edition of the *Lazarillo* is discussed by A. Rumeau, "Notes sur les 'Lazarillo,' " *BH* 66 (1964): 57–64, 257–293.

[27] *Carta VI*, "Del convento de Alcántara," in *Obras Poéticas*, edited by W. Knapp, pp. 306–314.

[28] GP II, 293–296.

Originally the fighting Christian knights had to observe vows of poverty and celibacy, although these rules were modified in the sixteenth century. A member of the order could now marry, and instead of the former "chastity," the knights now pledged themselves to defend the dogma of the Immaculate Conception. They were required to submit annual inventories of all their holdings: this served to pay lip service to the vow of poverty. One rule still valid was that the candidate had to retire temporarily, usually for a year's time, from the world before becoming *comendador*.

Mendoza's retreat, the monastery of San Benito, was located in Alcántara, the place where he now disposed of the revenues of two townships, Justicia and Solana.[29] It was a solitary edifice that crowned the summit of a steep rock above the town. Here, he had to conform to the austere discipline within the cloister and observe silence during the frugal meals he shared with the fraternity. From the height where the monastery stood (it is now in ruins), he could not even see the river Tagus with its Roman bridge below. The desolation of the locality, as his *Carta VI* shows, contributed to his depression. In this atmosphere, evidently, the falseness of his position became clear to him: he had joined a religious community not from religious conviction but for reasons thoroughly secular. For saving his honor as a gentleman among the *vulgo* he despised, he had sacrificed, as his own words seem to reveal, his name as an author and fame in posterity.

The poem, read in its literal sense, appears to be a lament about his inevitable parting from a *señora*. Before pledging himself to the order, he had ambivalent feelings about leaving her; indecision had torn him. Parting from her and from the world had resulted in a diminution, if not a complete annihilation, of his former self. The rapidity of his change of mood, the grief in his soul, overwhelms him. Taking leave from this *señora* has separated what is one; the pain of it kills him. But who is this *señora* whom (in quatrains forty-five and forty-six from the total of sixty-four) he accuses of cruelty?

> . . . And you, seeing me lost,
> Perhaps you do condemn me;

---

[29] Pero Pérez, "La Encomienda de Calatrava," *Revista del Centro de Estudios Extremeños* 6 (1930): 223–241.

> Are you not satisfied ruining me
> But must you step on the fallen?
> You will be cruel with me
> Who never embarrassed you,
> I succumbed to your arm
> Before I saw its strength. . . .[30]

The *señora* here addressed, it becomes clear, may not be a person as understood in the literal sense. Would any writer praise the "strong arm" of his lady? The lines that follow prove that this strong-armed woman is to be understood as a symbol for a quite different concept. She is a superhuman figure of a power overwhelming, destructive, and incompatible with the living; her arm is dangerous:

> It breaks *fueros* and laws,
> Denies friends and relatives,
> Made you kill many people,
> Defeating many kings.
> No one living ever saw you,
> You never threaten idly;
> But who, feeling your hand on him,
> Did ever regret it? . . .[31]

This, then, is no love poem. The *señora* from whom he so unwillingly parted, must be understood as Mendoza's concept of *fame*. What else could possibly be the meaning of the line "No one living ever saw you"?

With this explanation, many things seem to fall into place: the meaning of the poem, the anonymity of Mendoza's "Fábula" of 1553, the nonpublication of his "Cancionero," and perhaps the

---

[30]   (45)
Y tú, que me ves perdido
Quizá eres en condenarme;
¿No te basta derribarme,
Sino pisarme caido?

(46)
Conmigo serás cruel,
Que jamás te dí embarazo,
Y ántes me rendí á tu brazo
Que viese la fuerza dél.
Obras Poéticas, p. 312.

[31]   (47)
Quebranta fueros y leyes,
Niega amigos y parientes,
Que mataste muchas gentes
Y venciste muchos reyes.

(48)
Nadie te vió que viviese,
Nunca amenazaste en vano;
Pero ¿quién sintió tu mano
Que dello se arrepintiese?
Obras Poéticas, p. 312.

anonymity of the *Lazarillo*. No less vain than any other man, he could not have been averse to his own fame. It is inconceivable that he should not have entertained aspirations to the personal fame of an author. In his checkered career, his uncommon literary gifts provided the unity of his life. Some years earlier he had defined the merits of being a poet in his advice to his friend and fellow poet, Juan Boscán, to return to poetry:

> . . . Thousands admire you who listen to your song,
> And the people look up to you,
> Always expecting greater things.
> Go to bed early
> And get up at dawn
> To write what the world so admires. . . .[32]

When he wrote this, still dreaming of his own fame, he was young. But after the Emperor had dismissed him, slighting the many years he had spent in his service, he preferred to fame—a posthumous honor, as he saw it—the nomination to an ecclesiastical dignity usually conferred by the King on those whose services he found worthy of reward. Immortal fame would not have saved him from the actual derision of his former colleagues and rivals who were very much alive.

So he accepted the encomienda. Coincidentally, that August, his "Fábula de Adonis y de Hippómanes" was published not only anonymously but (as it has lately become clear) even against his will. A Venetian publisher appended this poem to a new edition of the works by Boscán and Garcilaso de la Vega by Alonso de Ulloa.[33] Though Mendoza must have learned about this publica-

---

[32] Admírente mil hombres que escuchando
   Tu canto están, y el pueblo que te mira,
   Siempre mayores cosas esperando.
   Con la primera noche te retira,
   Y con la luz dudosa te levanta
   A escribir lo que el mundo tanto admira . . .
Above from *Obras* by Boscán, first published Barcelona, Carles Amoros, 1543. Mendoza's epístola on folio cxxix. Boscán's reply starts fol. cxxxiiii. A Lisbon edition appeared the same year. Also in the edition of 1549, printed in León by Juan Frellon; Mendoza's epistle, pp. 459–473; Boscán's reply, pp. 474–495.

[33] *Las Obras de Boscán*, cf. note 25. About the editor Ulloa, cf. Othón Arróniz, "Alfonso de Ulloa, servidor de don Juan Hurtado de Mendoza, *Bulletin Hispa-*

tion, he never mentioned it or let on that he was the author of the "Fábula," his "most ambitious poetic work"[34] despite the fact that this work was stolen from him by Ulloa who at one time served him in the Venetian embassy. Mendoza took no apparent notice of Ulloa's theft, yet the publication of this poem must have reminded him that a collection of his poetry could have been his path to fame. There was his brainchild now, together with the works of Boscán and Garcilaso—famous poets, but both dead.

About the same time, he must have placed the *Lazarillo de Tormes* with a printer for anonymous publication in Antwerp, the place where he took sail to return to Spain. (There is no evidence so far that someone else stole that work also from him.) It is puzzling that, precisely at the time of his rejection of fame for himself, these two anonymous works should have appeared—the "Fábula" definitely by him, and the *Lazarillo*, which was declared to be by him about thirty years after his death (1607).

It might be said that the simultaneous appearance of two anonymous works at that particular time of Mendoza's renunciation was a mere coincidence. But the last lines of *Carta VI* contain a new metaphor, indicating that he is distinctly speaking of two sacrifices:

> . . . by staying here I pay
> For the madness of leaving,
> And I persist in regretting
> What I did and am not doing.
> Time and fortune will pass
> And I will always remain quiet;
> You will know late or soon,
> That my will is firm,
> And that having served you
> By fate and by free will,

---

nique 70, nos. 3–4 (1968): 437–457. Arróniz recently discovered that this well-known mediator between Spanish and Italian literatures was actually a scoundrel, acting in his youth for the French while serving both Mendoza in the last years of his Venetian embassy and subsequently also Mendoza's cousin and successor in that post. Although Arróniz does not mention this poem, one can deduce from the incidents he tells of Ulloa's life, that Ulloa, while still in Mendoza's house, must have got hold easily of the ambassador's poetry, but when he published this piece, he was out of Mendoza's reach.

[34] Batchelor, ed., *A ti, Doña Marina*, p. 39.

Twice I came to the same river
And did not drink. [italics added][35]

The image of the "river" might be another figure of fame, perhaps a symbol for literature. Twice, says Mendoza, he had come close to this river but did not drink from it. Twice, he had come close to literary fame, but had renounced it. He did so with infinite regret, but, as he believes, by his "free will" (*albedrío*)—although his will was conditioned by his necessity to be considered an honorable man. And to the loss of posterity, he kept the promise made here: "I will always remain quiet," meaning, he would hold to his vow of never publishing, although, as the *Carta VI* itself shows, he continued to write.

In his own words, then, he gave the key to the mystery of why and how he renounced fame. But at the same time, complex personality that he was, he could not refrain from telling the world of his sacrifice. Since he was a man of action at least as much as he was one of contemplation, it is not surprising that he also used the first occasion of being called to duty in the King's service to leave the surroundings that so utterly depressed him. After no more than eight or ten weeks of his year of probation had passed, he returned to the world, but he never returned to his quest for fame through popular literature. His noble effort of historiography, the *Guerra de Granada*, written almost twenty years later (and now almost the only work by which he is remembered), transcends that category.

[35]

(61)
Tal me veo en tal lugar,
Y tal de tí me aparté;
Allá me lleva la fe,
Detiéneme acá el pesar.
(62)
Mas con estar aquí pago
La locura del partirme,
Y páro en arrepentirme
Por lo que hice y no hago.

(63)
Pasen el tiempo y fortuna,
Que yo siempre estaré quedo;
Conocerás tarde ó cedo,
Que mi voluntad es una,
(64)
Y que habiéndote servido
Por hado y por albedrío,
Dos veces al mismo rio
He venido y no he bebido.
Obras Poéticas, p. 314.

15. A SPLENDID ERA ENDS,
1554–1559

I give thanks to God that He made me
decide to return to port.

Don Diego[1]

Outfitter of Philip's Armadas

In February, 1554, Don Bernardino de Mendoza was appointed Provider of the fleet that was to bring Prince Philip to England for his wedding and was then to continue its journey to the Netherlands, carrying army reinforcements to the Emperor. But Don Bernardino, who was "tired, old, and worn out," called upon Don Diego to assist him.[2] This gave Don Diego the opportunity to leave the monastery earlier than he had expected, yet in good grace. Of the bestowment of his *hábito* he was now assured.[3] "Service to the king," at any rate, was the only excuse—he was to use it also in the future to obtain release from his obligation of residence.[4]

[1] Mendoza to Doña Juana, September 20, 1557, from "Artamua" (Dartmouth), GP II, 325–327.

[2] Arras to Don Bernardino de Mendoza, February 20, 1554, Bibl. Pal., Rose-file.

[3] Arras to Mendoza, March 12, 1554, ibid.

[4] Pero Pérez, "La Encomienda de Calatrava," *RCEE* 4: 235; ". . . he sido informado que después que sois comendador de la dicha Encomienda no habeis residido en ella . . ."

Philip tarried in Spain until his sister Doña Juana, recently widowed of the heir of Portugal, was able to come to take over the regency of the Spanish kingdoms. (One of the dutiful Habsburg women, the young dowager princess had to leave behind her baby, now the heir of the Portuguese crown, born after the death of his father. She never saw her son again.)[5] Another month went by while the entire fleet of a hundred ships lay in La Coruña, waiting for good weather. The fleet sailed on July 13.[6]

It is not clear whether Don Diego went along. In the list of gentlemen accompanying the Prince—now King of Naples—there is mention of a Señor Don Diego Hurtado de Mendoza, whose escort of pages were sumptuously clothed in "silk of four colors, tawny and white and red and black."[7] But by now he had a number of eminent adult namesakes; it is impossible to claim that single Don Diego as ours. If he went, we hear nothing of his having been in England this time. He was not reported to have been back in Brussels, either, before the end of 1557. There is no news of any sort about him until he appears in Valladolid on April 18, 1556,[8] while the King was still in Flanders. Almost two years lack any documentation, as did the years of his youth, and those when he stayed so close to the Emperor that there was no official correspondence from him.

A remark of Arras in 1558—that he gave Don Diego the same room (in Brussels) that he had had when he came from Rome in 1553—lets us infer that he had been absent from Brussels in the

---

[5] Sebastian (1554–1578), who became King of Portugal at the age of three; he was killed in battle in Africa.

[6] The fact that Mendoza did the work for this armada has been heretofore unknown. But on October 25, 1567, working on his third armada for Philip, he wrote to Eraso about the rates of pay for enlisted men: "Tambien pretenden que las raciones no se les paguen respectivamente con el sueldo sino por entero y no tienen razon porque el que gana medio sueldo ha de ganar media raçion y entera el que gana entero. Yo lo he visto y hecho muchos años a en lo primero y sigundo . . ." ("This I have seen and done myself years ago, in the first and second [armadas]"), Mendoza to Eraso, Arch. Sim., Est., leg. 149, folio 299. He wrote to Philip II the same day, recalling even the armada of Tunis in the same connection; ibid., folio 298. On September 25, again to Philip II, he wrote that he was solving the problems by sending for the budgets of the years 1554 and 1557; ibid., folio 296. Sailing date of July 13, 1554, in *DIE* I, 564.

[7] Cf. Andrés Muñoz, *Viaje de Felipe II a Inglaterra*, p. 26.

[8] GP II, 297.

interim.[9] Most likely he was all the time in Spain. He may have returned to the cloister once his naval service was finished. But how long could he have stayed in that depressing environment? Or he might have lived the life he affected so much to prefer, "throwing his books about at his pleasure,"[10] and pursuing his gentlemanly hobbies in his own estates. If he did so, surely he would have written something, but on account of his break with "fame," whatever he might have composed during that time must be considered lost.

If he attended Philip's wedding, he must have returned to Spain on his own, and so far as we know now, with the exception of the brief notice that has him in Valladolid on April 18, 1556 (as *comendador de las Casas de Badajoz*), he reappears only in 1557. In April of that year, the Princess-Regent named him *proveedor general de la Armada Real de Laredo*, the fleet that was to assist Philip in his last, and victorious, war with Henri II.[11]

During the years from 1554 to 1557, the transition from Charles V's collapsing "Imperial" world empire to Philip's stable Spanish "royal" empire became complete. After the Emperor's abdication, the Habsburg dynasty split into two sub-branches, Austrian-Imperial (under Ferdinand, the former "King of the Romans," successor to Charles V as German Emperor) and Spanish-Royal. With a supreme effort that augured well for the stability of the new reign of Philip II, the Spaniards were finally on the way to victory from "the War" with France in the battle of St. Quentin on August 10, 1557. Also such small-scale settlements took place as Philip's cession of the finally beaten Republic of Siena to Duke Cosimo I, and his restitution of Piombino to Jacopo VI d'Appiano, the young lord formerly despoiled of the principality.[12]

[9] Arras to Vargas, from Brussels, February 6, 1558, Bibl. Pal., Rose-file.
[10] Arrojaré mis libros por el suelo,
 abriré o cerraré aquel que me plaze,
 y andaré salpicando, como suelo,
 por la vida que más me satisfaze.
 from "Epístola a Don Luis de Áuila," in C. Malcolm
 Batchelor, ed., *A tí, Doña Marina*, p. 170.
[11] GP II, 298, 299.
[12] Philip II to Iacopo Sexto, in London, May 29, 1557, Arch. Sim., Est., leg. 1049, folio 82.

Early in 1557, Philip II sent Ruy Gómez de Silva to Spain to organize that country's assistance in the new war effort against the French.[13] It was gratifying to Don Diego that the new King of Spain needed his expertise. That he was entrusted again with outfitting an armada has been interpreted as an inferior place in the Spanish administration, somewhat unworthy of the erstwhile ambassador in Rome.[14] But this explanation is incorrect. It was no diminution in rank to follow his much-honored brother Don Bernardino in the same position. The importance of this task can be gauged from the speculations about the reasons for the defeat of the great armada in 1588, which is often blamed on the fact that Medina-Sidonia, the great nobleman then in charge of the fleet, had no sea experience. The Mendozas from Granada had a special nautical know-how, as well as the other qualifications needed.

Don Diego, besides showing his experience as sea captain, acted also as an army general and absolute commander, statistician, minister of economy, and what not else. His office brought with it unlimited authority over men and property. He requisitioned supplies from all appropriate regions in Spain; he amassed ships and drafted and hired the men. It was in his power to prosecute, judge, and punish criminal offenses in connection with the armadas, and he went so far as to seize the moneybags of the Messieurs Schetz, agents of the Queen of Hungary, which were "standing around idly" while he had nothing to pay the men (government funds, as usual, were insufficient and delayed).[15]

He had to provision not only the vessels for many future months (thinking, for instance, of such items as casks of seasoned wood for drinking water, the salting of meat, requisitioning grape harvests for his supplies of wine), but also the poor villages and townships on the routes of march on which enlisted men were pushing their way through Spain to join the Armadas—lest the people be exposed to sacking and looting. At the same time, the vessels of grandees who brought the members of their own Houses, ostentatiously equipped with their precious mounts, were to be outfitted in style.

[13] Michiel Swian to the Doge from London, June 8, 1557, pp. 1146–1148, *Cal. St. P.*, Venetian, vol. 6, part 2, 1557.
[14] GP II, 297–327.
[15] GP II, 316.

To find room for the transport of three hundred horses, moneybags, and four thousand to six thousand men, Don Diego was empowered even to seize the merchant fleet from the hands of the wool traders and to have them put their wares ashore and empty their sacks— all with the promise of future indemnification. (As always, preparation for war went on over the hurts and spoils of the population.) It was also in Don Diego's power to appoint all high officials, although this took the form of recommendations to the Princess-Regent. Doña Juana, the twenty-two–year–old dowager, presumably raised no difficulties about approving his requests.

Such activity kept him in the midst of pulsating life. This was, in truth, just as congenial to him as study or high diplomacy, and probably much more so than his temporary cell in the monastery. Besides, not seeking fame or money for himself (he drew no salary or compensation for his own expenses),[16] this was merely a voluntary service, a token of Mendoza's loyalty to his master. Philosopher though he was, he did not dislike his dictatorial powers, requesting the highest officials to do what he ordered "without talking back, since I have known for many years how to order what is necessary."[17]

The magnitude of the job can be seen by the amount of money spent on it, two million ducats together with the English contribution, even though the allotted funds came trickling in by and by, and not entirely. The segment of the fleet that he took to England himself comprised twenty-five big vessels, seven of them armed with bronze artillery, carrying stabling for horse, victuals, ten companies of soldiers, rowers (there is no word of galley slaves), and also fifteen or sixteen smaller craft.[18] He went along on the last segment. After waiting many weeks for suitable weather, the fleet weighed anchor on September 1. Ruy Gómez de Silva had left the day before; he and Mendoza were to go and assist Queen Mary with the contribution she was making in her husband's war on the Continent.

---

[16] From papers "after Mendoza's death," December 6, 1576, Arch. Sim.. Rose-file.

[17] ". . . sin andar replicando porque ha muchos años que sé mandar lo que es menester . . . ," GP II, 306.

[18] GP II, 323.

On the way to England occurred one of the many instances in which Don Diego must have felt that his life was charmed. He had been in danger many times, in battles, assassination attempts, epidemics, and crossings, but this was perhaps the closest he came to disaster. Just before Dartmouth they ran into heavy weather. Mendoza wrote to the Princess-Regent:

Standing out to sea something like three leagues, it seemed to me, on the flagship, that the wind turned south, which, on this coast, means contrary wind. Against the opinion of mariners and pilots, I ordered a return to port. I did not wish to go forth to where we were standing before, although they tried to persuade me to do so, but it seemed very dangerous to me. When I sent word to lower the chain, and two pieces of it had been dropped, those on land did not wish to do it. I arrived with the flagship and found it still not lowered, running great danger of capsizing. I was forced to run aground. I ordered a vessel of Juan de Aguirre to cut the cables with all the sails on one side, and Pero Menéndez on the other. This opened it. It was all done so fast that the fleet could enter and we were able to drop anchor. Only two vessels were so foolish as to wish to stay behind, one at the mouth of the harbor, the other within.

Around ten o'clock at night the wind became so wild that several vessels tore loose from their anchorage and collided. By morning the storm was so heavy within port that five vessels capsized; two of them suffered no damage; a third was thrown straight back on land as though it were set on blocks—by means of a ditch it can be set afloat again. The other two were those further out near the mouth; on one of them was the contingent of Don Suero de Quiñones, one of the best of the armada; and the other was a medium-sized vessel with the contingent of a Captain Silvestre—they capsized and were lost. They carried thirty-six boxes of money, twenty-seven of which have been salvaged. We lost 130 men who dared to jump in because they knew how to swim.

I give thanks to God [he continues after more details] that He made me decide to return to port, because had we gone ahead, the entire fleet would have been lost, as were three or four vessels near here. Through the good fortune of His Majesty and Your Highness, the armada is saved; to my disgrace these two vessels were lost, although the damage is almost exclusively the Fuggers'.[19]

Within the following ten days he and Ruy Gómez went together

[19] GP II, 325–327.

to greet the Queen. (As it happened, Philip's men saw Mary after she had seen her husband for the last time. Philip had sailed from her in July, never to return.) Before September 30, Don Diego crossed from Dover to Calais.[20] Presumably he joined the King in his headquarters behind the army lines. He returned with the royal court afterward to Brussels, where he was again Arras' honored guest.

Changes in the Latter 1550s

Mendoza's mood of resignation, of acquiescence to forsaking fame, was profoundly jolted once he was again living in close touch with the court in Brussels. To his great annoyance he was now called on to account for every escudo spent in the enterprise of Siena—a matter he had considered closed when his accounts with the Emperor had been cleared five years back. And that was not the only instance forcing him to dwell on painful memories. In the spring of 1558, the French armies, in a last spurt of effort, succeeded in taking Calais from the English and were approaching Brussels under none other than Marshal de Termes, Mendoza's former antagonist, his first successor in the government ruling Siena, who had been the French ambassador in Rome. For a time it seemed that Termes might defeat the Spaniards again.

Yet the wheel turned in the Spaniards' favor: Don Diego's rival lost the battle on the beach of Gravelines (July 13, 1558), a victory toward which Mendoza's fleet of Guipuzcoan vessels, in conjunction with the English, had greatly contributed.[21] Termes himself was taken prisoner by the Count of Egmont, and after this decisive French defeat, peace was not far away.

With the old bitterness, something of Mendoza's old ambition seems to have reawakened. His attendance at court was conducive to it. He was on intimate terms with Philip II's close adviser Ruy Gómez, not to speak of Arras, Mendoza's best friend, who still played an important official role as chief architect of the Peace of Cateau-Cambrésis. (This agreement of 1559 would set the fate of Europe for decades to come.) In the knowledge of recently having

[20] Mendoza to Philip II, September 30, 1557, *Cal. St. P. Spanish*, vol. 13, 1554–58, no. 344.

[21] Pedro Aguado Bleye, *Manual de Historia de España*, II, 565.

done good services himself, and in a generally more joyful atmosphere with the approaching peace settlement, Don Diego saw himself restored to favor, yet without a high office in the new government that would be commensurate with this royal favor.

Notwithstanding his fine resolutions and resignations of the time when he had first left the world temporarily, Mendoza and his friends now apparently regretted that he did not belong to the group of high policy makers. One of his former secretaries in Rome, Pedro Ximénez, wrote to Arras: "I will never be happy until I hear that Don Diego has been properly employed, and employed as he deserves."[22] At around the same time, the Venetian ambassador in Brussels spread the word that "Don Diego, heretofore ambassador at Venice, . . . has now risen in repute, it being reported that the King will make him his maggiordomo."[23]

But if Don Diego's expectations rose once more, only to be disappointed, his reserves of moral strength saved him from despair. He tried to satisfy the royal accountants in Ghent, giving meticulous information, doing his best to recall the expenses of the Sienese fortress, brick by vanished brick. But he succeeded only in delaying, not closing, the uncomfortable investigations. He continued his affability at court, meanwhile living his preferred life with books and studies in Arras' best guest room.[24] On his galleys he had brought over nine Spanish horses and six steeds, most of them probably intended as gifts, not only for his host, but also for friends who had entertained him in former years, one of them the Cardinal of Trent, to whom he sent a magnificent horse.[25]

Now at the age of fifty-four or fifty-five, his eyesight was troubling him, and he appropriated the eyeglasses that the present Spanish ambassador to Venice kept sending to Arras, much as once upon a time, when he needed no glasses himself, he used to send spectacles to Cobos.[26] The situation seemed to repeat itself: Cobos,

[22] Ximénez to Arras, December 31, 1558, Bibl. Pal., Rose-file.

[23] Tiepolo to Doge and Senate, March 9, 1559, *Cal. St. P.* Venice, VIII, no. 38.

[24] Arras to Vargas, May 2, 1558, from Valenciennes, Bibl. Pal., Rose-file.

[25] Mendoza to Juan Vázquez de Molina, July 14, 1557, Arch. Sim., Est., leg. 1049, folio 30. Cardinal of Trent to Arras, January 7, 1558, Bibl. Nac., Madrid, Rose-file.

[26] *AC*, pp. 41, 42, 43, 44.

his former patron, husband of a Mendoza, had once been his best avenue to the Emperor. Now, Ruy Gómez, in a similar position, married to an even closer cousin of Don Diego, was also devoted to him. Gómez, Philip II's alter ego, was the grandson of the Portuguese doctor who had accompanied Empress Isabel to Spain. His wife was Doña Ana de Mendoza, great-granddaughter of the Grand Cardinal Mendoza. (She was later the famous Princess Eboli, with the dark patch over her right eye and dark secrets in her widowed life.) Since her marriage with Ruy Gómez had been contracted in 1553 (it was not consummated before 1559, when Gómez returned to Spain with the King), when Doña Ana was only thirteen, and when Don Diego, always fertile in ideas, was back at court, it is not improbable that this union was his idea, too. Or perhaps Gómez remained his friend simply because they were people who understood each other. Like Cobos and Arras, Ruy Gómez was a smooth and affable character, the mediating type, the only kind of man with whom Don Diego, often as harsh and blunt as the monarchs themselves, could sustain long friendships. But Don Diego had been much younger than Cobos. Now, his patrons Gómez and Arras were both his juniors, as was the King himself.

Ironically, all the futile tasks in which Mendoza had expended the best years of his career during the time of Charles V were now being accomplished without him. Philip II succeeded where the Emperor had failed. At last, for example, the French were turned out of Italy; the Farneses were attached firmly to the Spanish side; Siena, though ceded to Cosimo, had come to the Duke of Florence only after he had first been used by the Spaniards, having helped them reconquer Siena from the French (and besides, Philip remained, nominally, "suzerain" and even "vicar" over the one-time republic). But Spanish success had come despite Don Diego's unhappy efforts in the same direction. His past, however it was to be explained and excused, was still against him. Gómez was unable, even if he was perhaps willing, to effect a new promotion to high office in the foreign service for him.

Together with Don Diego's personal importance, the influence of his immediate family was also decreasing. When Mendoza had first been reunited in Spain with his brothers Don Luis and Don

Bernardino in the autumn of 1553, they were saddened by the belatedly arriving news that Don Antonio had died a year earlier,
shortly after he had gone as Viceroy to Peru. Closest to Don Diego
as always was Don Bernardino, whose guest he then was for an
indefinite time. Now Don Bernardino had died, in September,
1557, in consequence of his exertions in the battle of St. Quentin;
also Don Diego's assistant in Venice, his nephew Don Iñigo, son
of the late Don Antonio, fell in that battle. Don Bernardino seems
to have been the best loved of the brothers. He was the one with
whom Don Diego had contact most frequently. Don Bernardino
had been useful also to Don Antonio in Mexico; a close adviser to
Philip II, he became a member of the highest council of Spain, that
of Castile, in time to protect Don Antonio; the *visita* from Castile
had been making vast efforts to remove the Viceroy from his position.[27] (Don Bernardino's widow, Doña Elvira de Carrillo, was to
became the governess of Philip II's daughters.) Now Don Luis, the
oldest, and Don Diego, always remote from each other, were the
only brothers left.

Not long after the King had condoled with the Mendozas, Philip
II was again a chief mourner himself: the Emperor died in Yuste
on September 21, 1558, and Philip's wife Mary Tudor on November 17. By this time the peace negotiations were in progress, and
very shortly after the Peace of Cateau-Cambrésis was concluded
(April 1, 1559), the King and his court returned to Spain—the
famous return that dramatically underlined the start of the reign of
Philip as King of Spain and the Spanish-centered empire. Philip
II landed in Laredo on September 8,[28] and if Don Diego's arrival
was not simultaneous, it could not have been much earlier or later.
While Mendoza was still at Brussels, Grand Inquisitor Fernando
de Valdés had sent him a letter, summoning him for an interview.
Accordingly, in September, 1559, soon after he arrived with the
King and the court in Valladolid, Don Diego appeared before the
Inquisition.[29]

[27] Arthur Scott Aiton, *Antonio de Mendoza*, p. 166.
[28] Braudel, *La Mediterranée*, p. 776, nn. 1 and 2.
[29] J. A. Llorente, *Historia crítica de la Inquisición de España*, VII, 80; also
José Luis G. Novalin, *El inquisidor general Fernando de Valdés*, p. 344.

The Carranza Case

The profound change in the aspect of Spain after Philip's return as King had long been in preparation. Perhaps the situation had not been much different when Don Diego left the country with his armada two years before, or even when Philip went in 1554 into the turbulent half decade that was to keep him away. Yet 1559 was obviously the turning point. This fact could not be underlined more appropriately than by the great *auto de fé* that Valladolid celebrated hardly four weeks after the new King's arrival. This lit the flame of the successful Counter Reformation, whose patron was Philip II. And even before that event, only twenty days after his return, Don Diego went before the Inquisition—as a witness only, it is true, but never before had the Holy Office reached out toward him in any way.

In the first quarter of the century, a man like Don Diego had been able to grow up with an independent spirit; in the second quarter, when internal policies in Spain were tolerantly guided by Cobos, people still managed to live according to their own inclinations. The Grand Inquisitor himself, Don Alfonso Manrique, was an "Erasmian," and so was the primate of Spain, Cardinal Juan Tavera, Archbishop of Toledo. In the hands of Erasmian humanists, the Inquisition spared the lives of many educated people. A certain spiritual liberty still allowed men and women to question the validity of established religious practices and argue for the renewal of Catholicism, a reform from within. Not only did they dare to fight for individual liberty, but they also held illusions that their efforts could be successful—a sign that the atmosphere around them could not have been particularly oppressive.

But in 1546 Tavera was succeeded by Juan Siliceo, the first tutor of Philip II, who had been lax in teaching his pupil much of anything except ecclesiastical Latin, but who was a furious hunter of *conversos* (evidently the chief carriers of doubt and unsettling ideas), whom he set out to eliminate from positions in the Church. Also, Grand Inquisitor Manrique, in 1547, had been succeeded by Fernando de Valdés, a persecutor of sinister reputation. Cobos, ailing in 1546, died in 1547, and with this change of the principal actors in Castile, the stage was set for a new act in the religious and political tragedy. The "splendid" former period was at an end.

Other factors besides these few personalities had helped in the corrosion. The chief reason for the former relative freedom of conscience in Spain was not so much the presence of more lenient officials as the fact that the Emperor was almost continually absent. Perhaps, had he established himself there with any degree of permanence, as Philip II was to do, he also would have sanctioned and furthered the trend toward absolute intolerance. But while his absence was beneficial for his mother's country in one respect, it was harmful in others. Charles V made Spain pay for his military adventures elsewhere; at his abdication he left Spain with a national debt of twenty million ducats.[30]

There was, during that splendid period, a commercial boom from trade with the Atlantic area, with rising salaries and even more stiffly rising prices. But the boom was deceptive because Spain was improvidently exporting its raw materials; wool, silk, iron, leather, left the country, returning to it in a manufactured state with prices ten to a hundred times higher.[31] Added to this unfavorable trade balance was the fact that most banking, taken from the hands of Spanish Jews or Marranos, came into the hands of foreigners, Germans and Italians, who acted in the interests of banking houses in their home countries. Also, through the expulsion and persecution of the Jews, the Moors, as well as the Marranos and Moriscos—those of whom the commercial class was predominantly composed—Spain was increasingly feeling the lack of commercial knowhow.

While financial and commercial changes were gradual, the change in the aims of the Holy Office was abrupt, as was clear with the appointment of new men bent on persecution. In many cases, an accused person left alive in the splendid period was condemned to death immediately afterwards. If the victim had already died of natural causes, the persecutors dug up his body, burned that, and confiscated his property—the real reason for the majority of the persecutions. This happened, for example, to a hapless preacher, Juan Gil, a great favorite of the Emperor. Fray Domingo de Soto,

[30] Igual Ubeda, *La España del siglo XVI*, p. 52.
[31] Ramón Carande, *Carlos V y sus banqueros*, p. 125.

Mendoza's old antagonist but supposedly a friend whom the accused preacher trusted, was instrumental in condemning Juan Gil for alleged heretical tendencies.[32] Though Juan Gil ("Doctor Egidio") was still alive in 1553 when Don Diego returned to Spain for the first time, and in 1555 was even released after several years of captivity by the Inquisition, his case showed the trend of the times. As late as 1548, in Rome, Mendoza had described the Spanish way of living with a diversity of beliefs as something exemplary for the Germans to follow. But from that time on, Spain renewed its persecuting fervor. It had ebbed with the life of Queen Isabel. Now Spain was to do away with any still existing diversity of origin, belief, or opinion.

The letter from the Inquisition invited Don Diego to testify in the process of the Archbishop of Toledo, Fray Bartolomé Carranza de Miranda. Fernando de Valdés, the Grand Inquisitor, had just then successfully transgressed the usual power of the Holy Office in prosecuting a bishop who did not belong under his jurisdiction but only under that of the Pope.[33] He arrested Carranza on August 22, 1559, precipitating this unprecedented action so that he could present the King on his impending arrival with a *fait accompli*. Imprisoned on insufficient grounds as a suspected heretic, that highest Church official of Spain was to endure seventeen years of imprisonment only to be finally absolved, with qualifications. He survived his freedom for no more than two weeks.[34] While the original motive behind Valdés' persecution may have been his personal envy of Carranza's promotion to the see of Toledo (Valdés was Archbishop of Seville),[35] the affair became a test case in the

---

[32] See Adolfo de Castro y Rossi, *Historia de los Protestantes Españoles*, III, case of Juan Gil; also Novalin, *El inquisidor*, pp. 177–184.

[33] Novalin, *El inquisidor*, pp. 345–346, points out that Pope Paul IV, in audiences with Valdés' agent, his nephew Alvaro de Valdés, showed himself sympathetic to the Spanish inquisitor's demands, but before receiving his nephew's report, Valdés had arrested the Archbishop of Toledo anyway, and meanwhile the Pope died.

[34] An excellent, concise account of the Inquisition, including the Carranza case, is in J. H. Elliott, *Imperial Spain*, pp. 204–223.

[35] Novalin, *El inquisidor*, pp. 319–323, doubts that envy or revenge was Valdés' motive, suggesting that Carranza was headed for an inevitable clash with the Holy Office, with or without Valdés.

struggle of power between the Spanish monarchy against the papacy (with implications beyond the scope of Mendoza's life).

To build a case against the Archbishop of Toledo, the inquisitors contacted everyone known to have met Carranza during the sessions of the Council of Trent in 1545–1546. Carranza had been accused of having favored the arguments of the Lutherans in the matter of the sacrament of the Mass, and he was supposed to have said, in the presence of many members of the Council, *Ego haereo certe* ("I am certainly a heretic").[36] If these words could be proven, apparently the accused would be doomed. The Holy Office, needing corroboration from witnesses for this deposition, had waited for Mendoza's arrival from Flanders to summon him for this purpose. In the first "conversation" Mendoza had with the Inquisitor Riego on September 28, 1559, he said he could not remember that such a dispute had taken place in his presence but promised to search his own memory. Urged to name other possible witnesses, he obliged with the names of Dr. Alfonso Zorrilla, who had represented him in Trent during his absence, and the lawyer Dr. Velasco. The Inquisitor extracted from Mendoza his personal opinion that he did not hold the Archbishop of Toledo to be a good Christian, nor did he approve of his Catechism.[37]

At this first interrogation, Mendoza seems to have said as little as he possibly could get away with; his admission that Carranza did not seem a good Catholic to him may not have been volunteered, but, seeing that the inquisitor wished to hear just that, he could not deny it under oath. As we know, he had no sympathy for the Lutheran interference with Catholic tradition. He sincerely deplored any signs of imprudence in these matters. A trace of fanaticism, or of lack of clarity, of ambiguity in expression, were distasteful to Don Diego; they disqualified anyone from his concept of being a "good" Catholic, that is, a practical man who helped preserve the unity of the Church. And Carranza's faults that had brought him into trouble were a certain fuzziness of concept in his sermons and writings; besides, his unruly, egocentric, over-assertive personality had made him many enemies.

---

[36] Fray Bartolomé Carranza, *Documentos Históricos*, II, edited by J. Ignacio Tellechea Idiagoras, in *Archivo Documental Español* 19: 105.

[37] Ibid.

In fact, only two or three days before Mendoza's first interview, he was informed that Carranza had calumniated *him*.[38] The Archbishop enjoyed the privilege, in contrast to the average victim of the Inquisition, of learning the names of the witnesses; on being told that Mendoza was called in to testify, he affirmed having heard the former ambassador say things against religion himself (presumably at Trent). In the accused's mind must have lingered Mendoza's defense of Averroës for the sake of argument. So dangerous was the atmosphere that a chance remark like that, uttered in anger, might bring catastrophe on anyone. Despite Carranza's offense against him, it does not seem that Mendoza joined the persecutors in harming the accused, although his testimony sounds like slander of an innocent man. Knowing that not only the Archbishop's fate but possibly his own was in the balance, Don Diego would have been unwise to contradict their opinion of the victim, yet he nevertheless did not give the Inquisitors any shred of evidence they could use to convict him.

Only ten days later, Mendoza assisted at the great feast that these new scourges of Spain had especially prepared in celebration of the King's arrival. On October 8, Philip II and his entire court were regaled with the *auto de fé* of thirteen condemned "heretics" whose execution had been purposely delayed until that day so that the young monarch could witness the bonfire of their bodies. Among the spectators, Mendoza was understandably occupied with thoughts of his own recent testimony and that which he was required to give at his second appearance, scheduled for October 20. He heard one of the condemned, Fray Domingo de Rojas, say on the scaffold that the doctrine he had held was not his own but had come from others; just at this point the victim was "silenced."

This caused Mendoza to think and even to believe that, among the "others," Fray Bartolomé de Miranda might have been responsible for this victim's errors.[39] Yet he did not say so at his second interview, but only reaffirmed his criticism of Carranza's book.[40] He emphasized that, while in Brussels, he had advised the Duke of Arcos and Don Fernando Carrillo to get rid of this catechism that contained bad things. He also named the men Carranza had be-

---

[38] Ibid., p. 220.   [39] Ibid.
[40] Ibid., p. 122.

friended while in Italy, most of them followers of Juan Valdés. That he named all those names for his own protection, rather than to incriminate the accused, seems fairly obvious. The inquisitors knew Carranza's writings; if Mendoza shared this disapproval of them, this made himself look good without adding anything to the evidence. The men he named were either dead or in Italy.

We have no documents for the intervening two years, but on November 5, 1561, in Madrid, Mendoza was cited before the Archbishop of Santiago. He repeated his opinion that he did not think Carranza was a good Christian, and now told of his thoughts during the *auto de fé*. Asked if he hated thé accused Archbishop, Mendoza denied being his enemy, although he admitted that at his first visit he had been somewhat angry with him for having calumniated him, but that this would not prevent him from telling nothing but the truth, nor one word more.[41] Despite the Holy Office's keeping an eye on him over the years (he was called in for testimony again on June 5, 1562[42]), it appears that Mendoza had not helped the persecutors' case one bit. As Llorente says, "we must not forget that Don Diego de Mendoza is an extraordinary witness, giving no particular facts to substantiate anything."[43]

Doctor Zorrilla, the witness Mendoza had recommended, also denied having heard Carranza confess to being a "heretic." Even so, Mendoza's actual words, said under oath and in the presence of the most dangerous men in Spain, seem to disclose a certain eagerness to cooperate with the Inquisition: probably they were calculated to this effect. All the subtlety at his command was necessary to protect himself, especially since his relations with both the persecutor and the persecuted were extraordinarily complex.

Valdés had formerly been one of Cobos' friends; through his old patron's efforts, Don Diego since 1546 was the recipient of an annual stipend of fifteen hundred escudos from Valdés' archbishopric of Seville.[44] This suggests that there was no enmity between them at the time. In 1551, in fact, Mendoza recommended Valdés to the Emperor as a potential candidate for the cardinalate.[45] On the oth-

[41] Ibid., p. 220.
[42] *DIE* 5: 423, 424.
[43] Llorente, *Historia crítica*, VII, 83.
[44] Mocenigo, August 6, 1546, *Ven. Dep.* I, 614.
[45] Novalin, *El inquisidor*, p. 258.

er hand, in 1555, Valdés had tried to have arrested for heresy Don Diego's most prominent nephew, Don Iñigo López de Mendoza, then the fourth Count of Tendilla, *alcaide* of the Alhambra, because of steps the Count had taken to protect the Moriscos. And at that time Carranza, not yet under any indictment, had enthusiastically supported Valdés in his design.[46] Understandably, whatever sympathy Don Diego might have felt for Valdés until then would now have cooled, not to speak of his already low esteem for Carranza. The Inquisitor had been unable to proceed with his plan against the *alcaide*, however. The Mendozas had powerful friends at court, and Count Iñigo's father, Don Luis, second Marquis of Mondéjar, was the President of the Royal Council of Castile (equivalent to Chief Justice of the secular power).

Yet being a Mendoza was not in itself enough of a protection under all circumstances. If any witness ever showed himself uncooperative in the interrogation, what would his fate have been? Mendoza's behavior, obviously, was the only action he could have taken to turn suspicion away from himself without harming others. The "sage"[47] at court was simply alert to the fact that Carranza had incautiously exposed himself to danger. He was able to foresee how the trap would close on the unwary, just as he could foretell a storm at sea. This does not mean that he was on the side of the hunter.

Despite Mendoza's caution, it seems astonishing that he himself, a man who so easily made enemies, should have stayed clear of persecution. But fortunately for him at such a time, he now had no outstanding position that rivals might covet. And, besides, the Inquisition had different targets. Their nets were not equipped for so big a fish as a "philosopher" like Don Diego. Mendoza was no preacher; he would not try to change established doctrine. People who did that were the foremost victims in the time of Inquisitor Valdés. Nor had he been an "Erasmian," or a "Judaizer," or a "relapsed" Muslim. If it had ever come to analyzing his knowledge of heterodox philosophies, his expertise in all doctrines, his power of argumentation would have extricated him. Besides, his former

[46] The Tendilla incident (Novalin, *El inquisidor*, pp. 216–220) will be discussed in chapter 17.

[47] "el Sabio," L. Cabrera de Córdoba, *Historia de Felipe segundo, Rey de España*, p. 356.

antagonist in the matter of Averroës, Fray Domingo de Soto, who years before had helped deliver Doctor Egidio (Juan Gil) to the Holy Office, was now under prosecution himself.[48] De Soto had been a close friend of Carranza, in whose company he had come to Trent, and his testimony about the suspected catechism of the Archbishop had been so ambiguous as to catch him in contradictions, drawing suspicion upon himself, the most conservative of conservatives. De Soto died in September 1560, before they got as far as arresting him.

Many of us have lived in a similar climate. A growing constriction of accustomed freedoms is nothing new to the twentieth century. But historians of the nineteenth century (whose work, chiefly, has made us familiar with the sixteenth century in Spain), who lived and died in the illusion of a more rational world, were unable to imagine fully the apprehension, disgust, and sorrow that Don Diego and the remaining humanists must have felt. This specific period of terror lasted until 1566. Then Valdés, eighty-three and senile, was made to resign (he would live two more years). Into his awesome position stepped Diego de Espinosa (1502–1572), a friend and follower of Ruy Gómez—hence also of Mendoza. Espinosa's regime as Grand Inquisitor was less fertile in persecution and *autos de fé*, but he is held responsible for Philip II's increased oppression of the Moriscos of Granada and the ensuing civil war.

[48] Llorente, *Historia crítica*, V, 112, 113. Novalin, *El inquisidor*, discusses the incipient divergences between Valdés and De Soto on pp. 335–342.

16. AT THE COURT OF PHILIP II, 1559–1568

I will live my life without passion,
Far from disorder and turbulence,
Serving the King at my pleasure.
                    Don Diego[1]

The Old Bachelor

FROM THE END OF 1559 on, Don Diego's time for the next three or four months was taken up with idle ceremonies. The new bride of Philip II, the fourteen-year-old Elizabeth of Valois, daughter of Henri II, "Isabel of the Peace," was arriving from France. Perhaps to remind the King of the greatness of the House of Mendoza, the fourth Duke of Infantado, head of the clan, took it upon himself to escort her into Spain from the valley of Ronces-vaux, near the border.[2] The occasion became a resplendent reunion of the entire family, who traveled as guests of the Duke (he spent a thousand escudos per day), escorted by four thousand cavalry.

The spiritual head of the company, Cardinal Mendoza, Archbishop of Burgos (Francisco de Mendoza y Bobadilla, the "Coria" of the time of Paul III), conducted the marriage service in the

[1] C. Malcolm Batchelor, ed., *A tí, Doña Marina*, p. 168:
         Yo biuiré la vida sin pasión,
         fuera de desconcierto y turbulencia,
         siruiendo al rey por mi satisfación.
[2] P. Paris, *Négociations . . . relatives au Règne de François II*, pp. 166–168.

Duke of Infantado's palace in Guadalajara (February, 1560). Such was the pride of the Mendozas that the hostess, the Duchess of Infantado, asked by the King to give precedence to Isabel's companion of royal blood, Mme. de Rieux, refused to greet the new Queen in her own house, nor did she attend the wedding. Under pretense of illness, she withdrew with all the other female Mendozas to another of her residences to brood in splendid isolation.[3]

At this time, Don Diego's old, and now sole, brother Don Luis held the highest rank next to the King in government as President of the Royal Council; his son Don Iñigo López de Mendoza, fourth Count of Tendilla, was named special ambassador to Rome to congratulate the new Pope, Pius IV, on his election. Though this looks as if in the beginning of the sixties the progeny of old Count Iñigo stood as high with the monarch as they had done in previous times with any of the King's ancestors, it was a temporary flourishing, not comparable with their renown under Charles V and but a faint reflection of their power and influence in times of the Grand Cardinal.

Philip II's entourage had become so large and unwieldy that in 1561, after one more transfer with his court to Madrid, he decided to make Madrid the permanent capital. The greatest problem was to find adequate accommodation for all who were entitled to it. With the court were all the members of eight different Councils (of State, Royal, Indies, Holy Inquisition, Aragon, Italy, Chivalric orders, and Finance—six to sixteen persons in each); there were no less than thirteen embassies, whose order of precedence was: the papal nuncio, the ambassador of the Emperor "my uncle," those of France, Portugal, England, Venice, Genoa, the Duke of Florence, the Duke of Mantua, the Duke of Ferrara, the Duke of Urbino, the envoy of the Republic of Lucca, and a consul of the Duke of Savoy.

Separate households, going into the hundreds, were required for the servants of the King, Queen, Doña Juana, Prince Don Carlos, Don Juan of Austria (the King's half brother), and of the King's nephew Alessandro, Prince of Parma, son of "Madama" and Ottavio Farnese. It took years of new construction to cope with this housing shortage; meanwhile, such great personages as the King's majordomo and treasurer, or the ambassador of the King of France,

[3] Arteaga y Falguera, *La Casa del Infantado*, pp. 341, 342.

complained about the small, narrow, and unworthy houses allotted to them.[4] The King decreed that those who were not married had to double up; consequently Don Diego had to be satisfied with rented quarters in the house of a Doña Guiomar Flores, sharing it with a certain Pedro Valladares.[5] This shows that his relation with his brother, the Marquis of Mondéjar, had not become close even now.

Don Luis was not devoid of feelings for all his brothers: he had loved Don Bernardino. On learning of the latter's death, he had "bowed his head," returning to his own estates, refusing for a while to continue serving at court (of Regent Doña Juana at the time).[6] If he did not, during that extraordinary housing shortage, invite Don Diego to stay with him, he must have felt cool indeed toward the younger one. "God knows how glad I was to see letters signed by your own hand," Don Diego said, expressedly grateful, in his only extant letter to Mondéjar.[7]

In October, 1561, Don Diego took over the guardianship of a young orphan, a niece by marriage of his late brother Bernardino. This quasi-legacy of the brother who had been closest to him was to provide him with an interest and with a substitute for the family affection missing from his life. Doña Magdalena de Bovadilla, heiress to estates in Granada, was probably very young at the time her father died, although under the law of that time unmarried heiresses needed male guardians at any age.[8] A grandniece of Don Bernardino's widow, Doña Elvira de Carrillo, Magdalena was lady-in-waiting to Princess Doña Juana. She is known as a tiny person, but of a "high and most unusual intellect among her contemporaries, and as a great expert in Latin; highly gifted as a poetess and writer."[9] The fragments of her many years of correspondence with Don Diego reveal her wit and her sophisticated style.[10]

The Order of Santiago had legal claims on Doña Magdalena's

---

[4] C. Gutiérrez, *Madrid: De Villa a Corte*, pp. 7–52.

[5] GP II, 328.

[6] Letter to Ruy Gómez, Count of Melito, January 24, 1558, *DIE* 97: 344–345.

[7] *MRAE* 10: 218. The content suggests the date as that of the armada of 1557.

[8] On Magdalena, see GP II, 328–338.

[9] Serrano y Sanz, *Apuntes para una Biblioteca de escritoras españolas*, I, 160–164; also in *MRAE* 10: 423.

[10] Magdalena's correspondence with Don Diego in R. Foulché-Delbosc, *RH* 8, no. 25 (1901): 1–50.

estates. But for Mendoza's exertions during a lawsuit, her inheritance would have fallen to the King, and "once it gets into the hands of the King," wrote Don Diego, "it will never come back."[11] Apart from seeing to it that she was not robbed of her property, Don Diego devoted much of his time to this young girl. Her witty and responsive conversation, her exchange of poetry with him, drew him deep into the social life of the palace. It must have been his strong and reasonable argumentation, given "with a father's love,"[12] that made her agree to marry, in 1571, a first cousin, Don Jerónimo de Padilla, whom she had refused many times, even during the life of her father more than thirteen years before,[13] but whom, according to Mendoza, she "equaled in rank and person and ancestry. There are no better people in Spain than they."[14]

Outside that spiritual relationship, in his later fifties or early sixties he had some less-exalted feminine companionship, revealed by a pathetic note in his testament of 1575. He left a small legacy of an annual income for life to a boy who was being raised as his son in Valladolid in the house of Tomás de Avila, "although I do not think he is [my son]."[15] From the biographical sketch by Sédano in *Parnaso Español*, which is generally unreliable, it would appear that this supposed son was feeble-minded, yet—in a portrait in Mendoza's possession—the boy was said to look the image of him.[16]

It seems that women played an insignificant role in Don Diego's life. From the few hints here and there it appears, however, that he remained unmarried more by accident than by design. When he was a bachelor of almost fifty, at the height of his political influence, in the midst of the magnificence of his households in Rome and Siena, he professed that he would like to marry. Gonzaga offered him a match, "the sister of the Duke of Fernandina. He [Gonzaga] tells me she is a fine woman," Don Diego wrote Arras, remarking also that her estate was considerable. But he wished to find out the Emperor's opinion before committing himself. "In

11 Ibid., pp. 38, 44.
12 Ibid., p. 46.
13 *DIE* 97: 341.
14 Foulché-Delbosc, *RH* 8: 43.
15 GP II, 389.
16 López de Sédano, ed., "Noticia," introduction to *Parnaso español*, IV, x–xx; GP II, 400, where the portrait of the supposed son is described.

those cases a man has to take the opinion of his master as if it were that of his father. . . . Other marriage deals are being offered to me, but until I know from you [Arras] whether it is good to marry, or not, they are not worth a discussion. . . .[17] Among other Italian girls available to him were the wealthy daughters, Agnese, Vittoria, and Girolama, of Ascanio Colonna, head of the mighty clan, but "I have gone for none of them."[18]

The Bishop of Arras apparently did not presume to judge Don Diego's intentions, but, possibly somewhat doubtful, he asked the old bachelor whether he really desired to marry. "Yes, I would like to marry," Don Diego replied, "but I cannot do it until His Majesty pays me, and after the creditors are paid and I can take my leave. So as not to deceive the person who would have to live with me, or give her reason for discontent, it will have to be in Spain, since I shall not entertain such pretensions in Italy. . . ."[19] But by the time he cleared his accounts with the Emperor, he had his political disasters in Italy on his conscience. Then he was no longer in a position to take his pick from among the eligible women in Spain. From that time on women just continued to be his delighted audiences at court, as they had always been.

During the 1560s, years of external peace (apart from skirmishes in the Mediterranean and the growing revolt in the Netherlands) and internal stagnation in Spain, Don Diego lived uneventfully, serving the King, the new Queen, possibly the Prince Don Carlos, and certainly the Princess Doña Juana and her lady-companion, Doña Magdalena. He wasted his great gifts in idle conversation. When he might have produced his most important works, he trifled his time away at court. There is not even an anonymous work from the sixties extant that might be ascribed to him. Perhaps he found it impossible, after his close brush with the Inquisition, to take up writing again. The achievements of Valdés—the list of forbidden books, the new censorship edicts, and the encroachments of the Inquisition into the minds of all—could only hamper a free spirit, making a man like Mendoza cultivate nothing but safe, innocuous pastimes.

[17] *AC*, p. 293, n. 3.
[18] *AC*, p. 277.
[19] *AC*, pp. 293, 294.

Yet his life was not all ease and pleasure. The King, on the one hand, put him to work; on the other, he kept harassing him repeatedly with the citations of his accountants, who were never satisfied with Mendoza's declarations in behalf of his expenses in Siena, and who now examined his preceding accounts as well, as far back as his earliest services in Venice.

Despite its drawbacks, he undoubtedly preferred the atmosphere at court to the alternative he had, but which he positively neglected: he never took up his residence in his encomienda, those remote estates in Extremadura. The superiors of the Chivalric Order did not look kindly on his indifference. From the tasks they imposed on Mendoza in penance (besides the payment of fines) we can infer which other duties as a *comendador* of Alcántara it was his custom to disregard. It appears that he did not pray as he was obliged to do; he failed to wear at all times the habit of the order— the white mantle of his chapter, with the scapular and the cross of the order, which had to be worn over all his outer garments; and he neglected to confess in accord with certain rules at the three *Pascuas*: Christmas, Easter, and Pentecost.[20]

In the realm of politics, the court was split in two factions, one headed by the Duke of Alba, consisting chiefly of his own relatives, the other by Ruy Gómez. The latter, to which Don Diego stood close, included also Diego Espinosa, who was rising in power, Gonzalo Pérez (the King's secretary of state), and Gonzalo's son Antonio. In the circle of such powerful friends, Don Diego was able to hold his own against the great Alba, the man he most liked to tease. From the tone he formerly employed toward Alba, one can imagine that life at court, with its verbal thrusts and bitter differences of opinion, was never dull when Don Diego was around. His brother Don Luis, whose presence at court might have restrained Don Diego's sallies, retired in 1563, at seventy-four, from his position as President of the Royal Council; he died in 1566. Don Luis was replaced by Espinosa, whom Don Diego regarded as his friend.

From the King's point of view, the state of the world could hardly have been better. In his own country, he saw spiritual unification become a reality by his increased measures against the Moriscos of Granada. To be sure, the dangers in the Netherlands were

[20] Pero Pérez, "La Encomienda," *RCEE* 4: 223–241.

growing to such an extent that Philip's half-sister, "Madama," then governor of those unruly provinces, implored him to come to her assistance. Philip II never refused the request. In 1567 he ordered a mighty armada assembled, once more entrusting that enterprise to Don Diego.

With his empire, then, still under his control, the King should have been a happy man. He seems to have been genuinely fond of his attractive young wife. In 1563 he started to build his Escorial, the monument that was forever to give testimony of his filial devotion, his wealth, his grandeur, his faith. Yet all the reasons Philip II had for self-congratulation came to nothing in the face of his tragic flaw: Don Carlos, his only son and heir.

The existence of that mentally unbalanced youth in their midst caused monarch and court endless anxiety and embarrassment. Until the end of 1567, however, the King bore the cross of his son's presence with composure. The usually reliable reports of the Venetian ambassador about the state of affairs in 1567 bear witness to the fact that Don Carlos was a crazed fellow, given to increasingly uncontrollable rages.[21] All the courtiers lived in fear of him. Often, Don Carlos insulted, even struck the mighty Ruy Gómez, his majordomo, and such proud grandees as the Duke of Alba. The Venetian, with the uncanny foresight those envoys often revealed, predicted that this frequently feverish young man, intemperate in meals and choleric in manner, would not live long. Yet as late as the summer of 1567, the King had the intention of taking his rebellious heir along with him by sea, with a mighty armada, to the equally restless states of the Netherlands, "Our very dear and much beloved son," as he wrote in the commission he gave "Don Diego de Mendoça, Comendador de las Casas de Badajoz de la Orden de Alcántara," appointing his old and faithful vassal and factotum as Provider General of a new fleet on July 3, 1567.[22]

In 1567 Philip II had not left his realm for eight years. Even within "the Spains" he never traveled far, though he flitted back and forth continuously between Madrid and his pleasure palaces in Segovia and Aranjuez, and his temporary accommodations at the

[21] Alberi, *Relazioni degli ambasciatori veneti al Senato*, serie I, vol. V, *Relazioni di Spagna di Giovanni Soranzo*, pp. 119–121.

[22] R. Foulché-Delbosc, "Un point contesté de la vie de Don Diego Hurtado de Mendoza," *RH* 2 (1895): 248–254.

Escorial, which was rising under his supervision. So he was not believed when he let it be known that he was shortly coming to the aid of his sister, who expected him to act as once their father had done—at the request of their aunt, Queen Marie of Hungary— when he put down the revolt of Ghent. Even the Pope, Pius V (Saint Pius), relying on the reports of his nuncio at Philip's court, Archbishop Rossano, doubted the intentions of the King throughout 1566; he deemed it necessary to exhort Philip to make this expedition for the cause of religion.[23]

After the King reaffirmed his purpose,[24] the rumors abated somewhat, but in May, 1567, when the Duke of Alba made the journey alone (to establish his tyrannical rule over the Netherlands, making his name the most hated in Protestant history), a general incredulity started to buzz up again. This time Philip II spared neither money, men, nor pen and paper to prepare for the great armada on which he spent 200,000 ducats. There was nothing unreal about the bread, meat, fish, vegetables, oil, vinegar, salt, and the powder, cannon balls, munitions, wood, and nails that he ordered Don Diego to put together. Minor officials had been gathering ships and supplies from many parts of Spain long before Mendoza was put in charge over them. Don Diego had specific orders to hurry the enterprise and coordinate it as best he could, "you [Don Diego] being a person who understands more of these things than the afore named. Trusting in your loyalty, practical knowledge, diligence, and experience, and the great zeal you show in Our service, and because you did so well formerly in similar affairs, We have decided to name you and elect you as Our *proveedor general de la dicha Armada.* . . ."[25]

Don Diego left for Laredo on the ninth of July, finding things well prepared there. His underlings resented his appointment, begging the royal secretary Eraso not to underestimate their contribution, but as soon as Mendoza arrived, he generously gave them credit for all they had accomplished, and mollified them.[26] He

23 L. P. Gachard, ed., *Bibliothèque de Madrid et de l'Escurial,* pp. 87, 90–93. 100–102.

24 Ibid., November 15, 1566.

25 Foulché-Delbosc, "Un point contesté," p. 249.

26 Juan de Peñalosa to Eraso, July 10, 1567; to Philip II, same date; to Eraso, July 24, 1567; Mendoza to Philip II, July 27, 1567, Arch. Sim., Est., leg. 149, folio 284.

whipped things into their final shape so that the King could set out before the middle of August. But although his trunks were packed, his sister Doña Juana again appointed Regent of Spain, and his family and the court greatly inconvenienced by the general uproar of the preparations for the trip, Philip II never left for the Netherlands.

In September and October, Don Diego had the new task, traveling between Laredo, La Coruña, and Santander, of liquidating the armada, keeping the enlisted men satisfied with half pay, yet making sure they would be ready to go again by next April; he put boats, equipment, and supplies in storage, and, trying to prevent too great a loss for the royal treasury, he disposed of the victuals that not only were prone to spoil but were spoiled already. The ensuing correspondence was characteristic of the King, the son of the great Emperor of worldwide aspirations. For the eyes of Charles V, Don Diego had felt inspired to write résumés of world history, to analyze ideas and to describe peoples, states, and religious and political stratagems; he had searched the inside of the minds of popes and princes for his master.

But for the benefit of Charles' son, he had to employ his usually so eloquent and original pen in reporting on trifles unworthy of the ruler's time and attention: every detail about the unloading of ships, the dismissing of men, and whether the wine was still sweet enough to be sold without detection (he sold some of it to local taverns). He reported that the bacon and fish were so spoiled that they would not last until the next spring, and he urgently advised that the King should agree to sell the stuff as long as it was still possible and to lay in fresh stocks in the following year. In short, the King of all the Spains wanted to know, and received, Mendoza's pertinent information about every detail of prices and quality in these and other things about the armada that never was.[27]

Throughout it all Don Diego found it convenient to guide himself by his memory of all the armadas he had seen and assisted at, from that of Tunis, which had been prepared as long ago as 1534. Prices were higher now, but mainly, because higher wages were

---

[27] Mendoza to Philip II, October 5, 1567; to Eraso, September 25, 1567; to Philip II, September 25, 1567; to Eraso, October 25, 1567; to Philip II, October 25, 1567; Arch. Sim., Est., leg. 149, folios 294, 295, 296, 299, 298.

essential to lure the dwindling supply of men.[28] Otherwise, during a period of thirty-three years, technical matters in Spanish shipbuilding had not changed at all—the chief reason, perhaps, for the superiority of English equipment at sea only twenty years later.[29]

It should not be doubted that Philip II seriously intended to make the expedition on which so much of his prestige depended. The expenditure of hard cash speaks for itself, if nothing else does. But the fact is that his wings were clipped. How could the King move when his concern about the deterioration of his son increased every day? By January 19, 1568, he had him safely locked up in the palace—a fact that imprisoned Philip II himself hardly less than it did his son. For the remainder of the Prince's life, the King left the Madrid palace much less frequently than usual. Perhaps he distrusted even his most devoted men, the Prince of Eboli and his followers. (Seven gentlemen, altogether, protected by eight Spanish and German sharpshooters and halberdiers, were needed to restrain the prisoner, watching over his every movement.)[30]

When Mendoza returned to court by November, 1567, life there was far from normal. From January, though artificial entertainments continued to be staged, any apparent gaiety or amusement was pretense. Never before had Philip's environment sunk to such gloom, fear, and secretiveness. Except for the limited group of gentlemen who were chosen and sworn to watch the Prince day and night, no one, not even his Aunt Juana or the Queen, was allowed to visit Don Carlos.

The King seemed to be waiting for something. But even now he did not drop the plan of the armada, and Don Diego renewed his preparations in February, 1568.[31] The foreign ambassadors were mystified, pressing the embarrassed courtiers for news. On May 8, the French envoy, exasperated by Don Diego's evasive replies, said: "Of Don Diego de Mendoza one can only believe what one sees." In another letter of the same day to Catherine de' Medici, Fourque-

---

[28] Mendoza to Philip II, July 27, 1567, Arch. Sim., Est., leg. 149, folio 284.

[29] "dende el armada de Tunez aca que maquerdo . . . ," ibid., folio 298.

[30] J. A. Llorente, *Historia crítica*, V, 200.

[31] Fourquevaux to Charles IX, February 18, 1568, in *Dépêches de M. de Fourquevaux*, I, 328.

vaux noted that Don Diego had started ordering wines, munitions, and other equipment to be sent to Laredo. On June 25, the same ambassador was on tenterhooks about whether the fleet would sail; he reported that Don Diego was still at court. Yet by July 2 he was positive that Mendoza was making preparations to return to Laredo. And he predicted Don Diego's imminent departure for Laredo as late as July 21.[32]

The Day of Truth

We have no evidence of Don Diego's relations with young Don Carlos other than a record of an exchange of gifts. Once, the Prince gave him a small metal basin engraved all over in Arabic letters (valued at 1,865 maravedis); an antique (*litropia?*), decorated in gold and enamel lettering, costing 7,500 maravedis, and other things of greater value,[33] as well as a gold ring with a portrait of himself carved in cameo.[34] Don Diego gave the Prince a small kettle of either agate or jasper, worth at least two ducats,[35] and he left with him an illustrated parchment manuscript, showing shapes of stones and animals, a *lapidario*, "belonging to the College of the Cardinal of Valladolid from where it had been stolen."[36] Perhaps these tokens of affection hailed from an earlier time, when the Prince was still more tractable. The *lapidario* seems to suggest a time when he was still a child.

As Don Diego was not one of the guards now watching over Don Carlos, he was not in a position to see him. But, no doubt, the general apprehension pervading the court during that period—all the more ominous because the King arranged for the "oblivion" of the prisoner, insisting on "life as usual"[37]—took its toll from him, too. Like almost everyone else, Mendoza was becoming more touchy and excitable. Life at court was, at best, a life of make believe and pretense, but now it was one of monstrous concealments, of denials of the most obvious truths that, sooner or later, had to come out. In

---

32 Ibid., pp. 356, 358, 366, 368, 369.
33 *DIE* 27: 112, 113.
34 *RH* 2 (1895): 121.
35 *DIE* 27: 121.
36 Ibid., p. 93.
37 A. González de Amezúa y Mayo, *Isabel de Valois: Reina de España*, II, 462.

an oppressive atmosphere, for many years increasingly unnatural with mutual suspicion brought on by the ubiquitous Inquisition, the dark yet open secret about the Prince could only set the courtiers to shaking in their boots.

Meanwhile Don Carlos' fragile health was breaking down in his confined quarters, under the queer treatment that restricted his reading matter to breviaries but allowed him to gorge insensately on any food he desired, putting no limits on his destructive self-indulgence. On July 22 and 23, the news was given out that, after having confessed and received extreme unction, he was in his last agony.

This was the situation at the palace of Philip II on July 23, 1568. Anyone in his right mind, if he happened to have business at that stricken court, would have walked on tiptoe, not daring to raise his voice above a whisper. But in that unnatural environment, after months of a general numbness, several of the courtiers were perhaps close to losing their own minds. After so much restraint, something had to give; after the long silence of embarrassment, guilt, and death, someone had to shout. Why was Don Diego—aged sixty-four, white-haired and limping, the "sage" at court—the one to lose his temper in that ghostly atmosphere? He not only shouted, but even got into a personal fight with other courtiers in front of the King's chamber. This is a fact, but why did he do so? It is an enigma almost as deep as the entire case of Don Carlos. The several accounts about the affair were not written by eyewitnesses.

A correspondent of the Duke of Alba wrote:

On Friday, the 23rd, at the hour of noon, while the Prince was in a coma, Don Diego Hurtado de Mendoza and Don Diego de Leiva crossed swords with each other on account of some *motes* [epigrams]. They were in the palace, in front of the royal chamber, while the King was inside. The upheaval was great, and guards separated them with much difficulty. Although *alguaziles* [police] were present, they arrested no one. The fighting gentlemen were taken away, each by his own friends, and they went into different churches. They say that the noise drew His Majesty from his room and that he resented greatly, of course, the fact that such a thing could happen in the palace and at such a time. On the following day they were arrested and taken first to the *alcaldes* [chief of police], and afterwards Don Diego de Mendoza [was taken] to La Mota de Medina, and De Leiva to Simancas.[38]

Fourquevaux, the French ambassador, wrote: "Don Diego de Mendoza and Don Diego de Leyva put hand to sword on the 22nd in the palace corridors next to the chapel, and were separated without being hurt. They fled into two churches for asylum; nevertheless the King, your brother [actually, brother-in-law; addressee is the French King], ordered them brought out as criminals of lese majesty, violators of the freedom of his house. They are in danger, because he observes his rules pitilessly."[39]

Nobili, the Florentine ambassador, wrote his account a full week later; it is the one most frequently cited:

I must tell Your Excellency of an incident that happened in the palace on the 23rd, the same day the Prince was about to die. Don Diego de Mendoza, the old one, formerly ambassador in Rome, and Don Diego de Leva, natural son of Antonio de Leva, walking about in the hall of the Queen, had a dispute about some poems called *copule* here. There was some doubt about whether Don Diego de Mendoza had written them, and they started quarreling, so much so that by the time they left the hall for the upper corridors, they were so heated that Mendoza drew his dagger, pointing it at Don Diego de Leva who in turn drew his sword against Mendoza, giving him several blows. It was a very great rumpus, and His Majesty heard it and was extraordinarily upset, first, because such a thing is unusual in the palace, and second, because under those particular circumstances something worse might have been suspected. Both sought asylum in a church in order to escape justice and to make peace. Nevertheless, at midnight His Majesty ordered two *alcaldes* to get them out of the church and imprison them, and Don Diego de Leva was put in iron and chains. And the other night he ordered [one of] them taken into the fortress of Medina, and the other to Simancas, not without danger to the life of each of them. His Majesty contemplated punishing his guard for having let them escape from the palace, while they should have been arrested or killed.[40]

38 *Documentos escogidos del Archivo de la Casa de Alba*, p. 418.
39 Fourquevaux, *Dépêches*, I, 372.
40 Nobili to the Duke of Florence, July 30, 1568, Documenti dell' Archivio di Stato di Firenze, *Arch. Stor. Ital.* 8, serie III (1868), "Don Carlos di Spagna," p. 37; also *RH*, 2 (1895): 247.

The three reports are almost identical except that the first two have each culprit seek refuge in a different church (the first mentioning that each was saved through the help of his friends), while Nobili has both men fleeing into the same chapel and even making peace. And Fourquevaux errs in giving the date as the twenty-second instead of the twenty-third—which was in fact the last day of the Prince's life; he died between one and two hours after midnight.[41] In 1776, a letter by Don Diego to Cardinal Espinosa came to light; there he complained of being punished exceedingly when all he had done was "at sixty-four years of age to turn around to throw a dagger in the corridors of the palace."[42]

The King kept Mendoza for six months imprisoned in the grim castle La Mota of Medina. Then he pronounced sentence on him and on De Leiva. That is the only official document of this incident to survive; it speaks of "a question that occurred between Don Diego Hurtado de Mendoza and Don Diego de Leiva, who, having put hand to weapons against each other within Our palace, were apprehended. Our alcaldes of Our house and court proceeded against them, condemning them to certain pecuniary fines and to serve Us with their arms and their horse for the rest of their lives at a frontier which We will assign to them. . . ."[43]

None of the several reports, however, refers to the fact that more than just these two men were implicated. Mendoza himself, in a letter to Espinosa only more recently known, says that "in the same week they apprehended us—Don Diego de Leiva, and Don Diego

[41] *Documentos escogidos*, p. 418 n. During the seventeenth and most of the eighteenth century, the story was forgotten. Later historians embroidered the original. It was then said that the other caballero had drawn a dagger that Mendoza seized from him, throwing it "from the balcony" (López de Ayala, in an introduction to the fifth edition of *G. de Gr.*, Valencia, 1776), or "through a window, from which it dropped on the corridors of the Alcázar," (Cayetano Rosell, introduction to *Historiadores de sucesos particulares*, in BAE XXI, part one, p. xi). G. Ticknor added this picturesque though unsupported touch: "Some accounts say he afterwards threw out the courtier himself." (*History of Spanish Literature*, I, 473–474.)

[42] BAE XXI, part one, pp. xxvi, xxvii; RH 2 (1895): 237; AIH 2 (1911): 589; Bibl. Nac., Madrid, MS 18, 393, dated September 20, 1569, Rose-file. The date given in BAE, "1579," is erroneous.

[43] GP II, 364, January 27, 1569, El Pardo. First published by E. Señán y Alonso, *Don Diego Hurtado de Mendoza: Apuntes biográficos-críticos*, p. 53.

de Mendoça and Don Diego de Espinosa and Don Diego Sarmiento, Count of Rivadavia—and the three others are at liberty while I still remain captive in some respect. . . ."[44] From this it appears that all reports are far from presenting accurate facts. The only deed proved by Don Diego's own words is that in self-defense he handled a dagger (of another) and threw it about in the corridor of the palace. But why this happened, and why four men were involved and punished, has never been told.

The story handed out at the palace to the ambassadors gave as the cause of the scandal a disagreement over certain *coplas*. But evidently those rhymes were not worth fighting over even between two silly youths, much less between a person of Don Diego's caliber, and his temporary adversary, the son of the great general, Señor Antonio de Leiva (one of the personages most admired by Mendoza, and still remembered with veneration by him long after this incident). One set of the *motes* or *coplas* is said to have been written by Don Diego de Leiva to Don Diego de Mendoza, "saying his goodbys at the palace."[45]

The versifier (one can hardly call the author of those rhymes a "poet"), depicts in mocking terms how he decides, as he leaves a soirée in the "house of the Princess [Doña Juana]," the environment of Mendoza's ward Magdalena, to retire from court life. No more will he wrestle with the porters, ask Don Cristobal to recommend him, or make conversation with the great Duke of Arjona, *el de Sarriá* (the majordomo of the Princess), and bring along his freshly scrubbed pages to sit in the corners; no longer will he postpone his dinner for the privilege of a walk on the terrace, nor will he tip the dwarf to carry his messages which seem best when they are most nonsensical, or bribe more heavily the heavier guards, or the maid servants; nor will he press "Alejico" to tell him the inside news; nor will he say "nice to meet you" when he meets Don Francisco; no longer will he lie awake at night thinking up pretty things to say the next day. . . . He does not want to hear music on the terrace at all hours, or compete with hordes of other friends in sending *motes* to the ladies; he does not wish to dance . . . nor wear jabot and hose in the color of his lady. He does not like to get wet when his lady strolls on the gallery and it rains . . . and so on.

44 January 11, 1571, from Granada, GP III, 460.
45 *MRAE* 10: 425–426.

The other set is entitled "Reply of Don Diego de Mendoza (to the *coplas* of Diego de Leiva)."[46] In a tone just as flippant, it mocks line by line the *coplas* of the other, wondering why the author goes to so much trouble as to say goodby to the ladies, when, "so help me God, they are unaware of your existence."

If nothing else, that exchange of rhymes shows the inanity and futility of the pastimes at the court. Both, doubtless, are products of the same flirtatious and feline, perhaps female brain. It seems that Doña Magdalena herself might have penned both the first set and the reply to it, just to amuse herself at the expense of both gentlemen. In one of her letters she apparently refers to the incident in the palace, blaming herself for it.[47] Yet it is improbable that Mendoza, though he was irritable at the time, should have lost control solely because these *coplas* were teasingly ascribed to his authorship. This nonsense could not have been the real reason for such fateful happenings. Perhaps it is true that the two caballeros really came to blows, although, according to the chivalrous custom by which those nobles guided themselves, it was unheard-of that a young man (De Leiva was no more than thirty-five) should fight a man thirty years older.[48]

It seems much more plausible to suspect that the excuse of the *coplas* was an invention by the court, perhaps even by the contenders themselves: they must have given this as the reason for their quarrel to protect their lives. Because, knowing as we do, that Don Diego was outspoken, and that he was sharp enough to look through the pretenses and motives of most men, what remark might not have escaped him at a time when everyone, inwardly, was weighing the terrible guilt of the King? Upon learning that the Prince, who to many might have seemed unjustly punished by his father, was then at the point of death, what thoughts would have gone through the minds of those close at hand? Unspoken thoughts that at last spilt over into words for which other courtiers might have attacked Don Diego in their anxiety to silence him. For,

[46] William Knapp, ed., *Obras poéticas de Don Diego Hurtado de Mendoza*, p. 336.

[47] R. Foulché-Delbosc, Correspondence of Mendoza and Doña Magdalena de Bobadilla, *RH* 8 (1901): 9, 10.

[48] Foulché-Delbosc, "Un point contesté," *RH* 2 (1895): 236. There, Leiva's age is given as thirty-two.

though all the days at Philip's court, with their strict etiquette and fanatic religious ceremonial, were days of pretense, one of them— when someone in the palace might irresponsibly have uttered aloud what was unspeakable, but what everyone suspected, and when Don Carlos expired—was a day of truth on many levels.

On this day, the King awoke to the insight that he disliked Mendoza. Strong and self-willed personalities always grated on the King's nerves. The men he felt comfortable with were pliable, smooth, pleasant, moderate, and easy-going. Ruy Gómez de Silva was such a type; so, apparently, was Espinosa, friendliness personified according to Mendoza;[49] so was Antonio Pérez. It was unthinkable that one of them could ever forget himself to the point of disregarding the humility he owed the King.

But Don Diego was anything but subservient. In former times, his gifts as a clownish entertainer perhaps made up for his other faults. Adept at masking his intellect, he had succeeded in pleasing his young master, but only in a superficial way. Basically, he was too proud and frank to be a properly subdued vassal. And recently, during the months of ordeal with Don Carlos, there was no more occasion for any success with witticisms. Even more soured by this nervous strain than he usually was, Philip II grasped the opportunity of what he chose to call Mendoza's "crime" to get rid of his irritating presence. Never would he wish to see his face again. Now he had a pretext to banish this most loyal of his servants for what he had done. But in truth he was punishing Mendoza for what he, irrepressibly, was.

49 GP III, 449.

17. THE WAR OF GRANADA, 1569–1571

This dirty little war . . .
Don Diego[1]

The Native Returns

PHILIP II SAID that his cousin, the Duke of Savoy, had asked him to banish the "culprits" to Granada.[2] This amounted to a recommendation for mercy. The royal decree settling Mendoza's fate, issued on January 27, 1569, read: ". . . within the first fifteen days after leaving the prison where he is now, without entering Our court, he must go to Granada and appear there before the Marquis of Mondéjar, Our captain-general, to serve with his person, arms, and horse, in accord with the orders he will give him."[3]

On the face of it, if Mendoza deserved punishment, this seems a mild sentence. The very fact that he was sent home, in the custody of his nephew the Marquis Don Iñigo, shows that he was not guilty of anything. Otherwise, why would the King, who had the reputation of being merciless, let no harm at all come to Don Diego? Even in La Mota, the grim medieval fortress of Medina del Campo (the

---

[1] "esta suzia guerrilla," GP III, 457.
[2] E. Señán y Alonso, *Don Diego Hurtado de Mendoza: Apuntes biográficos-críticos,* p. 53.
[3] GP II, 364.

castle where the Catholic Queen had died and where once Cesare Borgia had been held captive), Philip II let the prisoner live at his ease with his own two servants and his reading and writing matter, not forbidding him to send and receive correspondence. Apparently, the order of "exile" to Mendoza's native town was little more than a measure to keep him safely removed from the King's presence.

Mendoza returned to Granada old, lame, punished, disgraced, and as he said, "in mortal sin."[4] On April 17, 1569, on the Alhambra, he gave himself over into the custody of his nephew.[5] As the King had commanded, he offered his person in Don Iñigo's service in the current war of the Moriscos that once more was making Granada a "frontier." But what had happened to Granada, integrated into Castile seventy-eight years before, where first his father and then his brother had ruled the population peacefully, in mutual trust?

While a new world had arisen in America, in the old world empires had shifted their centers, new religions had become powerful and disruptive, dynastic and religious wars had upset kingdoms, republics, and smaller principalities, and papal policies had changed with every new supreme pontiff. But back in Don Diego's native town nothing changed, except that the chiefs on the Alhambra now were his nephew and grandnephew, descendants considerably below the level of the impressive personality of his father.

The Moriscos had remained faithful Muslims. They were cautious enough, on the whole, to escape the Inquisition,[6] performing their preferred rites surreptitiously, but they clung openly to their customs: they continued to use their public baths; women dressed in balloon-type trousers with shapeless, padded leggings; outside their houses they covered their faces with a long pleated veil attached to their bonnets; they danced their Moorish dances; and all of them continued to speak Arabic. The contemporary Mendozas still supported their claim for tolerance, and the Church still perse-

---

[4] GP III, 449.

[5] Señán y Alonso, *Mendoza*, p. 15.

[6] K. Garrad, "La Inquisición y los Moriscos granadinos, 1526–1580," *BH 67*, nos. 1–2 (1965): 63–77.

cuted them. Only the emphasis had changed to their detriment. Under Philip II, the influence of the Mendozas was waning, while the King, the Church, and the Inquisition now felt and acted as one mind—the monarch's mind, whose rigidity brought on this war.

In 1569 the Morisco War, taking up where the last Morisco War had ended in 1501, rounded out a period just then ended, Spain's most splendid period, which had left only a few architectural traces in Granada. One of them was Charles V's Renaissance palace, whose bulk now dominated the Alhambra hill. It had been begun forty years before under the aegis of Don Luis, financed by the tribute the Moriscos paid for the Emperor's tolerance of their customs. The palace was unfinished; a giant block of marble and grey stone, its style and proportions clashed with the harmony of the indigenous structures. The aspect of the Italianate building might have reassured Don Diego that there really had been a time when intellectual and artistic currents from abroad had been welcome in Spain—the same time when he himself, also a relic now, had been fully active.

During the splendid period, the people of Granada had recovered from partial expulsion, shifts in landlords, occasional persecutions, and high taxes. Though squeezed by their annual tributes to the crown of Spain, they were able to keep Granada's silk industry flourishing and even to increase it until mid-century. In spite of much destruction of the fertile countryside and of Moorish irrigation channels during the war of conquest, mulberry trees were still growing all over the Alpujarra Mountains and around the Arab villages, where silkworms were raised in every hut (one of the many bonanzas introduced to Spain by the Arabs). This was a sufficient living for the frugal mountaineers; a living also for the remaining four thousand silk weavers and workers on Granada's Albaicin, a fine business for the three hundred silk merchants still active in Granada, and a princely income for the few great Castilian nobles (the Mendozas, Enriquez, and Bovadillas among them) who owned the silk-spinning villages, not to speak of the tributes in taxation to the crown. But from the mid-fifties on, with the finances of Spain in poor shape, the administrators of Philip II tried to enforce a lowering of prices, at the same time forbidding the export of silk. This, together, with the imposition of higher taxes, harmed the industry.[7] And then Philip II decided to revoke his father's pact with the Moriscos of Granada.

The change in the King's policy toward the Moriscos, perhaps influenced by his new adviser, Diego Espinosa (raised to cardinal in 1568), dates from 1566. In that year Don Luis, the second Marquis of Mondéjar, died at the age of seventy-seven. The Moriscos lost in him a venerable and powerful advocate. As Philip II well knew, it was due to the Mendozas' protection that the problem of assimilating the Moriscos had never been handled properly from the Christian point of view. Ten or eleven years earlier, Inquisitor-general Valdés had started to persecute them; every Morisco arrested for apparent relapse into Islam was being punished with confiscation of his property. At that time Don Iñigo López de Mendoza, then the fourth Count of Tendilla, in order to preserve economic stability and peace in his kingdom, petitioned the Pope to grant those of the persecuted who confessed and repented a breve of absolution and restitution of their goods. The result was that the *alcaide*, who was accused of heresy and very nearly arrested, drew upon himself the ire and suspicion of the Inquisition and of the Old Christians of Granada. But with both Charles V and Philip II absent from Spain, while a powerful section of the nobility stood behind the Mendozas, Valdés had been unable to proceed against the Granadines, both the *alcaide* and the people, as he desired.[8]

Frustrated in his design against the Moriscos, Valdés continued to concentrate on his specialty of detecting or suspecting heresies in other members of the Church. After the King's return to Spain, the opportunity for a new crusade against the Moors of Granada was ripening, but Valdés was too old and feeble to start anew in this direction. Only when he was replaced as inquisitor-general by Espinosa, who earlier had also succeeded Don Luis as President of the Royal Council of Castile, the King apparently felt the time for his long-desired change of the policy of toleration of the Moors had now come, and to Cardinal Espinosa he left the task of carrying it out.

[7] K. Garrad, "La industria sedera granadina en el siglo XVI y su conexión con el Levantamiento de las Alpujarras," *Misc.* (1956), pp. 5–8, 73–98, particularly pp. 91–96.

[8] J. L. G. Novalin, *El inquisidor general Fernando de Valdés*, pp. 216–220.

Espinosa, of the faction of Ruy Gómez and well-liked by the King, is a character difficult to assess. Since his name is linked with the fate of Don Carlos and the Morisco War, historians tend to find the worst epithets for him, "the king's evil genius,"[9] for example. But it seems, according to the evidence of the correspondence of Don Diego and Don Alonso de Granada Venegas with this Cardinal, that Espinosa was a creature of circumstances rather than an independent policy maker. When he showed himself inflexible, it was in behalf of Philip II's will. He appears to have been essentially weak; groomed to head those outwardly important positions as a tool to be guided by the King, through the agency of the infinitely dexterous Ruy Gómez, and also by others, even in minor matters.[10] Even though Espinosa and Ruy Gómez had the King's ear, therefore having been considered all-powerful, they do not appear to have influenced Philip's policies now that he was a man in his forties, although as Mendoza said, "the making of the monarch's mind depends largely . . . on the report he receives, which might be tinged with self-interest and passion, inclining him toward rigor and revenge. . . ."[11]

In the persecution of the Moriscos, then, Philip II was acting from his own deep motivation. He seems to have been chiefly driven by his faith to proceed so severely against those suspected "infidels," perhaps from genuine concern for the souls of those who relapsed from Christendom, or, at least, for the salvation of his own in case he neglected his duty. Charles V's last request to his son, unfulfilled as yet, was: "Throw the Moors out of your kingdoms!"[12]

Don Diego of course deplored this new trend that went diametrically against his own views (as shown in the *Guerra de Granada*) and against the interests of his family. But he remained on friendly terms with all who were carrying out the King's new

[9] Roger B. Merriman, *The Rise of the Spanish Empire*, vol. IV, *Philip the Prudent*, p. 86.

[10] ". . . El Cardenal haze lo que le ruega su amigo, que es D. Antonio [de Meneses] . . . ," Mendoza to Doña Magdalena, *RH* 8 (1901): 41.

[11] *G. de Gr.*, p. 62.

[12] Roger B. Merriman, "Charles V to his son," *AHR* 28, no. 3 (1923): 489–491.

measures, claiming that "servants" could not or ought not to be blamed for the deeds their master made them do—*amo y criado*. "It is not for the people to judge the ideas and motives of Kings."[13] All the same, while he was still at court, Mendoza must have aired his views; as a man of *libero arbitrio* he would never have withheld his opinion, though in this case, presumably, he was not asked. Not even the third Marquis of Mondéjar, then present at court, was ever consulted on the decision to revive the legislation against the Moriscos that had been in abeyance since 1526.

The new policy makers found that the texts of their new laws had been well prepared over forty years before. But formerly, the citizens of Granada had been able to buy their liberation from all the intended restrictions of their customs. Their initial tribute of eighty thousand ducats—used to start the palace of Charles V in the heart of the Alhambra—served to assuage the Emperor's crusading zeal against them. Now, Philip II, reviving the old laws, forbade the Moriscos to use their Arabic language, their baths, their dress, their very names, as well as other customs. They were to keep their doors ajar during any gatherings such as weddings, so that no trace of their heritage, even within the intimacy of their tiny homes, could escape his police.

Admittedly, communication between the Old Christian and Morisco elements had been deteriorating for some time preceding this *pragmática*. In 1553 the government had issued an order forbidding the Moriscos the use of arms (it was not enforced, nor was it enforceable); in 1555 the Inquisition under Valdés increased its harassment of the Moriscos, robbing them of their property under the slightest pretext of relapse into Islam; in 1560, the Cortes of Toledo issued a decree forbidding them to own Negro or Moorish slaves, while letting Christians retain this prerogative; and in 1559, the crown started confiscating their lands under the pretext that only those who could show hundred-year-old titles from the Nasirid epochs had a right to landed property.[14] When the newly dispossessed moved to the town of Granada, crowding the Albaicin and spread-

---

[13] *G. de Gr.*, p. 62.
[14] *G. de Gr.*, p. 12; Julio Caro Baroja, *Los Moriscos del Reino de Granada*, p. 14.

ing their discontent, they were denied their freedom of movement and ordered to go back where they came from.[15]

The decline in Morisco liberties was paralleled by steadily worsening relations between the military and civil local authorities, while the power of the police was increasing. Following the pacification in 1501–1502, the Catholic Kings coordinated the military power of the Captain-General of Granada (old Count Iñigo), until then supreme viceroy of the new kingdom, with a civic branch of government, the *audiencia* (chancelry), which had its seat on the Plaza Nueva in downtown Granada.[16] The innovation caused no difficulty as long as the *letrados* (jurists) in the civil service were themselves followers and friends of the Mendozas. But in 1535, Charles V, trying to clean a number of his cities from local patronage and graft, also replaced all the members of Granada's *audiencia* with new officials from other regions of Castile.[17] At about the same time, the second Marquis of Mondéjar (Don Luis) resigned in favor of his son Don Iñigo, fourth Count of Tendilla, from his position as captain-general and *alcaide* of the Alhambra to take part in the Tunis campaign. From then on, relations between the civil and military authorities changed for the worse.[18]

The young Don Iñigo (Don Diego's nephew), chief of the Alhambra from 1535–1561, was a man noted for his harshness of character. He and the chancelry fought over each other's transgressions of power in a deepening and endless struggle, animosity nearly culminating at the time—1555—when the Count tried to protect the Moriscos against their expropriation by the Inquisition. The situation deteriorated still further under his son, a violent man, who, as the fifth Count of Tendilla, took power over the *alcaidia* of the Alhambra in 1561 or 1562 when he was only eighteen or nineteen (his father retaining only the captain-generalship of Granada). Sensitive about being disrespectfully treated by the civilian chancellor on account of his youth, this grandnephew of Don Diego, another Don Luis, was exceptionally haughty and quarrelsome, hated

[15] Luis del Mármol Carvajal, *Historia del rebelión y castigo de los Moriscos de Granada*, I, 170.

[16] On the *letrados* and their growing power, see *G. de Gr.*, pp. 10, 11.

[17] Pedro Girón, *Crónica del Emperador Carlos V*, pp. 52, 53.

[18] Caro Baroja, *Los Moriscos*, p. 143.

by all except the Moriscos who were still protected by the Mendozas.[19] At that time, when many of the Moriscos were being expropriated, when the silk industry for various reasons was in a slump, when the liberty of movement of the Moriscos was interfered with while their protectors were losing power, Pedro de Deza, a high official of the Inquisition, was sent as the new president of the Chancelry to Granada, empowered to publish Philip II's pragmatic law.

The new law was noisily driven home to the public. The civilian body of government, its police, judge, and officers, marched in procession to the music of drums, trumpets, strings, and fifes, visiting every borough of the city, lending solemnity to the town crier's broadcasting of the text in both Arabic and Spanish.[20] The Moriscos, incredulous that it was impossible to buy themselves out of the hated *pragmática* this time, tried to soften up the authorities, from Deza to the King, for the better part of their year of grace—all of 1568. But gradually they understood. Their resentment changed into conspiracy. Construction on the palace of Charles V, already in progress for forty years, came to a halt. (In the still-unfinished octagonal corner, a hoisting crane continued to point its arm idly, accusingly, into the air for years to come.)[21] The tribute had ended. Unable, if not unwilling, to exchange one culture for another overnight—a people, as Mendoza expressed it, now "without a language, without support, caught in a trap, and reduced to servitude"[22]—the Granadines planned rebellion.

On Christmas Eve of 1568, a group of 50 mountaineers had seventeen long rope ladders ready to scale the forbidding walls of the Alhambra from the side of the ravine. Another troop of 150 broke through a gate into the city. The invaders marched through the

---

[19] *RH* 31 (1914): 11 contains the text of Ardila's chronicle. Abelardo Merino, *El Cardenal Mendoza*, p. 12, says that this chronicle is not the real Ardila whose [lost?] work, *Origen, descendencias y hazañas de la gran casa de Mendoza* is only partially included in *Historia de la casa de Mondexar*, MS in Bibl. Nac., Madrid, k. 100.

[20] José Palanco Romero, *Aben Humeya en la historia y en la leyenda*, p. 7.

[21] Cf. the engraving by George Hoefnagle, in *Gabinete de Estampas de la Biblioteca Nacional*; published, for example, in Luis Astrana Marín, *Vida ejemplar y heróica de M. de Cervantes Saavedra* II, opposite p. 192.

[22] *G. de Gr.*, p. 11.

Albaicin with shouts and martial music; they proclaimed the new era of Mohammed, and called upon their fellow Moriscos to rise.

In that snowy night, the Captain-General, Marquis Iñigo, and his son Count Luis, the *alcaide* of the Alhambra, were unable to stop the invasion. Taken by surprise, they had no army ready; all they could do during the darkness with their small garrison was to guard the thirty towers of the Alhambra until daybreak. But the plot failed. Had there been no hitch in the understanding between the mountaineers, hardy men from the Alpujarras, determined to fight, and the more sedentary city people who were supposed to "rise" that night, but did not do so—the city would have been theirs on the spot. The Albaicin did not then, nor ever, rise, nor would the Alhambra be assailed. Nevertheless, the civil war was on.

Although wars were fought only in the summer, armies of even the bitterest enemies hibernating during the winter months, the Moors, showing no consideration for the convenience of their enemies, struck at the beginning of the worst season. Marquis Iñigo had no choice but to pursue them through snow and ice into the Alpujarras, regions scarcely passable even in the best summer weather. In the mountains, all 182 silk-producing villages, each an almost inaccessible stronghold, were rebelling, eight thousand Moriscos ready to defend them. One of the younger city people who had fled into the mountains to join them, Don Fernando de Valor, a descendant of the ancient kings of Córdoba and, as the son of a wealthy Morisco, a Granadine city official—one of the "twenty-four"—was proclaimed King and thereafter known as Aben Humeya.

Place of Banishment

When Don Diego reached Granada on April 17, 1569, the war was at an impasse. His nephew was fighting a losing battle for his authority as captain-general, despite the fact that he had achieved a seemingly impossible military and political victory. Valiantly, Mondéjar had made war on those whom he would rather have pacified. Over snow-covered paths (there were no roads, only abysses, chasms, ravines, narrow trails, and steep cliffs) his "heavy-footed, burdened soldiery, unused to mountain warfare," was exposed to great travail, while the "light-footed, nimble" mountain folk were always gaining advantages.[23] Yet within two months Mondéjar succeeded in subduing all 182 rebellious villages. Recommending mild peace terms in the conciliatory Mendoza manner, he saw the rebellion as good as ended. But his view did not prevail against that of Deza, who did not want any agreement with the Moriscos. Against the captain-general's prerogative and wish, Deza had requested Mondéjar's enemy, the Marquis de los Velez of neighboring Murcia, to participate in the war, and Los Velez, who furnished numerous troops at his own expense, was also in favor of continuing hostilities.

The Marquis of Mondéjar wrote to the King frequently, explaining the situation, but Philip II, who did not care for his advice, did not even look at his letters.[24] (These would otherwise bear the King's marginal comments, as do practically all the letters he read.) Mondéjar's enemies in the administration decried as dangerous his recommendations for humaneness; they condemned from the outset his desire to negotiate with the Moriscos, since he was countering the King's intentions of rooting them out. Deciding to annihilate the enemy in an all-out war with fire and sword, the King sent his young half brother, Don Juan of Austria (the illegitimate son of Charles V and Barbara Blomberg, a German or Flemish woman), the future hero of Lepanto, to Granada to stress the importance of the war and, incidentally, by his presence, to reduce both Mondéjar's and Los Velez's authority.

Don Juan made his solemn and pompous entry into Granada, received by ten thousand troops. Oddly, many of these good Castilians dressed up *a la morisca* when the real Moriscos were forbidden their own costume. This was a few days before Don Diego, practically alone, made his own way up to the scenes of his boyhood, the place he had known and understood so well as "philosopher, Moor of Granada, or Marrano."

Mondéjar, who was not campaigning at the moment, did not use his uncle in the war. That is why Mendoza did not ride "with his arms and horse" in Marquis Iñigo's entourage until two months

[23] "Mémoire du Marquis de Mondéjar," in A. Morel-Fatio, ed., *L'Espagne au XVI. et XVII. siècle*, p. 22.

[24] Mondéjar to Philip II or to his secretary, from July 17 to September 10, 1569, Arch. Sim., Cámara de Castilla, leg. 2152, folios 58–70.

later when the Moriscos were rounded up in the Albaicin in preparation for their expulsion. Otherwise Mendoza was confined, under orders of the King, to some sort of house arrest. Perhaps the Marquis of Mondéjar and his son did not sympathize with Don Diego, whose "disgrace" they might have resented as a blemish on the family honor, although the young Count of Tendilla, his grandnephew, with his own record of violence, would have had no reason to call the kettle black. Mendoza, on his side, found little fault with his nephew's policies, though with his customary objectivity he also understood the blemishes in Marquis Iñigo's character. Concerning his grandnephew, even the veiled style of the *Guerra de Granada* shows nothing but criticism. Nonetheless, all faults of young Count Luis and his father considered, Mendoza preferred to see the Alhambra in their hands rather than in those of strangers.[25]

His own estate on which he installed himself with a considerable household was in the precinct of the Generalife. This was the "home" in the back of his mind nearly twenty years earlier during a difficult time in Rome, when he had spoken of his eventual retirement. But that idea probably had not been quite serious. It is unlikely that he ever really wished to retire. In the ups and downs of his political life, he would have had many occasions to bury himself in Granada. Instead, Granada long since signified little more than a backwater, a province. The Mendozas and such of their relatives and friends who, like Doña Magdalena de Bovadilla, owned estates in Granada, cherished their hometown chiefly for the income it produced for them while they preferred to live at court.

At this time the *alcaide* of the Generalife was Don Alonso de Granada Venegas y Rengifo, the son of Don Pedro de Granada Venegas y Mendoza, the half Moor who as a boy must have been Don Diego's neighbor and playmate.[26] Don Alonso, who was Don Diego's landlord, perhaps, or a co-owner or his host, but at any rate a neighbor, was one of the few friends Marquis Iñigo had left and probably the only sympathizer with his policy among the Christians of Granada. In 1568 Don Alonso spent many months at Philip II's court, hoping to persuade the King to leniency toward the Moriscos, but he only earned rebuffs. Returning with empty hands

[25] Mendoza to Prince of Eboli, April 13, 1570, *AIH* 2 (1911): 587.
[26] See chapter one.

from Madrid just in time to witness the start of the rebellion and to take part in Mondéjar's campaign, Don Alonso still was the agent through whom the moderates on both sides hoped for rapprochement.[27] The proximity of Don Alonso, whom he calls his *compañero*,[28] must have compensated Mendoza for the loss of a wider circle of friends: this worthy descendant of his own great-grandfather, the Marquis of Santillana, was also dedicated to poetry.[29]

Mendoza's house, within the precinct of the Generalife, "the first of the place"[30] as one came from the countryside in the east, does not exist any more. The two clues to its situation (his mentioning of "Genalarife" [*sic*] and calling it "the first of the place") lead to the locality near Fuente Peña, at the easternmost angle of the Alhambra hill, close to the modern entrance of the Generalife; an ancient gateway there still bears the coat-of-arms of the Granada Venegases.[31] Of the thirty towers of the Alhambra, nearest to it was the Torre del Agua. His entrance gate probably did not stand far from the end of the wild ravine between the Alhambra's hill Sabika and the hill of the Generalife. "Rocky Fountain," the name of the spot, is a toponym for an ancient trough cut right into the rocks (unearthed, partly preserved, in 1953).[32] The house, one of a group of country villas with the usual dependencies, orchards, vineyards, and fields, in back of it, must have had one of those views that more than justify the words of Alexandre Dumas: "God made the Alhambra and Granada/For the day He should weary of His dwelling."[33]

---

[27] Cf. E. Spivakovsky, "Some Notes on the Relations between Don Diego Hurtado de Mendoza and Don Alonso de Granada Venegas," followed by seven unpublished letters of Don Alonso, *Archivum* 14 (1964): 212–232; and idem, "Which Don Alonso Venegas?" *Renaissance News* 17, no. 3 (1964): 193–196.

[28] GP III, 458.

[29] Antonio Marín Ocete, *Gregorio Silvestre*, pp. 44–46.

[30] ". . . la primera del lugar . . . ," GP III, 452.

[31] I am most grateful to Don Jesús Bermúdez Pareja, director of the Museum of the Alhambra, for his kindness in showing me this location.

[32] Again I thank Don Jesús Bermúdez for this information.

[33] Hizo Diós a la Alhambra y Granada
Por si le cansa un día su morada.

Alexander Dumas, as quoted by Luis Seco de Lucena,
La Alhambra como fué y como es, p. 355.

When Mendoza formerly referred to this place of "retirement" as an abode of "poverty," he was speaking figuratively. While not living like a prince—or an Imperial ambassador in Rome—he still had the considerable staff of a country gentleman, with a major-domo, Juan de Agueras, at the head of them. Agueras spent much of his time traveling around Spain to Mendoza's encomiendas and benefices, collecting his revenues, partly in money, partly in produce. Don Diego had a private chaplain; he was surrounded by pages, lackeys, housekeepers, and other personal servants who were free men and women.[34] Only one, however, was intelligent enough to understand him, "mi mudo" (my mute one).[35] And he owned a number of male and female slaves (presumably black). A part of his belongings was still in a residence he had established in Laredo as provider of that nonexistent armada—a sign that he was in active duty up to the day of his "disgrace." Many of his books were either loaned out or left in his various establishments, but he had a good part of his collection of books, manuscripts, antiquities, paintings, sculptures, coins, and medals with him.[36]

In the course of his life, Mendoza had now accumulated enough paintings to furnish a long gallery, from portraits to biblical subjects and landscapes. In addition to the portraits of his father and his favorite three brothers, there were likenesses of the Emperor, "Madama," the Bishop of Arras, the wife of Cobos, and one portrait, already mentioned, that the executors of his testament believed to be his son (apparently because it resembled him, but it could have been one of his nephews): a boy dressed in black, with white stockings and jabot, in a red-painted wooden frame.[37] Among his Italian keepsakes, the likeness of Don Ferrante Gonzaga reminded him of great times, as did that of Pope Julius III, and that of Prospero Colonna. There were several portraits of Livia Colonna, the beautiful Roman woman; one of them (a supposed Veronese,

---

[34] Cf. the list of Mendoza's legatees in GP II, 369.

[35] GP III, 453.

[36] GP II, 397. More than a hundred of his books, mostly those of Italian literature (see the list in GP III, 536–557), were lent out to his relative the Duke of Infantado. At Mendoza's death, in his new household in Madrid, part of his estate was still in Laredo and another part in the house he still had in Granada; also, many pieces were in pawn with money lenders. GP II, 397. An inventory of his *objets d'art* was published by R. Foulché-Delbosc, *RH* 2: 289–303.

[37] GP II, 400.

now in the Prado) shows her sitting in an armchair, caressing a lap dog.[38] Mendoza also had an oil on canvas—probably a Titian— of an unknown Venetian lady, a half-figure, hatless, with white sleeves and a pearl necklace—perhaps, who knows, a likeness of his one-time Jewess.

His collection of sculpture, jewels, and other curios had increased through the "antiquities," probably of Roman origin, that he had found in his encomienda of Alcántara.[39] Those he added to the things he had found in the excavations of Siena, and to the Mexican treasures from Don Antonio. Pieces of Arabic culture had probably been in his possession from earlier times, and he could replenish them now; he also collected some four hundred Arabic manuscripts during his years in Granada.[40] Old coins, as we know, he had dug up since his student years in Spain; now he had a huge collection of coins and medals that was displayed in carved walnut boxes with drawers of ebony and walnut lined in satin and covered with black leather.

His banishment, then, was no physical hardship. Before his eyes spread the beautiful panorama of his childhood; he enjoyed the company and the care of his many treasures; he warmed his old bones in the Andalusian sun; he drank again the crystalline water of the Darro whose salubriousness he praised,[41] and he sustained himself on the produce of his own orchards and fields. Had he not always insisted that the best in life was to do as one pleases, "to throw his books on the floor, opening and closing them at random?" That he could do, all he wanted to. Materially, his life left nothing to be desired, but he chafed under the opprobrium of being in royal disgrace. He was weary, also, of solitude. Except for Don Alonso, whom he might now and then have challenged to a chess game on his "table of walnut,"[42] there was no one whose company he could even begin to enjoy.

Don Diego and the War

As long as the war continued, Mendoza did not derive much sat-

[38] On the speculation that Mendoza was in love with Livia, see GP II, 404–408.

[39] Arras to Mendoza, Brussels, April 17, 1554, Bibl. Pal., vol. 2318. Rose-file.

[40] GP II, 381.

[41] *G. de Gr.*, pp. 86, 87.

[42] GP II, 396.

isfaction from his enforced leisure. The efforts at pacification, openly solicited by the Marquis of Mondéjar and advocated behind the scenes by Don Alonso, were thwarted by Deza and his henchmen. In March, 1569, only a few weeks after Mondéjar's initial victories, and shortly before Don Diego arrived, Deza's police murdered in their prison the 150 elderly respectable Moriscos held there as hostages. The blood bath was immediately followed by spoliation of the wealthy victims that left their kin destitute. Such action infuriated Aben Humeya, precluding any further attempts at peace.

In Granada, a place boiling over with dissenting factions, Don Juan of Austria was unable for a long time to come to any decision, especially because every move had to be referred to Madrid and double-checked by the absent King himself. Philip II lacked the physical stamina to endure a stay near the battlefield, let alone take part in campaigns, but as an armchair strategist he did not miss the slightest detail. And trifling points of etiquette were as important to him as the gravest problems of policy. Revealing of his authoritarianism was his reaction upon learning from Don Diego's first letter to Cardinal Espinosa that Don Juan was being called "Highness" in Granada, instead of merely "Excellency" as decreed by the King.[43] Mendoza had recommended this procedure; there were so many "Excellencies" now in Granada, he wrote, that they overshadowed the title of the Prince. Besides, the Emperor himself had allowed persons of lower rank, like the Duke of Savoy (Philip II's cousin) to be addressed as "Highness." The King, reading every word from this wise but offensive courtier whom he never wished to see again, scribbled disagreeable comments in the margin of Mendoza's letter, but followed his recommendation—though in his very own way. He did not raise Don Juan's dignity, but decided to lower that of the dukes and marquises around the Prince, so that the "Excellency" of his brother would stand out properly.

The young Prince—only twenty-two—found himself in a bewildering situation between Deza and Mondéjar, each of whom was trying to deprive the other of authority, "each of them [said Don Diego] glad to see the other make mistakes, taking note of them as though they were conducting a law suit. Hence the city councillors think that, if they slander the Marquis, they are pleas-

[43] May 5, 1569, GP III, 446–448.

ing President Deza—and it is the King who has to pay for that."[44] Ordered by his brother to listen to the opinions of all his councillors, Don Juan was requested by Inquisitor Deza to punish forthwith all Moriscos for their sacrileges, to expel the entire Morisco population from Granada, and to wage a war of annihilation against the Moorish enemies in the mountains. At the Prince's other ear, the Marquis of Mondéjar explained how this kingdom was being destroyed together with the destruction of the Moriscos. None of the mountain towns could survive without them; their natives were a patient and industrious people who extracted excellent produce from a difficult soil, having built a silk industry under conditions so austere that no one else could do the same. Mondéjar advised that the leaders of the revolt be punished severely, to be sure, but that an agreement should be effected with the bulk of the population who belonged in this country.

Between the two opposing factions, Deza's was the more persuasive. Mondéjar was a harsh man who could not take contradiction, and Deza probably was a better speaker than he, a subtler mind. Besides, Deza's position, the uncompromising religious one, was after the heart and mind of the King. Under these circumstances, Don Juan found it impossible to make up his mind. Don Diego, informed of everything despite his official seclusion, understood the Prince's dilemma. He asked Cardinal Espinosa for permission to give Don Juan the experienced counsel his white hair entitled him to offer. But Philip II refused Mendoza's offer. "This would not do," he wrote in the margin of Don Diego's letter, "this would never have been convenient, and much less now." So afraid was he of Don Diego's influence on Don Juan even now that for a moment he considered removing Mendoza from Granada: "I am not sure that, considering his crime, he should even stay in that town."[45]

In June the King made a decision for Don Juan: he ordered him to go ahead with the total expulsion from the Albaicin. But neither the Prince nor his advisers were able to lure the frightened Moriscos out of their maze of narrow alleys and thousands of dark, barricaded hovels. Don Juan then proposed to take the Albaicin by force, smoking the people out and putting them to the sword. Only the Marquis of Mondéjar, whose objection to the expulsion had been

[44] GP III, 447.
[45] GP III, 448, n. 1.

overruled, was able to carry out the King's orders with minimal loss of life. For the last time, Mondéjar followed the tradition of his forefathers, going up the Albaicin with a small escort, appealing to the Moriscos as their friend and protector. He reasoned with them, presenting the people with the dreadful alternatives their resistance would draw upon them. The transfer from their homes, as decreed by the King, was intended solely for their own safety; with the imminent arrival of Christian armies from all of Spain, he could not guarantee that they would be left unmolested. So he persuaded the men to assemble in the largest churches, which they filled to the number of some 3,500. Once Mondéjar had the male population safely locked up, Don Juan joined him with all his forces to oust not only the Moorish men from the Albaicin and Granada, but also the much larger number of women, children, and old men who had been left in their homes.[46]

Among the policing officers, both Mendoza and Luis del Mármol Carvajal, the later historiographers, were there, where they helped and observed, while leading the subdued crowds down from the Albaicin to be assembled in the large lunatic asylum outside the city. Subsequently, all the Granadines, roped together in rows, were driven out of the realm. It was an outright victory for Deza who had advocated this move for a long time. "This exodus caused great compassion to those who knew how comfortably they used to live in their homes," says Mendoza. "Many died on the way, from effort, from exhaustion, from grief, from hunger, cut down by the very people who were in charge of guarding them, robbed, sold into slavery."[47] Even Mármol, who usually is not critical of the authorities, does not conceal his sympathy with the unjustly persecuted.[48]

As Don Diego was quick to notice, the evacuation undermined the very war effort. Once the basic population of Granada was removed, the additional soldiery coming in to enlist in the fight against the rebels found no households to lodge and feed them.[49]

---

[46] Morel-Fatio, ed., *L'Espagne*, appendix to "Mémoire du Marquis de Mondéjar," pp. 93, 94.

[47] *G. de Gr.*, p. 94.

[48] Mármol Carvajal, *Historia*, II, esp. p. 102.

[49] *G. de Gr.*, p. 95. Beginning January 19, 1569, the Count of Tendilla had lodged the incoming armies forcibly with the Moriscos on the Albaicin and elsewhere; Mármol Carvajal, *Historia*, I, 405–508.

This, in turn, helped to increase the demoralization of the Christian army; it was one of the countless mistakes plaguing the enterprise. In his many years in the field, Mendoza had never seen soldiers so intent on loot; so ill-trained for fighting, so prone to desert. The Emperor's Spanish armies (where mutiny was always latent, to be sure, and rape and sacking were the order of the day) and those of Philip II in Flanders and France acquitted themselves incomparably better, because, he thought, they were far from home, having nowhere to escape to. Here, with their first booty in hand, the men found it easy to run away to their homes. Besides, as Mendoza was the first to point out, this was truly a civil war, "Spaniards against Spaniards."[50]

Over the summer of 1569, infighting between the Christian authorities increased, while the Moors, recovering from their defeat in Mondéjar's winter campaign, reinforced themselves, regrouped, and presented a daily growing threat. Many places in the *vega* and in the sierras, often as close to Granada as two miles or less, fell to the Moors, while at night their marauders penetrated the outskirts of the city itself, stealing down over the Cerro del Sol and coming close to the Puerta de los Molinos, carrying off cattle, flour, and even the working people.

King Philip was snowed under by conflicting reports and complaints. In each letter, Mondéjar denounced his rival, the Marquis de los Velez, who was unable to do with an army of ten thousand what the former had already completed with three thousand. Mondéjar's son, the Count of Tendilla, asked many times unsuccessfully for men and provisions to reinforce the Alhambra, "the main bastion of this kingdom to prevent 'don Hernandillo' [Aben Humeya] from taking over." In one of his typical temper outbursts Count Luis wrote the King's secretary Vázquez that he would kill the Señor Don Juan if this kingdom were not helped in its danger —"I fear no one."[51]

Meanwhile the Prince, still under orders by his brother not to expose his person in any campaign, sat with tied hands in Gra-

---

[50] ". . . españoles con españoles . . . ," *G. de Gr.*, p. 22.

[51] Count of Tendilla to Juan Vázquez de Salazar, from the Alhambra, September 19, 1569: ". . . mato al señor Don Juan . . . No temo a nadie . . . ," Arch. Sim., Cámara de Castilla, leg. 2152, fol. 76.

nada; the Mendozas saw not only the last of their income-producing properties lost, but also those of the King himself; the royal armies continued to plunder and kill defenseless people, but fled at the first sight of fighting Moors, deserting with their spoils.

As a way out of the paralyzing dilemma, Don Diego strongly advised (through his letters to Cardinal Espinosa) an increase in Mondejar's authority over his rivals in the military, the Duke of Sesa and the Marquis de los Velez, who interfered with his strategy.[52] But the King was adamant in this point. All his moves had been designed to counter the policy of the Mendozas; he welcomed the opportunity to deprive them of power. With the respect he owed the rank of the Marquis, he proceeded against Mondéjar, but surreptitiously. He called him to court, ostensibly to invite the Marquis to his wedding (the King was marrying his niece, Anna of Austria, his fourth wife), and to report to him in person—and then he kept him there. The real reason for his recall was to keep Mondéjar safely, though honorably, removed from Granada.[53]

Almost simultaneously the fifth Count of Tendilla was foolish enough to play into his enemies' hands. He was apprehended in an insolent outburst against Deza, whom he threatened to kill. By order of the King, "perhaps [as Don Diego puts it] because of special displeasure with his house or with the person of the Count," Count Luis was then removed from his post on the Alhambra.[54] His position was given to his worst enemy, the Corregidor of Granada—no soldier, but one of Deza's collaborators. This man must have been a former underling of Don Diego's, for Mendoza complained the following year that he wished to live anywhere else rather than "under the rule of one who used to be under my own hand."[55]

Yet Don Juan's Council of War was still unable to move. "Granada does not learn the truth," wrote Mendoza to Ruy Gómez. "The Señor Don Juan listens, and the Duke [of Sesa] is raring to go, and Luis Quixada scolds, and the President [Deza] proposes,

[52] GP III, 449, 450.
[53] Mondéjar was permitted to return temporarily after the war was over, from February, 1571 until October, 1572. Caro Baroja, Los Moriscos, p. 208.
[54] G. de Gr., p. 158.
[55] Mendoza to Ruy Gómez, Prince of Eboli, April 13, 1570, AIH 2: 587.

and the Archbishop blesses, and Muñatones keeps nagging, and the Marquis of Mondéjar, my nephew, is over there [at court]; he is not missed here."⁵⁶

The Moors fared so well that their King Aben Humeya had the time of his life. "The news is," Don Diego wrote, "that the *reyecillo* [kinglet] lives as well as we do. He plays *cañas*, and after sitting at council, he dances all night with Christian women."⁵⁷ This went on while "every day the Moors come and eat grapes with us at the gate to Granada; if this goes on, as I fear it will, I think I will invite them to my house which is the first in the place. We give them a hard chase, but it's to no avail."⁵⁸

At last, only a drastic accidental change moved King Philip to let Don Juan go after the enemy: the murder of Aben Humeya by his own people in October, not long after Don Diego's reports on the *reyecillo*'s diversions. A jealous Moor whose woman he had taken killed the rebel king.

After Don Juan had not moved from downtown Granada for almost nine months, the news that he was to lead the armies from now on brought him men and officers from all parts of Spain, as well as from the veteran Spanish armies in Italy. His ultimate aim was the relief of Galera in the far northeast near Murcia. There, the Marquis de los Velez was bogged down, his armies demoralized before the forces of Aben Aboo, the new king of the Moriscos. But it was decided, before venturing further afield, to make Granada secure by conquering nearby Güéjar. This was a village, normally of 250 households, in the Sierra Nevada, at the source of the Genil, only fourteen miles from Granada by the road along the river. Since the impenetrable wall of the Sierra protects Güéjar from the back, the Christians thought this cul-de-sac to be practically impregnable. In the summer of 1569 the Moors had made it their stronghold and storage place for loot and provisions. From there,

---

⁵⁶ G. Ticknor, *Historia de la literatura española* (edition of 1851), II, note 8 to p. 71, 504, gives the complete text of this letter, which is often reproduced in mutilated form.

⁵⁷ Mendoza to Espinosa, October 3, 1569, GP III, 451, 452; also Caro Baroja, *Los Moriscos*, p. 180.

⁵⁸ GP III, 451, 452.

nightly parties of marauders descended on the *vega*, often sneaking directly into Granada. Spies had brought reports that the place held four to six thousand enemies; therefore Don Juan thought it feasible to approach that feared den of bandits only with an overwhelming force.

The day before Christmas Eve, with a force large enough to conquer a nation—nine thousand infantry and seven hundred cavalry —two armies, one under Don Juan, the other under the Duke of Sesa, set out from Granada's Puerta de los Molinos, intending to clean out that robbers' nest in the mountains. This "Conquest of Güéjar" was the first, and perhaps, only campaign of that war on which Don Diego went along. His description of it reads like a quixotic adventure.[59] He did not believe that Güéjar could possibly hold so many Moors. But the Prince, he saw to his astonishment, took his advice from strangers totally ignorant of the lay of the land. The few natives still about were not consulted. (Mendoza did not relent in reminding the court of this idiocy. "If the Mondéjars really did the King a disservice," he wrote Ruy Gómez, "he has had his revenge, and little good it has done his Majesty, because they served him well, and he does not appreciate them, keeping them away from the place they know.")[60] When two officers, whom Don Juan sent to reconnoiter, brought back the information that there were about six thousand enemies in Güéjar, Mendoza noted at once (but probably was not listened to) that this was an unsubstantiated guess. The men admitted having seen no one there; not once, through day and night, had they seen a light or fire lit, and, as Don Diego remarks, "this in the heart of winter, in this coldest of lands, with the sides of the mountain under snow."[61] Nor had they observed any changing of the guard; in short, since they had noted nothing whatsoever, the spies—instead of recognizing that there was in fact no one—believed that the Moors had been forewarned and were simply in hiding.

"Fear is always so much stronger than Truth," thought the old

---

[59] *G. de Gr.*, pp. 158–162. It is not impossible that an unknown young soldier named Cervantes took part in this campaign—less than two years before the Battle of Lepanto.

[60] *AIH* 2 (1911): 587.

[61] *G. de Gr.*, p. 157.

soldier Mendoza.[62] He could not imagine that Don Juan would fall for such bogus information. "If the enterprise sounded so difficult, why did he leave the direction to captains who had never been in wars or had never seen an enemy? In such a case experience was what counted most! Did the Prince perhaps have secret information? Had Güéjar been abandoned? Was his undertaking nothing but a feint?"

The Prince's sincerity was unmistakable, however, although Mendoza questioned that of his closest advisers who, for unaccountable reasons, though possessing good eyesight, later in this march mistook the Duke of Sesa's banners and armies for those of the enemy. To catch the enemy with a pincer movement, while avoiding the open road by the Genil River, Don Juan's army split in two parts: one column of four thousand infantry and three hundred horse under the Duke of Sesa was taking the short route over the "knives' edges" of the mountainous heights—the historian Mármol with them. The Prince, with another column of five thousand men and four hundred cavalry (among them Don Diego), took a longer, roundabout way.

Although both columns planned to converge in Güéjar at the same time, a comedy of errors made Don Juan's army lose the way (Don Diego commented that only the native soldiers could have guided them at night). Late in the afternoon, long past the appointed hour, when the young warrior arrived in Güéjar, "leading an orderly and well-selected army," as Mendoza said, "appearing to those of us who have been in the enterprises of the Emperor the image of the father's spirit and foresight and desire to take part in everything," the banners of the Duke of Sesa were already flying over Güéjar's walls, and not a Moor was to be seen. "The Duke sent a message that the enemies were routed, when in truth there were no enemies!" gibed Don Diego. "That is why the taking of Güéjar had more fame from afar than nearby, and the [ensuing] congratulations considerably outnumbered the enemies."[63] Later, Don Diego noted that, despite this easy "conquest," haste, disappointment, and inexperience had been the cause of leaving Güéjar insufficiently protected. The Moors, and with them the nightly

[62] *G. de Gr.*, p. 154.
[63] *G. de Gr.*, p. 159.

danger to Granada, soon returned, but by that time Don Juan, disgusted over his false start, had left town, rushing off to the real battlefields at the Almanzora River, where the rebellion was spreading rapidly.

Meanwhile, Don Alonso de Granada Venegas had returned to court, instructing the King and Cardinal Espinosa about the new Morisco kinglet Aben Aboo whom he knew. With a new Moorish leader, the chances of a peaceful settlement behind the scenes seemed improved. Philip II ordered Don Alonso to negotiate for a truce but to conceal that he had royal permission to do so. The King wished to appear to agree to such a deal only *post factum*, out of mercy and compassion. Don Alonso returned to Granada in time to take part in this "Conquest of Güéjar," but afterwards Don Juan disappeared before he could be informed of the intended peace negotiations. Don Juan's authorization was necessary to provide Don Alonso with a cavalry escort for the dangerous trip he was planning in order to meet with the enemy secretly. Don Alonso confided his worries to Espinosa, asking him for new official orders so that he could start out. "Without this I cannot go, because those here [Deza and his helpers, now the only ones in both military and civil command of the city] would think I am moved by self-interest, and my honor would suffer." He also implored the Cardinal to send help for the Generalife, "which is in danger of being lost; it would be a pity for a house like that to go to pieces. Here, nothing is done to sustain it. All of us who own property here, have a heart like Job."[64]

With the usual delays, Don Alonso was left waiting three months for the necessary orders and equipment to start out on his peace mission. Don Diego, one of those who felt like Job in his heart, was the only one to sympathize and wait along with him. At the same time, Don Juan, with his overwhelming army, gave a brilliant account of himself in the farther regions of the kingdom. But in Granada, on March 19, 1570, under the sole command of Deza, another expulsion was staged that now included every Moor still left behind the previous year. In addition, Deza's order comprised

---

[64] Alonso de Granada Venegas to Cardinal Espinosa, January 1, 1570, *Arch. Instituto de Valencia de Don Juan*, Envio 1–57; folio 9. published as E. Spivakovsky, "Some Notes," *Archivum* 14: 228–229.

all the Moorish inhabitants of the countryside just outside the city walls, whose labor had made the *vega* such a paradisiacal garden. This time eight thousand Moriscos were uprooted and sent away. But although Deza and his men triumphed in what they conceived to be such a pious enterprise, the government "burned with jealousy" says Don Diego, upon learning now of the peace mission entrusted from above to Don Alonso.[65] Yet, the local powers of the Inquisitor remained in force unhindered; Deza was now so powerful that Don Diego found it advisable to praise his government to Espinosa.[66]

It must have amazed Philip II that Don Juan now wrote him from the field in terms like Mondéjar's a year earlier and which the King had disregarded. Like the Marquis, Don Juan found reason to be critical of Los Velez, to complain about Deza, and to deplore the quality of many of his troops "who fled at the sight of the fewest Moors."[67]

At this time Philip II was preparing to meet the increasing danger in the Mediterranean from the Turks who had conquered Cyprus. Another "Holy League" between Venice, the Pope, and Spain was in the making. (This drove Don Diego into wistful memories of his rôle in the similar League thirty years back. He smarted over the King's neglect to seek his advice.)[68] But before sending his armies against the Turks, Philip II was impatient to bring about, first, the end of the Morisco rebellion. He and Cardinal Espinosa now urged Don Alonso more strongly than ever to attempt an understanding with Aben Aboo. No doubt the King was aware that he was in fact following the policies advocated in the first place by Mondéjar—but he never admitted it. He expressed his own autocratic sense of justice simply by promoting the Marquis, without apologizing for the wrongs he had done him, to the viceroyalty of Valencia.

[65] GP III, 458.   [66] GP III, 456, 458, 461.

[67] In *DIE* 28 are letters from Don Juan, written in Padules, May 1, 1570 to May 31; then from Andarax, June 4 to July 27, 1570, places where he was together with Don Alonso de Granada Venegas. From the tone he then took it appears that for the first time he understood the mischief of the anti-Morisco faction. Probably he was learning a thing or two from a side to which he had not listened while Mondéjar was its chief representative.

[68] GP III, 453; also, letter to Ruy Gómez, see note 59, above.

Meanwhile the Cardinal had seen to it that Don Diego's situation was somewhat improved. Apparently the few occasions when Mendoza left his house, such as when he witnessed the exodus of the Moriscos or went along to Güéjar, were in his line of duty, since he was under orders to assist in the war. Otherwise, he had been virtually a prisoner and therefore, as he conceived it, not responsible for his actions or his inactivity. Now he was technically free—though not permitted to leave Granada. It was gratifying that his master forgave to some extent the vassal's foolishness (*locura*) that had offended the authority of the King's house, "when I should have behaved better than the *mozos* [young fellows]." But he felt a deep regret about not being used in the present emergencies. He was embarrassed to sit around like "men without qualities" and not take a voluntary part in the war effort. He was ready to fortify and guard some spot, perhaps the coastal region of Almería, which was in great danger from the Turks.[69] But the King refused to use him.

At least, Don Diego was satisfied that Philip's mind was now set upon a fast end to the war, in contrast to the underlings who presently had a hand in the local affairs of Granada and who, as Mendoza reported, were interested in dragging the situation out for years to come. In Don Diego's allusions and veiled accusations directed to the Cardinal, he did not name any names except several times to commend, pointedly, the government and behavior of President Deza—as though Deza were not the leading spirit of those wanting to fight to the finish. This is somewhat astounding, although from the personal point of view of a lonely old man it might be understood. It seems that the Inquisitor, however pitiless in his policy, was the only one of all those now in leading positions in Granada who treated Don Diego with personal regard and perhaps even some deference, while all others took so little account of his presence "as though I were a basket."[70]

While Philip II was already pondering how to disband his armies with the least damage to his finances,[71] Don Alonso, deep in the

[69] GP III, 454, 455.
[70] GP III, 459–461.
[71] Don Luis de Requeséns, March 28, 1570, Arch. Sim., Cámara de Castilla, leg. 2152, folio 120.

Alpujarras in the midst of active warfare, established a correspondence with the "Black King." By the end of May, he was almost jubilant about the development of his mission. Many villages were prepared to surrender to him.[72] But in other regions fighting continued, and the city of Granada was again beset by marauders. Don Diego reported that "the enemies have come as guests to the gates of the place, each day carrying away cattle, people, flour, and even the millers." It was, he said, a "dirty little war," and "it ought to be ended fast by some great effort, and then the kingdom founded anew."[73]

In the spring and early summer, Don Diego suffered from a severe attack of sciatica that left him almost paralyzed; probably it was brought on by his exertions in the Christmastime expedition. He was unable to leave for a cure despite the King's permission (through Espinosa's mediation) to do so. But in the warmth of Granada's summer he recovered, and his good spirits returned by the end of June, when the war was dying down: "For my *compañero* [this must refer to Granada Venegas] the war has been over for days, because His Majesty uses him for a task which means an equal favor for me," he wrote on June 29 to the Cardinal. Since now there was practically peace, "but with suspicion, and racked by jealousies," he offered his services for armadas or anywhere else he might be useful.[74] Being restored to good health, he continued to be embarrassed not to do his bit in one of the theaters of the war effort.

When Don Alonso was halfway through with his mission, having pacified a number of villages and former nests of resistance, Deza and his men countered the promises Don Alonso had made to the Moors who surrendered peacefully to him. Instead of leaving those people alone, as Granada Venegas promised them in the name of the King, the Christians rounded them up, sending most of them

---

[72] Alonso de Granada Venegas, letters to the householders in Almuñecar and Bentomic and to the *reyecillo*, March 18, 1570; to the *reyecillo*, March 30 and April 1, 1570; to Philip II, April 1, 1570; to Vázquez de Salazar, April 2, 1570, Arch. Sim., Cámara de Castilla, leg. 2153, folios 141, 143, 140, 144; to Espinosa, May 21, 1570, *Inst. Don Juan*, see note 64, above. Cf. also Mármol Carvajal, *Historia*, II, 371–378.

[73] GP III, 456–457.

[74] GP III, 458.

to the galleys, selling others into slavery. The rest they planned to expel. Aben Aboo, reacting out of fear, suspected his contact man with Don Alonso, the trustworthy Habaqui, to have deceived him. He killed Habaqui and continued to fight.

This turn of affairs made Don Diego's heart sink again. We have no further correspondence from his companion Granada Venegas, but it is possible also to imagine his disappointment. Don Diego complained in August that he was not given anything to do. Had he not paid part of his *locura* with sickness, poverty, and humiliation?[75] He did not write to the Cardinal for the next four months, just the period in which he saw with regret and disgust how the Moors who had put their trust in his friend were now being treated so cruelly. For All Saints' Day, the first of November, those in Granada arranged a new general deportation.

Yet Aben Aboo continued to be active in the mountain fastnesses; there were still many pockets of resistance. Granada did not feel the pinch of that more remote guerrilla fighting so much. "Everything is now finished here," said Don Diego on January 11, 1571, "but the wounds are so deep that arms cannot cover them up." As "one who was born here and will not live long enough to recover what he lost," he wanted to tell Espinosa all about it.[76]

Perhaps on the spur of the moment, reflecting that he was not allowed to see this steadfast good friend and might never talk to him again,[77] Mendoza decided to put down what he had witnessed and heard—not only for his friend, but also for posterity, the best friend of those neglected in their lifetime. "The day will come that will disclose the truth hidden and suppressed by the malice of its century," he quoted Seneca, another Spaniard wronged by his sovereign, when he sent a copy of the manuscript of the *Guerra de Granada* to a friend. "He who thinks only of the people of his age is born but for few people."[78] Perhaps the recipient of those bitter but truthful words was Cardinal Espinosa; or it may have been

---

[75] August 6, 1570, GP III, p. 459.

[76] GP III, 459–461.

[77] Cardinal Espinosa died in September, 1572, while Don Diego was still in Granada.

[78] *BAE*, XXI, part one, p. 65. From Seneca, *Epistola* 79. I am grateful to Professor P. O. Kristeller for this rendition of the Latin quotation.

Jerónimo Zurita; there were not many possibilities, because by then Mendoza could count his public on his fingers. But among his first few readers was the King.[79]

The *Guerra de Granada* was a history of the war in which at first Don Diego was told to serve by way of punishment and where later he was not allowed to help, while he had to witness the growing disrespect to his proud and noble House and the destruction of his father's kingdom. By writing of that war, Don Diego freed himself from his disgust, from the neglect of his person, and from the studied uselessness to which he was condemned. On the events of the "dirty little war" he constructed a history worthy of Sallust or Tacitus, authors he diligently read in those days of enforced leisure.[80] Delving deeply in Arabic and Hispanic chronicles, polishing the Spanish style, usually so meandering, to the lustre and precision of his Latin models, searching for the causes of events, letting them speak for themselves (only occasionally stressing or implying a moral judgment), unsparing of his own blood relations, he put down a piece of truth.

I choose a narrow path, and though cumbersome, sterile, and inglorious [not unlike the trails in his Granadine mountains, he might have thought, compared to the commodious Roman highways], it may be of use to posterity. Manifold [were the] causes [of the war]: rebellion of outlaws, conspiracy of slaves, commotion of serfs, incompetence, hatred, ambitions and pretensions [of government authorities], lack of money, trifles, disdains and troubles, or not being believed and little appreciated [an obvious allusion to the treatment accorded those of Mondéjar], I hope the effort will make it worthwhile to look closely at the fact of how from slight beginnings and purely personal reasons arise the greatest troubles, difficulties, and damage to the entire community, almost beyond remedy. It will be seen that a war, locally thought to be of little account, is judged abroad to be of great impor-

---

[79] Jerónimo Zurita to Philip II, J. D. Dormer, *Progresos de la historia en el reyno de Aragón*, p. 128.

[80] Mendoza to Zurita, December 1, 1573, Dormer, *Progresos*, p. 570. On the *Guerra de Granada* and its bibliography, see GP III, 141–198. Add to GP's list: edition of M. Gómez Moreno, Madrid, 1948. See also E. Spivakovsky's papers in *Renaiss. News* 17 and *Archivum* 14.

tance, holding the attention of princes, friends and foes, of far and near.[81]

While Mendoza was at work on his history, the war ended with the death of Aben Aboo, who was murdered on March 15, 1571— like his predecessor, by his own people. His body, stuffed with straw and salt, propped up on a horse, was paraded through Granada. "Everything is now as usual here," reported Don Diego. "Deza has worked hard and ruled well. Of Moors: ten thousand and more remain, but they are dispersed and famished; they are waiting to cross over to Barbary as they always did. In the end, they will be finished off, [some] by going to Barbary, [others] by illness, famine, police roundups, and it will be done." "There is no more to say," he ended the last of his extant letters to Espinosa.[82] By now he reserved all he had to say for his work.

The authorities did not let the Moriscos vanish as naturally as Don Diego predicted they would. They hastened the process with a final expulsion that, all in all, led to the uprooting of 400,000 Granadine citizens and the complete desertion of 400 townships.[83] ". . . We saw the enemy," said Mendoza, "a bellicose people, armed, adept in their [mountainous] localities, assisted by Berbers and Turks, vanquished and subdued, uprooted from their land, dispossessed of their houses and goods; men, women, children led away, roped together; prisoners of war sold in auction or dragged away to live in lands far from their own: captivity and transmigration on the same scale as that of peoples one reads about in history; a doubtful victory and of such dangerous procedure that there was doubt at times whether God wished to punish us or the enemy. . . ."[84]

[81] G. de Gr., pp. 1, 2.
[82] March 23, 1571, GP III, 461–462.
[83] Miguel Lafuente de Alcántara, Historia de Granada, IV, 221; cf. also Caro Baroja, Los Moriscos, p. 56.
[84] G. de Gr., pp. 2, 3.

18. BENEFACTOR OF HIS KING,
TO 1575

> To prove my good conscience and my
> loyalty I declare His Majesty my uni-
> versal heir.
>
> Don Diego[1]

As soon as the kingdom of Granada was pacified, Philip II remembered that Mendoza had not yet cleared his old accounts. Six years before, the King had set his chief minister of finance, Don Francisco Gutiérrez de Cuellar, to disentangle facts from slander, faulty memories from actual obligations. That process had begun in 1559, when Don Diego was in Philip's good graces. It is likely that Mendoza's numerous enemies from the time of Siena, the Duke of Florence in particular, were the ones to set the King's officials on his trail, but from then on the heavy bureaucratic machine trapped them as well as Mendoza in its red tape.

It availed him nothing to remind the accountants again and again of the enormity of the enterprise of building the castle in Siena. The construction had continued through twenty months; wages and payments for materials had been swallowed up in a bottomless abyss. In 1559 the paymaster had acknowledged having received the money, a fact that alone should have served to clear

---

[1] ". . . Por sanear mi conciencia y mi lealtad, hago a su Magestad mi universal heredero . . . ," GP II, 389.

Mendoza. However, when his agents purchased materials necessary
for construction and supplies, they did not request receipts in his
name—for the reason that the details of the work were a military
secret, and his agents, when dealing with merchants and other
sources of supply, had to disguise themselves. This seems to have
been the usual procedure of occupation forces in alien territory. In
similar instances it was customary to believe a trusted minister's
oath. Mendoza had sworn many times to the truth of his statements. In April, 1552, his secretary Pedro Ximénez had gone to the
court of Charles V with a full accounting of all money received by
Mendoza up to that time, and that report had been accepted.[2]

But now it counted for nothing that his finances had been cleared
in 1553 under Charles V's rule in Brussels; that Mendoza had lost
his own accounts and a large portion of his goods when the people
of Siena sacked his premises, while another part of his documents
had been lost at sea; that he poured his own money, whatever he
had and was able to borrow, into the construction of the ill-fated
castle; that most witnesses of those times were now either dispersed
within the empire or were long since dead; and that Mendoza,
whose oath was not to be taken as false, repeatedly swore that he
owed nothing. The King was not satisfied.

When he used his old vassal once more—and without paying
him one maravedi—for the armada of 1567–1568 that never sailed,
Philip II had stopped harassing him. Afterward, with the outbreak
of the Morisco War, Gutiérrez de Cuellar was needed for greater
things. For the duration, the minister of finance was sent to Granada to keep an eye on Philip's financial interests in that convulsed
kingdom. But on July 13, 1572, the King wrote to Cuellar, who by
then had returned to Madrid, to take up his interrupted task again,
a task that now, with an ever-shrinking circle of old witnesses, with
memories still dimmer twenty years after the events, looked impossible.[3]

Soon, attorneys from the Chancelry and from Mendoza started
to travel back and forth between Madrid and Granada, with Don
Diego insisting he had to argue his own case in Madrid.[4] Now that

---

[2] Arch. Sim., Contaduría Mayor, no. 1414, Rose-file.

[3] Philip II to Cuellar, July 13, 1572, in R. Foulché-Delbosc, "Un point contesté de la vie de Don Diego Hurtado de Mendoza," *RH* 2 (1895): 272.

[4] Ibid., pp. 274–278.

Espinosa was gone, however, and even Ruy Gómez had died in his early fifties in 1573, there was almost no intermediary left between the unforgiving King and his superannuated vassal. But by 1574, Philip II, himself desirous of having the matter settled, gave in to the cogency of Don Diego's argument, conceding his coming to Madrid. He was to stay only for two months (that provision was disregarded later), and he was not allowed to set foot in the royal palace. A secretary of the King went to Granada to present this permit to the old courtier. Giving it the treatment customary for royal orders, Don Diego took the document in his right hand, kissed it, and put it on his head.[5]

Though that concession was made only for reasons of expediency, Don Diego felt encouraged to regard the King's permit as some sort of pardon. Since there was no trustworthy "ear" at the royal palace, which he never entered again, he now addressed Philip II directly. As long as he lived, he would always give his advice, even unasked, as he had done it with the father of his master. It grieved Mendoza, who had seen Spain grow so great during his life, to see it gliding from its eminence. Within the last three years, his country had taken hard blows: the over-celebrated victory of the Holy League over the Turks at Lepanto (1571) had turned to ashes. The league had rapidly fallen apart through a separate understanding of Venice with the Turk (a fact that surprised the world but not Don Diego, who had predicted it, wondering why no one else seemed to remember thirty years back).[6] The Turks, recovering quickly, achieved in the summer of 1574 an overwhelming victory over the Spaniards at Tunis and La Goleta. The wheel of fortune was reversed, the proud memory wiped out, and the event made painful because of young Don Juan of Austria's splendid but transitory victory over the same places shortly before.

Deeply moved by this news, Mendoza wrote to Philip II in September, 1574, after the fall and loss of Tunis and La Goleta with the Spanish garrison of five thousand men. The "meanest vassal" offered the King all that remained of his life—he was seventy— and of his goods in order to help his master. He gave the King the benefit of his advice about La Goleta, detailed, technical, experi-

[5] Ibid., p. 280.
[6] GP III, 453, 457.

enced. The King, upon reading it, might have regretted secretly
that he had not listened in time to this voice from the past.[7]

Within his own class, Don Diego was practically a stranger now.
He survived the few friends he had still left after his loss of reputation and was not in a position to make new ones in that late hour
of his life. But several nephews and cousins were around him, and
he had contact with a few intellectuals, the *letrados*, to whose circle
he really belonged by avocation, although formerly, as their Maecenas, he had not exactly mingled with them. He engaged in a com-
radely correspondence with Jerónimo Zurita, the noted historian of
the crown of Aragon,[8] who once had sent his young friend, the doctor Juan Páez de Castro, to Don Diego's house in Trent. Juan Páez
had also been dead several years.

Zurita must have been one of Don Diego's few contemporaries
to receive a copy of his *Guerra de Granada* not later than 1572,
possibly earlier, because (as mentioned above) the work might
have been seen by Cardinal Espinosa before he died that year. At
any rate, Zurita mentioned the work to Philip II on January 23,
1573, as though he were speaking of something known as well to
the King as to himself.[9] This fact disproves the generally held as-
sumption that Mendoza did not publish the *Guerra* out of fear of
the King's disapproval. His criticism of the war effort in the work
was no harsher than in his letters to Espinosa and Ruy Gómez that
Philip II could see at any time, and often did. In fact, by sending
his book to Zurita and, perhaps to Espinosa (doubtless also to Ruy
Gómez), he must have seen to it that Philip II himself would read
his history. The King and the few persons important to Mendoza
would have been the ones to know the truth as he had seen it—

[7] Modesto Lafuente, *Historia general de España*, X, 88–89, n. 1.

[8] About Mendoza's esteem for Zurita's work see D. J. Dormer, *Progresos de
la historia en el reyno de Aragón*, p. 185.

[9] Ibid., p. 128. Zurita writes to Philip II, recommending Deza for the office of
inquisitor-general as successor to Espinosa, early in 1573: ". . . y el 23 del
mismo Enero le dice, que en el memorial que habia remitido á su Majestad, se
olvidó de poner a D. Pedro de Deza, presidente de Granada, que fué muchos
años del Consejo de la inquisición, de quien D. Diego de Mendoza, lib. primero
de la *guerra de Granada*, núm. 7, fol. 10, dice fué 'Caballero que avia passado
por todos los oficios de su profesion, y dado buena cuenta dellos.' "

rather than the contemporary public that might criticize Philip II. His quoting Seneca shows that, as a historiographer, he was not averse now to posthumous fame.

Mendoza's letters to Zurita usually discussed books, such as the Arabic works he had gathered in Granada or the fact that the King wanted to acquire his library for the Escorial. After Don Diego received permission to come to Madrid, Zurita was the one whom he begged to find a house for him, if possible in his vicinity—" a house with a view, even though it does not look like much itself."[10]

As early as July, 1572, the King had cast his eye on Don Diego's collection of books and manuscripts, famous among the *cognoscenti*. Royal agents started to negotiate for it concurrently with the reopening of Mendoza's accounts; apparently Philip II's thoughts were evolving some sort of *quid pro quo*. Mendoza had sent his collection from Granada, along with other books that still remained in his various former residences, to the experts of the university of Alcalá for appraisal. But no bid was made or agreed upon by the time he left Granada in the latter part of 1574.

Before he settled down in Madrid, Mendoza went to Alcalá himself to take possession of his books again, "dusting them, and looking to see if they were rat-eaten, but satisfied that they had been treated well." For the first time in many years he saw all assembled the books he had left. It astonished him to find many authors whom he had forgotten, authors whose works he had read and annotated, "having learned so little out of them."[11]

Doubtless the first eight months in Madrid brought him some contentment through his reunion with his literary friends as well as with all his books, his entire collection now being under his roof. Ambrosio de Morales came to see him, and Mendoza told him that often when he had to travel, he had bought the same books of his favorite authors that he had been unable to take along, so that now he found two or three copies of the same works side by side, all of which he had underlined and annotated.[12]

---

[10] Mendoza to Zurita, Granada, December 1, 1573 and June 14, 1574; Dormer, *Progresos*, pp. 570–572.
[11] Mendoza to Zurita, Alcalá, November 18, 1574, ibid., p. 572.
[12] GP III, p. 472.

In the summer Mendoza fell ill. His name had not been fully cleared, and he had not seen his King. Philip II, his freely chosen master, vindictive by nature, was not a benefactor of this vassal who once ruined himself in his struggle to win a kingdom for the king, and who was still unjustly made to account for the money spent and lost in that useless struggle. Whether by design or by the government's usual procrastination neither the disposition of the Mendoza library nor the examination of the Mendoza accounts had visibly advanced by August, 1575, when the foot that had troubled Don Diego for many years became gangrenous. Three toes were paralyzed or dead; a bevy of surgeons debated whether to cut off the old man's toes, the foot, or the entire leg.

Several days before the operation, on August 6, Mendoza wrote his will. He was crowning the work of his life with an action that concluded everything that for some reason had been left undone. It cleared his relation with the monarch; it showed the world that Philip II had no claim on him. He stated that the examination of his accounts should be continued, so that it would be seen he owed the King nothing, and with the last words he was to write with his own hand, he declared: "And since I have accounts with the King, our master, concerning which I am being questioned, although the King knows very well that I do not owe him anything, to prove my good conscience and my loyalty, I declare his Majesty my universal heir."[13]

The day Mendoza made the will, the Duke of Infantado drew up an inventory of all his books, with a separate list of the hundred or so that Don Diego had lent him.[14] So, with notaries already taking stock of Mendoza's estate, rumors about the testament, which was closed and sealed four days before the day of surgery, were abroad and reached Philip II. Few people, the monarch least of all, may have cared during the last years whether Mendoza was dead or alive, but now the royal world watched his every breath.

On August 9, the keeper of the King's jewels, Hernando de Bri-viesca, informed another courtier of Don Diego's health and of the impending operation:

---

13 Ibid., p. 389.
14 Ibid., pp. 536, 551.

It seems to me that, whatever will be done to him, there is danger, because I am told he is very old. Therefore I went there to see what was going on. They tell me he made his testament and closed it, and when I was there, he confessed for the second time, before receiving the Holy Sacrament tonight. His nephew Don Luis de la Cueva is with him. He is said to be in good spirits. I am saying all this so that you may tell His Majesty I wished only to learn how he had disposed of his library, but since the testament was closed, I did not learn anything about it. I saw many books there, however, and many people, and it could well be that, when it comes to collecting them, there will be nothing left. It would be well, therefore, to have some plan ready. His Majesty, who usually has such good ones, should think of something and let me know, because it would be a pity to lose even a leaf of all the paper he has. . . .[15]

Promptly, Philip II dispatched his finance minister, Francisco Gutiérrez de Cuellar, to keep an eye on Don Diego's household. He also sent his secretary Antonio Pérez (then the official closest to the King, at the zenith of his good name and power) to watch the operation. Pérez wrote about it many years later when he himself was in exile. His eyewitness account of the event in which he was personally neutral sounds truthful; he also adduces Don Diego's grandnephew Don Francisco de Mendoza, son of the third Marquis of Mondéjar, as corroborator of the story. "When they proceeded to cut his leg off," Pérez said, ". . . after he had confessed and taken communion, ready for death, and anticipating his martyrium, he called his confessor and told him: 'Padre Ovando, stay with me and embrace me. We will say the Credo together with the blows of the irons; this way the pain of every cut will find me with a word of [the Credo] on my lips, so that however deeply it hurts, no complaint or moan shall escape my lips. . . .' "[16]

Mendoza survived his ordeal, and the next day Antonio Pérez brought him the King's pardon. In return, Pérez received the key to Don Diego's desk from his own hands. Later, Briviesca, the keeper of the royal jewels, also visited him. The dying man told him that he was "giving His Majesty his books, paintings, antiques, and

[15] Ibid., II, 391.
[16] Ibid., III, 243, 244.

everything else he has besides, and that he has sufficient proofs for all his accounts, and that he did not ask anything of His Majesty but that he let those accounts be rigorously examined. Afterwards he said the most excellent things about His Majesty."[17]

Three days later Don Diego's heart stopped.

By his last action he may have felt he made good, even bettered, his once-frustrated intention to present Philip, his young master, with a kingdom. During his banishment, when he was rejected by the King, his sense of frustration had deepened; he had even thought that he never had been of any use to his master "except among ship captains."[18]

Now his age-old ambition had come true after all. He had a gift of royal grandeur to give his King, a treasury of the mind. Bequeathing Philip II everything he owned, particularly his priceless manuscripts and books, Mendoza must have been content to become, in the end, his master's benefactor.

[17] Ibid., II, 392.
[18] ". . . sino para entre maestres de naos . . . ," ibid., III, 453.

EPILOGUE

With Mendoza disappeared the last of the few Spanish Renaissance men. Who else, in Spain, was equally at home in so many fields of interest? In the record of his life as a statesman, these universal interests might be counted as hobbies, though it would be a mistake to call him an amateur. An expert in the "humanist" disciplines[1]—grammar, poetry, history, and rhetoric—as well as in metaphysics, mathematics, theology, jurisprudence, and the natural sciences, he was totally an Aristotelian with his scientific philosophy of nature, his humanist preoccupation with the Greek text, and his study of Arabic philosophy, which also is based on Hellenic philosophy. Yet predominant in his complex personality was the statesman, the man of action, the diplomat. The diplomat overshadowed the philosopher, but perhaps the philosopher contributed to his failure in statesmanship. As governor of Siena, subconciously he himself might have brought on the revolt and loss of the republic—the greatest crisis of his political life—because his philosophical scruples, his humanist theories, prevented him from being a successful tyrant. This contradiction within the confluence

---

[1] As Paul Oskar Kristeller defined them in "Studies on Renaissance Humanism during the Last Twenty Years," *Studies in the Renaissance* 9 (1962): 21. Mendoza's use of the word "humanist" agrees with Professor Kristeller's definition; praising an *ilustrísimo autor*, Mendoza gives him these attributes: "gran filósofo, mayor teólogo, jurisconsulto célebre y perfecto humanista," in "Carta al Capitán Salazar," *Bibl. Clásica* 41: 436.

of so many streams of thought in his mind brings special interest to his place in history.

There is no contemporary of Mendoza (certainly no other Spaniard) whose reports of contact with foreign governments and peoples would offer an analogous illumination of the workings of power politics in the first post-Machiavellian decades. In the middle of the sixteenth century, the time of the Reformation, with its upheavals in the European balance of power between Spain, France, the Empire, the papacy, and smaller states, Mendoza's career provides a live commentary on the political events. The machinations of the rulers are revealed by his encounters—often detailed in his day-to-day proceedings—with the Senate of Venice, his government in Siena, the Duke of Florence, the Popes. His political life complements the reign of Charles V; he strides from one governmental mission to the next just as the Emperor proceeds, by means political or military, to attain universal monarchy. Both sovereign and minister are driven by the ambition to dominate the world; their arrogance becomes their hubris, and their grand design fails them both in the end, at the same time. Mendoza's role especially shows how the exertion of imperialist power, humanist ethics notwithstanding, inevitably entails moral corruption, hypocrisy, greed, and imbalance in the one who tries to wield this power. In an interplay of cause and effect (shown vividly in the correspondence of Mendoza the writer, at once entertaining and learned), the actions of this "imperialist" foreshadow what was to keep the world in unrest ever since.

The only author of his time "who knew how to combine in one and the same work the art of writing with that of thinking,"[2] Mendoza was regarded as the author of *Lazarillo de Tormes* for over three centuries. The "unknown" author of this work was a lofty poet, a great writer and humanist, yet a master of deliberate casualness also, as well as a comic genius. Mendoza was all that—the only Spaniard of that time who possibly could have written this

[2] ". . . es decir, que supo juntar en una misma obra el arte de escribir bien con el de pensar." Antonio de Capmany, *Teatro histórico-crítico de la eloquencia española*, III, 6.

masterpiece, which first appeared in 1553.[3] If his authorship of it were not now disputed, Mendoza's popular fame in Spain would be second only to that of Cervantes. But his name is usually omitted from the honor roll of Spanish Renaissance writers. His own wish, his intentional renunciation of fame, is responsible for this undeserved oblivion. Far from aspiring to publication, he avoided it in fact long before he revealed his reason for anonymity during his stay in the monastery. In his fifties, writing in Alcántara the lines pertinent to his decision, he professed to regret the choice between fame and religion he was forced to make. But it seems that even as a young student he left the literary world uncertain about the authenticity of his writings. It is impossible to say why as a youth he should have wanted to hide from a wider public. His oldest brother Don Luis, the stern head of the Mondéjar branch of the House of Mendoza, could possibly have forbidden him to publish. Or perhaps his equivocal stand on orthodox religion might have had something to do with his persistent anonymity.

In his poem from Alcántara (the only composition of his that seems to reveal something of his soul), there is a significant omission: the absence of any reference to religion. This is unusual for works produced in a monastery. That his last testament is drafted in deeply religious terms might not throw much light on his attitude of early years. Nor should the state of his soul, what he called his "conscience," be judged by his deposition in front of the Inquisitors, expressed in the presence of danger.

Yet Mendoza, despite his advocation of tolerance toward different faiths, was by no means irreligious. Some of the rare records of his faith—quite unsolicited—date from the period of the conclave after the death of Paul III. Then, the Emperor ordered him to keep in constant touch with the secret and sacred proceedings to effect the election of a Pope sympathetic to the Imperial side, and Mendoza, while doing his duty by the Emperor, took care that the capital sin of committing such interference would not be ascribed

[3] See E. Spivakovsky, "The *Lazarillo de Tormes* and Mendoza," *Symposium* 15 (1961): 271–285; and idem, "New Arguments in Favor of Mendoza's Authorship of the *Lazarillo*," ibid. (spring 1970).

to his conscience, but to those who gave him his orders.[4] He was, he said, "moved by honest zeal, not wanting the ruin of Christendom [through the election of an anti-Imperial Pope], but wanting to be an instrument toward [the salvation of Christendom], but I protest —the consequences resulting from this [renewed interference in the conclave] should be on your soul, not mine."[5] Further, he observed the cardinals displaying a self-interest that he had not expected in them "because they are sinning against the Holy Ghost."[6] He declared they were "devilish people, more confused within the conclave than the devils in Judas' kettle, and therefore it is no wonder that Popes like that [Paul III] issue from there; it is true that the Holy Ghost makes them righteous, but the tool damages the product. After what I have seen here, I am the most frightened man in the world, and I wish I did not have to witness it."[7]

At that time, reporting the "holy Christian death" of his nephew to a friend, he said that the proceedings of the conclave had made him "lose the little devotion I hitherto had."[8] And in his "Fable of Adonis and Hippomanes" he asked: "Is God every person's own agony?"[9]

Apparently, then, he was a believer, though perhaps out of habit rather than piety. Conventionally devout, as he had been before the conclave, he had felt free nevertheless to study other faiths and philosophies, as well as the natural sciences. Possibly he applied to his studies the doctrine of "twofold truth," but not in the hypocritical way the Averroists were erroneously said to have practiced it. The system of thought holding that the Christian could be a rationalist in philosophy as long as he remained a believer in his religion has been based on certain equivocations in the words of Averroës. Present-day criticism finds nothing of this "twofold truth" in Averroës. The doctrine itself "does not necessarily indicate secret disbelief . . . but rather the ideal of philosophical and

---

[4] Mendoza to Arras, December 8, 1549, AC, p. 141.

[5] Mendoza to Arras, December 21, 1549, AC, pp. 155–156.

[6] AC, p. 187, "porque pecan contra el Espíritu Santo . . ."

[7] AC, p. 183.

[8] Mendoza to Gutierre López de Padilla (erroneously dated March, 1550; content dates it to December, 1549), AIH 2 (1911): 275.

[9] "Es dios a cada uno su agonia?" C. Malcolm Batchelor, ed., A tí, Doña Marina, p. 127.

scientific liberty,"[10] an interpretation applicable to Mendoza's method of work and thought.

Although he was critical of the leading men of Catholicism, Mendoza accepted the edifice of the Church tolerantly. While he noticed (as well as any Protestant reformer) the wear that the abuses of its human element had occasioned in its fabric, he did not deem it necessary to pull down the entire structure. Yet he must have derived satisfaction in escaping now and then from its confines into the world of a wider human wisdom. These were harmless excursions that refreshed his mind. With the fields of classical and Arabic philosophy at his disposal, he helped preserve his individuality against the growing uniformity of thought for which such people as his former antagonist De Soto were preparing the ground.

Writing secular poetry in the Convent of San Benito of Alcántara was a dissenting act, as was his defense of Averroës at the Council of Trent. There he argued against the orthodox Thomist, not from the new Protestant position, for which he seems to have felt no sympathy, but from what he thought was Averroës' point of view. It amused him, of course, and he enjoyed teasing the rigid De Soto, who represented the unchangeable Church.

The poem from Alcántara, written most likely eight years after the Council of Trent, attests to Mendoza's continuing "otherness." His complaints there are unorthodox enough to support his growing reputation of being a catalyst for latent unorthodox opinion. Gradually he slid into the role of anonymous spokesman for a generally dissentient element expressing an amorphous rebellion. It was a vague and powerless movement, but it alleviated somewhat the stony conformity of thought exacted by the Spain of the Counter Reformation.

With the onset of the Counter Reformation in the 1550s—simultaneous with Mendoza's return to Spain—a mood of increasing anguish and despair, caused by the ubiquity of the Inquisition, pervaded the country. The literature reflecting this climate consisted chiefly of sermons, mystical devotional poetry, and homiletics. This anguished aspect of Spanish literature in the time of Philip II is

[10] P. O. Kristeller, "Paduan Averroism and Alexandrism," *Renaissance Thought II*, pp. 111–118.

now being explained as the result of a century-long persecution of the descendants of *conversos*. People who tried to conceal their embarrassing ancestry (often it included a parent or one or more grandparents or great-grandparents victimized by the Inquisition) sought refuge from their inherited fear of discovery of such "blemish" in the inner meaning of Christianity, in charity, in otherworldliness.[11] This mood deepened in the course of generations; eventually it found expression in great spiritual writers: Saint Theresa, Fray Luis de León, Fray Diego de Estella, the Blessed Juan de Avila—all of Jewish descent. Intellectualism itself was being stigmatized as an attribute of the "tainted." Since most of the intellectuals, the *letrados*, belonged to the middle class, consisting almost exclusively of *conversos*, very few writers were able to preserve a positive secular mind.

Perhaps this helps to explain why Mendoza, secure in his own privileged class, was able to maintain his stand from the beginning of that thought-crippling era. He fought almost playfully, and alone, against the monolithic control of conscience and mood. His former conversational assault against the rocklike Thomistic philosophy at the Council of Trent was but a prelude to the continuing manifestations of the independence of his mind. In his "otherness," he filled a role that was clear to his contemporaries. Whenever an anonymous pamphlet knocked the prevailing pompousness or bigotry, he was usually suspected to be the author—and very likely he was, as long as the style was witty and brilliant, or, as Juan Páez de Castro expressed it, "*suísimo*, even without his signature,"[12] which means "very much *his*."

Even though various literary critics do not now accept most of these anonymous writings as Mendoza's, it is revealing to study the character that his friends and countrymen attributed to him. It blends with his literary character as perceived in his correspondence and in his authentic publications. It is based on an undefinable "very-much *his*" quality, since apparently none of his contemporaries was large enough, courageous enough, or secure enough to

[11] See M. P. Hornik, ed., *Collected Studies in Honour of Américo Castro's 80th Year*, especially the articles by Antonio Dominguez Ortiz, A. A. Sicroff, Manuel Durán, and Francisco Márquez Villanueva.

[12] Páez de Castro to Zurita, from Quer, January 30, 1569, Dormer, *Progresos*, pp. 557, 558.

acquire such a reputation. Fame he had forsaken; therefore no monument honors him in Spain. No plaque recalls his presence even in Granada. But in the completenes of his unique personality be became a legend in his own time.

APPENDIX

A Note on Mendoza's Works, Published and Unpublished

Mendoza published nothing under his name during his lifetime. I attempted an explanation of this puzzling fact in chapter fourteen. A list of all editions of his *Poetry* is in GP III, 124–129; also C. Malcolm Batchelor, ed., *A tí, Doña Marina*. His *Prose*: Mendoza spoke of his Latin report of the expedition to Tunis to Conrad Gesner (GP I, p. 63), but this is apparently lost. See on this my " 'Lo de la Goleta y Túnez,' a Work of Diego Hurtado de Mendoza?" *Hispania* 23 (Madrid, 1963): 366–379. On Aristotle: Mendoza's "Paraphrasis de physico auditu en 14 quadernos" is unpublished; the autograph Latin manuscript is in El Escorial, MS F-II-6, folios 63-242. El Escorial has also two manuscript copies of Mendoza's Spanish translation of the *Mechanica*, one of them with marginal and textual corrections in Mendoza's hand (MS-f-III-15). The second (f-III-27), appears to be a clean copy of the first. It was published by R. Foulché-Delbosc, *R.H.* 5, nos. 13 & 14 (1898): 367–405. His *Guerra de Granada* was published more than fifty years after Mendoza's death by Luis Tribaldo (Lisbon, 1627).

Of all other works published under his name, there is no proof that he was the author. Among these are *Lazarillo de Tormes*, published anonymously in 1554 in Burgos, Alcalá, and Antwerp. See my "The *Lazarillo de Tormes* and Mendoza," *Symposium* 15 (1961): 271–285; and "*New Arguments in Favor of Mendoza's Authorship of the Lazarillo de Tormes*," ibid., spring issue, 1970. Other anonymous works attributed to him are "Carta del Bachiller de Arcadia," published in *Antología de humoristas españoles* (Madrid, 1957), pp. 98–105; "Respuesta del Capitán Salazar," ibid., pp. 105–110; "Libro de Chistes de Luis de Pinedo," ibid., pp. 93–98, of which the editor, José García Mercadal, says, p. 93: "Se le tiene por fruto de la labor de alguna de las Academias literarias que funcionaban en Madrid en el siglo XVI, la mayor parte de sus graciosas narraciones debieron de ser recogidas de sus labios"; "Diálogo entre Caronte y el ánima de Pedro Luis Farnesio," published in *Biblioteca Clásica* 41 (Madrid, 1907): 401–423.

On Mendoza's habit of spreading gossip and then denying his authorship, see his letter to the Duke of Alba, *AIH* 2, no. 18 (1911): 193, where he reports scandalous stories about the Cardinals Farnese and Ferrara, saying in the same breath: ". . . Y esto me lo han dicho por cierto; yo lo tengo por mentira. Suplico a Vuestra Signoria no me haga autor, porque lo desmentiré."

His famous anonymous letter of advice to the Emperor, the "Letter of Busseto," was published in 1604 by Prudencio de Sandoval, *Historia de la vida y hechos del emperador Carlos V*, book 25, paragraph xxx.

In the following I give a chronological list of the publications containing letters of Mendoza, without claiming completeness:

1604: Prudencio de Sandoval, *Historia de la vida y hechos del emperador Carlos V* (Valladolid, book 25, paragr. 30, has the first published letter attributed to Mendoza. In the 1681 edition the letter is on pp. 324–327.

1680: Diego J. Dormer, *Progresos de la historia en el reyno de Aragón.*

1845: Karl Lanz, *Staatspapiere zur Geschichte des Kaisers Karl V.*

1848: Adolfo de Castro, *El Buscapié* (Cadiz).

1852: Cayetano Rosell, ed., *Bibl. Autores Españoles* 21:1.

1862: J. J. I. v. Döllinger, *Beiträge zur politischen, kirchlichen und Kulturgeschichte*, vol. 1.

1873–1882: A. von Druffel, *Briefe und Akten zur Geschichte des 16. Jahrhunderts*, Beiträge zur Reichsgeschichte, 1546–1551, 3 vols. Letters of Mendoza in vols. 1–2.

1888: Pascual Gayangos, ed., *Calendar of State Papers*, Spanish, V, 2; 1536–1538.

1890: Ibid., VI, 1; 1538–1542.

1894: R. Foulché-Delbosc, ed., *Revue Hispanique* 1: 255–267.

1895: Gayangos, ed., *Cal. St. P.*, Spanish, VI, 2; 1542–1543.

1899: Ibid., VII; 1544.

1899–1900: A. Paz y Meliá, *Revista de Archivos* 4: 612–622.

1901: Foulché-Delbosc, ed., *Rev. Hisp* 8: 1–59.

1904: M. Hume, ed., *Cal. St. P.*, Sp. VIII, 1545–1546.

1907: Walter Friedensburg, ed., *Nuntiaturberichte aus Deutschland*, vol. 10 (1547–1548). Especially Appendix, pp. 529–702.

1910: Ibid., vol. 11 (1548–1549).

1911: C. Pérez Pastor, ed., *Memorias de la R. Acad. Española* 10:150–225.

1911a: Foulché-Delbosc, ed., *Archivo de Investigaciones Históricas* 2.
1912: M. Hume and Royall Tyler, eds., *Cal. St. P.*, IX, 1547–1549.
1914: Foulché-Delbosc, *Revue Hispanique*, vol. 32.
1929: *Archivo Histórico Español* (Madrid).
1935: *Algunas Cartas de Don D. H. de Mendoza*, Alberto Vázquez and R. Selden Rose, eds., Yale Romanic Series 10.
1943: A. González Palencia and E. Mele, *Vida y obras de D. D. H. de Mendoza*, vol. 3, appendices, pp. 276–469.
1947: Garrett Mattingly, ed. *Cal. St. P.*, Further Supplement, 1513–1542.
1954: R. Tyler, ed., *Cal. St. P.*, XIII, 1554–1558.

BIBLIOGRAPHY

Manuscript Sources

Arch. Flor.	Archivio di Stato di Firenze, Mediceo
Inst. D. Juan	Archivo del Instituto de Valencia de Don Juan, Madrid
Arch. Siena	Archivio di Stato, Siena
Arch. Ven.	Archivio di Stato, Venice
Arch. Sim.	Archivo General de Simancas
Escorial	Biblioteca de El Escorial
Bibl. Nac.	Biblioteca Nacional, Madrid
Bibl. Pal.	Biblioteca de Palacio, Madrid

Periodicals

A-A	Al-Andalus
AHR	American Historical Review
	Archives d'Histoire doctrinale et littéraire du Moyen-Âge
Arch. Stor. Ital.	Archivio Storico Italiano
AHE	Archivo Histórico Español
AIH	Archivo de Investigaciones Históricas
	Archivum, Universidad de Oviedo
	Atlante
BRAH	Boletín de la Real Academia de la Historia
BH	Bulletin Hispanique
Bull. Sen.	Bullettino Senese di Storia Patria
Ch. J. F.	The Chicago Jewish Forum
	Ciencia Tomista
	Franciscan Studies
	Hispania (Madrid)
	Hispania (U.S.)
	Hispanófila

JHI	*Journal of the History of Ideas*
MRAE	*Memorias de la Real Academia Española*
Misc.	*Miscelánea de Estudios Árabes y Hebráicos*
Quellen	*Quellen und Forschungen aus italienischen Archiven und Bibliotheken*
	Renaissance News
RABM	*Revista de Archivos, Bibliotecas y Museos*
RCEE	*Revista del Centro de Estudios Extremeños*
RH	*Revue Hispanique*
Riv. Stor. Ital.	*Rivista Storica Italiana*
	Romania
Schriften	*Schriften des Vereins für Reformationsgeschichte*
Stud. Stor.	*Studii Storici*
	Symposium

Books Cited Frequently

AC   Alberto Vázquez and R. Selden Rose, eds. *Algunas Cartas de Don Diego Hurtado de Mendoza, 1538–1552.* New Haven: Yale University Press, 1935.

BAE   *Biblioteca de Autores Españoles*

Cal. St. P.   *Calendar of State Papers*

Conc. Trid.   S. Merklé, ed. *Concilium Tridentinum.* 1901.

DIE   *Colección de Documentos Inéditos para la Historia de España.* Madrid, vol. I, 1842, and subsequent vols.

GP   Angel González Palencia and Eugenio Mele. *Vida y obras de Don Diego Hurtado de Mendoza.* 3 vols. Madrid, 1941–43.

G. de Gr.   M. Gómez Moreno, ed. *De la Guerra de Granada,* Commentarios por Don Diego Hurtado de Mendoza. Madrid, 1948.

MHE   *Memorial Histórico Español*

NB   *Nuntiaturberichte aus Deutschland.* Berlin: Gotha, 1892–1912.

Ven. Dep.   *Venetianische Depeschen vom Kaiserhofe.* 4 vols. Vienna, 1889–1895.

Books and Articles

Adriani, Giambattista. *Istoria de' suoi tempi.* Venice, 1587.

Affò, Ireneo. *Vita di Pierluigi Farnese.* Milan, 1821.

Aguado Bleye, Pedro. *Reyes Católicos: Casa de Austria.* Vol. II of *Manual de Historia de España.* 3 vols. Madrid: Escasa-Calpe, 1959.

Aiton, Arthur Scott. *Antonio de Mendoza: First Viceroy of New Spain.* Durham, N.C., 1927.

Alberi, Eugenio. *Relazioni di Spagna di Giovanni Soranzo.* Vol. V, series 1 of *Relazioni degli ambasciatori veneti al Senato.* Florence, 1839–1855.

Alberigo, Giuseppe. *I vescovi italiani al Concilio di Trento.* Florence, 1959.

Allison Peers, E., ed. *Critical Anthology of Spanish Verse.* University of California, 1949.

Amador de los Rios, José. *Historia social, política y religiosa de los Judíos de España y Portugal,* 3 vols. Madrid, 1871–1876. New edition, Madrid: Aguilar, 1960.

Amatus Lusitanus. *Centuria,* I. Venice, 1557.

————. *In Dioscoridis Anazarbei de medica materia libros quinque ennarrationes eruditissimae.* Venice, 1553 and Strassburg, 1554.

Andrews, Arthur I. "The Campaign of the Emperor Charles V against Tunis." Ph.D. dissertation. Harvard, 1905.

Aretino, Pietro. *Corrispondenza,* II. Bari, 1913.

Armstrong, Edward. *The Emperor Charles V.* 2 vols. London, 1902.

Arteaga y Falguera, Cristina de. *La Casa del Infantado, Cabeza de los Mendoza.* Madrid, 1940.

Atti del XII Congresso Internazionale di Filosofia, Venezia 1958. Florence, 1960.

Aymon. *Maximes politiques du Pape Paul III.* La Haye, 1716.

Balparda y las Herreras, Gregorio de. *Historia crítica de Vizcaya y de sus fueros.* Bilbao: Imprenta Mayli, 1933–1934.

Bardi, Angelo. "Istorie senesi del 1512 al 1556." MS in the Biblioteca Comunale of Siena: A. VI, 51, part II, a.1. 546.

Bartoli, Nerino. *Le congiure di Siena e la cacciata degli spagnoli del 1552.* Siena, 1931.

Bataillon, Marcel. *Erasme et l'Espagne.* Paris, 1937. Spanish trans., *Erasmo y España.* 2 vols. Mexico, 1950.

Batchelor, C. Malcolm, ed. *A tí, Doña Marina: The Poetry of Don Diego Hurtado de Mendoza.* Havana: Ucar, 1959.

Beltrán de Heredia, Vicente. *Domingo de Soto; Estudio biográfico documentado.* Madrid, 1961.

Bermúdez de Pedraza, Francisco. *Antigüedad y excelencias de Granada.* Madrid, 1608.

Bermúdez Pareja, Jesús. "El Generalife después del incendio de 1958," *Cuadernos de la Alhambra* 1 (1965).

Berrueta, Mariano D. *El Gran Duque de Alba.* Madrid: Biblioteca Nueva, 1944.

Bibl, Viktor. *Der Tod des Don Carlos.* Vienna and Leipzig, 1918.

Boom, G. H. de. *Eléonore d'Autriche: Reine de France.* Brussels, 1943.

Booth, Cecily. *Cosimo I: Duke of Florence.* Cambridge, 1921.

Boscán, Juan. *Las obras de Boscán, y algunas de Garcilaso de la Vega.* Edited by Alonso de Ulloa. Venice: Gabriel Gilito, 1553.

Bosque Maurel, Joaquín. *Geografía urbana de Granada.* Zaragoza, 1962.

Brandi, Karl. *Kaiser Karl V: Werden und Schicksal einer Persönlichkeit und eines Weltreiches.* 2 vols. Munich, 1937.

Braudel, Fernand. *La Mediterranée et le Monde mediterranéen à l'époque de Philippe II.* Paris: Librairie Armand Colin, 1949.

Burckhardt, Carl J. *Bildnisse.* Frankfurt a.M., 1958.

Bustani, Alfredo, ed. *Fragmento de la época sobre noticias de los Reyes Nazaritas o Capitulación de Granada y emigración de los andaluces a Marruecos.* Larache, 1940.

Cabrera de Córdoba, Luis. *Historia de Felipe segundo: Rey de España.* Madrid, edition of 1877.

Campana, L. "Monsignor Giovanni della Casa," *Studii Storici* 17.

Cantini, Lorenzo. *Vita di Cosimo de' Medici.* Florence, 1805.

Capasso, Carlo. *La Politica di Papa Paolo III e l'Italia,* I. Camerino, 1901.

―――. *Paolo III,* 2 vols. Messina, 1924 and 1933.

Capmany y de Montpalán, Antonio de. *Teatro histórico-crítico de la eloquencia española,* III. Madrid, 1787.

Cappelletti, Giuseppe. *Storia di Venezia,* VIII. Venice, 1852.

Cappelletti, Licurgo. *Storia della città è stato di Piombino.* Livorno, 1897.

Carande, Ramón. *Carlos V y sus banqueros.* Madrid, 1943.

Caro Baroja, Julio. *Los Judíos en la España moderna y contemporánea.* 3 vols. Madrid: Ediciones Arion, 1961.

―――. *Los Moriscos del Reino de Granada.* Madrid: Instituto de Estudios Políticos, 1957.

―――. *Razas, Pueblos y Linajes.* Madrid, 1957.

Carranza, Fray Bartolomé. *Documentos Históricos,* vol. 2. Edited by J. Ignacio Tellechea Idiagoras. In *Archivo Documental Español,* vol. 19. Madrid: Real Academia de la Historia, 1963.

Carriazo, J. de Mata. "Asiento de las cosas de Ronda, conquista y repartimiento de la ciudad por los Reyes Católicos." *Misc.* 3 (1954): appendix 1–139.

Cartwright, Julia. *Christina of Denmark: Duchess of Milan and Lorraine, 1522–1590.* London, 1913.

Castro y Rossi, Adolfo de. *El Buscapié.* Cadiz, 1848.

———. *Historia de los Protestantes españoles y de su persecución por Felipe II.* Cadiz, 1851.

———, ed. *Obras escogidas de filósofos.* Madrid, 1953.

———, ed. *Poetas líricos de los siglos XVI y XVII.* Vol. 32, part 1 of *Biblioteca de Autores Españoles.* Madrid, 1872.

Castro, Américo. *España en su historia.* Buenos Aires, 1948. English trans., *The Structure of Spanish History.* Princeton, 1954.

Cedillo, J. L. A., Comte de. *El Cardenal Cisneros.* 3 vols. Madrid, 1921–1928.

Cepeda Adán, José. "Andalucía en 1508." *Hispania* 22 (Madrid, 1962).

Cereceda, Feliciano. *Diego Láinez en la Europa religiosa de su tiempo (1512-1565).* Madrid, 1945–1946.

Cesaretti, Agostino. *Istoria del Principato di Piombino.* Florence, 1788.

Commines, Philippe de. *Mémoires.* Edited by Dupont. 3 vols. Paris, 1840–1847.

Cotarelo y Mori, Emilio, ed. *Cancionero de Antón de Montoro.* Madrid, 1900.

Cuadernos de Historia. Anexos de la Rivista Hispania, vol. 3. Edited by Salvador de Moxo. Madrid, Instituto Jerónomo Zurita, 1969.

Desjardins, Abel. *Négociations diplomatiques de la France avec la Toscane.* Paris, 1859–1886.

Documentos escogidos del archivo de la Casa de Alba. Edited by La Duquesa de Berwick y de Alba. Madrid, 1891.

Döllinger, J. J. I. von. *Beiträge zur politischen, kirchlichen and Kulturgeschichte.* Dokumente zur Geschichte Karls V., Philip II, aus spanischen Archiven, vol. I. Regensburg, 1862.

Dormer, Diego J. and Uztarroz, J. F. A. de. *Progresos de la historia en el reyno de Aragón.* Saragossa, 1680. Also, edition of 1878.

Druffel, A. von. *Briefe und Akten zur Geschichte des 16. Jahrhunderts.* Beiträge zur Reichsgeschichte, 1546–1551, vols. I and II. 1873–1882.

Durán, A. ed. "Romancero General," II. In *BAE*, vol. 16.

Durme, M. van. *El Cardenal Granvela.* Barcelona, 1957.

Edwards, William F. "The Averroism of Iacopo Zabarella," *Atti del XII Congresso Internazionale di Filosofia.* Florence, 1960.

Elliott, J. H. *Imperial Spain.* New York: St. Martin's Press, 1964.

Equiláz y Yanguas, Leopoldo de. *Reseña histórica de la conquista del Reino de Granada.* Granada, 1894.

Fernández de Bethencourt, Francisco. *Historia genealógica y heráldica de la Monarquía española, Casa Real, y Grandes de España.* Madrid, 1900.

Fernández de Retana, L. *Cisneros y su siglo.* 2 vols. Madrid, 1929–1930.

Fesenmair, J. *Don Diego Hurtado de Mendoza: Ein spanischer Humanist*. Munich, 1882.

Fita, Fidel. "Los judaizantes españoles." *BRAH* 33 (1898).

Fléchier, Esprit. *Historia du Cardinal Ximènes*. Paris, 1693.

Foulché-Delbosc, R. "Un point contesté de la vie de Don Diego Hurtado de Mendoza." *RH* 2 (1895): 208–303.

————. "Étude sur la *Guerre de Grenade* de don D. H. de Mendoza." *RH* 1 (1894): 101 ff.

————, ed. Letters of Mendoza. *RH* 1 (1894): 255–267.

————, ed. Mendoza's translation of Aristotle's *Mechanica*. RH 5 (1898): 367–405.

————, ed. Correspondence of Mendoza and Doña Magdalena de Bobadilla. *RH* 8 (1901): 1–59.

————. "Le portrait de Mendoza." *RH* 23: 310–313.

————, ed. Letters of Charles V to Mendoza. *RH* 31 (1914): 133–149.

————, ed. Rodríguez de Ardila, "Historia de los Condes de Tendilla." *RH* 31 (1914): 63–131.

————. "Les oeuvres attribuées à Mendoza." *RH* 32 (1914): 1–47.

————, ed. Letters of Mendoza. *AIH* 2 (1911).

Fourquevaux, M. de. *Dépêches de M. de Fouquevaux: Ambassadeur du Roi Charles IX en Espagne*. 3 vols. Paris: M. l'Abbé Douais, 1896, 1900, 1904.

François I. *Catalogue des Actes de François I*. Paris, 1889.

François, Michel. *Le Cardinal François de Tournon*. Paris, 1957.

Friedensburg, Walter. *Kaiser Karl V und Papst Paul III*. Leipzig, 1932. Also in *Schriften*, Jahrgang 50, Heft I, no. 153 (1932).

————, ed. *Nuntiaturberichte aus Deutschland*, X (1907); XI (1910).

Gachard, L. P., ed. *Bibliothèque de Madrid et de l'Escurial*. Brussels, 1875.

Gallego Morell, Antonio, ed. *Casa de los Tiros: Guías de los Museos de España*, XI. Granada, 1962.

Gallego y Burín, Antonio. *La Alhambra*. Granada: Patronato de la Alhambra, 1963.

Galluzzi, Riguccio. *Storia del Granducato di Toscana*, I, II. Florence, 1822.

García de Diego, Vicente, ed. *Marqués de Santillana: Canciones y Decires*. Madrid, 1942.

García Mercadal, José. *Antología de humoristas españoles*. Madrid, 1957.

Gardner, Edmund G. *The Story of Florence*. London, 1910.

Garrad, K. "La Inquisicion y los Moriscos granadinos, 1526–1580." *BH* 67, nos. 1–2 (1965): 63–77.

―――. "The Original Memorial of D. Francisco Nuñez Muley." *Atlante* 2 (1954): 198–226.

―――. "La industria sedera granadina en el siglo XVI y su conexión con el Levantamiento de las Alpujarras," *Misc.* (1956): 5–8.

Gayangos, Pascual, ed. Letters of Mendoza. *Cal. St. P.* 1888, 1890, 1895, 1899.

Gesner, Conrad. *Bibliotheca Universalis*, I, folio 205. Tiruci, 1545.

Gilson, Étienne, "Autour de Pomponazzi," *Archives d'Histoire* 28 (1961): 163–279.

Giordani, Gaetano. *Cronaca della venuta e dimora in Bologna del sommo Pontefice Clemente VII per la coronazione de Carlo V Imperatore.* Bologna, 1892.

Giovio, Paolo (Pauli Iovii). *Historiarum sui temporis.* 2 vols. Lutetiae, 1553–1554. Also in contemporary German trans., Jovij. *Wahrhafftige Beschreibungen aller chronickwirdiger namhafftiger Historien.* Frankfurt a.M., 1570.

―――. *Lettere*, vol. II, 1544–1552. Edited by Giuseppe Guido Ferrero. Rome, 1958.

―――. *La vita di Gonsalvo Fernando di Cordova: Il gran Capitano.* Florence, 1551. Translated from the Latin by L. Domenichi.

Girón, Pedro. *Crónica del Emperador Carlos V.* Edited by Juan Sánchez Montes. Madrid: Consejo Superior de Investigaciones Científicas, 1964.

Gómez Moreno, M. *Las águilas del Renacimiento español: Bartolomé Ordoñez, Diego Siloee, Pedro Machuca, Alonso Berruguete.* Madrid, 1941.

González de Amezúa y Mayo, Agustín. *Isabel de Valois: Reina de España.* 3 vols. Madrid, 1949.

―――. *Una Reina de España en la Intimidad.* Madrid, 1944.

González Palencia, Angel. *Don Luis de Zuñiga y Ávila.* Badajoz, 1931.

―――, and Mele, Eugenio. *Vida y obras de Don Diego Hurtado de Mendoza.* 3 vols. Madrid, 1941–1943.

Gosellini, Giuliano. *Vita dell' illustrissimo et generosissimo Sig. D. Ferrando Gonzaga.* Venice, 1579.

Granvelle, Cardinal (Antoine de Perrenot). *Papiers d'etat du Cardinal de Granvelle*, vol. VIII. Edited by C. Weiss. Paris, 1841–1852.

Graux, Charles. *Essai sur les origines du fond grec de l'Escurial.* Paris, 1880.

Gregorovius, Ferdinand. *Wanderjahre in Italien.* Dresden, edition of 1925.

Gronau, G. *Tizian.* Berlin, 1900. English trans., *Titian.* London, 1904.

Gudiel, Gerónimo. *Compendio de algunas historias de España.* Alcalá 1577.

Guidiccioni, Giovanni. *Lettere inedite di Monsignor Giovanni Guidiccioni da Lucca.* Lucca, 1855.

Gutiérrez, Constancio. *Los Españoles en Trento.* Cuenca, 1951.

———. *Madrid: De Villa a Corte.* Madrid, 1962.

Gutiérrez Coronel, Diego. *Historia genealógica de la casa de Mendoza.* Edited by A. González Palencia. Cuenca: Ayuntamiento de la Ciudad, 1946.

Guzmán, G. Avalos. *Don Antonio de Mendoza.* Morelia, 1941.

Hefele, Karl Joseph von. *The Life of Cardinal Ximénez.* London, 1860.

Henríquez de Jorquera, Francisco. *Anales de Granada,* I. Edited by Antonio Marín Ocete. Granada, 1934.

Henze, Anton. *Das grosse Konzilienbuch.* Starnberg, 1962.

Heynck, Valens. "A Controversy at the Council of Trent Concerning the Doctrine of Duns Scotus," *Franciscan Studies* 9, no. 1 (1949).

Hogenberg, Nicolas. *The Procession of Pope Clement VII and the Emperor Charles V.* Edinburgh, 1875.

Hornik, M. P., ed. *Collected Studies in Honour of Américo Castro's 80th Year.* Lincombe Lodge Research Library. Oxford, 1965.

Hurtado de Mendoza, Diego. *De la Guerra de Granada.* Comentarios, edited by Manuel Gómez Moreno. Madrid, 1948. Vol. 49 of *Memorial Histórico Español.*

———. *Guerra de Granada.* Edited by Baltasar de Çúñiga, with introduction "Breve Memoria de la vida y muerte de don Diego de Mendoza." Lisbon, 1627.

———. *La Vida de Lazarillo de Tormes.* Madrid, 1928. Vol. 79 of Biblioteca Universal.

Iongh, Jane de. *Mary of Hungary.* New York, 1958.

Jiménez de Quesada, Gonzalo. *Anti-Jovio.* Edited by Rafael Torres Quintero. Bogota, 1952.

Jover, José María. *Carlos V y los españoles.* Madrid: Ediciones Rialp, 1963.

Kamen, Henry. *The Spanish Inquisition.* New York: New American Library, 1965.

Keniston, Hayward. *Francisco de los Cobos: Secretary of the Emperor Charles V.* Pittsburgh: University of Pittsburgh Press, 1959.

Knapp, William, ed. *Obras poéticas de D. Diego Hurtado de Mendoza.* Madrid, 1877.

Kristeller, Paul Oskar. "Paduan Averroism and Alexandrism in the Light of Recent Studies," *Atti* 9 (1960): 147–155. Reprinted in Kristeller, *Renaissance Thought II: Papers on Humanism and the Arts.* Harper Torchbooks, TB 1163 (1965), pp. 111–118.

Lafuente de Alcántara, Miguel. *Historia de Granada.* 4 vols. Granada, 1846.

Lafuente, Modesto. *Historia general de España*, X. Barcelona, 1889.

Laiglesia, F. de. *Estudios históricos (1515–1555)*, I. Madrid, 1918.

Lanz, Karl. *Correspondenz des Kaisers Karl V.* 3 vols. Leipzig, 1844–1846.

Lanz, Karl. *Staatspapiere zur Geschichte Karls V.* Stuttgart, 1845.

Lautensach, Hermann. *Maurische Züge im geographischen Bild der Iberischen Halbinsel.* Bonn: Ferd. Dümmlers Verlag, 1960.

Layna Serrano, Francisco. *Historia de Guadalajara y sus Mendozas en los siglos XV y XVI.* 4 vols. Madrid: Aldus, 1942.

Lea, Henry Charles. *A History of the Inquisition of Spain.* 4 vols. New York: Macmillan, 1922.

————. *The Moriscos of Spain.* Philadelphia: Lea Brothers, 1901.

Lehnhoff, Otto. *Die Beichtväter Karls V.: Ihre politische Tätigkeit und ihr Verhältnis zum Kaiser.* Inaugural dissertation, Göttingen, 1932.

Lennep, S. A. van. *Les années italiennes de Marguerite d'Autriche*, Geneva, 1952.

Leva, Giuseppe de. *Storia documentata di Carlo V.* 5 vols. Venice, 1863–1896.

Liberati, A. "Onoranze rese a Don Diego di Mendoza nella sua venuta a Siena," *Bull. Sen.* 18: 364–368.

Litta, Pompeo. "La famiglia Appiani." Chapter 25 of *Famiglie celebri Italiane*, vol. II. Milan, 1825.

Llorente, J. A. *Historia crítica de la Inquisición de España.* Madrid, 1822.

López de Gómara, F. *Annals of the Emperor Charles V.* Edited by R. B. Merriman. Oxford, 1912.

Losada, Angel. *Juan Ginés de Sepúlveda.* Madrid, 1949.

Lynch, John. *Spain under the Habsburgs*, I. New York: Oxford Press, 1964.

Manucci, Aldo. *Vita de Cosimo I dei Medici Granduca di Toscana.* Pisa, 1883.

Marañón, Gregorio. *Antonio Pérez.* Madrid, 1954.

Maravall, José Antonio. *Carlos V y el pensamiento político del Renacimiento.* Madrid, 1960.

————. *Las Comunidades de Castilla: Una primera revolución moderna.* Madrid: Revista de Occidente, 1963.

Marcello, Pietro. *Vite de' Prencipi di Vinegia.* Venice, 1557.

Marín, Luis Astrana. *Vida ejemplar y heróica de M. de Cervantes Saavedra.* Madrid, 1948.

Marín Ocete, Antonio. *Gregorio Silvestre.* Granada: Facultad de Letras, 1939.

Marini, Caetano. *Degli Archiatri Pontifici.* Rome, 1784.

Mármol Carvajal, Luis del. *Historia del rebelión y castigo de los moriscos del reyno de Granada.* 2 vols. Madrid, 1797.

Martín Gamero, Antonio. *Historia de la Ciudad de Toledo.* Toledo, 1862.

Mártir, Pedro (Pietro Martire). *Epistolario de Pedro Mártir de Anglería.* Vol. X of *DIE.* Madrid, 1953. Also in *Anglerii Epistolarium.* 1670.

Mattingly, Garrett. *Catherine of Aragon.* Boston: Little, Brown and Company, 1941.

———. *The Armada.* Boston: Houghton Mifflin, 1959.

May, Florence Lewis. *Silk Textiles of Spain.* New York, 1957.

Mayans i Siscar, Gregorio. "Vida." Edition of *Guerra de Granada,* pp. v–lvi. Valencia, 1776.

Mazarío Coleto, María del Carmen. *Isabel de Portugal.* Madrid, 1951.

Memorias de la Real Academia Española, vol. 10. Edited by C. Pérez Pastor. 1911.

Merino, Abelardo. *El Cardenal Mendoza.* Barcelona: Editorial Labor, 1942.

Merriman, Roger Bigelow. *The Emperor.* Vol. III of *The Rise of the Spanish Empire.* 4 vols. New York: Macmillan, 1925.

———. *Philip the Prudent.* Vol. IV of *The Rise of the Spanish Empire.* 4 vols. New York: Macmillan, 1934.

Miscelánea de Estudios sobre Carlos V y su Época en el IV Centenario de su muerte. Homenaje de la Universidad de Granada. Granada, 1958.

Mitchell, R. J. *The Laurels and the Tiara.* New York, 1962.

Moeller, Ch. *Éléonore d'Autriche et de Bourgogne: Reine de France.* Paris, 1895.

Monografías de Ciencia Moderna, vol. 29. Consejo Superior de Investigaciones Cientificas [C.S.I.C.], 1951.

Morales, Ambrosio de. *Las antigüedades de las ciudades de España.* Alcalá, 1575. Dedication to Mendoza published in GP III, 470–474.

Morato, Nemesio. "Un catálogo de los fondos árabes primitivos de El Escorial." *A-A* 2 (1934): 87–181.

Morel-Fatio, A., ed. *L'Espagne au XVI. et XVII. siècle.* Heilbronn, 1878.

———. "Recherches sur Lazarillo de Tormes." *Études sur l'Espagne,* 1. série. Paris, 1888.

Mosto, Andrea da. *I Dogi di Venezia.* Milano, 1960.

Mulhacén, Marqués de. *Carlos V y su política mediterránea.* Madrid: Consejo Superior de Investigaciones científicas, 1962.

Muñoz, Andrés. *Viaje de Felipe II a Inglaterra.* Madrid, 1876.

Muñoz, Luis. *Vida y virtudes del venerable varón . . . Fray Luis de Granada.* Madrid, 1639.

Münzer, Hieronymus. "Viaje por España y Portugal en los años 1494 y 1495." Translated from the Latin by Julio Puyol. *BRAH* 84 (1924). Also in a new edition with prologue by Manuel Gómez Moreno, translated by José López Toro. Madrid, 1951.

Nifo, Agostino. *De immortalitate humanae animae adversus Petrum Pomponacium.* Venice, 1518.

Noailles, M. de. *Ambassades de M. de Noailles en Angleterre,* II. Leyde: Vertot, 1763.

Novalin, José Luis G. *El inquisidor general Fernando de Valdés.* Universidad de Oviedo, 1968.

O'Callaghan, J. F. "Don Pedro Girón: Master of the Order of Calatrava," *Hispania* 21 (Madrid, 1961), pp. 342–390.

Okey, Thomas. *The Story of Venice.* London, 1905.

Osorio, Antonio. *Vida y hazañas de don Fernando Alvarez de Toledo, Duque de Alba.* Madrid, 1945.

Pacifico, Pietro Antonio. *Cronaca Veneta della città di Venezia.* Venice, 1751.

Palanco Romero, José. *Aben Humeya en la historia y en la leyenda.* Granada, 1915.

Palandri, E. *Les négociations entre la France et la Toscane.* Paris, 1908.

Palencia, Alonso de. *Crónica de Enrique IV.* Edited by Paz y Melia. 5 vols. Madrid, 1904.

Paris, Louis, ed. *Négociations . . . relatives au Règne de François II tirées du Portefeuille de Sébastien de l'Aubespine.* Paris: Imprimerie Royale, 1841.

Pastor, Ludwig von. *Geschichte der Päpste,* V, VI. Freiburg i. Breisgau, 1909, 1913.

Paz y Melia, Antonio, ed. Letters of Mendoza, *RABM* 4 (1899–1900): 612–622.

Pecchiai, Pio. *Roma nel cinquecento.* Bologna, 1948.

Pecci, Gio. Antonio. *Continuazione delle memorie storiche critiche della città di Siena fino agli anni MDLII raccolte . . . ,* III. Siena, 1758.

Pérez, Pero. "La Encomienda de Calatrava," *RCEE* 4 (Badajoz, 1930): 233–241.

Pérez Pastor, C., ed. Testament of Mendoza, *MRAE* 10 (1911): 153–194.

Pescador del Hoyo, María del Carmen. "Cómo fué de verdad la toma de Granada," *A-A* 20 (1955): 259–344.

Pirenne, Henri. *A History of Europe.* New York, 1939.

Pomponazzi (Petri Pomponatii Mantuani). *Tractatus de immortalitate animae.* Edited by William Henry Hay II. Haverford College, 1938.

Pulgar, Hernando del. *Crónica de los Señores Reyes Católicos Don Fernando y Doña Isabel.* Valencia: Benito Monfort, 1780. Also, new edition by J. de Mata Carriazo. Madrid, 1943.

————. *Claros Varones de Castilla.* Edited by J. Domínquez Bordona. Madrid: Espasa-Calpe, 1942.

Prescott, William Hickling. *History of the Reign of Ferdinand and Isabella.* 3 vols. Boston, 1872.

Rachfahl, Felix. *Don Carlos.* Freiburg, 1921.

————. *Margaretha von Parma: Statthalterin der Niederlande.* Munich & Leipzig, 1898.

Ramos-Oliveira, Antonio. *Historia de España.* 3 vols. Mexico, 1952.

Rassow, Peter. *Die Politische Welt Karls V.* Munich, 1942.

————. *Karl V.: Der letzte Kaiser des Mittelalters.* Göttingen, 1957.

————. "Das Bild Karls V. im Wandel der Jahrhunderte." *Kölner Colloquium.* Cologne, 1960.

Relationen venezianischer Botschafter über Deutschland und Österreich, ed. Fiedler. In *Fontes Rerum Austriacum,* XXX. Vienna, 1870.

Remiro, M. Gaspar. "Granada en poder de los Reyes Católicos: Primeros años de su dominación," *Estudios Históricos de Granada.* 1911.

Rodríguez Garcia, F. *Cronica del Señoria de Vizcaya.* Madrid, 1865.

Romano, P. and Partini, P. *Piazza Navona nella storia e nell'arte.* Rome, n.d.

Romier, Lucien. *Les origines politiques des guerres de Religion.* Paris, 1913.

Rosell, Cayetano, ed. *Historiadores de sucesos particulares,* I. *BAE* XXI. Madrid, 1858; reprinted Madrid, 1946.

Roth, Cecil. *History of the Jews of Venice.* Philadelphia, 1930.

————. "The Origin of *Ghetto.*" *Romania* 60. Paris, 1931.

Saltini, Guglielmo Enrico. *Tragedie Medicee domestiche.* Florence, 1898.

Sánchez Montes, Juan. "Franceses, Protestantes, Turcos," *Monografías de Ciencia Moderna* 29 (1951).

Sandoval, Prudencio de. *Historia de la vida y hechos del emperador Carlos V.* Valladolid, 1604 (reprint, 1955). Some quotations are from the edition of Amberes, 1681.

Santa Cruz, Alonso de. *Crónica del Emperador Carlos V.* 5 vols. Madrid: Real Academia de la Historia, 1920–1922.

Sanuto, Marin. *Diarii.* Venice, 1879–1903.

Sarpi, Paolo. *Istoria del Concilio Tridentino,* II. Bari, 1933.

Schwarzenfeld, Gertrude von. *Karl V.: Ahnherr Europas.* Hamburg, 1954. English trans., *Charles V: Father of Europe.* London, 1957.

Seaver, Henry Latimer. *The Great Revolt of Castile: A Study of the Comunero Movement of 1520–21.* Boston & New York, 1928.

Seco de Lucena, Luis. *La Alhambra como fué y como es.* Granada, 1935.

Sédano, López de, ed. *Parnaso español; Colección de poesías escogidas,* IV. Madrid, 1776. Introduction, "Noticia," pp. x–xx.

Segni, Bernardo. *Storie Fiorentine,* II, III. Milan, 1805.

Señán y Alonso, E. *Don Diego Hurtado de Mendoza: Apuntes biográficos-críticos.* Jérez, 1886.

Serrano y Sanz, M. *Apuntes para una Biblioteca de escritoras españolas,* I. Madrid, 1903–1905.

Simonet, Francisco Javier, ed. *Descripción del Reino de Granada.* Madrid, 1860.

Solana, Marcial. *Historia de la filosofía española,* II. Madrid, 1941.

Sozzini, Alessandro. "Diario delle cose avvenute in Siena dai 20 Luglio 1550 ai 28 Giugno 1555." *Arch. Stor. Ital.* 2, serie 1 (1842).

Spini, Giorgio, ed. *Cosimo I de' Medici . . . , Lettere.* Florence: Vallecchi, 1940.

Spivakovsky, Erika. "The Shylock Myth." *Ch. J. F.* 18, no. 2 (1959–60): 131–134.

———. "A Jewess of Venice." *Ch. J. F.* 19, no. 2 (1960–61): 129–137.

———. "The *Lazarillo de Tormes* and Mendoza." *Symposium* 15 (1961): 271–285.

———. "¿Valdés o Mendoza?" *Hispanófila* 12 (1961): 15–23.

———. " 'Lo de la Goleta y Túnez': A Work of Diego Hurtado de Mendoza?" *Hispania* 23 (Madrid, 1963): 366–379.

———. "Building Castles in Spain." *Ch. J. F.* 22, no. 2 (1963–64): 114–117.

———. "Which Don Alonso Venegas?" *Renaissance News* 17, no. 3 (1964): 193–196.

———. "Diego Hurtado de Mendoza and Averroism." *JHI* 26, no. 3 (1965): 307–326.

———. "Some Notes on the Relations between Don Diego Hurtado de Mendoza and Don Alonso de Granada Venegas." *Archivum* 14 (1964): 212–232.

———. "El 'Vicariato de Siena,' Correspondencia de Felipe II, Principe, con Diego Hurtado de Mendoza y Ferrante Gonzaga." *Hispania* 26 (Madrid, 1966): 583–596.

———. "New Arguments in Favor of Mendoza's Authorship of the *Lazarillo de Tormes.*" *Symposium* 24, no. 1 (1970): 67–80.

Stahr, Karl. *Literarisches Taschenbuch.* 1847.

Stallwitz, Karl. *Die Schlacht bei Cérésole.* Inaugural dissertation, Berlin, 1911.

Strack, H. L. *Der Blutaberglaube bei Christen und Juden.* Munich, 1891.

Suárez Fernández, Luis. *Nobleza y Monarquía: Puntos de vista sobre la Historia castellana del siglo XV.* Valladolid: Facultad de Filosofía y Letras, 1959.

Ticknor, G. *History of Spanish Literature,* I. 1849.

Torre y Franco Romero, Lucas de. "Don Diego Hurtado de Mendoza no fué el autor de 'la Guerra de Granada.' " *BRAH* 64 (1914): 461–501; 65 (1914): 28–47.

Tyler, Royall. *The Emperor Charles the Fifth.* London & New York, 1956.

Tytler, Patrick Fraser. *England under the Reigns of Edward VI and Mary,* vol. II. London: R. Bentley, 1839.

Ubeda, Igual. *La España del siglo XVI.* Barcelona, 1957.

Usher, Abbott Payson, "Spanish Ships and Shipping in the 16th and 17th Centuries." In *Facts and Factors in Economic History,* pp. 189–213. Cambridge: Harvard University Press, 1932.

Valladar, F. de Paula. *Guía de Granada.* Granada, 1906.

Vasari, Giorgio. *Le vite de' piu eccellenti pittori, scultori e architetti.* Florence, 1550.

Vázquez, Alberto, and Rose, R. Selden, eds. *Algunas Cartas de Don Diego Hurtado de Mendoza: Escritas 1538–1552.* New Haven: Yale University Press, 1935.

Vázquez y Medina, Alberto. "El Fracaso de Don Diego Hurtado de Mendoza en Toscana." Ph.D. dissertation. Yale University, 1935.

Venetianische Depeschen vom Kaiserhofe. Edited by G. Turba. 4 vols. Vienna, 1889–1895.

Vilar y Pascual, Luis. *Diccionario histórico, genealógico y heráldico de las familias ilustres de la Monarquía Española.* 9 vols. Madrid, 1860.

Villa, R. "El Emperador Carlos Quinto y su corte," *BRAH* 45 (1883).

Werner, Karl. *Der Averroismus in der christlich-peripatetischen Psychologie des späteren Mittelalters.* Vienna, 1881.

Wolf, Ferdinand, in *Sitzungsberichte der Wiener Akademie der Wissenschaften,* I, II, Heft 1–5 (1848–1849).

Zeller, J. *La diplomatie française vers le milieu du XVIème siècle* Paris, 1881.

INDEX

In this index DD = Don Diego Hurtado de Mendoza.